THE NEW
TESTAMENT
ITS BACKGROUND, GROWTH,
AND CONTENT

Bruce M. Metzger

The New Testament

Its Background, Growth, and Content

~ THIRD EDITION ~
Revised and Enlarged

ABINGDON PRESS
Nashville

THE NEW TESTAMENT: ITS BACKGROUND, GROWTH, AND CONTENT

Copyright © 1965, 1983, 2003 by Abingdon Press

This book is printed on recycled, acid-free, elemental-chlorine–free paper.

Library of Congress Cataloging-in-Publication Data

Metzger, Bruce Manning.
    The New Testament : its background, growth, and content / Bruce Manning Metzger.—3rd ed., rev. and enlarged.
        p. cm.
Includes bibliographical references and indexes.
    ISBN 0-687-05263-7 (alk. paper)
    1. Bible. N.T.—Textbooks. I. Title.

BS2535. 3.M48   2003
225.6'1—dc21

2002155575

All Scripture quotations are from the New Revised Standard Version of the Bible, copyright © 1989, Division of Christian Education of the National Council of the Churches of Christ in the United States of America. Used by permission. All rights reserved.

06 07 08 09 10 11 12—10 9 8 7 6 5

MANUFACTURED IN THE UNITED STATES OF AMERICA

TO MY SONS
John Mackay Metzger
James Bruce Metzger

CONTENTS

PART ONE
THE BACKGROUND OF THE NEW TESTAMENT PERIOD

TABLE OF ILLUSTRATIONS

TABLE OF MAPS

PREFACE
TO THE THIRD EDITION

In the third edition of this book, quotations from the Scriptures have been taken from the New Revised Standard Version of the Bible (1989), replacing those from the Revised Standard Version (1952) used in the previous editions. Likewise, many pages contain one or more small changes in English style. Naturally, bibliographies and other quoted texts have been brought up to date.

Here and there the discussion has been expanded with additional information. For example, chapter 4 now draws attention to Scandinavian contributions to the study of the Gospels; chapter 9 mentions Sir Anthony Kenny's largely unnoticed stylometric study of the Pauline Epistles; and the four-page Appendix on the Canon of the New Testament has grown considerably and is now chapter 12. A glossary that briefly defines about one hundred items has been added at the back of the book, and there is an updated bibliography.

Perhaps the most obvious change compared with earlier editions is the presence of illustrations of *realia* that pertain to the New Testament and its times. It is hoped that these will be of assistance in visualizing statements made in the text.

Bruce M. Metzger
2002

PREFACE
TO THE SECOND EDITION

Most textbooks designed to introduce the student to the background and problems concerning the New Testament say little or nothing about those who were responsible for transmitting the Scriptures to us today. In view of the growing number of translations of the Bible, it seemed appropriate to add in the second edition an Appendix that deals with the role of scribes and translators in handing down the Scriptures through the centuries. Here a description is given of the materials and formats of ancient books, as well as some indication of the arduous task of copying manuscripts by hand. The second part of the Appendix focuses on English translations of the Bible, and describes briefly several of the major versions that are in current use.

As for the overall scope of the book, it did not seem necessary to add any other new topic or section. When the book first appeared several years ago, the section describing the recently developed discipline that German scholars call "redaction criticism" was the first to be published in an introductory textbook for American college students. Whereas some refinements have been made subsequently in the application of the discipline, no significant developments have taken place that need to be reported here. Consequently, apart from a few clarifications and corrections made here and there, the book remains a concise and, one trusts, adequate introductory account of the background, growth, and content of the New Testament.

Bruce M. Metzger
1983

PREFACE
TO THE FIRST EDITION

There are many ways of studying the Scriptures. When readers come to the Bible with the sole aim of securing spiritual guidance, they will ponder it from a devotional point of view. Their principal interest will not be with questions of who wrote what and when certain events happened, but in learning God's message for them now.

Another approach is to study the Bible from a literary point of view. The Old and New Testaments constitute a veritable library of sixty-six books that represent many types of literature—including law, history, sagas, poetry, prophecy, gospels, and letters. A host of problems concerning authorship, date of composition, sources utilized, and literary relationships will demand attention.

A third method of studying the Bible emphasizes the historical approach. It is not too much to say that every serious attempt to understand the Scriptures must be historically oriented. Only by being acquainted with the political, social, and religious background of the biblical era can the student understand the allusions to contemporary culture that the biblical writers assume will be obvious to their readers.

It is the aim of the present volume, which was written at the request of the Council for Religion in Independent Schools, to supply basic information concerning the content of the New Testament and important aspects of its historical background, as well as to let the reader see something of the critical processes by which scholars have sought to solve some of the chief literary problems of the Gospels. It would be out of place in a book of this kind to advocate novel theories, whether historical, literary, or hermeneutical. On the contrary, the author has attempted to present a balanced account that represents the consensus of present-day New Testament scholarship. The chief danger, as every writer who has attempted to popularize research knows, is that, in making the complex clear, one may also make it appear simple, or, in making the debatable plain, one may also make it appear certain. In more than one New Testament problem the balance of probabilities is close, and the student should be presented with differing interpretations of the evidence. In all historical research one must seek not only to learn what can be known of the past, but also to become aware of what, because of incomplete or conflicting testimony, cannot be known.

Though the concern throughout the book is with questions involving who, where, when, and what, the underlying presupposition of the author is that what is called the New Testament is not just a collection of interesting documents from antiquity, but something much more profound—that it is in very truth the New Covenant. The title "New Covenant" implies that the books contained in the collection witness to the belief that there now exists a new period or dispensation in the dealings of God with people. This new state has been brought about by God's decisive work in the life, death, resurrection, and lordship of Jesus Christ. Understanding the New Testament, therefore, involves far more than studying the several books as pieces of ancient literature; it involves also an appreciation of the testimony of those who experienced and recorded what God had accomplished in our behalf in and through God's only Son, Jesus Christ.

What has just been said implies that besides the New Covenant there is also a collection of books that Christians have inherited as Holy Scripture from their spiritual ancestors and that testifies to an earlier covenant between God and his people. Let it be clear at the outset that of all the "helps" that assist the reader to understand the New Testament, the Old Testament is by far the most important. In that earlier collection of books, one finds the religious presuppositions and historical background without which the thinking and experiences of the New Testament writers cannot be understood. For reasons of space, however, it is impossible in the present volume to give consideration to historical, literary, and religious questions concerning the Old Testament. In what follows it will be assumed that the student has, or will acquire, an adequate knowledge of the content of the Old Testament. Such a knowledge enables the Christian reader to perceive the working of divine providence through long stretches of history in the preparation of a chosen people, to whom at the fullness of time God sent forth his Son "to redeem those who were under the law, so that we might receive adoption as children" (Gal. 4:5).

It will be observed that in the following pages footnotes have been kept to a minimum. In another book intended for a different reading public it would have been appropriate to use them more frequently in order to provide full bibliographical references, or to explain ramifications of problems that are set forth here without elaborate qualifications. The author has likewise employed a minimum of technical phraseology, the significance of which would be unknown to the majority of his readers. Within these limits, however, an attempt was made to deal candidly with major problems of New Testament research and to avoid extreme or partisan positions that—as past experience teaches—are almost certain to be modified or abandoned in the future.

In conclusion, I wish to express my gratitude to my wife and to the members of the textbook Committee of the Council for Religion in Independent Schools for reading the manuscript of this book and for making helpful suggestions concerning both form and content. It should also be mentioned that chapters 4 and 6 contain material that the author presented in 1961 in the Adolf Olson Memorial Lectures at Bethel Theological Seminary, St. Paul, Minnesota.

Bruce M. Metzger
1965

ACKNOWLEDGMENTS

The National Council of Churches of Christ in the United States of America, for permission to quote from the New Revised Standard Version of the Bible, copyright 1989 by the Division of Christian Education, NCCCUSA.

Bastiaan Van Elderen, Calvin College, Grand Rapids, Michigan, and John McRay, Wheaton College, Wheaton, Illinois, who have spent much time in the Near East and whose photographs there were made available to the author.

William O. Harris, Librarian for Archives and Special Collections, Princeton Theological Seminary, who granted permission to reproduce several treasures in the Seminary Library.

Denise M. Schwalb, Faculty Secretary, Princeton Theological Seminary, who prepared the computer database for the present revision of this book.

PART ONE

THE BACKGROUND OF THE NEW TESTAMENT PERIOD

CHAPTER 1

THE POLITICAL AND SOCIAL BACKGROUND OF PALESTINIAN JUDAISM

The earliest followers of Jesus Christ were Jews of Palestine. All of the authors of the twenty-seven books in the New Testament were Jews, with the possible exception of Luke. In order to understand the New Testament, therefore, one must know something of Palestinian Judaism during the first Christian century. The external environment involving the political and social background is no less important than the inward aspects involving the cultural and religious setting (see chapter 2).

Palestine is a relatively small country, comprising just over 10,000 square miles. Its length is about 150 miles, and the average breadth of the wider part in the south is about 75 miles, becoming narrower in the north. Thus it is smaller than Switzerland, and not half as large as Scotland. It is about the size of the state of Maryland, and a trifle larger than Vermont.

The land is favored with a healthful climate, beautiful scenery, and a great variety and fertility of soil, capable of producing fruits of all climates, from the snowy north to the tropical south. Isolated from other countries by desert, mountain, and sea, yet lying at the hub of three continents, it was providentially adapted to be the home not only of the particularism of Judaism but also of the universalism of Christianity.

I. SURVEY OF THE POLITICAL HISTORY OF PALESTINE FROM ALEXANDER THE GREAT TO THE FALL OF JERUSALEM (A.D. 70)

In 586 B.C., the walls of Jerusalem succumbed to the invading armies of Nebuchadnezzar, the city was laid waste, and the majority of the Jewish people were deported to Babylon. Half a century later, after the Babylonian Empire had been overthrown by the Medes and the Persians, the Jewish exiles were permitted to return to Judea, which was now a province of Persia. Having arrived at Jerusalem about 537 B.C., they began to rebuild the temple, which was lying in ruins. After repeated exhortations by the prophets Haggai and Zechariah, the building was finally completed in 515 B.C. Subsequently the walls of Jerusalem were rebuilt under the supervision of Nehemiah (about 445 B.C.).

Persia, however, was not to remain in supremacy. In 334 B.C., Alexander of Macedon crossed the Hellespont, defeated the Persian satraps, and the next year gained the victory over the Persian hosts at Issus (the northeast angle of the Mediterranean Sea). After defeating Syria and entering Jerusalem with his armies, he went on to Egypt where he founded the city of Alexandria (331 B.C.). He then returned through Palestine to Persia, where he overthrew the Persian monarch Darius.

After further conquests, extending as far as the Punjab in India, Alexander's meteoric career came to an end in the summer of 323 B.C. Having marched to Babylon, which he intended to make the capital of his vast empire, he was stricken by a fever and died at the age of thirty-two years. He had appointed no one as his successor, and his seven ruling generals began to quarrel among themselves. The four generals who survived the period of rivalry and intrigues laid the foundations of four great empires within the vast area once under Alexander's rule. The most important of these, so far as the history of Palestine is concerned, were the Ptolemaic dynasty in Egypt and the Seleucid dynasty in Syria and the East.

After some wrangling concerning the allocation of Palestine, which lay halfway between Syria and Egypt, the country was finally annexed to Egypt by Ptolemy I in 320 B.C. During the following 122 years, the Jews were governed by a succession of their own high priests, subject to the overlords in Egypt. Most of the period was characterized by peace and security for the Jews. On the whole the Ptolemies were mild rulers, and made no attempt to interfere with the religious beliefs and practices of their subject peoples.

The comparative tranquillity of the Jews, however, came to an abrupt end at the beginning of the second century B.C. In 198 B.C., the vigorous and enterprising ruler of the Seleucid dynasty, Antiochus III, managed to wrest Palestine from Egyptian control and annexed it to Syria. Life for the Jews now became very different and extremely difficult.

The Seleucids felt themselves called to be champions of Greek culture (Hellenism) throughout their dominions, and encouraged the use of the Greek language and the adoption of Greek customs. Judea was no exception, and, as the result of the process of hellenization, there soon grew up a party in the nation, including many prominent and wealthy Jews, who abandoned the ancient practices in favor of the new sophistication. Indeed, it is a striking fact that the priests at Jerusalem seem to have taken a leading part in the spread of Hellenism. In the absence of any native secular head of the Jewish community, the high priests were the officials with whom the governing authority naturally had to deal, and they were thus the first to come under the influence of the new thought and customs.

A considerable number of the Jews, however, resisted the program of hellenization. Unlike most other subject peoples, the Jewish nation contained a conservative element that passionately clung to their ancestral traditions. This group, called the Hasideans (= the Pious), resented the introduction of the Greek language and all that this entailed. They protested the adoption by Jewish dandies of broad-brimmed hats, so stylish among the pagans because the god Hermes was pictured wearing one. They opposed the erection of a gymnasium in Jerusalem, with an adjoining racetrack. The religious situation went from bad to worse when even the priests became regular attendants at the races, which were opened with invocations to pagan deities. The sophisticated Jews who had adopted foreign customs were, in the eyes of the orthodox Hasideans, traitors to the time-honored ways of their ancestors.

The political situation also took a turn for the worse. In the succession of the Seleucid dynasty, Antiochus Epiphanes became ruler in 175 B.C. Though he himself delighted in the epithet "Epiphanes" (which means "the manifest god"), his victims called him Antiochus Epimanes ("Antiochus the insane"). How appropriate the nickname was may be seen from the following. After an unsuccessful attempt in 169 B.C. to conquer Egypt, Antiochus returned through Palestine in a spirit of wild vindictiveness. Deprived of the prize that he had coveted, Antiochus treated the city of Jerusalem as though it had been the cause of his defeat. Gaining possession of the city by treachery, he sacked and burned it, plundered the temple, and massacred many of the citizens. Antiochus determined once and for all either to convert or exterminate those whose devotion to the Laws of Moses seemed to imply disloyalty to Syria. His victims were those who clung to Judaism, and above all the Hasideans. The observance of the sabbath, the rite of circumcision, and the possession of a copy of the Hebrew Scriptures were made crimes punishable by death. Jewish worship was abolished, and pagan altars were erected in many of the cities of Judea. The royal edicts were enforced with the utmost cruelty, and, for the first time in history, we have reliable and detailed records of widespread and bitter religious persecution. The climax of desecrating sacrilege came when, in December 167 B.C., a sow was sacrificed on the great altar of burnt offering in the temple area.

1. THE MACCABEAN REVOLT[1]

For some months, as it seems, the Hasideans suffered without retaliation; a group even allowed themselves to be slaughtered by the Syrians rather than break the sabbath by defending themselves. But a new spirit arose. The attempt to compel Jews to offer a pagan sacrifice on an altar at Modein, northwest of Jerusalem, led to an outbreak in which the king's commissioners and his guards lost their lives. The leaders among the revolt were an elderly priest named Mattathias and his five sons, who subsequently fled to the hills and embarked on a program of armed resistance. With a troop of fanatical followers, Mattathias ranged up and down Judea, hiding by day, attacking by night, pulling down pagan altars, forcibly circumcising children, and, as far as he was able, guaranteeing safety in the observance of the Mosaic Law. For about a year the old man withstood the rigors of this rough life and then he died (166 B.C.), urging his sons to "show zeal for the law, and give your lives for the covenant of our ancestors" (1 Macc. 2:50). The conduct of the struggle he bequeathed to Judas, his third son, who was nicknamed, Maccabeus ("the Hammerer").

---

1. Primary source material for the Maccabean period includes the two books of the Apocrypha entitled 1 and 2 Maccabees (see pp. 44-45).

By avoiding pitched battles and by harassing the Syrians with vigorous and persistent guerrilla warfare, the Jewish patriots won victory after victory. The first really large army led against them was commanded by a prominent Syrian general named Lysias, who might have put down the revolt. But in 165 he heard of the death of Antiochus, who had been conducting a military campaign against the Parthians on his eastern frontier, and agreed to a compromise with Judas and his party. The temple in Jerusalem was to be purified and restored to its original purpose, and the Jews were to be accorded religious freedom. The rededication of the temple was accomplished, in December 164, exactly three years after it had been defiled by the sacrifice of swine's flesh. A festival to celebrate this restoration was instituted, and was kept annually thereafter. This was the winter festival of Dedication, alluded to in John 10:22; today it is celebrated by Jews as the festival of Hanukkah (also spelled Chanukah).

Judas Maccabeus had now won for the Hasideans all that they most earnestly desired. He and his family, however, seem to have been dissatisfied with what they had achieved and undertook a career of actual conquest, leading to complete independence for the Jewish people. In 160 B.C., Judas fell in battle, and his younger brother Jonathan, who was already high priest, assumed command of the army. During the leadership of Jonathan, the Syrians were occupied with internal conflicts, intrigues, and murders that culminated in civil war, so that not only was Judea left in peace, but the favor of the Jews was actually sought. Jonathan strengthened his position internally and externally, even making treaties with the Romans and with the Spartans. He was treacherously slain by Trypho, a Syrian general, in 142 B.C., and the leadership fell to Simon, the last remaining son of Mattathias. In the same year, Demetrius II, king of Syria, granted the Jews complete political independence. Coins were struck bearing the legend "Shekel Israel," and contracts were dated "In the first year of Simon the great high priest and commander and leader of the Jews" (1 Macc. 13:42). This period of national freedom lasted for almost eighty years (until 63 B.C.), being the only such period of political independence that the Jews knew from 586 B.C. until the mid–twentieth century.

The Jewish nation, however, lacked leaders who could weld the people into a strong unit. The nation was divided into two major parties. On the one hand there were the supporters of the Maccabean priest-princes, aiming first at political power. Eventually this party came to be known as the Sadducees. On the other hand, over against them, and regarding them with a prejudice that at times amounted to bitter hatred, were the descendants of those who had supported Judas Maccabeus down to the rededication of the temple in 164, but who then withdrew their aid, on the ground that religious freedom was all they needed. From this group of Hasideans arose the party known as the Pharisees.

Political power naturally remained with the Sadducees. After Simon and two of his sons were treacherously slain in 134 B.C. by his son-in-law Ptolemy, John, the only son who escaped, assumed the power and was known as John Hyrcanus. He was a worthy grandson of the doughty Mattathias and embarked on a career of

Figure 1.1. Foundations of Samaritan Temple on Mount Gerizim
(Courtesy of John McRay.)

These ruins of the temple, which had been destroyed in 128 B.C., remained a center of Samaritan worship, particularly for the observance of Passover. They would have been visible to Jesus and the Samaritan woman from Jacob's well (John 4:12), thus giving point to her query (John 4:20) concerning the place at which people should worship—Mount Gerizim or Jerusalem.

genuine conquest. He subjugated the territory east of the Jordan, and the Idumeans were compelled to adopt Judaism as their faith, a step that was to have momentous consequences for the Jews a century later. John also overran Samaria to the north, captured the city of Shechem (known today as Nablus), and destroyed the Samaritan temple on Mount Gerizim. After a long and prosperous reign (134–104 B.C.), John died a natural death and was succeeded by his son Aristobulus, a cruel and unprincipled man who killed his mother and brother. He changed the theocracy into a kingdom, calling himself a king, but retained at the same time the high priesthood. During his short reign of one year, Galilee to the north of Samaria was conquered, and the Galileans, most of whom were Gentiles, were forcibly converted to Judaism.

During the following years the country was torn by dissensions between the Sadducees and the Pharisees. Finally civil war broke out. Weakened by internal strife, Judea became an easy prey once again to foreign domination. For several years the Romans under the able leadership of Pompey had been closing in upon Syria and neighboring kingdoms. After attempting to negotiate with both Jewish factions, Pompey, armed with unprecedented forces, took possession of Jerusalem in 63 B.C. The Jewish kingship was abolished, and Judea became formally subject to Rome. It was required to pay tribute, but was left for a time until 40 B.C. under native rulers. Thus almost exactly one hundred years after the triumphs of Judas Maccabeus, Judea once more, and finally, fell into the control of a foreign power.

2. THE ROMAN PERIOD AND THE HERODIAN DYNASTY[2]

A new stage of Jewish history began when Antony and Octavius placed the Jews under the rule of a powerful Idumean chieftain named Herod. Though appointed king *de juro* in 40 B.C., it took Herod three years to subjugate the unwilling inhabitants of Judea and to become king *de facto* by the capture of Jerusalem in 37 B.C. With Herod the Great there began a notable dynasty, the house of the Herods. In figure 1.2, an abridged genealogy lists the several Herods who are mentioned in the New Testament.

---

2. Besides the New Testament, the chief sources of information concerning the Jews during this period are the writings of the Jewish historian Flavius Josephus (see pp. 89-90).

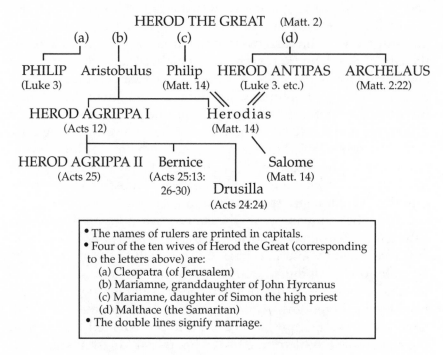

Figure 1.2. Abridged Genealogy of the Herodian Family
(from The New Testament: Its Background, Growth, and Content *by Bruce Metzger © 1965-1983 by Abingdon Press. Used by permission.)*

Herod the Great was a descendant of the Idumeans who had been conquered by John Hyrcanus during the previous century and had been compelled to adopt a semblance of Judaism. Herod's private life was unsavory, and characterized by cruelty. Over the years he killed two of his ten wives, at least three sons, a brother-in-law, and a wife's grandfather. When he himself was about to die, knowing that the people would rejoice at his demise, he commanded that the leading Jews be shut up in the arena at Jericho and put to death when he expired. Thus he craftily planned that though there would be no mourning *for* his death, there would be mourning *at* his death. Fortunately, however, when the news of his death in 4 B.C. arrived, these prisoners were set free, and the passing of the tyrant was welcomed as a relief. Herod's propensity to bloodshed is reflected in his command, issued after he had heard of the birth of a "king of the Jews," that all the children in and around Bethlehem who were two years old or under should be killed (Matt. 2:16).

But despite Herod's domestic tragedies and private crimes, he proved himself to be an able ruler and made some attempt to consider Jewish sentiment. He tried to conciliate the Jews by rebuilding their temple on a much grander scale. The old area was enlarged to twice its former dimensions, and the temple complex was embellished with enormous carved masonry (Mark 13:1).

After the death of Herod the Great, his kingdom was divided among three of his sons in accordance with the provisions of his

Figure 1.3. The Emperor Augustus (63 B.C.–A.D. 14)
(Courtesy of the Vatican Museums.)
In 27 B.C. the Roman Senate bestowed on Gaius Caesar Octavianus the honorific title *Augustus* (Latin for "venerable, majestic") in gratitude for the peace and prosperity that he had brought to his domain. Shortly after his death a marble statue, now in the Vatican museum, was erected in Rome to honor him not merely as a human deliverer from conflict and struggle, but as a divine "savior-king." The reliefs on his armor, his bare feet, and the cupid on a dolphin (a symbol of Apollo) indicate his divine status.

will, which had to be confirmed by the emperor Augustus. These sons of Herod the Great were Archelaus, Philip, and Herod Antipas.

Archelaus inherited the southern portion of Palestine, embracing Samaria, Judea, and Idumea. Instead of allowing him to be called king, however, Augustus permitted him to adopt only the title of ethnarch, which carried much less prestige than that of king. After his father's death, a rebellion broke out in Jerusalem during the Passover season, and Archelaus had to quell it with armed forces, killing some three thousand persons, among whom were many pilgrims visiting the holy city for the festival. Thus, at the very beginning of his reign, Archelaus gained for himself an evil reputation, and it is easy to understand the alarm of Joseph, who, with Mary and the infant Jesus, had gone into Egypt to escape Herod the Great's edict: "When [Joseph] heard that Archelaus was ruling over Judea in place of his father Herod, he was afraid to go there. And after being warned in a dream, he went away to the district of Galilee" (Matt. 2:22).

Some years later the principal men of Judea and Samaria sent representatives to the emperor at Rome to complain of Archelaus's tyrannical cruelty. They succeeded in their object, and in the ninth year of his reign (A.D. 6) he was deposed and banished to Vienne in Gaul, while his wealth was confiscated and put in the emperor's treasury. Judea, Samaria, and Idumea were now put under the jurisdiction of Roman governors, one of whom (Pontius Pilate) later condemned Jesus to be crucified.

Philip, another son of Herod the Great, inherited the northern and northeastern parts of Palestine, including Ituraea and Trachonitis, Gaulanitis, Auranitis, and Batanea. His rank was that of tetrarch (literally, "ruler of a fourth part"), a title that carried even less prestige than that of ethnarch.

Philip's rule was mild and peaceful. He rebuilt the ancient city of Panias and named it Caesarea in honor of Caesar Augustus. In order to differentiate this city from others of the same name it was usually called Caesarea Philippi (that is, Caesarea of Philip). The Gospels narrate that on one occasion Jesus went north from Galilee into the district of Caesarea Philippi (Matt. 16:13), the only journey that he took into the territory of Philip.

Another son of Herod the Great, Herod Antipas (called simply Herod in the New Testament), was tetrarch of Galilee and Perea.

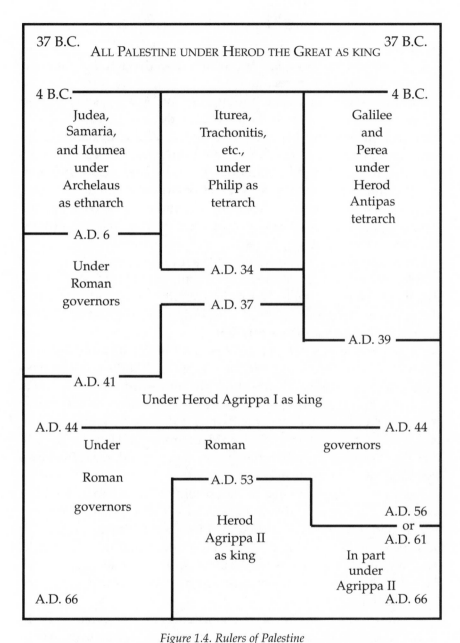

Figure 1.4. Rulers of Palestine
(from The New Testament: Its Background, Growth, and Content *by*
Bruce Metzger © 1965–1983 by Abingdon Press. Used by permission.)
Outline of the rulers of Palestine from the accession of Herod the Great to the
beginning of the Judeo-Roman war. (The three vertical columns of the chart correspond to three geographical areas of Palestine.)

Since most of the life of Jesus was spent within the area ruled by Herod Antipas, this member of the Herodian dynasty figures most prominently in the Gospels.

Herod Antipas married a daughter of Aretas, king of the Nabatean Arabs, whose capital was Petra. But afterward, while visiting with his half-brother, Herod Philip (not Philip the tetrarch), he became enamored of his host's wife, Herodias, a daughter of Aristobulus and granddaughter of Herod the Great. Consumed by his passion, Herod Antipas arranged to divorce his lawful wife and to take Herodias instead. Resenting the injury inflicted upon his daughter, Aretas declared war against Herod and eventually defeated his army in A.D. 36.

Herodias was the prime mover in the murder of John the Baptist. Because John had been fearless in rebuking Herod for his unlawful marriage, Herodias held a grudge against him and contrived through her daughter Salome, whose dancing pleased Herod, to have John beheaded (Mark 6:17-29).

On one occasion, Jesus warned his disciples against the leaven of Herod (Mark 8:15); on another, the Pharisees, manifesting an unexpected interest in Jesus' safety, brought him word that Herod was planning his death (Luke 13:31). Jesus' comment on the latter occasion ("Go and tell that fox") shows that he saw through the cunning design of Herod to be rid of him, for Herod's uneasy conscience made him fear that Jesus was John the Baptist risen from the dead (Matt. 14:1-2).

Herod Antipas happened to be present at Jerusalem at the time of Jesus' trial and crucifixion. Because Jesus was from Galilee, and hence under Herod's jurisdiction, Pilate sent him to Herod for adjudication. Herod was glad, for he thought that now he would have an opportunity of seeing Jesus perform a miracle, but he was disappointed, and with his men of war treated Jesus with contempt and mocked him (Luke 23:6-12).

When Herod Antipas, at the insistence of Herodias, went to Rome to ask to be advanced from the rank of tetrarch to that of king, the emperor Caligula banished him to Lyons in Gaul (A.D. 39), because Herod Agrippa I had sent letters to Rome accusing Antipas of being in league with the Parthians, inveterate enemies of the Romans. Herod's domain was then given to Herod Agrippa I.

Herod Agrippa I was the son of Aristobulus, who had been executed in B.C. 7 by his father, Herod the Great, for plotting against his life. In A.D. 37, he became king over those parts of Palestine that his late half-uncle Philip had governed as tetrarch. In A.D. 39, as was mentioned above, the emperor banished Herod Antipas and added his territory of Galilee and Perea to the kingdom of Agrippa. Two years later, the emperor Claudius added Judea and Samaria to Agrippa's dominions, which now equaled those of his grandfather, Herod the Great (i.e., all of Palestine).

According to the book of Acts, Herod Agrippa I laid violent hands upon some who were leaders in the early church. He killed James, the brother of John, with the sword, and proceeded to arrest Peter also (Acts 12:1-3). Herod's own death came not long afterward (A.D. 44), sent, as was widely believed, as a punishment for his overweening pride (Acts 12:21-23; Josephus, *Antiquities*, XIX.viii.2).

At the time of Herod Agrippa's death, his son, Herod Agrippa II, was only seventeen years of age. The emperor Claudius therefore transformed Palestine into the status of a Roman province and placed it under the rule of governors. About A.D. 53, Herod Agrippa II acquired the tetrarchy of Philip, and in 56 or 61 (the date is disputed) Nero added Galilee and Perea to his kingdom. It was before Herod Agrippa II and his sister Bernice, while they were visiting the governor Festus at Caesarea, that the apostle Paul pled his cause (Acts 25:13–26:32).

The history of the Jews during the remaining years until the fall of Jerusalem in A.D. 70 can be told quickly. The feelings of the Jewish people were frayed by many and varied indignities, real and imagined, which the Roman overlords committed. The occasion for armed resistance was the rather infelicitous demand on the part of the governor Gessius Florus, in May of A.D. 66, for seventeen talents from the temple treasury. The sum was comparatively small, and as governor he was probably within his rights in making the demand. The Jews, however, regarded his assessment as sacrilegious robbery of the sacred treasury that had to be resisted at all costs.

After his demand had been refused, Florus came to Jerusalem with a military contingent to enforce payment. His way to the temple was barred by the populace. The leaders of the Jews, including Herod Agrippa II, seeing the danger of revolt, attempted mediation, but in vain, for popular passion was too highly inflamed to listen to reason. The force that Florus had brought with him was insufficient to quell the Jewish mob; he therefore retired to Caesarea.

In other parts of Palestine, fighting broke out between Jew and Gentile. In the autumn of A.D. 66, the Jews put to flight a considerable force, a circumstance that convinced the more fanatical that the Almighty was fighting for them. But before the end of 67, Galilee was subdued by Vespasian (at whose side Herod Agrippa II fought), and by the middle of the next year practically all of Judea was conquered. The news of the death of Nero made it imperative for Vespasian to attend to other matters, and for more than a year the Jewish war was suspended. For one reason or another the actual besieging of Jerusalem did not begin in earnest until the spring of A.D. 70, when Titus arrived before its walls. The

Figure 1.5. Brass Coin of Vespasian
(Courtesy of the Princeton Theological Seminary.)

Brass coin of Vespasian commemorating the destruction of Jerusalem in A.D. 70; struck in 71 when Vespasian was Consul for the third time.

The legend around the leaureated head of Vespasian is IMP(erator) CAE(sar) VESPASIAN(us) AUG(ustus), P(ontifex) M(aximus), TR(ibunitia) P(otestate), P(ater) P(atriae), COS III.

On the reverse side, IUDAEA CAPTA. On the left side of palm tree, a captive standing with his hands tied behind his back; behind him are shields. On the right, a female figure seated on a cuirass, weeping. In the exergue, S.C. (Senatus Consulto) is inscribed.

horrors of the siege of five months' duration are described in pitiable detail by the Jewish historian Flavius Josephus in books 5 and 6 of his *History of the Jewish War Against the Romans*. At last, after frightful suffering amid the rigors of famine, the city fell into the hands of the Romans, who looted the temple and razed it to the ground (September, A.D. 70). Captives and spoils were carried to Rome for Titus's triumphal procession, and Roman coins were minted bearing the legend *Iudea Capta*. Thus a break in Jewish history occurred that can be compared only with the catastrophe of 586 B.C. Untold numbers of Jews had perished during the four years of warfare, many thousands were sold into slavery or kept for gladiatorial games, and only a remnant remained in Judea.

The country was now made an imperial province, governed by a legate who remained at Caesarea and had at his command a legion that was stationed at Jerusalem. The name of the land was changed from Judea to *Palaestina* (land of the Philistines), to symbolize the utter extinction of the Jewish nation. A rethinking of Judaism— and to some extent also of Christianity—was necessitated by the cessation of the temple worship. Greater importance came to belong to the Jews of the Dispersion, and the predominantly Gentile character of the Christian church became increasingly more pronounced.

A last attempt at restoring an independent national organization took place during the reign of the emperor Hadrian (A.D. 117–138). In A.D. 132, when the emperor issued a decree changing Jerusalem into a Roman colony, another Jewish revolt broke out under the leadership of Simon bar Coseba, nicknamed Bar Cochba, "Son of the Star." Recent discoveries in caves near the Dead Sea have shed new light on some of the refugees trapped there by the Roman forces; these discoveries include documents issuing from the rebel leader himself. After a bitter struggle, in A.D. 135, this revolt also was crushed, and Hadrian's plan was carried out. The devastated city of Jerusalem was completely rebuilt, now on a Roman plan, and called Colonia Aelia Capitolina (*Aelia* after the family name of Hadrian, and *Capitolina* in honor of Jupiter Capitolinus, the Roman god Jupiter as worshiped in his great temple on the Capitoline Hill in Rome). On the site of the ancient Jewish temple a pagan temple was erected to Jupiter Capitolinus, and all Jews were forbidden under pain of death to set foot within Jerusalem.

II. THE ROMAN PROVINCIAL SYSTEM

The Roman Empire achieved what previous empires had attempted with only partial success—the welding of many nationalities and peoples into one unified whole. Because of its peculiar genius for law and government, Rome was able to maintain a more or less stable civil order for nearly half a millennium.

The secret of Rome's success where others had failed lay in its wise provision for differing kinds of local supervision and control. The emperor was the effective head of the state, but under him were many aides to whom he delegated certain of his own powers and prerogatives. Newly subjugated territories were brought under Roman jurisdiction as provinces or subject kingdoms. In 27 B.C., the emperor Augustus divided the thirty-two existing provinces into two categories. The senatorial provinces (eleven in number) continued to be governed by ex-consuls and ex-praetors, appointed by lot under senatorial supervision. The imperial provinces (twenty-one in number) were under the direct control of the emperor, to which he sent his own agents who were responsible to himself alone.

The senatorial provinces were, on the whole, the older, richer, and more peaceful territories, which had long since been subjugated and where there was no danger of an uprising. Such a province was governed by a proconsul, that is, one acting for the consul. He was appointed to serve for one year, though occasionally the appointment was renewed. The proconsul had no legionary troops under his command and was attended by quaestors, who collected the revenues and paid them into the treasury managed by the senate.

However, imperial provinces were usually the newer, frontier areas that had been recently added to the empire and within whose boundaries were many revolutionary elements, seething and ready to assert themselves. Such a territory was kept under the surveillance of the emperor himself, who appointed an agent to serve for as long or as short a time as seemed good to the emperor. There were two kinds of imperial provinces. The larger ones were governed by a legate (his full title was *legatus Augusti pro praetore*), who served in the capacity of both military governor and chief magistrate. The smaller imperial provinces were ruled by a governor who bore the title of *praefectus;* from the time of the emperor Claudius (A.D. 41–54), however, it became customary to call such a governor the *procurator Augusti.* When Archelaus was deposed by the emperor Augustus in A.D. 6, Judea, Samaria, and Idumea were formed into a division of the prefecture of Syria; it was called the province of Judea and put under Roman governors. These governors were in some degree subordinate to the legate of Syria, but within Judea their authority was absolute. The Roman garrison stationed in the province was at their command, and all important matters came before their judgment seat. They had the power of life and death *(ius gladii)*, and their sentences were executed by the military.

The governors of Judea commonly resided at Caesarea by the sea, but they were accustomed to go up to Jerusalem at the festivals and sometimes to winter there, and they visited other cities of their dominion as occasion required. When in Jerusalem, they would occupy the palace erected by Herod the Great. Pontius Pilate was governor[3] of Judea from A.D. 26 to 36, and it was during his rule that Jesus was condemned to death by crucifixion.

In addition to the Roman provinces, there were also a considerable number of semi-independent kingdoms within the orbit of the Roman Empire. Part of the Roman genius for adapting the form of government to local situations can be seen in the policy of allowing, whenever feasible, the native rulers of annexed territories to continue their jurisdiction over their people, though answerable to Rome. If the country was of fairly great importance, the title *king* was permitted to its ruler, but in smaller and less significant areas the subject prince was given the title of *ethnarch* or *tetrarch.* The name tetrarch means, strictly, a person who rules over a fourth part (it goes back to Philip of Macedon's dividing Thessaly into four districts called tetrarchies), but eventually the word came to be used loosely of any petty subject prince.

Slightly higher in prestige was the title ethnarch, which was used with various meanings, ranging from "chief" to "governor." It was used, like tetrarch, to designate a ruler over a territory not great

---

3. An inscription contemporary with Pilate's tenure of office, found at Caesarea, calls him "prefect of Judea." Later Jewish and Roman historians, such as Josephus and Tacitus, refer to him as "procurator of Judea," but they probably use this title, which had become current in their day, anachronistically of Pilate. Throughout the New Testament, Pilate and his successors are designated by the general term "governor."

Figure 1.6. The Pontius Pilate Inscription
(Courtesy of Bastiaan Van Elderen.)

The only reference to Pontius Pilate in an inscription came to light in 1961 at Caesarea Maritina, the city of Pilate's residence in Israel. The stone had been reused in the construction of a landing between flights of steps in an open theater. Despite the poor condition of the stone three lines may be partially reconstructed:

]TIBERIEVM
PON]TIVS PILATVS
PRAEF]ECTVS IVDA[EA]E

Apparently the first line refers to some important building, perhaps dedicated in honor of the Emperor Tiberius.

enough to be classified as a kingdom. Sometimes the Roman emperor would deliberately assign a new ruler the title tetrarch or ethnarch as though he were on probation, and if he was successful in his rule (gauged in large part by the quantity of revenues he managed to collect), he would eventually be advanced to the rank of "king."

III. THE LANGUAGES CURRENT IN PALESTINE

Fastened to the top of the cross on which Jesus was crucified was an inscription that was written in Hebrew, Latin, and Greek

(John 19:20). This trilingual inscription accords with what is known from other sources to be a fact, namely that Palestine was a cosmopolitan country in which several different languages were current.

Latin was the official language of the conquerors. It was used by the governors as well as by the soldiers of the Roman army of occupation. Very few Palestinian Jews knew more than the most common of everyday Latin words that had been, so to speak, naturalized wherever the Roman garrisons had been stationed. These were words such as "centurion," "legion," "denarius," "praetorium," "colony," and the like. The trial of Jesus before Pontius Pilate would obviously have required the use of an interpreter.

The Greek language, on the contrary, was widely understood in Palestine, particularly in the north, which was commonly called "Galilee of the Gentiles." Here, more frequently than in Judea to the south, Jews would come into contact with Greek-speaking Gentiles, and, in order to hold one's own in the marketplace, bilingualism was an economic necessity. As was explained earlier, this bilingualism had its historical roots in the second century before Christ, when the Seleucid rulers promoted the deliberate policy of grecizing the Jewish population of Palestine. Though the Maccabean reaction had temporarily delayed the process of hellenization, inevitably more and more of Greek culture and language permeated Palestine. It is safe to say that at the time of Jesus most educated Palestinian Jews of the upper classes knew at least some Greek, especially those living in Jerusalem and the larger cities.

The third language in common use in Palestine was Aramaic, the mother tongue of the great majority of Jews. Though the rabbis and learned scribes still had a fluent command of the classical Hebrew of the Old Testament, for the ordinary Jewish populace Hebrew was approaching the status of a dead language. During the exile in the sixth century, the Jews had begun to use Aramaic, a Semitic language related to Hebrew somewhat as Spanish is related to Portuguese. At the beginning of the Christian Era, in the synagogues of Palestine as well as of Babylon, the text of the Old Testament was read not only in the original Hebrew, but also rendered in an Aramaic paraphrase, called a Targum,[4] for the benefit of those Jews in the congregation who knew little or no Hebrew.

Several of the seven different Western Aramaic dialects were current in Palestine. The dialect used in Galilee was recognizably different in pronunciation from the southern dialect spoken in and around Jerusalem. The difference may be described as twofold—pronunciation and vocabulary. The former was the more distinctive feature, and in many instances resulted in a changed orthography. According to rabbinic sources, the northern brogue of the Galileans was characterized by a vague or indistinct utterance of certain letters, and by the confusion or suppression of others, especially the gutterals. Thus, Peter's accent betrayed his northern origin to a Jerusalemite bystander during Jesus' trial before Caiaphas in Jerusalem (Matt. 26:73). Galilean must not be regarded as a later and more degenerate form of Judean, any more than Aramaic itself should be regarded as a corrupt form of Hebrew. In any complete statement it would be necessary to distinguish the vernacular and the literary language of Palestine.

Other dialects of Western Aramaic used in the period of the New Testament include Samaritan Aramaic and Nabatean Aramaic. The Samaritan dialect was a very early form of Aramaic. On the whole, it was more akin to Galilean than to Judean, but was closer to Hebrew than either. Samaritan pronunciation, continued in use today in the small community of Samaritans at and around Nablus (the ancient Shechem), differs in some respects from other Aramaic dialects. The Nabateans, who earlier had been nomads, reached their culmination under King Aretas IV (9 B.C.–A.D. 40), whose ethnarch endeavored to arrest Paul at Damascus (2 Cor. 11:32). All these forms of Western Aramaic were mutually understandable.

---

4. The Targums are interpretative renderings of all the books of the Hebrew Scriptures (with the exception of Ezra, Nehemiah, and Daniel). At first the Targum was oral, a simple paraphrase in Aramaic, but eventually in written form it became elaborate and incorporated explanatory details inserted here and there into the translation. The functions of these glosses were various, including the harmonizing of conflicting texts, the resolving of textual difficulties by interpreting obscure words or simplifying syntax, and the strengthening (or occasionally even negating) of the force of the scriptural passage. There also was a tendency to avoid direct reference to the ineffable name of God (Yahweh), and anthropomorphisms generally were avoided. For further discussion, with examples of such modifications, reference can be made to the present writer's book *The Bible in Translation: Ancient and English Versions* (Grand Rapids: Baker Academic, 2001), pp. 20-24.

By way of summarizing, it is altogether probable that Jesus grew up in his home at Nazareth using Aramaic as his mother tongue. In later life he doubtless acquired some facility in speaking Greek and in reading Hebrew. His teaching and preaching to the common people would have been carried on in Aramaic; his debates with the learned scribes may have been conducted in Hebrew. When he occasionally conversed with non-Jewish persons (for example, the Roman centurion and the Syro-Phoenician woman), he probably used Greek, the lingua franca of the Greco-Roman world.[5]

---

5. For additional information, the following may be consulted: Joseph A. Fitzmyer, "The Languages of Palestine in the First Century A.D.," in *A Wandering Aramean: Collected Aramaic Essays* (Missoula: Scholars Press, 1979), pp. 29-56; Klaus Beyer, *The Aramaic Language: Its Distribution and Subdivisions* (Göttingen: Vandenhoeck & Reprecht, 1986); Michael O. Wise, "Languages of Palestine," *Dictionary of Jesus and the Gospels*, Joel B. Green and Scott McKnight, eds. (Downers Grove, Ill.: InterVarsity Press, 1992), pp. 434-44; and Alan Millard, *Reading and Writing in the Time of Jesus* (New York: New York University Press, 2000).

CHAPTER 2

THE CULTURAL AND RELIGIOUS BACKGROUND OF PALESTINIAN JUDAISM

Although it is needful for the student of the New Testament to know something of the political and social conditions of Palestinian Judaism outlined in the previous chapter, it is even more necessary to be acquainted with the cultural and religious background of Jesus and his contemporaries. What books influenced the thinking of Jews in Palestine? How did Jewish beliefs and aspirations find expression in the rise of religious sects and parties? Who were the scribes and rabbis, and what was the nature of the piety fostered by the synagogues? The answers to these and similar questions bearing on the inward, spiritual life of Palestinian Jews are of central importance in understanding the matrix in which and from which the Christian church emerged.

I. SURVEY OF INTERTESTAMENTAL JEWISH LITERATURE

The Bible of Jesus and his earliest followers was the Hebrew Scriptures, which today are called the Old Testament. The most important of the ideas and ideals that molded the intellectual and religious life of Jews came from the Laws of Moses and the writings of the Hebrew prophets. It is obvious that no one can fully understand the New Testament without taking into account the thirty-nine books of the Old Testament, and it is assumed that the readers of the present book have some knowledge of the contents of the Old Testament.

During the centuries between the close of the Old Testament period and the opening of the New Testament period, the Jews continued to produce religious literature. Much of this was on a distinctly lower level than that included in the Hebrew Scriptures, and was never regarded by Palestinian Jews as possessing the same religious authority as the books of the Old Testament. At the same time, most of these intertestamental books were widely read, and exerted a lasting influence on religious life and thought.

In contrast to the authoritative or canonical literature of the Old Testament, these intertestamental books were called *apocryphal*, a term that originally meant "hidden." Traditionally, fifteen such books, or parts of books, belong to the Apocrypha, but besides these there are many other similar works that also are apocryphal.[1]

The intertestamental literature falls into several literary categories. According to their subject matter these books may be classed as *(a)* historical; *(b)* legendary or novelistic; *(c)* didactic or sapiential; and *(d)* apocalyptic. The following are representative examples in each category.

(a) About one hundred years before the beginning of the Christian Era an ardent admirer of the Maccabean patriots wrote, perhaps at Jerusalem, the story of the three brothers—Judas, Jonathan, and Simon—who had freed Judea from her Syrian oppressors and restored the purity of her worship (see chapter 1). The First Book of the Maccabees is a stirring narrative told by one who was proud of the achievements of the sons of Mattathias. The unknown author depended upon annals and archives of historically valuable materials, and he put this material together in a sober and straightforward account. Taken as a whole, 1 Maccabees is an exceedingly valuable source of information concerning the Maccabean uprising and its aftermath, covering about forty years (175 to 134 B.C.).

The Second Book of the Maccabees deals with a period of about fifteen years, extending from before the accession of Antiochus Epiphanes (175 B.C.) down to the year 160 (see p. 25). Thus the book

---

1. The books traditionally called the Apocrypha were included in the King James Bible (1611) between the Old and New Testaments. They have been available since 1957 in the Revised Standard Version, both as a separate volume and bound at the close of the Bible. For a convenient edition with introduction and notes, the *Oxford Annotated Apocrypha* (New York: Oxford University Press, 1965) may be consulted. For a condensed version of each of the fifteen texts, see the present writer's *Introduction to the Apocrypha* (New York: Oxford University Press, 1957).

is in the main parallel to the first part of 1 Maccabees, though independent of that work. Unlike the sober and unadorned style of 1 Maccabees, the unknown author of 2 Maccabees chose to write in the artificial and florid style of what is called "pathetic history," so popular in Alexandria at that period. As a result, his book is a rhetorical and melodramatic account, historically somewhat less trustworthy than 1 Maccabees.

A special aim of the author seems to have been the honoring of the temple at Jerusalem. Not only does he frequently refer to it with obvious affection and reverence (as in 2:19, 22; 3:12; 5:15-21; 14:31; 15:18), but he is concerned to relate fully the circumstances connected with the institution of a great national festival of the Jews—the annual festival of Dedication, commemorating the purification of the temple three years after its desecration by Antiochus Epiphanes. Likewise, 2 Maccabees throws light upon the development of doctrine among Palestinian Jews during their struggle with the Seleucid dynasty. The author makes it clear that he holds rather fully developed doctrines of Providence, of retributive justice, and of the resurrection of the body. Furthermore, his description of the frightful persecution and martyrdom of a Jewish mother and her seven sons, who refused to renounce their faith (chap. 7), became for Jewish and Christian readers alike an object lesson worthy of devout imitation.

(b) Among the purely legendary or novelistic books of intertestamental literature are the stories of Tobit and Judith. The former is an entertaining and moralizing narrative written about 190–170 B.C. A devout Jew in Nineveh named Tobit has the misfortune of losing his eyesight after having performed the pious act of providing honorable burial for members of his race who had been the victims of persecution. Subsequently, his son Tobias goes on a long journey to Media in order to reclaim a sum of money that had been left in trust with a friend of the family named Gabael. The adventures of the young man, accompanied on his journey by the angel Raphael, who is disguised as a traveling companion and guide, are both entertaining and edifying. Managing to overcome a foul demon that threatened his life, Tobias marries a beautiful girl; he also obtains a concoction that, on his return home, effects a cure on his father's blind eyes. Though the story reminds one of the *Arabian*

Nights tales, it proved to be valuable for inculcating lofty moral standards in personal life and in family relationships. For example, Tobit's exhortation given to his son just before his son started his journey includes the Golden Rule in a negative form: "What you hate, do not do to anyone" (Tob. 4:15). It is not surprising that a book that manages to combine religious and ethical teaching with an entertaining story of travel, love, adventure, conflict, and a happy ending had a wide circulation.

The book of Judith is another adventure story that attained wide circulation. It reflects the belief that God will defend his people if they observe his Law; otherwise he will allow their foes to prevail. The heroine of the stirring tale is a Jew who combines the most scrupulous observance of the Mosaic Laws with a grim and cunning bravery in the face of great personal danger. In the midst of war between the Assyrians and the Jews, the city of Bethulia is in grave danger of being destroyed. When it seems that all hope must be abandoned, Judith undertakes to outwit Holofernes, the general of the Assyrian forces.

As compared with the story of Tobit, which inculcates such virtues as gentleness and kindliness, the plot of the book of Judith is strenuous, not to say fierce and almost vindictive. The name of the heroine was doubtless chosen to suggest her as a counterpart to that doughty warrior, Judas Maccabeus. The story relates how, during a banquet held in Judith's honor in his tent, Holofernes drinks much more wine than he had ever drunk at one time before. While he lies on his couch in a drunken stupor, Judith seizes his scimitar and, with a prayer to God for strength, cuts off his head.

Two ancient "detective stories" that circulated among the Jews just prior to the beginning of the Christian Era were eventually added to the Greek translation of the book of Daniel. One of these, the story of Susanna, is a literary gem; it is based on the motif of the triumph of virtue over villainy, the narrow escape from death of an innocent victim falsely accused of adultery. While inculcating lessons of morality and trust in God, the plot also grips the reader's interest from the outset. The other tale, which in literary technique is much inferior to the story of Susanna, is entitled Bel and the Dragon. In it the author heaps ridicule upon the folly of idolatry and seeks to discredit heathen priestcraft.

(c) Two books of the Apocrypha—the Wisdom of Solomon and Ecclesiasticus—belong to that genre of ancient literature known as sapiential or Wisdom literature. The authors of this type of literature were called wise men or sages, and they exercised almost as much influence in personal and national life as did the priest and the prophet.

The treatise known as the Wisdom of Solomon attempts to unite the conventional piety of Orthodox Judaism with the Greek philosophical spirit current in Alexandria during the first century B.C. By means of enthusiastic and verbose repetition, the unknown author, who impersonates King Solomon, lauds wisdom as the only true guide for life and condemns materialism as voluntary ignorance.

Ecclesiasticus, otherwise known as the Wisdom of Jesus Son of Sirach, has many affinities with the Old Testament book of Proverbs. The author, who wrote the treatise in Hebrew about 180 B.C., is concerned with wisdom chiefly as it relates to practical ethics and to general human conduct regulated by divine statutes. One of the famous chapters of Sirach deals with the honor that is due physicians (chap. 38).

(d) Apocalyptic is the name given to that type of literature that purports to reveal the future (the Greek word *apokalypsis* means literally "unveiling, revealing"). The book known as 2 Esdras is a typical example of apocalyptic literature. Written sometime in the first Christian century, and attributed to the ancient Israelite leader Ezra, the unknown author makes a valiant attempt to reconcile the earthly calamities of the Jews with the righteous government of God. In common with other apocalypses, 2 Esdras includes many symbols involving mysterious numbers, strange beasts, and the disclosure of hitherto hidden truths through angelic visitants.

Another apocalyptic work, though not included among the fifteen books traditionally called the Apocrypha, is the book of Enoch, also known as 1 Enoch or Ethiopic Enoch. This is a long, rambling work, the product of several authors who lived during the period from about 200 B.C. to about A.D. 100. It embodies a series of revelations, of which the antediluvian Enoch is the professed recipient, on such matters as the origin of evil, the angels and their destinies, the nature of Gehenna and Paradise, and the preexistent Messiah. The entire work, which was written in

Hebrew or Aramaic, is preserved in an Ethiopic translation; portions of the book are extant also in Aramaic, Greek, and Latin.

Besides 1 Enoch, several other Jewish and Jewish-Christian pseudepigrapha (that is, writings that circulated under false titles) were produced during the period just before and just after the rise of Christianity. These include the Assumption of Moses, the Sibylline Oracles, Slavonic Enoch, the Psalms of Solomon, the Testaments of the Twelve Patriarchs, the Book of Jubilees, the Histories of Adam and Eve, and the Ascension of Isaiah.[2]

The importance of the intertestamental apocryphal and pseudepigraphic literature lies in the information that it supplies concerning the development of Jewish life and thought just prior to the beginning of the Christian Era. The political fortunes of the Jews from the time of the Maccabean uprising onward; the emergence of what has been called normative Judaism, which became characteristic of the religion of the Pharisees; the lush growth of popular belief in the activities of angels and demons; the growing preoccupation with the doctrine of original sin and its relation to the "evil inclination" in every person; the blossoming of apocalyptic hopes relating to the coming Messiah, the resurrection of the body, and the vindication of the righteous—all these subjects and many others receive additional light from the intertestamental literature.

II. SECTS, PARTIES, AND CLASSES WITHIN PALESTINIAN JUDAISM

The total population of Palestine in the first century of the Christian Era was probably between one and a half million and two million persons. Of this number approximately 500,000 to 600,000 were Jews, the majority of whom lived in Judea, in the southern part of Palestine. Here was located Jerusalem, the capital of the country, with a Jewish population variously estimated to have been between 25,000 and 95,000. The northern part of the country, Galilee, where Jesus spent most of his life, was predominately non-Jewish in population, and hence was often called "Galilee of the Gentiles" (Isa. 9:1; 1 Macc. 5.15; Matt. 4:15).

---

2. An English translation of these pseudepigrapha is available in the edition prepared by R. H. Charles, *The Apocrypha and Pseudepigrapha of the Old Testament*, vol. 2 (Oxford: Clarendon Press, 1913), and, with many additional texts, in James H. Charlesworth, *The Old Testament Pseudepigrapha*, 2 vols. (Garden City, N.Y.: Doubleday, 1983, 1985).

According to the Jewish historian Flavius Josephus (A.D. 37–100), there were three chief religious sects in Palestine—the Pharisees, the Sadducees, and the Essenes. In the days of Herod the Great the number of adult male Jews who belonged to the sect of the Pharisees was slightly above six thousand. When this number is compared with the total number of Jews in Palestine it will be seen that, contrary to a commonly held opinion, the proportion of Pharisees to the total Jewish population was relatively small. It is probable that most of the Pharisees lived in or near Jerusalem.

1. THE PHARISEES

Of the origin and the antecedents of the Pharisees there is no record. It is commonly surmised that they were the successors of those who in earlier generations were called the Hasideans (= the Pious) in distinction from their worldly and indifferent country-men. The group (as was mentioned in chapter 1) probably arose prior to and during the Maccabean uprising in reaction to the hellenizing process that the Seleucid rulers attempted to impose on the Jews. After the Maccabean uprising ceased to be a struggle for religious liberty and became a contest for political supremacy, most of the Hasideans lost interest in it. The Pharisees appear first under that name during the rule of John Hyrcanus (135–105 B.C.). Though its etymology has been disputed, the word *Pharisees* is generally interpreted to mean "the separated ones."

In describing the beliefs and practices of the Pharisees, it is customary to begin with a statement of Josephus: "The Pharisees are a group of Jews who have the reputation of excelling the rest of their nation in the observance of religion, and as exact exponents of the laws" (*Jewish War*, I.v.2). It was this accurate interpretation of the Mosaic Law, and scrupulous adherence to it, that characterized the religiosity of the average Pharisee.

In distinguishing the Pharisees from the Sadducees, Josephus enumerates several doctrines held by the former and denied by the latter (*Jewish War*, II.viii.14; *Antiquities*, XVIII.i.3). They are the following:

(*a*) The Pharisees held the doctrine of foreordination, and considered it consistent with one's free will. The Sadducees denied that history was divinely controlled, insisting on the individual's freedom to direct one's life and thus history itself.

(b) The Pharisees believed in the immortality of the soul as well as the resurrection of the body. They held that individuals are rewarded or punished in the future life, according as they have lived virtuously or viciously in this life. The Sadducees derided these beliefs.

(c) The Pharisees had highly developed views of angels and demons, but the Sadducees rejected the developed doctrine of the two kingdoms with their hierarchies of good and evil spirits (compare Acts 23:8).

(d) The Pharisees recognized as the supreme authority in religion the written Hebrew Scriptures and the oral tradition that comprised an accumulated body of pronouncements of Jewish teachers down through the generations. Conversely, the Sadducees accepted only Scripture and, therefore, rejected all beliefs and practices not taught in the Old Testament.

Though these doctrinal differences serve to distinguish the Pharisees from the Sadducees, they do not constitute the essence of Pharisaism. Pharisaism is the final result of that conception of religion that makes religion consist in conformity to the Law, and promises God's grace only to the doers of the Law. It was the scrupulous adherence to legalistic traditions that created the Pharisaic ethos. In most religions there is an ever-present tendency to regard outward formalism as more important than inward disposition of the heart, and in Pharisaism this natural tendency often became so strong as to give rise to the modern use of the name *Pharisee* to describe a self-righteous formalist or hypocrite.

It must not be supposed, however, that all Pharisees were nothing but hypocrites. At first, when it was dangerous to be known as an opponent of Hellenism, Pharisees were men of strong religious character and devout commitment to God. Subsequently Pharisaism became an inherited belief, the profession of which was popular, and men of less heroic mold joined its ranks.

As in other religious movements, the proportion of sincere, earnest adherents came to be outnumbered by those who were characterized by less worthy motives. Even the Jewish Talmud itself acknowledges the existence of several kinds of Pharisees, not all of whom were good and upright. It differentiates seven varieties, and vividly characterizes five of them with descriptive adjectives that hold them up for ridicule: (a) The "wait-a-little" Pharisee always has an excuse for putting off doing a good deed. *(b)* The "bruised" or "bleeding" Pharisee, in order to avoid looking at a woman, shuts his eyes and stumbles against the wall so as to bruise himself and bleed. *(c)* The "shoulder" Pharisee wears, as it were, his good deeds ostentatiously upon his shoulders, where all can see them. *(d)* The "hump-backed" Pharisee walks about stooped over in mock humility. *(e)* The "ever-reckoning" Pharisee is continually counting up his good deeds to balance them against his bad deeds. *(f)* The "God-fearing" Pharisee stands in awe and dread of God. *(g)* "God-loving" or "born" Pharisee is a true son of Abraham and a genuine Pharisee.[3]

It will be recalled that John the Baptist called the Pharisees and the Sadducees "a brood of vipers" (Matt. 3:7), and that Jesus severely denounced the Pharisees for their self-righteousness, their hypocrisy, and their inattention to the weightier matters of the Mosaic Law, while being very punctilious concerning minute points (Matt. 5:20; 16:6, 11-12; 23:1-39). Jesus' scathing rebukes are sometimes assumed to mean, "Woe to the party of the Pharisees, none of whom are any good!" In light of all the evidence, however, it appears that Jesus' "woes" are to be understood as directed against those kinds of Pharisees who were unworthy of the heritage of the Hasideans. According to the Gospels, Jesus was on friendly terms with some of the Pharisees, such as Simon, who made a banquet for him (Luke 7:37). On another occasion certain Pharisees warned him that Herod was seeking his life (Luke 13:31). Other Pharisees, however, whose religious formalism and hypocrisy Jesus had denounced so vigorously, took a prominent part in plotting his death (Mark 3:6; John 11:47-57).

2. THE SADDUCEES

The word *Sadducee* probably comes from the name Zadok, which was often written *Saddouk* in Greek. Among prominent Jews who bore the name Zadok, it is customary to trace the Sadducees back to the high priest Zadok who officiated in David's reign (1 Chron. 16:39; 24:3, 31) and in whose family the high priesthood remained until the political confusion of the Maccabean times.

---

3. For these types see Rabbi Kaufmann Kohler in *The Jewish Encyclopedia* (New York: Funk & Wagnalls Co., 1905), IX, p. 665.

During the program of hellenization of Palestine imposed by the Seleucid rulers, it was the Sadducean high priests who came in touch with foreign influences. As their political authority grew, their religious devotion waned, and the author of 1 Maccabees regarded such leaders as renegades and traitors to the heritage of their fathers (1 Macc. 1:15).

In Jesus' time, the Sadducees were a small group numerically, but they exercised a widespread influence in politics and religion. Judging from what Josephus tells us, they were educated men, and mostly of prominent positions *(Antiquities, XVIII.i.4)*. Sociologically, the Sadducees represented the sophisticated, urban class that was centered in Jerusalem. Many of them were wealthy landholders. They had no following among the masses, whose sympathies, Josephus says *(Antiquities, XIII.x.6)*, were largely on the side of the Pharisees.

Doctrinally, the Sadducees differed from the Pharisees in the several respects previously mentioned. The most basic of these was the rejection of the accumulated oral traditions by which Pharisees interpreted and expanded the Mosaic Law. From this point of view the Sadducees were conservative theologically, while liberal politically.

3. THE ESSENES

The Essenes, which were the third major Jewish sect, are not mentioned in the New Testament. According to information given by Philo, Josephus, and Pliny, they numbered about four thousand and devoted themselves to a simple and abstemious life. The stricter Essenes refrained from marriage. Admission to the communal life of the group was gained only after a period of probation of three years, and upon joining the sect, members turned over their property to a common treasury. The chief religious exercises involved ritual washings and baptisms; stated periods for prayer, beginning at sunrise; and the continuous reading and study of the Hebrew Scriptures. The Essenes believed that the promises of God foretold through the prophets were being fulfilled in the history of their own community.

The Essenes did not participate in the animal sacrifices at the temple in Jerusalem, not because they advocated more spiritual principles of worship, but because they held that the temple worship was polluted. They wore white robes as symbolic of inward purity. Their interpretation of the sabbath law was even more rigid than that of the Pharisees.

There were colonies of Essenes in various towns of Judea, but the wilderness west of the Dead Sea was a favorite location for their settlements. About the middle of the twentieth century, the ruins of a monastic-like community near Qumran were unearthed, and in neighboring caves several scrolls, sealed within jars, were discovered, as well as hundreds of fragments of scriptural and apocryphal fragments in Hebrew, Aramaic, and Greek. Both the buildings and the scrolls are dated by archaeologists and palaeographers approximately to the period 100 B.C. to A.D. 100. The manuscripts, which are called the Dead Sea Scrolls, belonged to a large library that included most, if not all, of the Old Testament books (of some, such as Psalms, Deuteronomy, and Isaiah, there are a dozen or more fragmentary copies), a number of apocryphal works, and half a dozen writings belonging specifically to the sect. The latter, especially the so-called Manual of Discipline, give us a fairly detailed insight into the group's beliefs and practices.[4]

4. THE HERODIANS

A dozen theories have been proposed concerning the origin and views of the Herodians; according to most scholars, it seems clear that they were neither a religious sect nor a political party. The term apparently denotes an attitude and an outlook, and refers to Jews of influence and standing who supported the Herodian rule, and hence also that of the Romans, by whose authority the Herodian dynasty was maintained. In such allegiance they were definitely in the minority, for most Palestinian Jews were strongly opposed to that regime.

---

4. Several English translations of the Dead Sea Scrolls are available, including those by Geza Vermes, Michael Wise, Martin G. Abegg Jr., and Edward M. Cook, *The Dead Sea Scrolls: A New Translation* (San Francisco: HarperSanFrancisco, 1996); Geza Vermes, *The Complete Dead Sea Scrolls in English* (New York: Allen Lane/Penguin Press, 1997); Florentino García Martínez, *The Dead Sea Scrolls Translated*, Wilfred G. E. Watson, trans., 2nd ed. (Leiden: Brill, 1996). The last has been issued as a Study Edition in two volumes, with the (unpointed) Hebrew text, edited by Florentino García Martínez and Eibert J. C. Tigchelaar (Leiden: Brill; Grand Rapids: Eerdmans, 2000), paperback.

For twelve authoritative studies on the Dead Sea Scrolls and related literature, see Joseph A. Fitzmyer, S.J., *The Dead Sea Scrolls and Christian Origins* (Grand Rapids: Eerdmans, 2000).

In the Gospels, the Herodians are mentioned as enemies of Jesus, once in Galilee (Mark 3:6), and again at Jerusalem (Matt. 22:16; Mark 12:13). On the latter occasion they combined with the Pharisees in seeking to entangle Jesus with the question, "Is it lawful to pay taxes to the emperor, or not?" They expected that Jesus would have to commit himself as favoring either nationalism or submission to a foreign power. Asking to see a denarius, he responded, "Give to the emperor the things that are the emperor's, and to God the things that are God's."

Figure 2.1. A Silver Denarius of the Emperor Tiberius
(Courtesy of the Princeton Theological Seminary.)

Denarii commemorating the Emperor Tiberius (A.D. 14–37) have been found in almost every country within the Roman Empire. Design of this specimen: Head of Tiberius laureate, with legend: TI(berius) CAESAR DIVI AUG(usti) F(ilius) AUGUSTUS ("Tiberius Caesar Augustus, son of the divine Augustus"). Reverse side: a seated female (probably his mother, Livia) in the role of Pax ("Peace"), holding a (olive?) branch and a scepter; the legend is a continuation of the emperor's titles, PONTIF(ex) MAXIM(us).

5. THE ZEALOTS

The party of the Zealots, described by Josephus as the "fourth philosophy" among the Jews (*Jewish War*, II.viii.1; *Antiquities*, XVIII.i.1 and 6), may have been founded by Judas the Galilean, who stirred up a rebellion against the Romans in A.D. 6 (Acts 5:37). The Zealots opposed the payment of tribute by Israel to a pagan emperor on the ground that this was treason against God, Israel's true King. In religious beliefs they agreed with the Pharisees, and in spirit they revived the zeal shown by Mattathias and his sons during the Maccabean uprising. Though the rebels were defeated and Judas was killed, members of his family continued to keep alive the aspirations for liberty and independence.

Modern scholars have questioned whether the Zealots of the Jewish revolt that began in A.D. 66 existed as a distinct party in the early part of the first century. But there is little doubt that Israel always had her feisty bands of patriots ready to support the struggle for national independence. Confusion arises through the mention of the word *Zealots* in many obscure passages.

About the middle of the first century, another patriotic agitator from Egypt gathered a group of some four thousand militant Jewish nationalists. Since they had armed themselves with concealed daggers, they were called *Sicarii*, that is, the Assassins (Acts 21:38; Josephus, *Jewish War*, II.xiii.3). Zealots were active throughout the war of A.D. 66–70, a war that resulted in the fall of Jerusalem. The last pocket of Zealot resistance continued to hold out for three more years at Masada near the Dead Sea, a palace-fortress planned by Herod the Great as a refuge for himself. In April A.D. 73, on the night before the Romans finally breached the walls on the upper terrace, the last de-fenders killed their wives, their children, and then themselves rather than surrender (see Josephus's account in his *Jewish War*, VII.viii).

That Jesus had a former Zealot in his apostolic band (Luke 6:15; Acts 1:13), as well as Matthew, who had been a tax collector for the hated Romans, is an illuminating commentary upon the breadth of his appeal to persons of the most diverse backgrounds.

6. THE COMMON PEOPLE

The great majority of Palestinian Jews (more than 90 percent) were unaffiliated with any of the sects and groups previously mentioned. These multitudes were known as the people of the land (*'am ha-arets*). In the earlier books of the Old Testament, this term meant merely the common people, as distinct from rulers and aristocracy. After the return from the exile, the phrase was sharpened to designate those Palestinians whose Judaism was mixed or suspect, and with whom the more scrupulous Jews could not intermarry

(Ezra 9:1-2; Neh. 10:30-31). In New Testament times the term came to mean specifically all those who, either through ignorance or indifference, failed to observe the Mosaic Law and all its ramifications. The antipathy of the Pharisaic elite for the common people finds expression in John 7:49, where the designation "this crowd" is applied with scornful contempt to the ignorant masses who do not know the Law. So deep-seated was the Pharisees' disdain for the people of the land, who were regarded as immoral and irreligious, that they avoided as far as possible all contact with them. According to rabbinical law they were not to be summoned as witnesses, nor their testimony admitted in court. No secret was to be entrusted to them, nor should one of them be appointed guardian of an orphan. A Pharisee could not eat with a member of the *am ha-arets*, and marriage between the two classes was condemned in terms of abhorrence (the Pharisees' judgment was that "their women are unclean vermin").

Now Jesus was friendly with this class of people, and freely associated with them. Though the Pharisees regarded them as worthless outcasts, he was sympathetic toward their plight and referred to them as "sheep without a shepherd" (Matt. 9:36). As a result of Jesus' taking their part, and his own neglect to observe the minutiae of Pharisaic rules (such as the ceremonial washing of the hands before eating—Mark 7:1-5; Luke 6:1-5; 11:37-41), he was regarded with animosity by the religious leaders of his day.

Summary: The spread of Greek culture throughout the Near East following the conquests of Alexander the Great was for the Jews the beginning of long years of struggle for the maintenance of their distinctive national and religious life. The dominant Hellenism threatened to absorb or destroy all that was characteristic of traditional Hebrew thought and practice. Hence there arose among the Jews, at various times and under various names, a nationalistic party—those who, by emphasizing what was distinctive in Judaism, sought to maintain the old isolation and resist the incursion of Gentile ways and ideas. It was during this struggle between Judaism and Hellenism that the more important Jewish sects and parties emerged. The struggle had a twofold aspect: religious and political. The Pharisees, for example, embodied the principle of rigid observance of the Mosaic Law with its overgrowth of rabbinic traditions, and the Essenes outdid the Pharisees by withdrawing into small communities. In the political sphere, the Zealots were the extreme party seeking independence, saying that God alone was their King. Conversely, the principle of moderation and the practice of concession found expression on the religious side in the sect of the Sadducees and on the political side among the Herodians. In addition to the common people (the *'am ha-arets*), the chief sects and groups that are mentioned in the New Testament may be categorized as follows:

	Extremists	*Moderates*
In religion:	Pharisees	Sadducees
In politics:	Zealots	Herodians

III. SCRIBES AND RABBIS: THEIR DUTIES AND METHODS OF TEACHING

From time immemorial in the Near East, professional scribes performed a useful service as public secretaries. In ancient Israel, an amanuensis was employed to take down in writing what another dictated (Jer. 36:4, 18, 32). When, however, one reads in the New Testament of scribes, an entirely different type of work is envisaged. The change from a generally secular to a religious function came about during and after the exile. While in Babylon, the priestly caste became specialists in, and guardians of, the Mosaic Law. The most noted of these earlier scribes was the priest Ezra (Neh. 8:9), who was "a scribe skilled in the law of Moses" and "had set his heart to study the law of the LORD, and to do it, and to teach the statutes and ordinances in Israel" (Ezra 7:6, 10). In this latter respect he was the prototype of scribes of New Testament times, who were professional interpreters and teachers of the Hebrew Scriptures.

In the Gospels, the scribes are sometimes referred to as "lawyers," that is, experts in the sacred Mosaic Law, which was in theory the sole legislation, civil and religious, governing the Jewish people. They are also occasionally called "teachers of the law," or simply "teachers." It is easy to see how persons of such an occupation came to occupy a high position in the estimate of the common people. Their services were needed not only at Jerusalem, but in the villages throughout Judea and Galilee as well (Luke 5:17).

The titles that were bestowed upon the scribes indicate the extraordinary respect accorded them by the populace. The usual title was the Hebrew appellation *rabbi,* meaning literally "my great one." In the period just after the New Testament times, this mode of address became a title that was used in talking not just to scribes, but about them as well (not simply, as in the New Testament, "Rabbi, what do you say . . . ?" but, "The rabbi said . . . "). Other common titles used in addressing a scribe, besides "my great one," were "master" and "teacher."

The scribes required of their students the most absolute reverence, surpassing even the honor felt for one's parents. According to their reasoning, one's father had brought his son only into this world, whereas one's teacher, who instructs a pupil in divine wisdom, brings him into the life of the world to come.

All the labors of the scribes, whether educational or judicial, were to be gratuitous. Therefore, in addition to teaching and transmitting the Law, Jewish scribes had to depend upon other means of obtaining a livelihood. Thus, Paul's trade was that of a tentmaker (Acts 18:3); other rabbis were stonemasons, leatherworkers, carpenters, and the like.

Most scribes belonged to the party of the Pharisees, but such phrases as "the scribes of the Pharisees" (Mark 2:16) and "certain scribes of the Pharisees' group" (Acts 23:9) are generally taken to imply that there were scribes with other sectarian affiliations, such as Sadducean scribes. The stereotyped phrase, "scribes and Pharisees," which occurs so often in Matthew and Luke, reflects the prominence of the status of the professional members of the Pharisaic party over those who were nonprofessional. Thus, not all Pharisees were scribes, nor were all scribes members of the Pharisaic sect.

The professional employment of scribes was a threefold one: they were concerned with *(a)* the more careful theoretical development of the Law itself; *(b)* the teaching of the Law to their pupils; *(c)* the practical administration of the Law in pronouncing legal decisions. Each of these aspects of their work deserves further comment:

(a) The theoretic development of the Law itself. In addition to the Ten Commandments, the Old Testament contains many other precepts and statutes. Within the five books of the Pentateuch (the Torah of the Hebrew Bible) Jewish scribes had counted a total of 613 commandments, 248 being positive and 365 negative. Some of the Mosaic Laws are expressed in very general terms, and these had to be made explicit and particular.

Thus, in order to obey the commandment forbidding work on the sabbath day (Exod. 20:8-11), one needed to know which activities constituted work and which did not. Obviously, for example, threshing grain and lifting burdens on the sabbath were work and were therefore prohibited. But many other activities might also fall into the same category, and these needed to be determined in order to avoid violating the divine commandment. In the course of the centuries it was decided that one might be allowed to walk through a grain field on the sabbath when the grain was ankle-high, but not if it were knee-high; for then one's legs would strike the ripened seeds of the grain, and, by such action, one would thresh some of the grain. Again, a poultice might be placed on a boil on the sabbath in order to prevent it from becoming worse, but not in order to promote its healing. If a cotton wadding that was worn in one's ear happened to fall out on the sabbath, it might not be replaced, for this was judged to constitute lifting a burden. Even certain actions, not unlawful in themselves, were forbidden on the sabbath lest they should become the occasion of actions deemed to be labor. Thus, a woman was forbidden to look in a mirror on the sabbath lest perchance she see a gray hair and be tempted to pluck it out, which would involve "working."

Occasionally, scribal ingenuity was exercised to provide relief from legislation that proved to be too restrictive. Thus, a sabbath day's journey (Acts 1:12) was the maximum distance (roughly about three fifths of a mile) that according to the scribes, one was permitted to walk beyond one's dwelling on the sabbath. Eventually, however, scribes devised ways of allowing a trip twice this distance. For example, if at the boundary of a sabbath day's journey a man deposited prior to the sabbath food for two meals, on the sabbath he could travel up to that point, constitute it his dwelling, and then proceed an equal distance beyond it.

Even the most trivial problems were debated with great earnestness by scribes. It was agreed, for example, that if one threw an object into the air and caught it with the same hand one had violated the sabbath commandment, but there was some doubt about one's guilt if the object were thrown into the air with one hand and caught with the other hand. Though such discussions among the scribes may seem to be unworthy of serious attention, it must not be forgotten that the Pharisees' determination to obey all of God's commands led them to seek out in ever more precise detail what did and what did not violate the Divine Law, as interpreted by the decisions of the scribes. The accumulated body of such legal pronouncements was called "the traditions of the elders" (Matt. 15:2; Mark 7:3, 5) and was transmitted orally until about A.D. 200 when it was reduced to writing in the Mishnah (see p. 63). More than once, Jesus came into conflict with the scribes when he rejected the unwritten tradition, regarding much of it as either superfluous or contrary to the original intention of God.

(*b*) The second chief task of the scribes was to teach the Law. The ideal of Pharisaic Judaism was that every Israelite should have a professional acquaintance with the Mosaic Law. If this were unattainable, then the greatest possible number of people were to be raised to this ideal elevation.

Elementary schools were established in connection with the synagogues, where children were taught to read from the Hebrew Scriptures, to write, and to do simple arithmetic. More advanced instruction in the Mosaic Law was provided by noted scribes who gathered about themselves followers, called disciples (literally "learners"). These disciples were followers both in the literal and in a figurative sense. When the scribe walked down the road, his disciples would follow a few feet behind him, for it was thought unseemly that learners should walk side by side with their master. Discussions and lectures on the Law were held in chambers connected with the outer court of the temple (Luke 2:46) or in a room of the synagogue. Not only was the instruction imparted directly to one's disciples in these schools, but on occasion learned scholars held public disputations with one another in the presence of their followers.

The method of teaching was by the indefatigable exercise of the memory. The object was that the pupil should learn with accuracy the entire matter, with its thousands upon thousands of minutiae. To accomplish this end, the teacher was obliged to repeat the material again and again to his pupils. Hence in rabbinic terminology "to repeat" *(shanah)* meant also "to teach."

Among the more mature students the scribe would introduce several legal questions for discussion. At the close of the discussion, during which previous decisions by earlier scribes were cited, the teacher would sum up his doctrine in a crisp aphorism. This material in turn became part of the oral tradition that was transmitted to succeeding generations of students.

Since all knowledge of the Law was strictly traditional, a pupil had only two duties: one was to commit everything faithfully to memory, and the other was never to teach anything other than that which had been delivered to him. The rabbis had a saying that the ideal pupil was like a limed (that is, a concrete) cistern, which never loses a drop of water that is put into it. The obligation of the pupil to reproduce to the next generation exactly what his master had taught him extended not only to ideas, but even to the manner of expression and the choice of words. Among the more strict groups, such as the Essenes, the pupil took an oath "to impart to no one a knowledge of the doctrines in a different manner from that in which he has received them himself."[5]

It will be obvious that in many respects Jesus of Nazareth was like a typical Jewish scribe. He gathered about himself a group of disciples who had responded to his call, "Follow me." They addressed him as "Rabbi" (see John 1:38; 4:31; 9:2; Mark 9:5; 11:21; 14:45; and others), and on one occasion asked him to compose and teach them a prayer, as John the Baptist had done for his disciples (Luke 11:1-2; see pp. 184-86). To assist his followers in remembering his teaching, Jesus cast noteworthy sections of it in a rhythmical structure (see pp. 165-66).

In other respects, however, Jesus differed in his teaching methods from contemporary teachers. His hearers soon discovered that, unlike the scribes who quoted from and appealed to the authority of earlier scribes, Jesus taught "as one having authority" himself (Matt. 7:28). Moreover, one of the peculiarities of Jesus' manner of teaching—not paralleled, so far as is known, by any Jewish teacher

---

5. Hippolytus, *Refutation of All Heresies,* ix.18, end.

before or since—was to preface his pronouncements with the word *amen* (usually translated *"Verily* I say to you . . . "). It will be pointed out later (p. 182) what significance this idiosyncrasy has for an understanding of his person and authority; here it is sufficient to call attention to the fidelity with which this mannerism in his teaching has been transmitted, first orally for a generation or more and then in written form in the Gospels.

(*c*) The third chief task of scribes was that of applying the Law. This they did by making pronouncements regarding the legality of certain actions and by issuing authoritative judgments concerning cases brought before them.

The technical terms used of rabbis when issuing authoritative decisions was "binding" or "loosing"; "to bind" was to declare an action unlawful, and "to loose" was to declare it lawful. Thus Rabbi Jochanan said, "Concerning gathering wood on a feast day, the school of Shammai binds [that is, forbids] it—the school of Hillel looses [that is, permits] it."[6]

In Judea, local courts that tried cases were composed of at least three judges. Cases concerning offenses punishable by death, however, were decided by twenty-three or more judges. The great council or Sanhedrin of Jerusalem was composed of seventy persons, and was presided over by the high priest, making seventy-one in all. In New Testament times, the great Sanhedrin included three kinds of members—the high priests (that is, the acting high priest and those who had been high priest), the elders (that is, tribal and family representatives of the lay aristocracy), and the scribes (these legal experts were chiefly from the Pharisaic party).

The authority of the Sanhedrin was dependent on the presence or absence of a national monarch. Under Herod the Great it possessed only a shadow of power. Under Roman governors, however, it was in practice the chief governing body in the land, regulating religious matters in complete freedom and civil matters within the limits set down by Rome. It had a body of police under its command and could make arrests on its own authority (Matt. 26:47; Mark 14:43). Capital cases required the confirmation of the

---

6. The power of binding and loosing, which, according to Matthew 16:19 and 18:18, Jesus promised to Peter and to the other disciples, was the power to decide with authority questions of faith and morals in the early church.

Roman governor (John 18:31), though the governor's judgment was usually in accordance with the sentence of the Sanhedrin.

When in session, the members of the Sanhedrin sat in a semicircle, so as to be able to see one another. At each end stood a clerk of the court, one to record votes of acquittal and the other votes of condemnation. The decision of acquittal required a simple majority, whereas a sentence of condemnation required a two-thirds majority. Disciples of the scribes were permitted to attend the proceedings and could speak in favor of acquittal, but not for condemnation. In capital cases, the arguments for acquittal were presented, then those for condemnation. If one spoke in favor of acquittal he could not later reverse his opinion, whereas if one spoke for condemnation he could later change his view.

It was before such a body that Jesus was tried (Matt. 26:59; John 11:47). Some time later Peter and John were interrogated by the council (Acts 4:5-7, 15; 5:27, 34). Stephen was taken before the council (6:12), though his murder appears to have been an illegal act of mob violence. Several years later Paul made his defense before the council (Acts 22:30; 23:15). The Sanhedrin was abolished at the time of the destruction of Jerusalem in A.D. 70.

After the fall of Jerusalem, Jewish scribes continued their work of the theoretical development of the Law and its codification. The retention in the memory of a vast number of details, which were continuously augmented by additional pronouncements, eventually became so burdensome that about A.D. 200 a leading Jewish scholar, Rabbi Jehuda, ventured to commit the "tradition of the elders" to writing. This material, in Hebrew, is called the *Mishnah*, and comprises sixty-three tractates grouped in six major divisions that cover the whole range of Pentateuchal legislation.[7]

Reducing the traditional Law to writing did not, of course, prevent further elucidation and the accumulation of still other legal pronouncements. These traditions were collected at two great rabbinical schools, one in Palestine and the other in Babylonia, and were transmitted orally in Aramaic. Called the *Gemarah*, each of

---

7. These are named according to the general content of each, "Seeds," "Set Feasts," "Women," "Damages," "Hallowed Things," and "Cleannesses"; they total about eight hundred pages in Herbert Danby's standard English translation, *The Mishnah* (London: Oxford University Press, 1933).

these two similar though distinct commentaries on the Mishnah is a veritable encyclopedia, embracing jurisprudence, theology, philosophy, ethics, natural science, mathematics, history, legend, and folklore. One is constantly led from one subject to another, on the theory that the variety serves to keep the mind agile.

Once again the enormous amount of materials that were continuously being accumulated imposed a severe strain on the memory, and in the fourth century the Gemarah of the Palestinian school of rabbis was reduced to writing. This, with the text of the Mishnah, is called the Jerusalem Talmud. In the fifth and sixth centuries, the Gemarah that had been developed by the rabbinical schools in Babylonia was reduced to writing, constituting, with the basic Mishnah text, the Babylonian Talmud. The Babylonian Talmud is about four times the length of the Jerusalem Talmud.

IV. THE TEMPLE AND ITS RITUAL

The temple in Jerusalem was the focal point of the Jewish worship of God. Built by Solomon a thousand years before the Christian Era (1 Kings 6:1), the temple was destroyed in 586 B.C. when the Jews were deported to Babylon. After their return under Zerubbabel, the erection of another temple was authorized by King Cyrus of Persia (Ezra 6:3-5). Completed in 515 B.C. the restored temple was far less magnificent than the original had been (Ezra 3:12). In order to curry favor with the Jews, King Herod the Great undertook to rebuild their temple on a much grander scale.

Fully described by Josephus (*Antiquities*, XV.xi; *Jewish War*, V.v.) and in the Mishnah (tractate "Middoth"), the temple complex, involving courts and cloisters for the priests as well as the temple proper, stood within an area of about twenty-six acres, called "the court of the Gentiles." This court, which Herod surrounded with magnificent marble colonnades, was open to Jew and Gentile alike and was the center of a busy life. Within this was a second, smaller court enclosed by a stone balustrade between five and six feet high, on which were inscriptions, some written in Greek, others in Latin characters, forbidding all persons except those of the commonwealth of Israel from entering the enclosure. Two of these warning notices have been discovered; they read, "Let no man of another nation enter inside the barrier and the fence around the temple. And whoever is caught will have himself to blame that his death ensues." Within this area, the temple proper stood upon the highest ground. It was built of great blocks of white stone. Its interior had the length and breadth of Solomon's temple (1 Kings 6:2), but its height was sixty feet (exclusive of an upper chamber), instead of forty-five feet.

The altar of burnt offering, made of unhewn stone, stood before the temple entrance. To the north of the altar was the place where the sacrificial victims were slaughtered and prepared for burning on the altar. A laver for the priests' ablutions stood to the west of the approach to the altar. Within the temple proper, the furniture, as in Old Testament days, included the altar of incense, the seven-branched golden lampstand, and the table made of acacia wood overlaid with gold for the bread of the Presence (Num. 4:7). A special interest attaches to the latter two in that they were among the temple spoils carried to Rome by Titus to adorn his triumph at the fall of Jerusalem in A.D. 70, and are still to be seen depicted among the sculptures on the Arch of Titus in the Roman Forum.

The principal act of Jewish ritual in the temple during the days of Jesus was the daily or "continual" burnt offering, presented every morning about 9:00 and every afternoon about 3:00 in the name, and on behalf, of the whole community of Israel. The detachment of priests on duty in the rotation of their divisions slept in the adjoining cloisters. Before dawn the priests who wished to be available for the morning service bathed and robed, and then assembled in a room for the drawing of lots to determine those of their number who should officiate (Luke 1:8-9). By successive lots priests were designated for several duties, such as removing the ashes from the altar of burnt offering, preparing the wood for burning the sacrifice, the slaying of the lamb, the throwing of the blood against the altar, the cleaning of the lampstand, and the preparing of the meal offering of choice flour and the drink offering.

At dawn, the gates of the temple enclosure were thrown open, and soon afterward delegations of men from Jerusalem and the immediate neighborhood, as well as Jews who might have come from more distant places, would begin to assemble in the court on three sides of the temple. Women took their places in the court of women, which was more distant from the temple and on a lower level.

Figure 2.2. The Arch of Titus in Rome
(Courtesy of John McRay.)
Standing at the south gateway to the Roman Forum, the Arch was erected in
A.D. 81 by the Emperor Domitian and the Senate to commemorate the fall of
Jerusalem in A.D. 70.

Figure 2.3. Bas-relief inside the Arch of Titus
(Courtesy of Alinari/Art Resources.)
This bas-relief inside the Arch of Titus features the precious objects that the
Romans took away from the temple at Jerusalem. Jewish prisoners are seen on
the right.

The officiating priests met together in a room for a short devotional service, after which there commenced the solemn ritual of
the offering of incense and the burning of the sacrificial lamb.
When the priests entered the temple with a censer of incense,
the worshipers outside prostrated themselves in adoration and
silent prayer (Luke 1:10). After coming out of the temple, the priest
pronounced a benediction from the steps of the temple porch,
and the several parts of the sacrifice were placed upon the altar
and burned. The pouring of the drink offering (a libation of
wine, between three and six pints in quantity) was now the signal
for one of the choirs of Levites to begin chanting or singing the
psalm appointed for the day (1 Chron. 6:31-32). The choir was

accompanied by instrumental music, including the harp and psaltery (lyre) and several kinds of wind instruments (compare Ps. 150:3-5). At intervals two priests blew on silver trumpets, at the sound of which the people again prostrated themselves.

With the close of the psalm the public service was at an end, and the private sacrifices were then offered. These were various expiatory or thank offerings, presented by pious Jews at their own expense. One of those prescribed by the Mosaic Law was offered forty days after the birth of a child. Ordinarily it comprised a lamb one year old for a burnt offering and a young pigeon or a turtledove for a sin offering, but families who could not afford a lamb were permitted to substitute a second pigeon or turtledove (Lev. 12:6-8; Luke 2:22-24).

The order of the afternoon service differed from the morning service only in that the incense was offered after the burning of the sacrificial animal instead of before. The lamps, also, on the seven-branched golden lampstand were lighted for this service.

V. THE SYNAGOGUE AND ITS WORSHIP

The importance of the synagogue as a molding influence upon the development of Judaism can hardly be overestimated.[8] Strangely enough, however, there is an almost total absence of information concerning its origin. There is no mention of synagogues in either the Old Testament or in the intertestamental Jewish literature, except perhaps a passing reference in Psalm 74:8 ("they burned all the meeting places of God in the land"). Despite the lack of historical information relating to the rise of the synagogue, there is general unanimity of opinion among scholars that it had its origin during the Babylonian exile after the destruction of the temple at Jerusalem in 586 B.C. Probably devout Jews, far from their homeland, felt the need of having special places where they could meet for common prayer, particularly on the sabbath. It is natural that they would assemble at the dwelling place of a prophet for religious instruction (Ezek. 14:1; 20:1). Whether during the exile houses for such meetings were appointed cannot be determined. In any case, after the Jews returned from exile and during

---

8. See Lee I. Levine, *The Ancient Synagogue: The First Thousand Years* (New Haven: Yale University Press, 2000).

the pre-Maccabean period, they built for themselves religious meeting places in addition to the rebuilt temple at Jerusalem.

At the beginning of the Christian Era, synagogues were to be found in almost all Palestinian cities and towns, as well as in many centers throughout the Mediterranean world. Jews at that time regarded the synagogue as an institution of almost immemorial antiquity, going back to Moses himself (for example, Josephus in his *Against Apion*, ii.18). In the larger cities there were many synagogues (though a Talmudic tradition that Jerusalem had 480 synagogues is a gross exaggeration), and Jews of differing nationalistic backgrounds or interests would gravitate to one or another synagogue in accordance with their preference (compare Acts 6:9).

Archaeologists have discovered the remains of ancient synagogues in Palestine dating from the early Christian period. They were of no fixed size or shape, but most of them were rectangular in ground plan, having two rows of columns that divided the interior into a central nave and two side aisles. Corresponding to the layout of the interior there were usually three entrances—a middle door and two smaller doors at the front of the building. The synagogue was generally built on the highest point of the town, and was frequently oriented with the front doors facing toward Jerusalem.

Of the furnishings in the synagogue, the most important was the chest or closet, called the "ark," in which were kept the Hebrew sacred scrolls of the Law and prophets. Near the location of the ark was a raised platform, on which the reader of the Scriptures and the prayer leader stood. Most of the excavated ancient synagogues were provided with one or two rows of stone benches running along two or three walls. People who could not be thus accommodated apparently stood during the service or sat either on wooden chairs or on mats spread out in the center. The "best seats in the synagogues," which the scribes and Pharisees sought to occupy (Matt. 23:6; Mark 12:39; Luke 11:43; 20:46), were those in front of the platform and facing the congregation. A special chair, called "Moses' seat" (Matt. 23:2), was allotted to one of the scribes, who was presumably the most distinguished scholar of the community.

The supervision of a local synagogue was in the hands of a body of elders. In order to constitute a congregation, a minimum of ten "men of leisure" were required. There was no resident priest or rabbi who had charge of conducting the services. Instead, one of the laymen of the congregation was appointed to serve as "the leader (or official) of the synagogue" (Luke 8:41; Acts 18:8, 17). Besides having under his care the general oversight of the building, the ruler was responsible for maintaining order during the services. It also was the ruler's duty to select each week the persons who would read the Scripture lessons and otherwise participate in the service.

Aside from the leader of the synagogue, the only other permanent official was the *hazzan,* or attendant. Besides being in charge of cleaning and lighting the synagogue, during the service itself the *hazzan* had the special duty to bring the sacred scrolls from the "ark" to the reader standing on the platform, and to replace them when the reading was finished (Luke 4:17, 20). He also performed a variety of other services, including the blowing of the trumpet three times at sunset on Friday evening to announce the beginning of the sabbath, when all labor should cease, and the flogging of criminals who had been condemned by the council (Matt. 10:17; 23:34; Acts 5:40).

The order of a typical synagogue service in New Testament times probably consisted of the following four parts:

(*a*) The service was opened with an invitation to prayer, consisting of the proclamation by the leader of the words, "Bless ye the Lord who is to be blessed." To this the congregation responded with the acclamation, "Blessed be the Lord who is to be blessed forever," and then continued with the recitation of what was in effect a confession of faith. This was called by its first word the *Shema'* (meaning "hear") and was made up of three paragraphs from the Pentateuch (Deut. 6:4-9; 11:13-21; and Num. 15:37-41), beginning, "Hear, O Israel: The LORD is our God, the LORD alone."

(*b*) The next part of the service was the prayers, called "the lifting up of hands." In contrast to the first part of the service, in which all took part, the prayers were said by an individual chosen for the purpose; the congregation, however, responded with the word "Amen" at the close of each collect. (This mode of prayer in the public service was taken over by the early church, as is attested by 1 Cor. 14:16).

The most important of the Jewish prayers from the second Christian century onward was the collection known as the "Eighteen Benedictions" (the *Shemoneh 'Esreh*). Every Jewish person was expected to recite the Eighteen Benedictions every morning, afternoon, and evening. During the first Christian century, at least six and perhaps as many as twelve of the eighteen collects were incorporated into the synagogue service.

(c) The liturgy was followed by the reading of a lesson from the Mosaic Law. The five books of the Pentateuch (Genesis, Exodus, Leviticus, Numbers, and Deuteronomy) were divided into 154 (or more) sabbath pericopes, or sections, so that the whole Pentateuch was read through in three or three-and-a-half years. It was the *hazzan's* duty before the service to adjust the roll so that it would open at once to the lesson. On sabbath morning at least seven persons took part in the reading, and no one was to read fewer than three verses. After each verse the reader would pause and an interpreter would give an Aramaic translation (called the *Targum*) for the benefit of the common people who no longer understood classical Hebrew.

After the Law came a lesson from one of the Old Testament Prophets, chosen at the discretion of the reader (see Luke 4:16-21). This lesson was also rendered into Aramaic by an interpreter, who translated three verses at a time. Strangely enough, the Psalms appear to have had no place in the usual service.

When a competent person was present, the reading of the Scriptures was usually followed by an exposition of one or both of the passages (see Luke 4:21). If a stranger were present in the service, the leader of the synagogue would ordinarily make a point of inviting him to speak to the congregation a "word of exhortation" (Acts 13:15).

(d) The service was closed by a priest pronouncing the priestly, or Aaronic, benediction contained in Numbers 6:24-26. If no priest was present, a layman would give the benediction in the form of a prayer. The congregation responded with "Amen."

The full order, as sketched above, was followed at the principal service of the week, held on the forenoon of the sabbath. At other services, such as those held daily in the larger towns, and at the regular Monday and Thursday services, some of the parts were abbreviated or omitted.

The influence of the synagogue was both extensive and pervasive. Jesus and his disciples would have been educated as children at a synagogue school, and upon reaching thirteen years of age would have taken their place as worshipers in the regular services. What they knew of the words of the scriptures they had learned in the synagogue from their studies and from the oral readings and expositions.

The synagogue influenced the piety not only of Jews but of some Gentiles as well. Earnest souls, dissatisfied with the creeds and cults of paganism, turned to the Jewish synagogue and its ethical monotheism. Many such persons became associate members of the synagogue, and participated in its worship, even, in some cases, building a synagogue (Luke 7:2-5). It was Gentiles of such a background who responded favorably to the earliest Christian missionaries and evangelists (Acts 13:42-48; 14:1-2).

The synagogue thus played a conspicuous part in the preparation for the coming of Christianity. Not only did synagogues throughout the Mediterranean world become seedbeds of the church, but also Judaism supplied the institutional forms of Christian worship and even, in some cases, the words of prayers and liturgies themselves.

CHAPTER 3

THE PHILOSOPHICAL AND RELIGIOUS BACKGROUND OF GRECO-ROMAN PAGANISM

The earliest followers of Jesus had been nurtured in Palestinian Judaism. When they carried the message of Christianity to cities and villages throughout the Mediterranean world, they encountered a wide spectrum of philosophies and religions in the Greco-Roman world. In Athens, Paul addressed Epicureans and Stoics (Acts 17:18), and at Ephesus he clashed with the promoters of the religion of Artemis (Acts 19:23-41).

Genuine belief in the reality of the ancient gods and goddesses of classical mythology had long since given way to widespread agnosticism. Through their plays Euripides and Aristophanes ridiculed the foibles and follies of the Olympian deities, and Euhemerus explained that the gods were originally men who had distinguished themselves either as warriors or benefactors of mankind, and who after their death were accorded divine honors from their grateful people.

Though rationalism had destroyed the foundations for belief, the pendulum swung for many from skepticism toward credulity. The growth of superstition and astrology, the consultation of horoscopes and omens, the use of amulets and charms, the honor given to exorcists and charlatans of all kinds who preyed upon the gullible—such was the understandable reaction to a crude and skeptical materialism. Divine honors were conferred not only upon deceased Roman emperors, but also toward the end of the first Christian century Domitian began to require that sacrifices be offered before his image, and demanded that his subjects address him as "Lord and God." Though the old deities were dead, devotees of the exotic mystery religions brought new gods to the Greco-Roman world from the East. Their popularity is testified to by the remains of temples and places of meeting that archaeologists have unearthed in cities and villages throughout the Roman Empire—except within Judea. Many persons, being promised ritual purification and spiritual salvation, were initiated into several of these cults, like a mistrustful capitalist who spreads his investments over as many ventures as possible to reserve at least something in the next financial crisis. This was the secret sickness of the mystery religions; their adherents believed, and yet they did not believe. What has been aptly termed "the failure of nerve" characterized the moral and religious vacuum that many felt but could not overcome despite the panaceas offered by a welter of competing teachers, philosophers, priests, astrologers, and quacks.

I. SCHOOLS OF PHILOSOPHY IN THE GRECO-ROMAN WORLD

1. PLATONISM

Among the numerous schools of philosophy that flourished in the Greco-Roman world, primacy of honor belongs to the system associated with the great Plato (427–347 B.C.), a pupil of Socrates. From Socrates' teaching, Plato learned his method of dialectic—the questioning of common assumptions; from his teacher's character he gained the conviction of indispensable primacy of ethical goodness in all the relations of life. For forty years he taught at a school that he had established on the outskirts of Athens near the grove sacred to the hero Academus (hence the "Academy," which had a continuous life until its dissolution by the emperor Justinian in A.D. 529). With the exception of a small collection of epistles, Plato's extant writings are in the form of dialogues, often with Socrates as the principal speaker and with various critics or pupils, after whom the dialogues are usually named, taking part in the discussion. Unsurpassed in literary artistry, intellectual breadth, and moral seriousness, Plato's dialogues have exercised a deep and pervasive influence upon subsequent Western culture.

The leading doctrine of Platonism is the view that true reality is found, not in the objects of sense, but in the "idea" or "form" that lies behind each class of objects and of which they are but unsubstantial shadows. By grasping and participating in the eternal forms, which belong to the higher world, the soul attains its true well-being and is lifted above the flux of "becoming." The soul's eternal home is in the world beyond the senses, whereas the body with its sensual life is but its prison house and grave. To fulfill one's destiny one must escape the material world, search for the good, the true, and the beautiful, and thus become assimilated to the divine.

2. EPICUREANISM

The Greek thinker Epicurus (342–270 B.C.) was a far greater person than the word *epicure*, derived from his name, might lead one to suppose. A man of blameless character and amiable disposition, Epicurus gathered about him, in the garden that he had purchased at Athens, a brotherhood of devoted followers who came to be known either as Epicureans or "the philosophers of the Garden."

Epicurus distrusted the dialectic and metaphysics of Plato as dealing with words, not things. Suspicious of abstract terms, he appealed to the common sense of the plain man. He held that the senses, as the one and only source of all our ideas, provided the sole criterion of all truth. On this basis he taught that the greatest good lies in independence of external things and in reliance upon the inner life or character. Consequently, one's wisdom lies in the pursuit of pleasure, which Epicurus equated with freedom from pain and from fear, a state one attains by the avoidance of excesses of all kinds. The gods, if they exist, live in serene detachment and have nothing to do with human existence. Death brings a final dispersion of the atoms that constitute one's body and soul.

Among the more noteworthy followers of Epicurus was the Roman poet Lucretius (about 99–55 B.C.), whose didactic poem *De Rerum Natura* ("Concerning the Nature of Things") manages to set forth abstruse philosophy in majestic hexameters of great power and beauty.

3. STOICISM

The Stoic school took its name from the circumstance that its founder, Zeno of Citium in Cyprus (about 336–263 B.C.), lectured in the Painted Porch (Stoa), a colonnade at Athens decorated with elaborate frescoes. Unlike Epicureanism, which tended to foster atheism and self-indulgence, Stoicism encouraged the development of religious and moral fiber. The universe, Zeno taught, was not meaningless, nor was one's place in it determined by blind fate.

Pervading the whole of the material order is divine Reason, and one's duty is to live in accordance with this Reason or *Logos,* which manifests itself in the order and beauty of the world. The soul is a divine spark or seed of the universal Reason, imprisoned within the body. Thanks to this soul, a person can rise above adverse circumstances, and in the face of difficulties can maintain a dignified tranquillity (hence the modern usage of the word "stoical").

The ethical teachings of later Stoics, such as Seneca (a contemporary of the apostle Paul), Epictetus, and Marcus Aurelius, contain superb examples of moral maxims. Since, however, there is no personal God, the Stoic creed, though noble and elevated, always remained a philosophy and never made a religious appeal to the masses.

Like other educated men of his day, the apostle Paul was acquainted with a certain amount of Stoic teaching. In order to establish contact with his audience at Athens, he included in his Areopagus address several sentiments that were widely held among Stoics: "In him [God] we live and move and have our being. . . . For we too are [God's] offspring" (Acts 17:28). Likewise Paul's Letters contain occasional phrases that have a Stoic ring. Thus, the apostle's assertion, "I have learned to be content with whatever I have" (Phil. 4:11), would have been recognized by a Stoic as his own language. At the same time, however, the parallelism is more in the realm of words than basic idea, for the theological presuppositions and the springs of Paul's actions were very different from those of a Stoic philosopher; the source of his contentment, he goes on to declare, is found in his relationship to the personal and transcendent Deity ("I can do all things through him who strengthens me," Phil. 4:13).

4. CYNICS

Of the lesser Socratic schools, one of the more interesting was that of the Cynics, whose founder, Antisthenes, was an older contemporary of Plato. Of his pupils the most famous was the churlish and eccentric Diogenes of Sinope (about 412–323 B.C.), who lived in a huge jar or tub and, when asked by Alexander the Great what he could do for him, replied, "Get out of my light!"

The Cynics taught a simplicity of life that all could follow. By practicing an extreme frugality one would learn to be independent of externals and thus attain true happiness. One's salvation lies in a return to nature: let us therefore live like the beasts (the word *Cynic* means "like a dog") and then we will not be vexed with the artificial conventions of the world, its ambitions, its censure, and its praise. Let each face the changes and chances of life with the optimistic nonchalance of the great sage himself: "Bury me," said Diogenes, "face downward, for everything is soon going to be turned the other way up."

Going out into the streets and fields, the wandering Cynics brought philosophy to common people. In their preaching and exhorting they developed the literary form known as *diatribe*. Though in modem usage the word is confined to denunciation, originally a diatribe was like a homily or sermon, and was characterized by a lively and vivid semiconversational style. The literary form of the Pauline Letters often resembles that of the Cynic diatribe, particularly in the use of a series of questions and answers (for example, Rom. 3:1–4:12; and 1 Cor. 6:2-19, with the repetition of "Do you not know . . . ?").

5. OTHER PHILOSOPHICAL SYSTEMS

Besides the philosophical schools already mentioned, during the early Christian centuries many others flourished. Though the greatness of Aristotle (384–322 B.C.) was not fully appreciated in antiquity, some of his followers attempted to popularize his encyclopedic teaching.

The Skeptics, who looked back to Pyrrho of Elis (about 365–275 B.C.) as their founder, held that, because of the contradictions in sense perceptions and in opinions, knowledge and conviction are unattainable. One's attitude toward life, therefore, should be a cautious suspension of judgment, absolute indifference to outward things, and conformity to prevailing custom.

The Eclectics, as their name suggests, selected what they regarded as the best features of various philosophical systems and acknowledged no single teacher as their master.

On the borderline between philosophy and religion—with a strong dash of mysticism thrown in as well—was Pythagoreanism. Pythagoras of Samos, who flourished in the latter part of the sixth century B.C., paid great attention to numbers and their application to weights, measures, and the theory of music (the octave). He gathered about himself a group of followers to whom he communicated secret symbols and metaphysical lore, including belief in the transmigration of souls. Members of the Pythagorean brotherhood were vegetarian in diet and regarded the body as the seat of all impure passions. Every evening they would make an examination of their conscience; going over the events of the day that was past, they would ask themselves, "In what have I transgressed—doing what I ought not to have done, or leaving undone what I ought have done?"

During the last century B.C. there was a revival of interest in Pythagorean symbolism and mysticism, and even the Stoic philosopher Seneca confessed himself fascinated by its teachings. Ultimately certain aspects of Pythagoreanism were adopted and adapted by various Gnostic systems of the early Christian period. Though Gnosticism took many different forms, a characteristic teaching of all Gnostics was the fundamental antithesis between the material and the spiritual universe. The spiritual element in a person could receive redemption only through gnosis, "spiritual enlightenment," which was the supposedly revealed knowledge of God and of the origin and destiny of humankind. The systems of Gnostic teaching range from those that embody much genuine philosophical speculation to those that are wild amalgams of mythology, astrology, and magical rites drawn from all quarters.

II. MYSTERY RELIGIONS IN THE GRECO-ROMAN WORLD

As was mentioned in the introductory paragraphs of this chapter, the vacuum left by pervasive agnosticism concerning the traditional Greco-Roman gods and goddesses was filled, at least in part, by the growing popularity of what are called the mystery cults.[1] Most

---

1. For further information on the mystery religions, the following may be consulted: Harold R. Willoughby, *Pagan Regeneration: A Study of Mystery Initiations in the Graeco-Roman World* (Chicago: University of Chicago Press, 1929); Joscelyn Godwin, *Mystery Religions in the Ancient World* [with many illustrations] (San Francisco: Harper & Row, 1981); Marvin W. Meyer, ed., *The Ancient Mysteries: A Sourcebook* (San Francisco: Harper & Row, 1987); Robert Turcan, *The Cults of the Roman Empire* (Oxford: Blackwells, 1996); and the present writer in the following three items, "Methodology in the Study of the Mystery Religions and Early Christianity" in *Historical and Literary Studies; Pagan, Jewish, and Christian* (Grand Rapids: Eerdmans, 1968), pp. 1-24; "The Second Grade of Mithraic Initiation," ibid, pp. 25-33; and "A Classified Bibliography of the Graeco-Roman Mystery Religions" [3,647 titles of books and articles] in *Aufstieg und Niedergang der Römischen Welt*, II, 17 (3) (Berlin and New York: n.p., 1984), pp. 1259-1423.

of these were imports from the East and had a certain fascination arising from their novelty, as well as from the vow of secrecy that was imposed upon the initiates not to disclose the content of the ritual or the doctrine. The chief mystery cults were those of Eleusis, Mithra, Isis, Dionysus, and Cybele or Magna Mater.

1. THE ELEUSINIAN CULT

The most highly regarded cult of antiquity, for which even Plato, who generally spoke depreciatingly of such cults, had only words of respect, was that located at Eleusis, a small town about fifteen miles west of Athens. The ritual commemorated the ancient myth of Persephone, the daughter of Demeter, "giver of goodly crops," who was carried off by Pluto to the underworld to be his bride. Distracted with grief, the mother searched frantically for her lost daughter. In retaliation, she refused to allow crops to grow, and consequently no offerings were made to the gods. Finally an arrangement was made with Pluto whereby Persephone was permitted to be with her mother for a portion of each year. Overjoyed at the restoration of her daughter, Demeter instituted the Eleusinian mysteries, through which the initiate was assured of a happy future life. During the portion of each year while she had her daughter, Demeter allowed crops to grow. This story, it need scarcely be remarked, provided an explanation for the cycle of changing seasons.

The Eleusinian rites involved preliminary instruction in the "lesser mysteries," celebrated in March at Agrae, a suburb of Athens on the banks of the Ilisus, and the "greater mysteries," celebrated in September. These latter comprised stages of initiation, each becoming more solemn. Cleansed by baptism in the sea and sprinkled with the blood of a sacrificial pig, the candidates marched in festal procession to Eleusis. Here, within the huge Hall of Initiation (which has been excavated), the priests took part in a religious pageant dramatically reenacting the Demeter myth, and the initiates, as spectators, shared the emotions of the goddess.

2. THE MITHRAIC CULT

More archaeological remains of Mithraism have been found than of any other mystery cult. Originally a god worshiped by the ancient Indo-Iranians, Mithra became prominent in the Zoroastrian pantheon as mediator between mortals and the god of light (Ahura

Mazda). Carried westward first by the Persian military and later by the Roman, the Mithraic cult spread far and wide. It was introduced into Rome itself at the time of the emperor Trajan (A.D. 98–117) and became the prevailing religion among the Roman legionaires.

The devotees of Mithra (the cult was restricted to men) met in small chapels or sanctuaries located in caves or partly underground crypts. In the center of the apse stood a statue depicting the most significant work of Mithra, the tauroctony. This was the rep-

Figure 3.1. The Mithraic Tauroctony
(Courtesy of the Vatican Museums.)

resentation of Mithra, clad in a cape and pointed cap, in the act of slaying a bull. With his left knee astride the bull, which has been forced to its knees, and his left hand grasping and pulling back the snout of the animal, Mithra plunges a short dagger into the neck of the bull. From the wound there spring three stalks of grain. Other animals in the tableau are a dog, which seeks to lick the blood flowing from the wound, a serpent in the foreground, a scorpion attacking the genitals of the bull, and often a raven bringing a message to Mithra. Many tauroctonies are so carved as to represent all these figures within a semicircular grotto, along the edge of which are depicted other scenes involving exploits of Mithra—such as his rising out of a rock, his carrying away a bull, and his riding to heaven in a four-horse chariot with the sun god—as well as the signs of the zodiac. The full significance of all these is not known, but it is supposed that the devotee saw in the central act of the slaying of the bull Mithra's overcoming of evil and the bringing of life and vegetation to humankind.

According to information preserved by early church fathers, Mithraism had an elaborate ritual of initiation that involved seven stages: the grade of the raven, the bridegroom (or *nymphus*), the soldier, the lion, the Persian, the courier of the sun *(heliodromus)*, and the father. During the ceremony the celebrants wore costumes and masks appropriate to the grade of initiation (for example, a huge papier-mâché bird's head and wings that could be flapped; a soldier's panoply; a lion's head and skin; the distinctive garb of a Persian). There was also a ceremony of baptism and a sacramental communion involving bread and water.

The most elaborate rite of Mithraism, which it had appropriated from the cult of Cybele (Magna Mater), was the taurobolium or blood bath. The initiate, who was naked, crouched in a pit covered with a grating over which a bull, garlanded with flowers, was slaughtered. As the warm blood streamed over the devotee, he would eagerly drink in some of the life-giving fluid. Inscriptions dating from the early Christian period and commemorating the performance of this rite indicate that the initiate believed that he had been reborn for twenty years or, in some cases, for eternity.

Figure 3.2. A Mithraic Ritual Meal
(Courtesy of the National Museum of Bosnia and Herzegovina, Sarajevo.)

A fourth-century relief found at Konjic in Dalmatia (today Bosnia and Herzegovina) depicts several Mithraic devotees of differing grades. The two central figures behind the table are almost a head taller than the others, and may represent the two highest grades (the *heliodromus* and the father). To the left and right stand four other devotees of lower rank, serving those behind the table. From their masks, the raven and the lion are clearly recognizable, and the figure wearing a Persian cap is also identifiable. Unfortunately, the head and torso of the fourth attendant have been destroyed.

A small circular three-legged table stands in the foreground. This table, to which the viewer's attention is deliberately drawn, is seen from above in defiance to demands of perspective. On it lie small round loaves or bread-rolls, each scored with a cross so that they can more easily be broken apart. The symbolic lion to the left of the table is present also in other scenes of a ritual meal.

3. THE ISIAC CULT

The essential elements of the myth of Isis and Osiris, preserved in pyramid texts and in a treatise by Plutarch, include the following: Osiris, a wise and beneficent king, fell victim to the plotting of his wicked brother Set, or Typhon, who hacked Osiris into fourteen pieces and dispatched them to different parts of Egypt. Isis, wife and sister of Osiris, searched out and found all but one piece of the dismembered body, which she reassembled and carefully embalmed. After a ceremonial lament over the corpse, in which her sister Nephtys joined, by means of magical rites Isis revivified Osiris, who then received the title "Lord of the Underworld and Ruler of the Dead."

Through miniature passion plays in chapels dedicated to Osiris, and by means of funerary rites performed over the body of a deceased person, the benefits of spiritual rebirth were held to be conferred. An Egyptian text testifies to the hope of a future existence for one who had shared in Osirian rites: "As truly as Osiris lives, he also shall live; as truly as Osiris is not dead, shall he not die; as truly as Osiris is not annihilated, shall he not be annihilated."

During the Hellenistic age, Ptolomy Soter (323–283 B.C.) modified the cult by replacing Osiris with a new, syncretistic god named Serapis. The reformed Isiac religion spread throughout the Mediterranean world and many Greek and Latin authors refer to the warm devotion that was felt for Isis, who was revered as the giver of security and happiness in this life and the next. Isis is virtually the only ancient divinity who displays only love or concern for her devotees. Women, in particular, found special satisfaction in the worship of Isis, and often her temples were located near a Mithreum. Roman coins bearing images and inscriptions honoring Isis and Serapis were minted as late as the fourth Christian century.

The popularity of the Isaic cult was fostered by impressive ceremonials, some public and others private and secret. Detailed descriptions of elaborate processions of Isiac priestesses and crowds of devotees have been provided by Latin and Greek authors of the second century A.D.[2] Dressed in appropriate costume or vestment, the participants carried a variety of objects, such as lamps, a winnowing fan, mirrors, palm branches, a miniature altar, and other objects of religious significance.

Along with such written accounts, the artist of a finely crafted representation from the second century, now in the Vatican, depicts

---

2. Apuleius, *Metamorphoses*, XI.8 , and Clement of Alexandria, *Stromata*, II.iv, 35, 1.

visually the solemnity of such processions. An Isiac priestess strides first, with a serpent (living?) wrapped around her left arm. She is followed at a discrete distance by a sacred scribe, bald-headed, with a band around his head in which two feathers (quill pens) are sticking. He reads from a scroll held in front. Behind him strides a prophet, holding a pitcher or jug in his veiled hands. A maidservant with corkscrew curls follows, carrying a ladle and making "music" on a sistrum.[3]

4. THE DIONYSIAC CULT

Dionysus (also known as Bacchus or Father Liber) was the god of wine and of animal life. In order to attain communion with their god, the devotees of Dionysus (called Bacchantes) drank wine until

Figure 3.3. An Isiac Procession
(Courtesy of the Vatican Museums.)

---

3. The sistrum was an instrument consisting of a handle attached to a thin metal frame through which passed a number of metal rods, which were loose or fitted with loose rings. In either case, a jingle was produced by shaking the sistrum, presumably to frighten away evil spirits. It is still used in Nubia.

thoroughly intoxicated, experiencing thus the influence of their god. Another realistic sacrament was the feast of raw flesh. The initiates, after indulging in a wild, whirling dance that induced a frenzied delirium, tore asunder a goat or a fawn and devoured the dripping raw flesh. Such orgiastic rites, called *Bacchanalia,* were celebrated in Crete as late as the third and fourth centuries of the Christian Era. The Greek historian Herodotus (450 B.C.) describes Dionysus as the god "who drives people to madness" (4.79). Euripides' play *The Bacchae* tells how the women of Thebes pursued the king of their city (who had opposed the introduction of the cult), caught him, and tore him limb from limb. In their ecstasy, he appeared to them to be a deer. Only after they had killed him did Dionysus clear their minds allowing them to see what they had done while in the god's power.

The Greeks feared this cult at first and took steps to ban it, but to no avail. The second-century B.C. Latin historian Livy describes how Bacchic rites spread rapidly through Rome until the worshipers numbered in the thousands, whereupon the Senate proscribed the ceremonies (Livy, book xxxix, 8-19). The government executed hundreds of its adherents, but the cult soon flourished again. Archaeological artifacts give us some gauge of how powerful and widespread this cult was.

5. THE CULT OF CYBELE

The rites of Cybele or Magna Mater ("the Great Mother") flourished first in central Asia Minor and from there spread westward. The myth told of the death of Attis, a shepherd lad who was the consort of Cybele, and of his subsequent restoration by the goddess. Celebrating her principal rites in the springtime, her devotees would work themselves into a frenzy of excitement, during the course of which they gashed their arms and sprinkled the blood on their altars, while her priests went so far as to emasculate themselves. Those who could afford the expense underwent the rite of the taurobolium (see p. 81). This religion was officially introduced into Rome in 204 B.C. to ward off the Carthaginian threat; native Romans, however, were not permitted to take part in it until about the beginning of the Christian Era.

As is the case of other mystery cults, the myth of Cybele and Attis represents the annual dying of vegetation in the autumn and its coming to life again in the spring. As late as the fourth century, a Roman emperor, Julian the Apostate, wrote an elaborate philosophical interpretation of the cult.[4]

The question of how far the theology of the apostle Paul may have been influenced by one or another of the mystery religions is discussed on pages 280-81.

---

4. Other ancient religions contained features that resembled the Magna Mater cult. Thus the Babylonian Ishtar (known to Old Testament writers as Ashtoreth) had as her consort Tammuz, who was slain (Ezek. 8:14), and the Syrian goddess Atargatis loved and lost Hadad (Zechariah knew of the lamentations for Hadad, Zech. 12:11).

PART TWO

ASPECTS OF THE LIFE AND TEACHING
OF JESUS CHRIST

PALESTINE—A.D. 30

During the Ministry of Jesus

TETRARCHY OF PHILIP

TETRARCHY OF HEROD ANTIPAS

UNDER PONTIUS PILATE

DECAPOLIS

(from The New Testament: Its Background, Growth, and Content *by Bruce Metzger © 1965-1983 by Abingdon Press. Used by permission.)*

CHAPTER 4

SOURCES FOR OUR KNOWLEDGE OF THE LIFE AND TEACHING OF JESUS CHRIST

The sources for our knowledge of the life and teaching of Jesus Christ fall into two categories—those written by non-Christian authors of the early centuries of our era, and those written by Christian believers about their Lord. Before the historian can utilize these materials, however, it is necessary to examine them critically; that is, one must inquire into such matters as their date and authorship, the oral and written sources utilized by the authors, the modification of the material during its oral transmission, the special interests or bias of the authors, and similar questions.

I. NON-CHRISTIAN SOURCES—JEWISH AND PAGAN

The non-Christian source materials concerning Jesus, though scanty in extent, are definite in their testimony concerning his historical existence and the basic facts of his public ministry and death under Pontius Pilate, the procurator of Judea.

1. JEWISH SOURCES THAT REFER TO JESUS

The earliest non-Christian witness to the historicity of Jesus Christ is the Jewish historian Flavius Josephus. Born about A.D. 37 or 38, he was the son of a Jewish priest named Matthias and claimed kinship with the Hasmonean dynasty. During his late teens, Josephus spent three years in close association with the Essenes and under the spiritual guidance of a hermitlike ascetic named Bannus. At the age of nineteen he joined the party of the Pharisees, remaining, at least nominally, a member of this group until his death, about A.D. 100. Josephus's personality was far from attractive. A member of the priestly aristocracy whose opportunism accommodated itself to the Roman yoke, he was vain, self-satisfied, and far too obsequious. In his autobiography he includes, with naive vanity, many laudatory details about himself; for example, that while still a boy at the age of fourteen, he was so advanced in learning that the chief priests and the leading scholars of Jerusalem used to come regularly to him for precise information on some particular in the Jewish Laws!

During the Jewish revolt, which resulted in the fall of Jerusalem in A.D. 70, Josephus counseled his people to surrender to the Romans. Unable to dissuade them from pursuing their fanatical and futile resistance, he went to Rome where he settled down as friend and pensioner of the emperor Vespasian, whose family name, Flavius, he adopted.

While at Rome, Josephus occupied himself with literary endeavors, and about A.D. 77 published his *History of the Jewish War Against the Romans*. Some sixteen years later he finished his great work, the celebrated *Antiquities of the Jewish People*. This is a lengthy account in twenty books of the Jewish people from the earliest times; Josephus begins his narrative with the creation of the world and traces the fortunes of the Jews down to his own day (A.D. 93). Besides his autobiography, which he issued shortly before his death, he also wrote a treatise entitled *Against Apion*, in which he defended himself and his countrymen against the anti-Semitism of such Gentile antagonists as Apion, an erudite literary critic who had made slighting references to the Jews in his *History of Egypt*.

Such, in brief, is a thumbnail sketch of the author who has supplied the earliest non-Christian testimony concerning Jesus and his followers. In the *Antiquities of the Jews*, two passages refer to Jesus; the longer one (XVIII.iii.3) is the following:

> About this time [namely, after an altercation between Pilate and the Jews over using temple funds for the building of an aqueduct in Jerusalem] arose Jesus, a wise man, if indeed it be right to call him a man. For he was a doer of marvelous deeds, and a teacher of men who gladly receive the truth. He drew to himself many persons, both of the Jews and also of the Gentiles. He was the Christ. And when Pilate, upon the indictment of the leading men among us, had condemned him to the cross, those who had loved him at the first did not cease to do so, for he appeared to them alive on the third

day—the godly prophets having foretold these and ten thousand other wonderful things about him. And even to this day the race of Christians, who are named from him, has not died out.

Elsewhere in the *Antiquities* Josephus refers to the trial of James, a leader of the Christians, before the Sanhedrin (XX.ix.1). In this passage, Josephus identifies James by calling him "the brother of Jesus, the so-called Christ."

For the past several centuries the significance of these two passages has been hotly debated by historians. On the one hand, it is pointed out that the bald statement, "He was the Christ," and the references to Jesus' resurrection and to his being more than human are totally contrary to what one would expect a non-Christian writer to report. Furthermore, though Eusebius, a church historian of the fourth century, knew and accepted Josephus's testimony to Jesus as the Messiah, another ecclesiastical writer, Origen, who lived in the first half of the third century, does not seem to have known the passage, since he says specifically that Josephus remained a Jew and did not believe Jesus to be the Christ. Many scholars have therefore concluded that sometime prior to the fourth century the passage was interpolated into the *Antiquities* by Christian scribes while recopying Josephus's works.[1]

On the other hand, scholarly opinion about the famous *testimonium Flavianum* in Josephus's *Antiquities* has been shifting to a defense of the essential authenticity of the passage on the basis of an examination of a tenth-century Arabic version of Josephus made by Agapius, a Melchite bishop of Hierapolis in Syria. An Israeli scholar, Shlomo Pines,[2] having compared the Arabic and Greek texts, found the following differences: (1) Agapius's version of Josephus assumes the humanity of Jesus. (2) His account does not refer to Jesus' miracles, but rather to his good conduct and virtue. (3) The appearance after three days is mentioned as a "report."

---

1. Because Josephus was deemed a renegade to Judaism, Jewish scribes were not interested in preserving his writings for posterity, and all manuscripts of his writings are the work of Christian copyists. When his *History of the Jewish War* was translated into Old Slavonic, in the twelfth or thirteenth century, about two dozen passages that refer to Jesus were interpolated either by the translator or by subsequent scribes. For an English translation of the passages see Henry St. John Thackeray's edition in the Loeb Classical Library (New York: G. P. Putnam's Sons, 1928), III, pp. 635-58.

2. Shlomo Pines, *An Arabic Version of the Testamonium Flavianum and Its Implications* (Jerusalem: Israel Academy of Sciences and Humanities, 1971).

(4) A disclaimer, "perhaps," is inserted before the statement that "he was the Messiah." Such differences led Pines to conclude that the Arabic version may preserve a form of text that is close to the original, untampered text of Josephus. Furthermore, other Jewish scholars (such as Paul Winter, L. H. Feldman, and Geza Vermes) have pointed out that the literary style of the Greek account is altogether like that of Josephus, and that the most that needs to be assumed is that an original, shorter account about Jesus was somewhat embroidered by a Christian scribe who added several clauses in order to make Josephus's testimony still more explicit. Moreover, it is also conceivable that Christian omissions as well as Christian interpolations may have taken place, and that Christian copyists, adding material in praise of Jesus, may also have omitted whatever they thought derogatory to his person.

The present status of the debate over the value of Josephus's testimony to Jesus is that almost all scholars regard the shorter passage in the *Antiquities* (XX.ix.1), where the reference to Jesus is introduced in a casual, almost offhand manner and where Josephus speaks of him as the "so-called Christ," as undoubtedly genuine. However, it is probable that the longer passage has been expanded, but not totally interpolated, by an overzealous Christian scribe.

Another Jewish witness concerning Jesus and his followers is the Babylonian Talmud. Though reduced to writing in the fifth and sixth centuries, it contains, as was mentioned in a previous chapter, an accumulation of much earlier materials, some of which go back to the first Christian century. Amid this vast collection of Jewish traditions, there are half a dozen references to Jesus. Some of these are much distorted and reflect the slander and animosities that unhappily characterized both Christians and Jews in their relations to each other.

The Talmud makes the following statements about the founder of Christianity. (1) Jesus, under the name of Ben Pandera (that is, Son of Pandera), is said to have been born out of wedlock, his mother having been seduced by a paramour named Pandera. (2) He is said to have been in Egypt where he learned magic, whereby he was able to perform many marvelous works in order to deceive the people. (3) He called himself God. (4) He was tried by the Sanhedrin as a deceiver and a teacher of apostasy. (5) He was executed on the eve of the Passover, either by crucifixion or (as an alternative tradition states) by being stoned and then hanged. (6) He had five disciples, whose names are given as Matthai, Neqai, Netzer, Buni, and Thodah.

It is commonly agreed by both Jewish and Christian scholars that these Talmudic traditions add nothing new to the authentic history of Jesus contained in the Gospels. In general, they confirm early Christian tradition by giving independent—and even hostile—testimony that Jesus of Nazareth really existed. It is noteworthy also that the Talmud refers to Jesus' power to perform miracles (though it attributes them to his knowledge of magic) and to his claim to be the divine Son of God. The defamatory account of his birth seems to reflect a knowledge of the Christian tradition that Jesus was the son of the Virgin Mary, the Greek word for virgin, *parthenos*, being distorted into the name Pandera.

2. PAGAN SOURCES THAT REFER TO JESUS

The earliest Latin author who refers to Christ is Pliny the Younger (ca. A.D. 62–ca. 113). While Pliny was governor of Bithynia, a Roman province in Asia Minor, he consulted with the emperor Trajan concerning the line of action he should take with the Christians, who had been increasing in numbers throughout his province. A serious economic consequence of their growth was the falling off of the sale of animals designed as sacrificial offerings in pagan temples. In a letter written to Trajan about A.D. 112 (*Epist.* x.96), Pliny states that the Christians are accustomed to assemble together regularly on a certain day, and "to sing responsively a hymn to Christ as if to a god" *(carmen Christo quasi deo dicere secum invicem)*.

The evidence from the Roman historian Tacitus (ca. A.D. 55–ca. 117) is still more explicit. In his celebrated *Annals*, a vivid and tersely phrased work drawn up about A.D. 115, Tacitus describes the persecution of the Christians at Rome. He relates that Nero, disturbed by a rumor accusing him of having deliberately started the great fire that destroyed half the city of Rome in A.D. 64, tried to throw the blame for the catastrophe on the Christians, and he delivered them up to the most appalling tortures—such as having them dipped in tar and then setting them on fire to illuminate his race track at night, or turning ferocious animals upon them in the amphitheater. "Their name," Tacitus adds, "comes from Christus, who in the reign of Tiberius as emperor was condemned to death by the procurator Pontius Pilate" (*Annals*, xv. 44).

The importance of this testimony to the historicity of Christ is hard to exaggerate. Tacitus is universally acknowledged to be one of the most reliable of Roman historians, whose passion for sober and accurate reporting was joined with a critical sense rare in his time. It is significant that he fixes the date of Jesus' death in terms of the reigning emperor as well as the procurator of Judea.

A third Roman writer who refers briefly to Christ and the Christians is Suetonius (ca. A.D. 70–160). While secretary to the emperor Hadrian, and hence having access to the official archives, Suetonius wrote a popular history under the title *The Lives of the Twelve Caesars*. Published about A.D. 120, this work is biographical in style, containing many gossipy sidelights concerning the foibles of the emperors. In the section that deals with Nero (chap. xvi), Suetonius says that this emperor "inflicted punishments on the Christians, a sect that professes a new and mischievous superstition." In the section concerning the emperor Claudius (chap. xxv), he makes reference to the expulsion from Rome of the Jews, "who had been continually stirring up trouble under the influence of Chrestus."[3] The disturbances were probably the result of agitation and rivalry between Jews and Christians; the misspelling of the name "Christus" is understandable on the part of a pagan author who obviously had very little interest in or sympathy for the new sect.

The total testimony concerning Jesus that is preserved in early non-Christian authors is not extensive, yet the scantiness of evidence should occasion no surprise. Sophisticated Roman authors of the first Christian centuries had not our reasons for being interested in Jesus. What had happened in a remote corner of the empire among the despised race of the Jews appeared relatively unimportant in comparison with other more congenial topics. As for Josephus, there were special considerations that kept him from

---

3. Compare Acts 18:2, which also refers to Claudius's edict expelling the Jews from Rome in about A.D. 49.

enlarging on the history and significance of Jesus. In writing books that were intended to exalt and defend his people in the eyes of Roman readers, it is natural that he would say as little as possible about messianic agitators, whose activities only served to disturb the status quo and to bring a reproach against the Jewish people.

However, the early non-Christian testimonies concerning Jesus, though scanty, are altogether sufficient to prove (even without taking into account the evidence contained in the New Testament) that he was a historical figure who lived in Palestine during the early years of the first century, that he gathered a group of followers about himself, and that he was condemned to death under Pontius Pilate. Today no competent scholar denies the historicity of Jesus.[4]

II. CHRISTIAN SOURCES— CANONICAL AND APOCRYPHAL

Jesus, so far as is known, left none of his teachings in written form, preferring rather to impart his instruction orally. In subsequent years, his followers saw the advisability of drawing up in more or less fixed form written accounts of what they remembered of his life and teaching. The four Gospels that are included in the New Testament were among the first such literary productions. That they were transmitted and regarded as canonical, while other first-century gospels (compare Luke 1:1) perished, is no doubt to be explained as the survival of the fittest. Certainly the apocryphal gospels of the second and succeeding centuries are feeble both in literary and spiritual power when compared with the four canonical Gospels.

In the following survey, attention will be drawn to what is known or can be deduced concerning the composition, mutual relations, individual characteristics, authorship, and date of the earliest Gospels (both canonical and apocryphal) as witnesses to the life and teaching of Jesus Christ.

1. THE CANONICAL GOSPELS

When the four canonical Gospels are compared with one another, it is perceived at once that three of them—those attributed to Matthew,

---

4. For a fuller account see Robert E. Van Voorst, *Jesus Outside the New Testament: An Introduction to the Ancient Evidence* (Grand Rapids: Eerdmans, 2000).

Mark, and Luke—have much in common and, in general, present the life and teaching of Jesus from the same point of view. They are usually called the *Synoptic Gospels* (from the Greek word *synopsis*, a seeing together), and in many particulars the three differ from John's Gospel. The Synoptics take for their chief theme Jesus' ministry in Galilee; the Fourth Gospel gives prominence to his work in Judea. Though Jesus' betrayal, arrest, trial, crucifixion, and resurrection are so important that they are reported by all four evangelists, the only prior incident recorded in detail by all four is the miracle of the feeding of the five thousand. Another marked difference concerns the reporting of the teaching of Jesus; the Synoptics contain much teaching about the kingdom of God, whereas John refers to the kingdom of God only once (3:5) and includes no example of Jesus' typical parables. However, John records at length Jesus' teaching about himself, and this is usually in the form of extended discourses.

During the past two centuries an enormous amount of research has been devoted to the study of the four Gospels. The earlier stages of this investigation involved the literary analysis of the written Gospels. At the close of World War I, attention was shifted to the preliterary stages of the Gospels, and what is called *form criticism* was applied to the units of tradition about Jesus that had circulated by word of mouth before they were incorporated in written Gospels. More recently the pendulum of scholarly research has begun to swing away from preoccupation with the oral period of the transmission of Gospel materials and now concentrates on examining the Gospels as unified compositions by literary authors, each with its own emphasis and point of view. A summary of the contributions of each of these three stages of research must now be given.

(i) Literary Criticism of the Synoptic Gospels

When the text of the Synoptic Gospels is set forth in parallel columns, it can be readily seen that there is very extensive agreement among them in content, arrangement, and even in wording.[5] The substance of 606 of the 661 verses of Mark reappears in some-

---

5. It is recommended that the material in the following section be studied by consulting a harmony of the Gospels, such as *Gospel Parallels,* 2nd ed., B. H. Throckmorton, ed. (Nashville: Thomas Nelson, 1992).

what shortened form in Matthew, and about 350 of the 661 verses of Mark reappear in Luke. Stated in another way, of the 1,068 verses of Matthew, about 500 contain the substance of 606 verses of Mark, while rather more than half of Mark's material (about 350 out of 661 verses) is embodied in Luke's 1,149 verses. Furthermore, Matthew and Luke have each about 235 verses in common, comprising chiefly discourse material, which are not in Mark.

Not only do all three Synoptic Gospels have a great deal of material in common, they also show an undeniable agreement in other points. For example, occasionally citations are made from the Old Testament in a form that is identical in all three Synoptics, though differing from both the Hebrew original as well as the Greek translation of the Old Testament (e.g., Matt. 3:3; Mark 1:3; Luke 3:4; and Matt. 11:10; Mark 1:2; Luke 7:27). Moreover, all three Gospels sometimes agree in style, vocabulary, and collocation of words involving extremely rare terms (e.g., Matt. 9:1-17; Mark 2:1-22; Luke 5:17-39), or even mere transitional phrases (e.g., Matt. 8:16; Mark 1:32; Luke 4:40; and Matt. 19:13; Mark 10:13; Luke 18:15).

It is obvious from these data that there is some kind of literary relationship among the Synoptic Gospels. Of several possible relationships, the one that has approved itself to most scholars is the priority of Mark. This is the theory that Matthew and Luke followed Mark's historical narrative, making its language fundamental to their own accounts, arranging its material to conform to their own purposes in writing, and adding material from other sources, oral and written. In support of this view it is customary to point not only to the implications of the data set forth above, but also to the following features that suggest the primitive character of Mark's Gospel.

(*a*) When the sections of Mark and Luke differ in sequence, Matthew agrees with Mark; but when the sections of Mark and Matthew differ in sequence, Luke agrees with Mark. Furthermore, Matthew and Luke never agree in sequence against Mark.

(*b*) In style and language, Mark is decidedly less polished than Matthew and Luke, and it would be contrary to all analogy that well-written documents should be so revised as to produce a cruder one.

(*c*) Phrases in Mark that are difficult or that might be misunderstood are absent from the parallel passages in Matthew and Luke. For example, the statement in Mark 2:26 that Abiathar was high priest when David entered the house of God is contrary to the account in 1 Samuel 21:1-7, and is omitted in the parallels in Matthew 12:3 and Luke 6:3. Again, the command, "You shall not defraud," which is included in a list of the commandments in Mark 10:19, is deleted by Matthew and Luke in their parallel accounts as being inappropriate among the Ten Commandments.

(d) In the early church, there was an increase of respect for the apostles, who came to be regarded as the pillars of the church. Matthew and Luke often soften Mark's blunt and sometimes uncomplimentary statements regarding these leaders of the church. For example, Matthew omits Mark's statement about their hardness of heart (Mark 6:52), their unseemly dispute as to who of them was the greatest (Mark 9:33-37), and their inability to comprehend Jesus' teaching (Mark 9:32). Luke softens Mark's account (Mark 14:71) of Peter's vigorous cursing, transforming it into a gentle disavowal, "Man, I do not know what you are talking about!" (Luke 22:60). Luke also omits Jesus' stinging rebuke of Peter, when he said, "Get behind me, Satan!" (Mark 8:33).

(e) A natural development of reverence for Jesus in the primitive church is reflected in the Gospels by such details as the following. Only once does Mark use "the Lord" to refer to Jesus (Mark 11:3); Matthew, however, uses it nineteen times and Luke sixteen. Conversely, both Matthew and Luke suppress or weaken references in Mark to such human emotions of Jesus as grief and anger (Mark 3:5) and amazement (Mark 6:6), as well as Jesus' unrequited love (Mark 10:21); they also omit Mark's statement that Jesus' friends thought he was beside himself (Mark 3:21).

(f) The later Gospels omit what might imply that Jesus was unable to accomplish what he willed; for example, Matthew and Luke do not repeat Mark's statements that Jesus "could no longer go into a town openly" (Mark 1:45) or that "he intended to pass by them" (Mark 6:48). Furthermore, they also omit questions asked by Jesus that might be taken to imply his ignorance. For example, the questions in Mark 6:38; 9:16, 21, 33 are absent from both Matthew and Luke, and the questions in Mark 5:9, 30; 8:12; and 14:14 are all omitted by Matthew.

(g) Side by side with softening in Matthew and Luke of what might lessen the majesty of Jesus' person is a readiness to heighten what illustrates it. Whereas Mark says that "they brought to him all who were sick or possessed with demons. . . . And he cured many . . . and cast out many demons" (Mark 1:32, 34), Matthew reports that "they brought to him many who were possessed with demons; and he cast out the spirits with a word, and cured all who were sick" (Matt. 8:16). In accordance with the implication of the phrase "with a word" in the last reference, more than once in telling of Jesus' miraculous work Matthew uses the word *instantly*, thereby insisting that the healing took place immediately (e.g., Matt. 15:28; 17:18). Likewise, according to Matthew, the fig tree that Jesus cursed withered at once, and the disciples were amazed at the sudden withering (Matt. 21:19-20), whereas Mark indicates that they did not notice the withering until the next day (Mark 11:20-21).

(h) Here and there the phrasing adopted by Matthew and Luke in reporting Jesus' words seems to reflect a later stage of theological understanding than that in Mark. For example, in the parable of the wicked tenants, according to Mark 12:8, when the owner of the vineyard sent his son to the vineyard to get some of the fruit, the tenants "seized him, killed him, and threw him out of the vineyard." Matthew and Luke, however, finding in the parable a parallel to what happened to Jesus when he was crucified *outside* the city walls, alter the sequence of clauses so as to read, "they threw him out of the vineyard and killed him" (Matt. 21:39; Luke 20:15).

These examples, which will be appreciated most fully if they are examined by consulting a harmony that gives the text of the Gospels in parallel columns, are more than sufficient to prove that Mark's Gospel is the most primitive of the Synoptics, and that where the three report the same incident, Matthew and Luke seem to have depended upon Mark's account, occasionally modifying its words in accordance with their own purposes.

Almost as widely held in Synoptic research as the priority of Mark is the view that the material common to Matthew and Luke, but not in Mark, was derived from a common source. This material, as was mentioned above, embraces about 235 verses and contains chiefly sayings of Jesus, though some narrative material, including the miraculous healing of the centurion's servant, is present as well. It is customary to refer to this hypothetical source by the symbol Q (standing for the German word *Quelle*, meaning "source").[6] Though several scholars believe that this material circulated only in oral form, most hold that it was reduced to writing, perhaps in Aramaic and then in Greek, before it was utilized by Matthew and Luke. A diagram that represents the relationship of the Synoptics and Q is as follows:

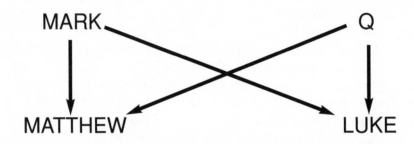

This basic theory of Synoptic relationships, called the two-source theory, has been enlarged and refined in various ways. The question has been raised, for example, as to what sources may have provided the approximately 300 verses in Matthew that have no parallel in any of the other Gospels, and the 520 verses of similar material in Luke.[7] Of the latter, the most considerable block of material is incorporated in the great central section of his Gospel (between Luke 9:51 and 18:14), which contains many distinctive parables of Jesus, such as those of the good Samaritan, the rich fool, the lost coin, the lost sheep, the prodigal son, the unjust steward, the unjust judge, and the Pharisee and the tax collector. Several British scholars (notably B. H. Streeter and Vincent Taylor) argued in the twentieth century that the present Gospel According to Luke went through several distinct stages of expansion, and that originally it began with what is now 3:1. This earlier Proto-Luke, as it is called, was formed when Luke combined his distinctive material with Q. Later he learned of Mark's Gospel and issued an enlarged edition of his own work, incorporating in it significant portions of Mark. Though there are certain features in Luke that seem to support this view (for example, the presence of an elaborate chronological framework at 3:1-2, which seems so appropriate for the opening of

---

6. David R. Catchpole, *The Quest for Q* (Edinburgh: T & T Clark, 1993).

7. The special sources of Matthew and Luke are frequently referred to by the symbols M and L.

a Gospel), the theory of Proto-Luke has not received the approval of most of New Testament scholars.

(ii) Form Criticism of the Gospels and Its Aftermath

Shortly after World War I, several scholars, dissatisfied with the increasingly meager results of the literary criticism of the Synoptic Gospels, began to investigate the Gospel traditions from a different point of view. They asked themselves what is likely to have happened during the transmission of the teachings of Jesus and the narratives about his ministry during the generation or two when they circulated by word of mouth before being reduced to writing. Several German scholars, including Martin Dibelius and Rudolf Bultmann, analyzed and classified the units of Gospel materials into such literary forms as pronouncement stories (i.e., short, succinct narratives that find a climax in a significant pronouncement made by Jesus, such as in Mark 3:31-35), miracle stories, parables, stories about Jesus, "I" sayings, and legends.

In addition to undertaking the analysis of the units of the Gospels, form critics also sought to reconstruct the conditions in the primitive Christian community in which the first unconscious shaping of the Gospel materials took place. This "situation in life," as it is called, included early missionary preaching, sermons, liturgy, and catechetical instruction, as well as controversies and disciplinary measures in the early Christian church.

The benefits derived from this kind of analysis of the Gospels were very real. Instead of concentrating on a scissors-and-paste type of literary criticism, attention was directed to the practical interests and needs of the early church in which the Gospel traditions circulated. It was more fully appreciated that the history of Jesus was never viewed as a mere incident of the past; it was seen rather as a vital power always operative, challenging, and controlling the lives of his followers in the present. Such continued use of his words and deeds was bound to shape their telling and to bring out what was deep and rich in every event.

Form critics have pointed out, for example, that the accounts of Jesus' miracles were preserved in the memory of the early Christian community mainly by being preached. This preaching involved the recital of how Jesus "went about doing good and healing all who were oppressed by the devil" (Acts 10:38). Keeping to the demands of oral style and following the rabbinical pattern, the first preachers described the miracles of Jesus with a minimum of excess verbiage concerning irrelevant details of time, place, and circumstance. The account was whittled down to brief notes involving three phases: (1) the illness and condition of the sufferer; (2) the action of Jesus the wonder-worker; (3) the saving effect of his power. This crisp brevity and concentration on what is essential characterize most of the Synoptic healing narratives.

Other units of Gospel materials were preserved, and sometimes modified, because the early church recognized their usefulness in answering current questions. Form critics have reminded us that as the church grew in numbers and diversity of membership, it was confronted with many pressing problems. As each difficulty arose, memories of Jesus were rekindled and relevant words of his were recounted. What, for example, was to be done with Gentiles who wished to join the primitive church? Some urged that they must first become Jews. It was helpful to recall how Jesus had dealt with non-Jews. Not only had he commended on more than one occasion members of the despised race of the Samaritans, but in healing the servant of a Roman centurion he had offered to enter the Gentile's house, even though strict Jews looked upon such an act as ceremonially defiling. What is more, he gave full praise to the man's peerless faith: "Truly I tell you, in no one in Israel have I found such faith" (Matt. 8:10). This conduct of Jesus lived on in the memory of his Jewish followers and played an important share in persuading the majority to accept Gentile converts just as they were.

Again, the early church had its conflicts with a hard core of Jewish Christians who insisted on coupling observance of the Mosaic Law with their allegiance to Christ. It was encouraging to remember that Jesus had faced similar controversies in his encounters with the Pharisees. His solution of these thorny problems provided ammunition in controversies that beset the early church. The frequent rehearsal of his conflicts resulted in a clearly defined literary form that form critics call the pronouncement story. The pattern is easy to detect in the Gospels: everything in the narrative is pared down to bare essentials in order to place emphasis on the concluding pronouncement made by Jesus. The story in Mark 2:23-28 provides an apt illustration. First a single sentence describes the situation: "One sabbath he was going through the grainfields; and as they made their way his disciples began to pluck heads of grain" (v. 23). Next follows the objection not only as Jesus heard it from the Pharisees but also as the early Gentile Christians heard it from their critics: "Look, why are they doing what is not lawful on the sabbath?" (v. 24). This objection is met with a rebuttal by Jesus, culminating in a memorable pronouncement that later would serve as a principle of action for the expanding church: "The sabbath was made for humankind, and not humankind for the sabbath; so the Son of Man is lord even of the sabbath" (vv. 27-28).

It will be seen from these examples that the discipline of form criticism has enlarged our understanding of the conditions that prevailed during the years when the Gospel materials circulated by word of mouth. There is no reason to doubt that a significant proportion of the words and events included in the Gospels are there not only because they figured in the life of Jesus, but also because they served some vital need in the life of the early church. Since, moreover, many of the sayings of Jesus were preserved mainly by being preached, they were liable in this way to a certain, or rather an uncertain, amount of modification with a view to bringing out the point of them in one or another set of circumstances in the primitive church. What each evangelist has preserved, therefore, is not a photographic reproduction of the words and deeds of Jesus, but an interpretative portrait delineated in accordance with the special needs of the early church.

The inference drawn by some form critics, however, that such interpretation has deformed the original meaning of Jesus' teaching is not justified by the literary argument. Reinterpretation and development need not involve deformation, but may be entirely homogeneous with the original meaning, whose full vitality is thus unfolded for the benefit of the whole church.

There were several circumstances that tended to prevent the free invention of Gospel traditions. One was the presence of original eyewitnesses (Luke 1:2), who would have acted as a check upon wholesale distortion of Jesus' words and works. Another was the rabbinical method of teaching that Jesus seems at times to have employed when impressing his message upon the memory of his disciples, thus guaranteeing a high degree of fidelity in its transmission.

Noteworthy among scholarly examinations of ancient Jewish and early Christian methods of transmission of tradition is Birger Gerhardsson's landmark study *Memory and Manuscript: Oral Tradition and Written Transmission in Rabbinic Judaism and Early Christianity*.[8] Here he departs from the form-critical approach and directs biblical investigation to the prehistory of the written Gospels. Gerhardsson's viewpoint is that the primary setting for the early Christian transmission of the Jesus tradition is tradition itself.

Gerhardsson's subsequent publications, especially *The Origins of the Gospel Traditions*,[9] present a Scandinavian alternative to continental form-criticism in biblical studies. Acknowledging the creative character of early Christian interpretation, Gerhardsson declares that "it is one thing to take these changes in the transmitted material in all seriousness, and quite another thing to presume that the early church freely constructed the Jesus traditions, placing the words of early Christian prophets and teachers in Jesus' mouth, and so on."[10] Other scholars have subsequently taken up Gerhardsson's insights for a symposium edited by Henry Wansbrough.[11]

It is not, however, merely by such development in scholarly research that one is assured of the essential fidelity with which the Gospel traditions of Jesus' teaching were passed on to the next generation. A consideration of the actual state of the evidence will lead one to the conclusion that there was no large-scale introduction of extraneous materials into the Gospels. The fact, for

---

8. Birger Gerhardsson, *Memory and Manuscript: Oral Tradition and Written Transmission in Rabbinic Judaism and Early Christianity*, 2nd ed. (Uppsala and Lund: C. W. K. Gleerup, 1964).

9. Birger Gerhardsson, *The Origins of the Gospel Traditions*, English translation (Philadelphia: Fortress Press, 1979).

10. Birger Gerhardsson, dust jacket of his *The Origins of the Gospel Traditions* (Philadelphia: Fortress Press, 1979).

11. The symposium is entitled *Jesus and the Oral Gospel Tradition* (Sheffield: Academic Press, 1991). Also worthy of consideration are two monographs written by Gerhardsson's pupil Samuel Byrskog, *Jesus, the Only Teacher: Didactic Authority and Transmission in Ancient Israel, Ancient Judaism and the Matthean Community* (Stockholm: Almqvist & Wiksell, 1994) and *Story as History—History as Story: The Gospel in the Context of Ancient Oral History* (Tübingen: Mohr Siebeck, 2000).

Several of Gerhardsson's out-of-print studies have been reissued under the title *The Reliability of the Gospel Tradition* (Peabody, Mass.: Hendrickson, 2001), with a ten-page foreword by Donald A. Hagner, who contrasts Gerhardsson's careful handling of evidence with the skepticism of the "Jesus Seminar."

instance, that certain of Jesus' parables were recast in the retelling so as to deal more directly with new problems in the developing church, so far from supporting the opinion of some scholars that the early Christian communities invented a large part of the contents of the Gospels, points rather to the tenacity with which the church retained the words of Jesus and merely readapted them to meet new situations. Furthermore, the total absence of parables in the teaching of the apostles, as reported in the book of Acts and the twenty-one Letters of the New Testament, indicates that, so far from their being the creation of the early church, the Gospel parables reflect the authentic teaching method and message of Jesus.

A simple test can be made to determine the extent to which extraneous materials have been taken into the Gospels. One of the most influential figures in the early church was the apostle Paul. His Letters, which date from the time when many of the Gospel traditions were taking shape, abound in pithy sentences and spiritual insights that could easily have been transferred to Jesus and presented as oracles of the Lord. If it be asked how many times this has happened, the answer must be *Not once!*

Furthermore, it is noteworthy that Jesus' followers felt obliged to transmit his sayings even though some were not understood at the time and others became increasingly embarrassing to the church. For example, the Synoptic Gospels contain passages that indicate that Jesus expressed an attitude toward little children and toward animals that was very remarkable in that age (Matt. 6:26; 10:29; 18:1-6, 10-14; Mark 9:36-37; 10:13-16; Luke 12:6). Since there is no evidence that this attitude was appreciated in the early church, where the child suggested childishness rather than childlikeness (1 Cor. 3:1; 13:11; Eph. 4:14; Heb. 5:12-14), it was the evangelists' faithfulness to historical memory that led them to represent their master as dealing with children and speaking of animals in a way they themselves did not understand, but felt to be characteristic of him.

Likewise, the Gospels preserve more than one saying attributed to Jesus, which as the years went by, became more and more embarrassing to the church. For example, the difficult sayings of Jesus to his disciples, "Truly I tell you, you will not have gone through all the towns of Israel before the Son of Man comes" (Matt. 10:23), and "Truly I tell you, there are some standing here who will not taste death until they see that the kingdom of God has come with power" (Mark 9:1), both of which seem to predict the imminent end of the age, were retained despite the embarrassment that must have been felt increasingly as time passed without their being fulfilled in the way that many thought they must be fulfilled. The early church could have allowed such sayings to fall into oblivion, yet these and others have been faithfully preserved despite strong pressures to modify or forget them.

(iii) Theological Analysis of the Individual Gospels

In reaction against the excesses of certain form critics, at the close of World War II several New Testament scholars shifted attention away from the analysis of individual units in the Gospel tradition and concentrated on the Gospels as unified compositions of literary authors. These scholars (Günther Bornkamm, Hans Conzelmann, Willi Marxsen, and others) came to recognize what had been overlooked by many who were preoccupied with minute analysis of sources, namely that each Gospel possesses a unique literary quality, and that the reader must seek to discover the leading theological insights and purposes of its author. This method of Gospel research, called "redaction criticism," was not altogether new, for during the nineteenth century more than one New Testament scholar applied something like it in studying the characteristics of each individual evangelist.

It is obvious that, despite the many similarities among the three Synoptic Gospels, each evangelist has produced a distinctive presentation of the common gospel message. The most obvious reason that accounts for their variety is that each writer had access to a somewhat different body of oral traditions regarding Jesus' words and works. Moreover, since each evangelist had in mind a special reading public, he would naturally choose to emphasize those details which, in his view, were most suited to communicate the message of the gospel to that reading public. The natural consequence is that each evangelist as a literary artist has drawn his own distinctive portrait of Jesus Christ. A unified outlook pervades the component parts of each Gospel and is apparent in the connective tissues by which each writer has linked together the various parts of his narrative.

Most readers of the New Testament have in their minds a composite picture of the life of Jesus Christ, made up of features drawn from all four Gospels (see the following chapter for such an outline). An effort must be made here to isolate the individual characteristics of each Gospel in order to appreciate the special contribution made by its author to our understanding of the person and work of Jesus Christ.

(a) The Gospel According to Matthew contains many features that indicate that it was written to convince Jewish readers that Jesus is their royal Messiah. It begins with a genealogy that traces Jesus' ancestry from Abraham, regarded by Jews as "the father of the faithful," through King David and all the succeeding kings of Judah. Born at Bethlehem, the city of David, the infant child is adored as king of the Jews by wise men from the East (2:1). As a royal teacher of his people, Jesus sets forth in his "inaugural address" (the Sermon on the Mount, chaps. 5 to 7) the traits and temperament of those who would be citizens of his domain.

Much of the matter peculiar to the Gospel of Matthew is concerned with the Jews or with the fulfillment of Old Testament prophecies. All of the Gospels mention Jesus' Davidic lineage, but Matthew emphasizes this relationship by alluding to it much more often than does any other evangelist. In addition to what he has in common with one or more other Gospels, he includes also the testimony of the two blind men (9:27), the multitude (12:23), the Canaanite woman (15:22), the crowds at the triumphant entry into Jerusalem (21:9), and the children in the temple (21:15)—all of whom recognize Jesus as the Son of David. Only Matthew among the evangelists refers to Jesus as king of the twelve tribes of Israel (19:28), and as the one who is to rule over a kingdom prepared from the foundation of the world (25:34). In short, the special aim of Matthew is to show that Jesus is the legitimate heir to the royal house of David.

In this connection, Matthew's appeal to the fulfillment of prophecy is a noteworthy feature of his Gospel. All four evangelists quote Old Testament prophecies that they regard as fulfilled in the person and work of Jesus, but Matthew includes nine additional such prophetic proof texts, all of which are characterized by a certain verbal literalism of the type that would make special appeal to persons of Jewish background. Thus, he finds allusions in the Old Testament to Jesus' birth from a virgin (1:22-23), to the return from Egypt (2:15), the lamentation over the slaughter of the Bethlehem children (2:17-18), the abode of Jesus in Nazareth (2:23), Jesus' preaching in Galilee (4:14-16), Jesus' taking peoples' infirmities and bearing their diseases (8:17), Jesus' desire to avoid popular disturbances (12:17-21), Jesus' habit of teaching in parables (13:35), and the purchase of the potter's field (27:9-10). Matthew's emphasis upon Old Testament prophecies is designed to show that the mission of Jesus was neither haphazard nor capricious, but was part of a well-ordered and divinely prearranged whole.

There are other special characteristics of Matthew's Gospel, such as the evangelist's singular fondness for groups of threes,[12] but what has been cited will be sufficient to make it clear that his whole Gospel is pervaded by those features that would make it specially appealing to Jews and Jewish Christians.

(b) The Gospel According to Mark was evidently written for a Gentile reading public, and probably for the Romans in particular. The evangelist is careful to translate Aramaic and Hebrew phrases and names, such as *Boanerges* (3:17), *talitha cum* (5:41), *ephphatha* (7:34), *Abba* (14:36), and the cry of dereliction from the cross (15:34). Still more significant is that he explains Greek expressions by their Latin equivalents; thus he informs his readers that the two coins that the poor widow placed in the offering box in the temple were the equivalent of the Roman *quadrans* (12:42), and he identifies the "court" of Pilate's palace as the *praetorium* (15:16). Obviously such pieces of information would have been of interest primarily to Roman readers.

The evangelist is concerned more with what Jesus did than what he said, and events rather than discourses make up the bulk of his Gospel. In relating Jesus' activities, Mark's narrative gives the

---

12. The orderliness of Matthew's arrangement of materials and his penchant for grouping in threes can be seen from the following: There are three divisions in Jesus' genealogy, three incidents in Jesus' childhood, three illustrations of righteousness (6:1-18), three prohibitions (6:19–7:6), three commands (7:7-20), three miracles of healing (8:1-15), three miracles of power (8:23–9:8), three miracles of restoration (9:14-17), a threefold "fear not" (10:26, 28, 31), three sayings regarding little ones (18:6, 10, 14), three questions (22:15-10), three parables of warning (24:43–25:30), three prayers in Gethsemane, three denials of Peter, three questions of Pilate, and three incidents that vexed the Pharisees. A few of these items are shared by Matthew with one or more evangelists, but most of them are peculiar to his Gospel.

impression of vigor; in this, the shortest of the four Gospels, the Greek word translated "immediately" or "then" occurs more than forty times in but sixteen chapters. The Gospel opens with an account of Jesus receiving baptism at the hands of John the Baptizer (Mark 1:4-11), followed by the commencement of Jesus' public ministry. About one fourth of the entire Gospel deals with the events of the last week of Jesus' life, leading to his crucifixion and resurrection.

No Gospel brings into clearer light the full humanity of Jesus. As was pointed out earlier (p. 98), Jesus asks questions, apparently for the purpose of gaining information, and displays such human emotions as grief, anger, and amazement. He sleeps from fatigue (4:38) and declares that he, though the Son, is ignorant of the Father's appointed time (13:32).

It would be entirely wrong, however, to conclude that Mark regarded Jesus as no more than a mere man. On the contrary, throughout his Gospel there is a pervasive undertone of testimony to Jesus as the divine Son of God. Starting from the opening sentence ("The beginning of the good news of Jesus Christ, the Son of God"), Mark records the application of the title "Son of God" to Jesus on the part of demoniacs (3:11; 5:7), in the high priest's question (14:61), and at the end of Jesus' life in the centurion's cry, "Truly this man was God's Son!" (15:39). To these must be added the words of the voice from heaven at the baptism, "You are my Son, the Beloved" (1:11), and at the transfiguration, "This is my Son, the Beloved; listen to him!" (9:7). In accordance with the implications of the title "Son of God," Mark represents Jesus as knowing what is passing in men's minds and hearts, and the circumstances of their lives (2:5, 8; 8:17; 9:33-35; 12:15, 44); and Jesus foresees and foretells the future, whether his own (10:32-33) or that of individuals (10:39; 14:27) and communities (13:1-8).

In the earliest manuscripts of the New Testament, the Second Gospel breaks off suddenly at 16:8 with the words, "for they were afraid." What follows in verses 9-20 is an early attempt to provide a more or less suitable ending for what was soon recognized as a most unsatisfactory close for a book that presents "the good news of Jesus Christ"—which is what "the gospel of Jesus Christ" means. Whether Mark was prevented by death from completing his

Gospel, or whether the original copy was accidentally mutilated, losing its final sheet (or sheets), no one can say.

(c) The Gospel According to Luke was written in order to attract and win to Christianity cultured Greek readers such as Theophilus, to whom it is dedicated (1:3-4). It is obvious from a number of features that the evangelist envisages a Gentile rather than a Jewish reading public. Thus, the Third Gospel makes comparatively few quotations from the Old Testament, which would have been a strange and almost unknown book to most non-Jews. For the same reason Luke seldom appeals to the argument from prophecy. Furthermore, instead of using the Jewish word *rabbi,* Luke is the only New Testament author who employs the classical Greek equivalent *(epistatēs),* a word meaning "master" (5:5; 8:24, 45; 9:33, 49; 17:13). In passages where Mark uses the Hebrew word *amen,* Luke usually substitutes a native Greek word meaning "truly" or "verily."[13]

Luke includes details that describe the graciousness of Jesus' personal character and his concern for people of all races and classes. The universal aspects of his mission are emphasized. Unlike Matthew, who traces Jesus' lineage from Abraham, Luke carries Jesus' genealogy beyond Abraham to Adam himself (3:23-38). Like the other Synoptic writers, Luke applies to the work of John the Baptist the words of Isaiah, "The voice of one crying in the wilderness: 'Prepare the way of the Lord' " (Luke 3:4; Isa. 40:3), but unlike Matthew and Mark, he extends the quotation from Isaiah so as to include the prediction that "all flesh shall see the salvation of God." This is one of several passages in which Luke indicates that Gentiles will have an opportunity to accept the good tidings of the gospel (compare 2:32; 24:47).

Only Luke recalls that Jesus commended members of a despised nation, the Samaritans (10:30-37; 17:11-19). In his account of Jesus' commission to the twelve apostles, who according to Matthew were bidden to "go nowhere among the Gentiles, . . . but go rather to the lost sheep of the house of Israel" (Matt. 10:5-6), Luke says nothing about restrictions on the apostles' activities (9:2-5). Luke's

---

13. In the Synoptic Gospels, *amen* occurs in Matthew thirty times; in Mark, thirteen times; and in Luke, six times. In John, where it is usually doubled *("amen, amen"),* it occurs twenty-five times. (For the special significance of Jesus' use of *amen* to preface his pronouncements see p. 182.)

Gospel also includes fuller information than the other Synoptics concerning women and the new place of importance that they hold among the followers of Jesus (7:36-50; 8:3; 10:38-42).

Another characteristic of the Third Gospel is its emphasis on what has been described in modern times as "the social gospel." Luke depicts particularly what may be called Jesus' humanitarian concern: his deep sympathy for the plight of the poor, the oppressed, and the outcast. Whereas in Matthew's account of the Sermon on the Mount Jesus is quoted as saying, "Be perfect . . . as your heavenly Father is perfect" (Matt. 5:48), Luke's account of Jesus' sermon concludes with, "Be merciful, just as your Father is merciful" (6:36). Instead of the Matthean form of the first Beatitude, "Blessed are the poor in spirit, for theirs is the kingdom of heaven" (Matt. 5:3), Luke reports Jesus as teaching, "Blessed are you who are poor, for yours is the kingdom of God" (6:20). Only Luke adds after the Beatitudes a series of woes directed against those who are rich and full (6:24-26). Luke alone recalls that on one occasion Jesus said to his host:

> When you give a luncheon or a dinner, do not invite your friends or your brothers or your relatives or rich neighbors, in case they may invite you in return, and you would be repaid. But when you give a banquet, invite the poor, the crippled, the lame, and the blind. And you will be blessed, because they cannot repay you, for you will be repaid at the resurrection of the righteous. (14:12-14)

In Luke, an exhortation to almsgiving and voluntary poverty occurs frequently (6:20; 12:33; 14:33; 16:25). This Gospel alone records Zacchaeus's public renunciation of his earlier life of dishonesty as a tax collector (19:8). Only Luke speaks of the Pharisees as "lovers of money" (16:14).

Finally, mention must be made of the high quality of Luke's literary style. Of all four evangelists, he is preeminently a person of broad culture, capable of writing an elegant style of Greek. As a gifted literary artist he produced what has justly been described as "the most beautiful book in the world" (Ernst Renan).

(*d*) In comparison with the Synoptics, the Fourth Gospel is quite independent in (1) style, (2) content, and (3) theological emphasis.

(1) The Gospel According to John is at once the most simple and yet the most profound of the four Gospels. Though John's vocabulary is far less extensive than that of any of the other evangelists, he makes impressive, almost majestic, use of a limited number of fundamental words and phrases by the expedient of repetition. Characteristic words that appear many times are "love," "truth," "light," "witness," "sin," "judgment," and "life." His syntactical construction is also severely plain, almost childlike, and shows a marked fondness for linking sentences with the words "and" or "then." At the same time the author's ability in character drawing is surprising; such persons as Nicodemus (chap. 3), the woman of Samaria (chap. 4), the man born blind (chap. 9), and Pilate (chap. 19) stand out with dramatic vividness.

(2) A large part of the Fourth Gospel consists of discourses of Jesus. These discourses are not individual sayings or even collections of sayings (as in the Sermon on the Mount); they each develop a particular theme. Furthermore, it is a characteristic of the Johannine discourses that Jesus is often interrupted by questions or objections from the hearers, a feature that never occurs in the Synoptics.

There is a fundamental divergence between John and the Synoptics in the outline of the chronology and geography of the ministry of Jesus. The Synoptics confine Jesus' public ministry largely to Galilee, and, because they mention only one Passover, the reader may get the impression that Jesus' ministry lasted less than one year. John, however, mentions at least three Passovers during Jesus' ministry (2:13, 23; 6:4; 12:1), and four journeys of Jesus to Jerusalem, preceded by an earlier period of Jesus' preaching in Judea.

Scholars have differed in their evaluation of the historicity of John's account. On the one hand, it is obvious that the fourth evangelist was guided by theological rather than simple historical interests. For example, already in the first chapter of his Gospel he provides a fairly complete record of the disciples' conception of their master and his work; and he does this by means of seven titles given to Jesus: the Word (of God), the Lamb of God, Rabbi (or Teacher), the Messiah (or Christ), the King of Israel, the Son of God, and the Son of Man. A comparative study of the other Gospels reveals that these titles were given at various times throughout the early ministry of Jesus, or even during his postresurrection life, and that the realization of their significance was the result of a long evolution.

On the other hand, an examination of the same first chapter shows that the evangelist has recorded valuable historical data, not immediately discernible in the Synoptic Gospels; for example, that Peter, Andrew, John, Nathaniel, and Philip—perhaps even Jesus himself—had originally been for some time followers of John the Baptist, or that the change of Simon's name to Peter took place at an early stage of Jesus' public ministry (as Mark 3:16 and Luke 6:14 also attest) and hence not as late as the incident at Caesarea Philippi, where Matthew 16:18 places it.

In recent decades, there has been a growing tendency among scholars to acknowledge that the Fourth Gospel preserves independent reports concerning Jesus' public ministry in Judea and Jerusalem, thus supplementing the information given by the Synoptic Gospels concerning his ministry in Galilee. A careful reading of the Synoptics will disclose hints that Jesus had labored in Jerusalem for a considerable time or on several occasions prior to the only visit during his ministry that they explicitly record—the one that eventuated in his crucifixion. For example, Jesus' lament over impenitent Jerusalem ("How often have I desired to gather your children together as a hen gathers her brood under her wings, and you were not willing!" Matt. 23:37; Luke 13:34) clearly implies earlier visits to the city and efforts to win followers there.

(3) The theological emphases in the Fourth Gospel differ from those in the Synoptics. Instead of beginning with the genealogy of Jesus, the evangelist commences with the preexistence of the Word of God, who, being the source of life and light for all creation (1:1-4), became incarnate in Jesus Christ (1:14). Throughout his Gospel, John represents the mission of Jesus as the climax of God's self-revelation, bringing believers that light which consists of the highest truth (8:12-32), and that life which consists of spiritual union with God (17:22-23; 20:31).

The person of Jesus is emphasized in the Fourth Gospel. Though the earlier Gospels preserve sayings of Jesus that are powerful expressions of his lofty self-consciousness ("I tell you, something greater than the temple is here; . . . something greater than Solomon is here!" Matt. 12:6, 42), this aspect of his teaching is not stressed in them. However, in the Fourth Gospel, Jesus speaks freely in the first person; for example, "I am the bread of life" (6:35), "I am the light of the world" (8:12), "I am the resurrection and the life" (11:25), and "The Father and I are one" (10:30).

From such data as these concerning the style, content, and theological complexion of the Fourth Gospel, it must be concluded that the evangelist has given us a highly individualistic portrait of the person and work of Jesus. Whereas the Synoptics preserve the sayings of Jesus more exactly in their original language and form, the fourth evangelist employs more freely his own modes of thought and language in reporting and interpreting the discourses of Jesus. The fact, however, that the Gospel of John was soon placed side by side with the Synoptics indicates that the early church realized that Jesus' promise, as reported by John, had been fulfilled, "The Holy Spirit . . . will teach you everything, and remind you of all that I have said to you" (John 14:26).

(iv) Date and Authorship

Very little has been said thus far about the identity of the several evangelists and the date of the composition of each Gospel. Actually not much is known about these matters. The text itself of each Gospel is anonymous and its title represents what later tradition had to say about the identity of the author. Of course the probabilities are that such traditions contain at least a substantial hint as to identity of the evangelist. Sometimes, however, internal considerations are such as to cast doubt upon the full accuracy of the later tradition. In the case of the First Gospel, the apostle Matthew can scarcely be the final author; for why should one who presumably had been an eyewitness of much that he records depend so slavishly upon the account given by Mark, who had not been an eyewitness? As a solution of this difficulty it has often been suggested that what Matthew drew up was an early collection of the sayings of Jesus, perhaps in Aramaic, and that this material, being translated into Greek, constitutes what scholars today call the Q source. In that case, the first Gospel was put together by an unknown Christian who utilized the Gospel of Mark, the Matthean collection, and other special sources. The name of Matthew was subsequently transferred from the collection of sayings to the completed Gospel.

According to traditions reported by several church fathers of the second and third centuries, the Gospel of Mark embodies what John Mark (Acts 12:12, 25; 15:37) wrote down at Rome from the preaching of Peter. Its colloquial style and graphic description of incidents in which Simon Peter figures prominently, or which must have had special interest for him (for example, Mark 1:16-20; 1:29–3:1; 1:35-38; 14:27-31, 32-42, 54, 66-72), give the impression of being derived directly from the reminiscence of Peter himself. Furthermore, in 1:36 the disciples are called "Simon and his companions," and in 16:7 the women are commissioned to tell to "his disciples and Peter" that the risen Christ is going ahead of them into Galilee.

Early tradition makes Luke a native of Antioch in Syria, and indicates that he became a Christian during the early decades of the expansion of the church among the Gentiles. The information supplied by Paul that Luke was a physician (Col. 4:14) is quite in accord with the cultured literary style characteristic of his two volumes (Gospel and Acts). Not having been a disciple, Luke had to depend upon information derived from others concerning the life and teaching of Jesus, and he tells us that he was diligent in seeking out eyewitnesses of Jesus' ministry (Luke 1:1-4).

The Fourth Gospel refers to its author as "the disciple whom Jesus loved" (John 21:20, 24). From a comparison with the other passages where this same expression occurs (13:23; 19:26; 20:2; 21:7), it appears that John the son of Zebedee is meant, and with this conclusion early and widespread Christian tradition agrees. At the same time, it is clear that others were also involved in its composition and authentication (compare the statement at the close of the Gospel, "We know that his testimony is true." [21:24]). The markedly different style of the book of Revelation, also attributed to a person named John (Rev. 1:1, 4, 9; 22:8), raises perplexing questions. No simple solution to the problem of authorship is possible, but it is probable that the Fourth Gospel preserves Palestinian reminiscences of Jesus' ministry. Tradition places the composition of the Gospel of John at Ephesus toward the close of the first century.

When the Synoptics were written has been much debated. Some scholars have been impressed by the abrupt ending of the book of Acts, where nothing is said about the outcome of the trial for which Paul had been brought to Rome. If Luke ended his book in this unsatisfactory way because he published it before the trial had been held, then Acts must be dated about A.D. 63 and the Gospel of Luke about 61. Therefore Mark, one of Luke's sources, must have been published toward the end of the fifties.

However, those who are not convinced that Acts was published shortly after the last event that it records usually date the Lukan Gospel in the seventies or eighties, and Mark sometime in the late sixties.

The date of the Gospel According to Matthew is unknown, except that it is later than Mark. Most scholars date it in the years just before or after the fall of Jerusalem in A.D. 70.

Summary. Over the years scholarly investigation of the Gospels has concentrated on the several stages of the transmission of the words and deeds of Jesus. Most of Jesus' teaching was in Aramaic, though occasionally he probably also used Greek. After his Aramaic sayings had been translated into Greek they continued to circulate by word of mouth, along with accounts of Jesus' activities during his public ministry. Those who had been with Jesus, as well as their disciples, brought to recollection what he had said and done, thus providing the church with guidance in doctrinal, liturgical, and practical matters.

The recounting of Jesus' teaching and activities entailed a certain amount of modification in order to bring out more clearly their meaning when applied to new situations. A generation or two after Jesus' public ministry, and on the basis of what was remembered in churches of Palestine and beyond, each of the four evangelists put into writing his account of the gospel, which means "the good news." The four accounts differ because they incorporate differing formulations of Jesus' words and deeds; they also differ because each evangelist emphasized what he felt was most valuable for the special reading public he had in mind and, therefore, chose among the traditions what was most suitable to accomplish his purpose. The four accounts agree in essentials because they are not imaginative compositions but go back to a historical person who had made a profound impression upon his followers. Furthermore, the Synoptic Gospels agree in many sections because, in drawing up their Gospels, the first and third evangelists used Mark's Gospel as well as a common source containing chiefly Jesus' teachings (Q).

Thus, each portion of the Gospels can be investigated as to its contribution to the total purpose of the evangelist, as well as its earlier function in the life of the church while it was transmitted by word of mouth. It is only by studying the Gospels on these two levels that one comes to a full understanding of the third level on which all else is based. This is the historical level of the earthly life of Jesus—his words and deeds.

It is obvious that it would be unwarranted to regard any of the Gospels as a journalist's verbatim report of what happened yesterday. What the evangelists have preserved for us is not a photographic reproduction of all the words and all the deeds of Jesus, but something more like four interpretative portraits. Each of these portraits presents distinctive highlights of Jesus' person and work, and, taken together, the four provide a varied and balanced account of what Jesus said and did.

2. THE LETTERS OF PAUL

The Letters of the apostle Paul also bear witness to some of the events in the life and ministry of Jesus Christ. Though Paul probably had never seen Jesus in the flesh, his acquaintance with Peter, James, and other early leaders of the Jerusalem church provided him with information regarding the life and teaching of Jesus. Here and there in his Letters, written in the late fifties and early sixties, he includes more historical data concerning Jesus than is usually realized.

Paul's knowledge of Jesus was not limited to the bare fact that Jesus had lived upon the earth; he had a definite idea of the story of his life, and was careful to distinguish between pronouncements made by Jesus on ethical problems and his own pronouncements (1 Cor. 7:10-12). In addition to quoting the eucharistic words of Jesus (1 Cor. 11:23-25), Paul's Letters contain a fairly large number of allusions to sayings of Jesus, so many, that some scholars have thought it likely that Paul may have had in his hands a collection of Jesus' sayings.[14]

---

14. The following are several examples (the references in parentheses are to those words of Jesus, now preserved in the Gospels, to which Paul may be alluding): Rom. 12:14 (Matt. 5:44); Rom. 14:14 (Matt. 15:11); 1 Cor. 5:4 (Matt. 18:20); 1 Cor. 13:2 (Matt. 17:20; Mark 11:23); 1 Cor. 13:3 (Mark 10:21; Luke 12:33); 2 Cor. 10:1 (Matt. 11:29); Gal. 4:17 (Matt. 23:13; Luke 11:52); 1 Thess. 4:8 (Matt. 10:40; Luke 10:16).

In evaluating the weight of Paul's knowledge of Jesus, the historian finds it significant that the Pauline Letters confirm the broad outlines of the testimony of the Gospels.

3. APOCRYPHAL GOSPELS

Besides the four Gospels that are included in the New Testament, many others were written both before (compare Luke 1:1) and after the four canonical ones. It was particularly in the postapostolic age that the production of these noncanonical gospels flourished. From the writings of the church fathers we know the titles of about forty such gospels; the text, in more or less complete form, of about a dozen has survived.[15]

One of the oldest is the Gospel of Thomas, dating from the first half of the second Christian century. Besides three small fragments in Greek preserved among the Oxyrhynchus papyri (P.Oxy. 1, 654, and 655), in 1945 the entire Gospel of Thomas in Coptic was discovered in Upper Egypt at Nag Hammadi (the ancient Chenoboskion). Here thirteen leather-bound codices, kept in a storage jar, came to light, containing in various degrees of preservation more than forty (mainly Gnostic) works, nearly all previously unknown.[16]

Unlike the canonical Gospels, the Gospel of Thomas has no narrative framework but consists entirely of 114 sayings (called *logia*) attributed to Jesus. A few of these are similar to those in the canonical Gospels: others are totally different. For example, "Jesus says, A city built upon a high hill [and] fortified cannot fall nor can it remain hidden" (logion 23, similar to Matt. 5:14*b*). Another is, "Jesus says, Give to Caesar what belongs to Caesar; give to God what belongs to God; and give to me what is mine" (logion 100; parallels to the first two phrases are in Matt. 22:21 and Luke 20:25). Logion 102 has no parallel in the New Testament but seems to echo

---

15. For an English translation, see Wilhelm Schneemelcher's edition of Edgar Hennecke's *New Testament Apocrypha,* English trans. By R. McL. Wilson, 2 vols. (Philadelphia: Westminster Press, 1992, 1993) or J. K. Elliott, *The Apocryphal New Testament* (New York: Oxford University Press, 1993).

16. An English translation of the Coptic Gnostic library was edited by James M. Robinson, *The Nag Hammadi Library in English* (Leiden: E. J. Brill, 1977; 3rd ed., 1988). This was completely revised by Richard Smith, who also provided an afterword (San Francisco: HarperCollins, 1990), paperback. Majella Franzmann deals with Nag Hammadi and Jesus research in her book *Jesus in the Nag Hammadi Writings* (Edinburgh: T & T Clark, 1996).

Figure 4.1. Gnostic Books
(Courtesy of the Institute for Antiquity and Christianity, Claremont Graduate University, Claremont, Calif.)
Gnostic books discovered in 1945 near Nag Hammadi, Egypt.

Figure 4.2. The Jabal al Tārif Cliffs
(Courtesy of the Institute for Antiquity and Christianity, Claremont Graduate University, Claremont, Calif.)
The Jabal al Tārif Cliffs, where the Gnostic books were found in a jar.

one of Aesop's fables: "Jesus says, Woe to the Pharisees, for they are like a dog sleeping in the manger of oxen, for neither does he eat nor does he allow the oxen to eat." Also, altogether unlike anything in the canonical Gospels is logion 77: "Split the wood, I am there; lift the stone, and you will find me there." This pantheistic saying suggests that Jesus is coterminous with the material of this world. Likewise, totally uncharacteristic of Jesus are the enigmatic logion 105: "Jesus says, He who will know the father and the mother will be called the son of a harlot," and the antifeminist concluding sentence: "Jesus says . . . , Every woman who makes herself a male will enter the kingdom of heaven" (logion 114).

The Nag Hammadi codices also preserve the text of the Gospel of Philip, which follows the Gospel of Thomas in codex II. Very likely a translation of an original Greek work dating from the second or third century, the Coptic version is dated to about A.D. 350. Unlike any of the canonical Gospels, the work is a compilation of reflections on the question of salvation, loosely linked by catchphrases. In addition to quoting five sayings of Jesus from Matthew and three from John, it contains eight brief enigmatic "new" sayings of Jesus. Among several extracanonical stories about Jesus are (a) his ability to change his appearance to suit the nature of those to whom he was revealing himself (57:28–58:10); (b) his three female companions were each named Mary (59:6-11), though Mary Magdalene alone received many kisses from him (63:32–64:2); and (c) the result of mixing seventy-two colors together was a vat of white (63:25-30). Throughout there are echoes of the influential teaching of Valentinus, a second-century Gnostic theologian, including the restoration of Adam's original androgynous nature.

Whereas some of the apocryphal gospels were written to provide support for heretical ideas that were current in sections of the early church, others were drawn up to satisfy the curiosity of Christians in the postapostolic church regarding aspects of Jesus' life that are passed over with little or no comment in the four canonical Gospels. In particular, people were curious about what had happened to Jesus during his infancy and childhood. When people are curious, they generally try to satisfy their curiosity. In this case, despite the absence of historical information, the imagination of pious Christians ran riot. Reasoning that what could have happened might have happened, and that what might have happened did happen, stories about Jesus began to circulate in what are called Infancy Gospels. They are all of poor literary quality and devoid of historical value.

The two most widely circulated Infancy Gospels are the Book of James and the Infancy Gospel of Thomas. The former, also known as the "Protevangelium," consists in the main of a highly embellished account of the events connected with the birth of Jesus. The latter is a collection of folkloric tales of Jesus' childhood from the age of five to twelve years. It begins with an account of how the boy Jesus, five years old, was playing with other children on the sabbath at the ford of a brook, making mud pies. After Jesus had fashioned twelve sparrows from the soft clay, he clapped his hands and the sparrows took flight and went away chirping!

When Jesus was six years old, his mother gave him a pitcher and sent him to draw water at the well. In a crowd at the well, he stumbled and the pitcher was broken. But Jesus was not daunted; he spread out the skirt of the garment that he was wearing, filled it with water, and brought it to his mother.

When Jesus was eight years old he helped Joseph, his father, in the carpenter shop. An order had come in from a rich man to make him a bed. Accidentally, Joseph cut one of the two pieces of the wood for the bed too short, and did not know what to do. Jesus instructed Joseph, "Lay down the two pieces and make them even at the end next to you." Then Jesus stood at the other end, took hold of the shorter beam, and stretched it, making it equal in length to the other.

Occasionally a story is told in the apocryphal gospels that implies that Jesus could be petulant and ill-tempered. A certain schoolmaster, Zacchaeus by name, came to Joseph and offered to teach Jesus, starting with the alphabet. He told Jesus all the letters from Alpha to Omega clearly, with much questioning. But Jesus looked at the teacher and said to him, "How can you, who do not know the Alpha according to its nature, teach others the Beta? You hypocrite, first, if you know it, teach the Alpha, and then we will believe you concerning the Beta." Then he began to question the teacher about the first letter, and he was unable to answer him.

On another day when Jesus was walking through the village, a boy ran and dashed against his shoulder. This so exasperated Jesus that he cried out, "You will never get where you are going," and the boy immediately fell down and died.

The chief appraisal that the historian can make about these and similar stories is that the apocryphal gospels presuppose the existence of the four canonical Gospels. Such stories tell us more about the interests and mentality of the unknown Christians whose active imagination drew up such texts than they do about Jesus himself. Sometimes apocryphal gospels are referred to as "excluded books of the Bible." Even a casual acquaintance, however, of these gospels and their credentials will convince the reader that no one excluded them from the Bible; they excluded themselves.[17] (See also the Appendix: "The Formation of the Canon of the New Testament," pp. 311-21.)

---

17. For a discussion of the contents and character of New Testament apocryphal accounts of Jesus, see J. K. Elliott, *The Apocryphal Jesus: Legends of the Early Church* (New York: Oxford University Press, 1996).

CHAPTER 5

A SUMMARY OF THE LIFE OF JESUS CHRIST

I. THE CHRONOLOGY OF THE LIFE OF JESUS CHRIST

In the Greco-Roman world, several methods of reckoning eras were commonly employed. One that came into wide use counted the number of years from the founding of the city of Rome (A.U.C. = *ab urbe condita*). During the first half of the sixth century A.D., a new method of reckoning time was proposed by a Scythian monk named Dionysius. He must have been a little man, for he is generally called Dionysius Exiguus ("Denys the Little"). Held in high respect as a theologian, mathematician, and astronomer, Dionysius took the birth of Jesus Christ as the starting point for the Christian Era. Dates were now computed "in the year of the Lord" (A.D. = *anno Domini*). By the time of Charlemagne (about A.D. 800), Dionysius's system had supplanted the mode of reckoning the years A.U.C. Unfortunately, however, Dionysius erred in his calculations by at least four years. Instead of correlating Jesus' birth with A.U.C. 754, he should have placed it sometime prior to A.U.C. 750, which was the year of the death of Herod the Great. The actual year of the Nativity is therefore sometime prior to 4 B.C. (how much prior will be discussed below). By the time Dionysius's error was discovered, it was too late to attempt to rectify the mistake and to alter all previously dated documents.

It should be noted that there is no year 0, and therefore from 1 B.C. to A.D. 1 is one civil year; and from 4 B.C. to A.D. 4, for example, is seven years.

For the historian, three pivotal dates to be determined in the life of Jesus Christ are the date of his birth, the date of his baptism and of the beginning of his public ministry, and the date of his crucifixion. If these three dates can be ascertained, it will be possible to reckon other events in his life as so many years before or after them. The scanty and sometimes conflicting evidence in the Gospels, however, makes it exceedingly difficult to attain certainty for any of these pivotal dates.

1. THE DATE OF THE BIRTH OF JESUS

The New Testament provides no precise information concerning the year, the month, or the day of the Nativity. A fixed point from which to start is the fact that Jesus was born before the death of Herod the Great; for, according to Matthew 2:1-9, Herod was troubled by the arrival of the wise men from the East asking where the king of the Jews had been born. From Josephus we learn that Herod died on or before Passover, A.U.C. 750 (that is, on or before April 4, 4 B.C.). How long before this date Jesus was born is not known. Matthew and Luke tell of certain events that occurred between his birth and Herod's death, including the presentation at the temple forty days after his birth, the visit of the wise men, the flight into Egypt, and the murder of all the children in and around Bethlehem who were two years old or younger (Matt. 2:16). Whatever view is taken of the order of these events, they can scarcely have occupied less than two or three months.[1] Therefore, the birth of Jesus took place no later than January of 4 B.C. or December 5 B.C., and it may have occurred up to two years earlier (Matt. 2:16).

The custom of celebrating December 25 as the birthday of Jesus did not arise until about the third or fourth century. Prior to that time it was customary to celebrate January 6 as the time of the coming of the wise men. According to the Lukan account (2:1-20), Jesus was born when Judean shepherds were out-of-doors at night. Since the rainy season in Palestine usually begins in December, it is not likely that this was the month of the Nativity. When it was, we do not know. Some have thought that the choice of December 25 may have had a connection with the pagan celebration of the *Dies Solis Invicti* ("Day of the Invincible Sun"). Although there is no proof, it

---

1. It is not likely that the Magi had come with their rich gifts prior to the presentation at the temple, otherwise Joseph and Mary would not have been justified in pleading poverty as an excuse for making the cheaper of the two permissible offerings (Luke 2:22-24; compare Lev. 12:8). Therefore it is quite anachronistic to represent (as some artists have done) the Magi as present with the shepherds adoring the newborn child.

may be that the early church chose this date to celebrate the birth of Jesus in order to provide Christians with an alternative festival in place of the one held in honor of the sun-god, who was often identified with Mithra.

2. THE DATE OF THE BAPTISM OF JESUS AND THE BEGINNING OF HIS PUBLIC MINISTRY

Several pieces of evidence bear upon the date of the baptism of Jesus and the beginning of his public ministry. Luke places the beginning of John the Baptist's preaching in the wilderness "in the fifteenth year of the reign of Emperor Tiberius" (Luke 3:1). Though this chronological datum appears to be simple and unambiguous, its exact interpretation is disputed. Tiberius Caesar had been exercising coregency with Augustus Caesar in the years just prior to the latter's death in August A.D. 14, but he did not come to full imperial authority until September 17, A.D. 14. We do not know whether Luke intends to include the period of coregency or not. If he does not, the fifteenth year of Tiberius's reign was A.D. 29. In Syria, however, it was customary to date regnal years from October 1, so that the second year of Tiberius's reign would have begun on October 1, A.D. 14; his fifteenth year therefore would have run from October 1, A.D. 27 to September 30, A.D. 28. If a period of coregency was included, a correspondingly earlier date is required.

The Gospels provide two other chronological data, neither of which is altogether specific. Immediately after his account of the baptism of Jesus, Luke states, "Jesus was about thirty years old when he began his work" (Luke 3:23). If Jesus was born about 5 or 4 B.C., this would be about A.D. 26 or 27. At the season of Passover, not long after Jesus' baptism, the Fourth Gospel represents the Jews as saying that the reconstruction of the temple complex was forty-six years in building (John 2:20). Since, according to Josephus, Herod the Great began the work of reconstruction in the eighteenth year of his reign (i.e., 20 or 19 B.C.), the forty-sixth year would be A.D. 27 or 28.

In light of these somewhat conflicting data, it appears that Jesus was baptized and began his public ministry sometime between about A.D. 26 and 28; a date early in 27 is perhaps as likely as any.

3. THE DATE OF THE CRUCIFIXION OF JESUS

The length of Jesus' ministry and, consequently, the year of his death are to be fixed by the number of Passovers that elapsed from the time of his baptism. As was mentioned earlier, if we had only the Synoptic Gospels, we might infer that Jesus' ministry lasted but one year. John, however, refers to at least three Passovers (2:13; 6:4; 13:1), and it is highly probable that the festival referred to in John 5:1 was also a Passover. If so, Jesus' ministry included four Passovers, at the last of which he died.

If, then, Jesus was baptized early in A.D. 27, his first Passover thereafter was in April of that year, and he died in the spring of A.D. 30. (Those who think that John 5:1 does not refer to a Passover, date Jesus' death in A.D. 29.)

The chronology of the last week is complicated by a difference in dating the Last Supper. According to John 13:1 and 29, the Last Supper was held prior to the festival of Passover. The Synoptics, however, treat the Last Supper as a Passover celebration (Matt. 26:19; Mark 14:12; Luke 22:13).

This discrepancy has occasioned much debate as to whether (1) the Synoptics are right and John is wrong; or (2) John is right and the Synoptics are wrong; or (3) whether there is a way of harmonizing the two traditions. Perhaps the least unsatisfactory solution of the problem is to assume that the two traditions reflect divergent methods of calculating the time of Passover. It is known that the sect at Qumran followed a solar calendar, according to which the Passover always fell on a Wednesday. Most Jews, however, followed a lunar calendar, according to which in A.D. 30 the full moon fell either on Thursday, April 6, or on Friday, April 7. Since Jewish authorities in the time of Jesus determined the beginning of the month by observation of the new moon, when the weather was cloudy opinion might differ as to the exact time that the celebration should take place. It is possible, therefore, that different groups of Jews celebrated Passover that year according to two different reckonings, and that both are reflected in the Gospels.

The hour of the Crucifixion is variously given by different evangelists. According to Mark 15:25, Jesus was crucified at the third hour (= 9:00 A.M.). According to John 19:14, the trial before Pilate

126

was not quite over by the sixth hour (= noon), and therefore the Crucifixion took place still later.

Attempts have been made to prove that John used a different mode of reckoning the hours of the day from that in common use, namely that he calculated from midnight to midday (so that when John says "sixth hour" he means 6:00 A.M. and the discrepancy vanishes). But there is no evidence to support such a supposition, which has the appearance of a fiction proposed by despairing harmonizers. Others have suggested that, since the apostles carried no watches, different persons estimated the time quite diversely. But, for writers who seem to be intent on giving the time with some exactness, a discrepancy involving about four hours seems to be greater than one would think probable. Perhaps, with Jerome in the fourth century, we may presume that an error has crept into the transmission of the manuscripts of either John or Mark. Since the Greek letter that stands for 3 is the gamma (Γ) and the character that stands for 6 is the digamma (Ϝ), a sleepy copyist, early in the transmission of the text of the New Testament, may have mistaken one for the other.

All four Gospels put the Crucifixion on Friday and date the Resurrection three days later. It was usual among the Jews, with whom a new day begins at sunset, to reckon time inclusively and to count parts of days as whole days. Therefore, the time from Jesus' death Friday afternoon until sunset on Friday was counted as one day, Saturday was the second day, and the period from sunset on Saturday until early Sunday morning was the third day.

The uncertainty about dates in the life of Jesus arises from the circumstance that most early Christians were not interested in details of chronology. In their eyes, far more important than dates was the assurance that, according to God's prearranged plan (Gal. 4:4-5), the Savior of the world and the Lord of the church had come into the world, had taught, suffered, died, and was gloriously raised from the dead (Acts 10:37-41; 26:22-23).

II. THE EARLY YEARS OF JESUS' LIFE

Matthew and Luke record several details concerning the circumstances of Jesus' birth, and each tell the story from a specific point of view. In Matthew's account the narrative is unfolded as though it were seen from Joseph's point of view, and in Luke's account from Mary's point of view. The two Gospels are in agreement on the central features: (1) Mary, the mother of Jesus, was a virgin at the time of his birth; (2) Joseph, to whom Mary was betrothed, was a descendant of King David; (3) though Joseph was the legal father of Jesus, Jesus' conception was due to the Holy Spirit; (4) Jesus was born in Bethlehem during the reign of Herod the Great; and (5) in accordance with an angelic command, the child was named Jesus, signifying that he would save his people from their sins.[2]

However, each account differs in certain other details. Matthew tells of the visit of the wise men, the flight into Egypt, and Herod's command to kill the infants in and around Bethlehem. The special material in Luke is considerably more varied, owing to his reporting the conception and birth of John the Baptist as well as the birth of Jesus. Interspersed in his narrative Luke includes half a dozen poetic passages, three of which are widely used in the church as liturgical hymns. These canticles are known by the first words of their Latin translation; namely, the *Magnificat* (1:46-55), attributed to Mary in most manuscripts; the *Benedictus* (1:68-79) of Zechariah, the father of John; and the *Nunc dimittis* (2:29-32) of Simeon, a devout Jew of Jerusalem. The Lukan genealogy of Jesus (Luke 3:23-38) differs from Matthew's (Matt. 1:1-17) in many generations after David, though both agree in tracing his lineage through David to Abraham. The only scriptural account of Jesus as a boy is given by Luke, who relates how, at twelve years of age, Jesus was found in the temple, which he called his Father's house (Luke 2:49).

How far the reports of Jesus' birth and infancy in Matthew and Luke are sober history and how far they are poetic and theological interpretations has been debated at length. There is not space here to say more than that a century ago some of the details of the account (such as the census throughout the Roman Empire under Augustus, Luke 2:1) seemed to contradict what was known at that time from secular history, but many of these details are now seen to be in harmony with more recently discovered archaeological data. It should be added, however, that Luke's statement that the census was conducted while Quirinius was governor of Syria (Luke 2:2) still remains in conflict with what Tacitus and Josephus report concerning the sequence of governors of Syria. In such cases, the cau-

---

2. Jesus is the Greek form of the name Joshua, which means "Jehovah is salvation."

tious historian will await acquisition of further information that may resolve the discrepancy.

Regarding the central affirmation, found not only in the Gospels but also in the Talmud, that Joseph was not the biological father of Jesus, different readers will react in accordance with their general religious and philosophical orientation. For Christians, the all-important truth of the Gospel narratives is their testimony to the reality of the Incarnation. Though Muslims, for example, acknowledge that Jesus was born of the virgin Mary, they deny that he is the divine Son of God. Classical Christianity, which affirms the reality of the Incarnation, has regarded it as entirely congruent that he whose death had an outcome so different from that of all other men also came into the world in a different way, namely, that he was "conceived by the Holy Ghost and born of the virgin Mary."

III. THE BAPTISM AND TEMPTATION OF JESUS CHRIST

1. JOHN THE BAPTIST

All four evangelists agree in placing the beginning of Jesus' public ministry within the framework of the ministry of John the Baptist. The latter was a typical "holy man" of the Near East. According to the Gospels (Matt. 3:1-6; Mark 1:6; Luke 3:1-6), John retired from society and lived like a hermit in the vicinity of the Jordan River. Taking Elijah for his model (2 Kings 1:8), John wore rough garb and subsisted on such fare as he could find in the wilderness. Like Elijah also, he was fearless in his rebukes directed toward both kings and the multitudes.

Neither the New Testament nor Josephus, who mentions the preaching of John (*Antiquities*, XVIII.v.2), informs us how the Baptist acquired notoriety. In any case, however, his fame became widely known, and many sought him out in his solitude. A forceful preacher, John urged his fellow countrymen to repent of their sins, receive baptism in the Jordan, and live a life of righteousness. Specifically, John spelled out in practical terms just what this new life should involve for each candidate for baptism. Those who had earthly possessions should share them with the poor. Tax collectors, notorious for their dishonesty, were told to adhere to the prescribed tax rates and no longer to overcharge, pocketing the surplus. Soldiers were to refrain from bullying, false accusing, and mutineering (Luke 3:10-14).

Among the crowds who came from towns and cities to hear John were representatives of the Pharisees and the Sadducees. As John looked upon them he thought of a scene that he had more than once witnessed in the wilderness, when the parched brushwood caught fire and the reptiles rushed from their lairs in terror. "You brood of vipers!" he cried, "Who warned you to flee from the wrath to come?" Then he challenged them to relinquish their pride of descent from Abraham, and to bear fruit that befitted repentance (Matt. 3:7-10; Luke 3:7-9).

If John's message had been merely in terms of ethics and what people should do, as the account in Josephus implies (*Antiquities,*

XVIII.v.2), it is difficult to understand the reason for the feverish pitch of popular excitement that his preaching aroused. Doubtless many an Essene would have agreed with both the message and the need for baptism. But what made John's ministry so thrilling to every Jewish heart was the strong messianic hope present in his message. He declared that nothing less than the Day of the Lord was at hand, and that at long last God would vindicate his people and deliver them from oppression. Referring to the coming judgment in terms that Palestinian peasants could

Figure 5.1. A Winnowing Fork
(Courtesy of Bastiaan Van Elderen.)
This was a forklike shovel, with which the threshed grain was thrown into the wind, thus separating the chaff from the grain (Matt. 3:12; Luke 3:17).

comprehend, John compared the coming of the Messiah to a farmer using a winnowing fork to separate the wheat from the chaff; the wheat he would gather into his garner, but the chaff he would burn with unquenchable fire (Luke 3:17-18). Since God was soon to invade history, and since judgment was so near at hand, the Baptist's message took on a somber aspect. John had to tell his hearers that the nation as a whole was utterly unprepared for the Messiah. It was for this reason, and not merely for the sake of inculcating general ethical standards, that John called the nation at large—every class and every individual—to repentance as the indispensable preparation for participating in the blessings of the new epoch. As an outward symbol of an inward change, he baptized in the Jordan all who received his message with faith.

Despite similarities with other Semitic holy men, there were two highly original features in the ministry of John the Baptist. Unlike the washings and baptisms practiced by Pharisees and Essenes, which were repeated daily, John's rite of baptism was performed once for all. In this respect it was similar to the rite of proselyte baptism by which a Gentile entered Judaism. The other unique characteristic of John's preaching was his insistence that in the coming judgment the privilege of belonging to the chosen people would count for nothing: "Do not begin to say to yourselves, 'We have Abraham as our ancestor'; for I tell you, God is able from these stones to raise up children to Abraham" (Matt. 3:9; Luke 3:8). In effect, John excommunicated the whole nation and received back such as would repent and be baptized.

2. THE BAPTISM OF JESUS

One day, probably early in A.D. 27, there appeared among the Baptist's followers one who particularly attracted his attention. This was Jesus, a kinsman of John's (John's mother Elizabeth was a cousin of the virgin Mary). Up to this time Jesus had been in the carpenter shop at Nazareth; now he joined the crowds that were streaming into the Jordan wilderness and presented himself for baptism. When Jesus emerged from the water, the Synoptic Gospels report that the heavens opened and the Spirit of God, in the form of a dove, descended and alighted on him (Matt. 3:16; Mark 1:10; Luke 3:21-22). At the same time, a voice came from above acknowledging Jesus to be God's beloved Son. The evangelists thus indicate the full endowment of Jesus with spiritual power for his subsequent ministry.

By receiving baptism at the hands of John, Jesus showed his acceptance of John's twofold message of impending doom for the wicked and the imminent coming of the kingdom of God. His own preaching at first echoed the Baptist's call to repentance (Matt. 4:17; Mark 1:15). In this sense, the beginning of Jesus' ministry was merely a chapter in the history of the Baptist's movement.

Questions were bound to rise in the early church regarding the implications of Jesus' baptism. Since John's rite was a baptism of repentance, many would ask how it was that Jesus, whom the church regarded as sinless and needing no repentance, should have submitted to such a rite. Doubtless the reply, more often than not, would recall the dialogue reported by Matthew in which John hesitates to baptize Jesus ("I need to be baptized by you, and do you come to me?" Matt. 3:14). Jesus reassures him, "Let it be so now; for it is proper for us in this way to fulfill all righteousness" (Matt. 3:15). Here it is plain that personal penitence is absent. To fulfill all righteousness is to leave nothing undone that God had shown to be his will. For the crowds, John's baptism signified a break with a sin-ful past and a new start upon a reformed life. For Jesus it denoted a break simply, the entrance upon a new phase in the accomplishment of his mission. His reply expresses his realization that the time had come to leave behind the carpenter shop at Nazareth and to devote himself to his special work. Since for Jesus the Baptist's message and movement were from God (Matt. 21:25; Mark 11:30; Luke 20:4), by submitting to baptism he dedicated himself to God's work that John had announced.

3. THE TEMPTATION OF JESUS

According to all three Synoptic Gospels (Matt. 4:1-11; Mark 1:12-13; Luke 4:1-13), immediately after his baptism Jesus was led by the Spirit into the wilderness to be tempted by the devil. Nowhere does the Bible describe the appearance of the devil, though Paul declared that he can disguise himself as an angel of light (2 Cor. 11:14); the notion that he has horns, hoofs, and a tail is derived from folklore. The testing in the wilderness grew out of Jesus' experience at his baptism, when a divine voice proclaimed that he was the beloved Son of God. For forty days Jesus fasted and wrestled with questions of how and for what purpose he should utilize the extraordinary powers that he was conscious of possessing. The first temptation, to turn stones into bread, was a temptation to use these powers for his own advantage. The second temptation,[3] to cast himself down from the pinnacle of the temple, expecting to be supported, as it were, by a celestial parachute, was a temptation to win a large following by means of miracle and magic. The third temptation, to secure the kingdoms of the world by bowing in temporary homage to the devil, was a temptation to acquire power over secular kingdoms by temporizing with evil. In short, the several temptations were enticements to selfish security, cheap popularity, and worldly power.

The narratives of Jesus' temptation must rest upon what he saw fit to tell his disciples during subsequent months. No one in the early church would have invented such a tale about the Messiah, for temptation by the devil plays no part in previous anticipations of the role of the Messiah. The story was remembered because of what it contributed to the early church's understanding of the significance of the person and work of Jesus.

It soon came to be appreciated that Jesus' temptations had far-reaching significance. They involved the necessity of his deciding at the beginning of his ministry what kind of Messiah he would be, the strategy by which he would accomplish his work, and the extent of his warfare against evil. The decisions that he made in the wilderness he carried out again and again in later months when confronted with similar temptations. Thus, the temptation at the end of his life to avoid personal suffering by calling upon God for twelve legions of angels (Matt. 26:53), he denied for the same reason that led him in the wilderness to prefer to suffer the pangs of hunger rather than help himself by utilizing more than human resources. An early Christian theologian perceived that, had Jesus succumbed to the temptation to extricate himself from unpleasant circumstances by means that are not available to ordinary humans, he would have been "unable to sympathize with our weaknesses" (Heb. 4:15). Since, however, Jesus "in every respect has been tested

---

3. It is the second temptation in Matthew's account; in the Lukan account it is the third temptation. The same temptation may have presented itself more than once.

as we are, yet without sin" (Heb. 4:15), he could become "a merciful and faithful high priest in the service of God, to make a sacrifice of atonement for the sins of the people. Because he himself was tested by what he suffered, he is able to help those who are being tested" (Heb. 2:17-18). Thus, according to this interpretation, the essence of the devil's temptation was to entice Jesus into doing what would have prevented his full participation in the human predicament.[4]

More than once during his ministry Jesus must have faced a recurring temptation to win a large following by overawing the crowds with displays of his might and power. Rather than secure adherents by turning stones into bread or by performing other spectacular feats, he determined that the strategy of his messianic work was to teach by word and example so that individuals would recognize and accept God's offer of grace and power to all who repent and accept the claims of the kingdom. In accordance with his conception of faith as free decision rather than coerced opinion, Jesus determined at the beginning of his ministry that his miracles would be secondary, an aid to the faith of those who on other grounds were inclined to believe, not portents to overwhelm the minds of those who had no real sympathy for himself or his aims.[5]

IV. THE PUBLIC MINISTRY OF JESUS CHRIST

Form criticism has reminded us that for a generation or more most of the materials in the Gospels circulated orally, mostly as separate units. Only rarely were geographical and chronological details mentioned as a setting for an individual story. When, therefore, the evangelists set about putting these materials into a connected whole, they had only meager hints as to when and where Jesus' sayings and deeds ought to be placed. One can understand, therefore, why specific chronological data occur so infrequently and why such colorless words as "then," "again," and "thereupon" appear so often in the Gospel accounts. Furthermore, the fragmentary nature of our records is obvious. For example, though Jesus pronounced woe upon Chorazin, a city by the Sea of Galilee, for its

---

4. If it be asked, Would not Jesus have been better able to sympathize with those who are tempted if he had actually sinned? the answer must be in the negative; it is only the person who never yields who has felt the *full* intensity of temptation.

5. This insight into the nature of Christ's temptations is powerfully set forth by Fyodor Dostoyevsky in his novel *The Brothers Karamazov* in the famous chapter "The Grand Inquisitor."

unbelief despite the mighty works that he had done in it (Matt. 11:21; Luke 10:13), not one incident in the Gospels is identified as having occurred in Chorazin. It is obvious that a modem biographer simply does not have available sufficient information to warrant writing a detailed life of Jesus Christ. However, the Gospels disclose several relatively clear stages in the public ministry of Jesus, and by taking these into account one is able to reconstruct the broad framework of his activities with some approximation to certitude. Within such a framework the historian, aware of the limitations imposed by the nature of the materials, seeks to draw up a more or less coherent interpretation of the literary evidence, recognizing that frequently the resulting account rests upon only the most tentative judgments of historical sequence.

As was pointed out earlier in the section on chronology (p. 125), Jesus' baptism and the beginning of his public ministry took place probably sometime early in A.D. 27, and his death occurred probably on April 7 of A.D. 30. The time between these dates can be divided into three periods, each roughly one year in length. Each of the three periods has special features of its own. The first may be called the year of obscurity, partly because the records of it that we possess are scanty and partly because during it Jesus seems to have been only slowly emerging into public notice. Most of Jesus' activity during this time of approximately eight months seems to have been spent in Judea.

The second period was the year of public favor, during which his fame as a teacher and healer extended far and wide. Most of his activity during this period, lasting approximately fifteen months, was confined to Galilee.

The third period was the year of opposition. Now public favor ebbed away, and Jesus' enemies multiplied, until at last they managed to secure his execution. The first part of this final year was spent in Galilee, and the last part in other parts of Palestine.

1. THE YEAR OF OBSCURITY

Among Jesus' early followers were several who had formerly been John the Baptist's disciples. Notable among them were two pairs of brothers, Andrew and Peter, and Philip and Nathaniel (John 1:35-51). With his small band of disciples Jesus ascended from the valley of Jordan to the higher country of Galilee. There, in the village of Cana, he performed the first of his miracles (John 2:1). After a brief stay at Capernaum, where he was afterward to carry on a large part of his ministry, Jesus again went southward to Jerusalem at the time of Passover (John 2:12-13).

At Jerusalem, his first recorded act (John 2:14-22) was an act of stern rebuke. According to the Talmud, the temple markets held in the court of the Gentiles were under the control of the high-priestly clan and so were called "the bazaars of the sons of Annas." Here were sold unblemished sheep and oxen and doves that were intended for sacrifice. Indignant at what he regarded as the profanation of God's house, Jesus made a whip of cords and drove out the traders and money changers.[6] It was an act worthy of a prophet intent on reforming flagrant abuses of God's service; but his words, "Stop making my Father's house a marketplace!" indicate that he claimed to be more than a prophet (John 2:16).

After the Passover, Jesus retired from Jerusalem and returned to the Judean countryside (John 3:22-24). Here he began to preach, as the Baptist was still doing, the necessity of repentance. For a time both worked for the spiritual quickening of the nation. When Jesus finally began to attract more disciples than John did, some of the Baptist's followers became envious, and Jesus decided to go back to Galilee (John 3:25–4:3). Thus the first period of his ministry closed, during which the nation was gradually made aware of his presence as a teacher and healer.

2. THE YEAR OF PUBLIC FAVOR

The year of public favor, as it may be called, was characterized by the increase of popular excitement, particularly in Galilee, over the person and work of Jesus of Nazareth. Without benefit of modern means of publicity, ever greater numbers of persons came under the influence of Jesus' teaching. During most of this period he made Capernaum the focus of his ministry. This commercial town, situated on the northwest shore of the Sea of Galilee, was the seat of a tax collector's office and was apparently also a Roman military post. Here Jesus healed the Roman centurion's paralyzed

---

6. The position of this account illustrates the difference of organization between the Fourth Gospel and the Synoptics. Since the latter compress Jesus' entire ministry within one year, the place for them to tell about the cleansing of the temple is in connection with his visit to Jerusalem to celebrate Passover, just prior to his death. See page 142.

Figure 5.2. Remains of a Synagogue in Capernaum
(Courtesy of Bart D. Ehrman, University of North Carolina at Chapel Hill.)
The surviving building represents a structure that was built on the site that Jesus would have visited several centuries earlier (Mark 1:21; John 6:59). Beneath the floor, archaeologists have found pottery from the first century A.D., which establishes that date for the construction of the floor.

servant (Matt. 8:5-13; Luke 7:1-10), Peter's mother-in-law when she was prostrate with a fever (Matt. 8:14-17; Mark 1:29-31; Luke 4:38-39), a demoniac (Mark 1:21-28; Luke 4:31-35), and other persons afflicted with various diseases. The number of his followers increased rapidly, and on more than one occasion his audience totaled four or five thousand persons (Mark 6:30-44; 8:1-9). From the larger crowd of disciples Jesus chose a smaller group of devoted followers to carry on his work; these were designated apostles[7] (Matt. 10:1-4; Mark 3:13-19; Luke 6:12-16). Apparently all of the twelve apostles were Galileans except Judas Iscariot, who (according to tradition) came from Kerioth in southern Judea.

---

7. The word *apostle* means "one sent as a messenger or representative."

According to John 5:1, Jesus went again to Jerusalem to participate in the celebration of a festival. At this time he healed a lame man on the sabbath, and at once a conflict with the Jewish rulers broke out (John 5:2-47). Soon after the altercation Jesus returned again to Galilee, where his popularity continued to grow.

Besides performing works of healing, Jesus also preached and taught his followers. The several portions of what is called the Sermon on the Mount (Matt. chaps. 5–7), as well as the collection of parables in Matthew, chapter 13, embody what his hearers remembered of his messages during this period. Besides setting forth the spiritual nature of the kingdom of God, he taught that an individual's relation to himself would determine that person's destiny in the day of judgment (Matt. 7:21-23; Mark 10:29; compare Matt. 25:31-46).

There is not space here to set forth in further detail the progress of Jesus' work and influence during his year of public favor. By consulting a harmony of the Gospels, where the accounts are conveniently set forth in parallel columns, the student will be able to gain a general impression of the extension of Jesus' influence, characterized both by profound teaching concerning the kingdom of God and by tender compassion extended to those in physical and spiritual need.

3. THE YEAR OF OPPOSITION

During the year of opposition, what had been previously only occasional displays of hostility by scribes and Pharisees against Jesus increased in number and in intensity. The common people had early sensed a profound difference between the direct and forthright manner of Jesus' teaching and the methods of the scribes (Matt. 7:28-29; Mark 1:21-22; Luke 4:31-32). It is understandable that the latter were envious of his success in teaching, which endangered their own position.

The Jewish leaders had what were, in their opinion, serious grounds of opposition against Jesus. He rejected their elaboration of the Mosaic Law and rebuked them for paying so much attention to the detailed rules that had accumulated in their traditions that they neglected the weightier matters of justice and mercy (Matt. 23:23). He did not himself practice, nor did he encourage his disciples to practice, the many ritual acts of purification (such as the ceremonial washing of the hands before meals) that were generally considered to be the marks of a pious person (Mark 7:1-2). It was especially in the observance of the sabbath that the differences between him and contemporary religious teachers became most apparent. In the face of the scribes' multiplication of sabbath laws (see pp. 59-60 above), Jesus declared that "the sabbath was made for humankind, not humankind for the sabbath," and boldly implied that he was lord of the sabbath (Mark 2:27-28).

The waning of Jesus' popularity among the crowds was occasioned both by the increase of outward opposition on the part of the Jewish rulers, as well as by the demands that he laid upon those who desired to be his followers (Mark 8:34-38; 10:21-22; John 6:60-66). After the feeding of the five thousand, the throng wished to make him king (John 6:15). When they learned, however, that he was unwilling to conform to their ideas of a Messiah who would fulfill their material and national desires, many even of his disciples "turned back and no longer went about with him" (John 6:66).

One of the most important incidents of the gospel record occurred in the region of Caesarea Philippi, northeast of Galilee. The worship of the Greek god Pan had long prevailed here, whence it was called Paneas. The town was enlarged by Philip the tetrarch, and its name altered to Caesarea in honor of the Roman emperor Tiberius Caesar (Josephus, *Antiquities,* XVIII.ii.1; *Jewish War,* II.ix.1). It is in such a setting that the Synoptic Gospels report a conversation between Jesus and Peter arising from Jesus' question, "Who do people say that I am?" (Matt. 16:13-16; Mark 8:27-30; Luke 9:18-20). The outcome of that conversation was Peter's declaration that Jesus was truly the long-expected Messiah. Though the disciples had already been committed to Jesus, such a declaration on Peter's part was by no means a matter of course, for Jesus was not the kind of Messiah that most Jews had been expecting. They had been looking for a Messiah who, as the anointed king of Israel, would deliver God's people from the Roman overlords and make Jerusalem the center of the whole world.

Earlier in his ministry Jesus seems to have preferred to keep his messiahship in the background. Public proclamation of his messiahship would have aroused false, worldly hopes of political upheaval. Before proclaiming himself as Messiah, Jesus needed to

Figure 5.3. A Grotto Sacred to Pan and the Nymphs
(Courtesy of John McRay.)
Caesarea Philippi had earlier borne the name Paneas, which commemorated a nearby cave or grotto where the old inhabitants had worshiped Pan, the so-called universal god who was represented as half-man and half-goat. An inscription beneath one of the niches (where a statue had stood) reads, "To Pan and the Nymphs."

In this unique setting, where Judaism touched both the worship of nature and the worship of man (i.e. the emperor), Jesus called upon his disciples to commit themselves to him as Messiah (Matt. 16:13-26).

make clear by his teaching and by his example what kind of Messiah he was. That Peter had now come to appreciate, even dimly, Jesus' mission was a triumph of faith, for which Jesus pronounced him blessed (Matt. 16:17).

After Peter's acknowledgment of Jesus as Messiah, Jesus began to teach the disciples more of what his messiahship meant. Instead of worldly honors, or even the continuation of a humble life in Galilee, it meant sufferings and death (Matt. 16:20-21; Mark 8:30-31; Luke 9:21-22).

It is in such a context that the Synoptic evangelists place, one week later, the narrative of Jesus' transfiguration (Matt. 17:1-8;

Mark 9:2-8; Luke 9:28-36), a mysterious experience in which Jesus is revealed in heavenly glory as the Messiah. According to Luke's account, the event, which apparently took place at night (Luke 9:32), began as prayer and grew into an intense religious experience, which Matthew describes as a vision (Matt. 17:9). Moses and Elijah, representatives of the Law and the prophets, appear and converse with Jesus about his approaching death. Then a bright cloud overshadows them, and a voice from the cloud declares, "This is my Son, the Beloved; listen to him!" (Mark 9:7). Thus for the reader, as originally for the disciples themselves, the story of the transfiguration sets the seal of divine approval on Jesus' teaching, so recently given, concerning the way of the cross, and attests also his divine nature as the Messiah.

Henceforward Jesus apparently preached less to the multitudes and devoted himself to instructing his disciples in humility, self-sacrifice, and love, preparing them for his death and for carrying out their responsibilities in the future (Matt. 18:1-35; Mark 9:33-50). It was now probably the early autumn of A.D. 29, and leaving Capernaum for the last time, Jesus resolutely "set his face to go to Jerusalem" (Luke 9:51).

It is impossible to determine the exact sequence of Jesus' subsequent journeys, for Luke's special section (9:51–18:14), on which we are mainly dependent for information concerning this period, contains few precise chronological and geographical details. It appears that Jesus passed through Samaria and, crossing the Jordan, labored in the regions east of the Jordan known as Perea and the Decapolis. The latter, which means literally "the Ten Cities," was a federation of about ten towns populated chiefly by Greeks who had come there in the wake of Alexander's conquest three centuries earlier.

At the beginning of this period of Jesus' itineration, he sent out seventy disciples to prepare for his own coming into the several cities and villages that he was intending to visit (Luke 10:1-16). The Seventy were in possession of something of Jesus' power, and after returning from their mission they were able to report with joy that even the demons were subject to them in his name (Luke 10:17). The third evangelist places in this same period some of the more beautiful of Jesus' parables, including the parables of the good

Samaritan, the lost sheep, the lost coin, the prodigal son, the unjust steward, the importunate widow, and the Pharisee and the tax collector (Luke 10:30-37; 15:3-32; 16:1-14; 18:1-14).

According to the Fourth Gospel, toward the close of Jesus' journeys in Judea and Perea, he performed at Bethany, a village near Jerusalem, one of his most notable miracles—the raising to life of Lazarus, who had been dead four days (John 11:17-44). The miracle was so stupendous and performed so near Jerusalem that it had a profound effect upon the people of the capital; and the Sanhedrin, under the leadership of Caiaphas, the high priest, decided that the influence of Jesus could be destroyed only by his death (John 11:45-54).

4. THE LAST WEEK[8]

As Jesus approached Jerusalem, an atmosphere of intense expectation increased among his followers. Luke comments, "They supposed that the kingdom of God was to appear immediately" (19:11). It was at this juncture that Jesus quite deliberately offered himself publicly as the Messiah, in fulfillment of the apocalyptic prophecy of Zechariah (Zech. 9:9). Unlike the warrior king of popular expectation, however, Jesus chose to ride into Jerusalem on a donkey's colt (Matt. 21:2-7), illustrating the peaceful character of the Kingdom he had come to inaugurate.

The roads to Jerusalem were thronged with crowds consisting partly of those who had been accompanying Jesus, and partly of those who, having heard of the raising of Lazarus, flocked out of Jerusalem to see him. They welcomed him with enthusiasm, and began to shout, "Hosanna to the Son of David! Blessed is the one who comes in the name of the Lord! Hosanna in the highest heaven!" (Matt. 21:9; Mark 11:9-10; Luke 19:38). It was a messianic demonstration such as he had formerly avoided, but now he yielded to it. The crowd grew larger as the procession moved to the gate of the city, and the more exuberant cut leafy branches from the trees, as the procession passed (Mark 11:8), and waved them in joyful exultation. Jesus' triumphal entry into Jerusalem occurred on what came to be called Palm Sunday.

---

8. For a detailed commentary on the Passion Narratives in the four Gospels, see Raymond E. Brown, S.S., *The Death of the Messiah: From Gethsemane to the Grave*, 2 vols. (New York: Doubleday, 1993).

At this point in the narrative, Matthew (21:12-13) and Luke (19:45-46) insert the account (which John places at the beginning of the public ministry; see the note on p. 136) of the cleansing of the temple of the traders and money changers who profaned it. Whenever it was that Jesus purged the temple (or even if he did so both at the beginning and again at the close of his public ministry), the act was filled with symbolic meaning, setting forth an important aspect of his understanding of his messianic work, namely the purging of contemporary Jewish religion from commercialism and materialism.

When evening came, Jesus left the city (Mark 11:19), going to Bethany to spend the night in the home of his friends Mary, Martha, and Lazarus.

The following morning Jesus returned to Jerusalem, and engaged in teaching and in controversies with religious leaders of his nation. The stories of these controversies reflect the mounting tension between Jesus and the authorities. A delegation from the Sanhedrin came to demand his credentials for his acts. Jesus countered by inquiring about the credentials of John the Baptist—whether his baptism was from heaven or from men. When they refused to commit themselves, Jesus, with scathing rebuke and warning, told them the parable of the wicked tenants, the point of which was that to reject God's messengers, and finally his Son, will result in being rejected by God (Matt. 21:33-46; Mark 12:1-12; Luke 20:9-19).

Representatives from the Pharisees and the Herodians, who were politically antagonistic to each other, confronted Jesus with an adroit question by which they thought they could catch him, however he would answer it: "Is it lawful to pay taxes to the emperor, or not?" (Mark 12:14). Then Sadducees, who denied the Resurrection, posed a question in an attempt to make the doctrine of the Resurrection appear ridiculous (Matt. 22:23-33; Mark 12:18-27; Luke 20:27-40). An individual scribe inquired about the most important commandment (Matt. 22:34-40; Mark 12:28-34; Luke 10:25-27). In his replies, Jesus proved to be more than a match for them, and at length let loose a storm of indignation, denouncing openly the formalism and hypocrisy of scribes and Pharisees (Matt. 23:1-36).

As he left the temple area, Jesus sadly remarked to one of his disciples that the magnificent structure would be destroyed. Later that evening as he sat on the Mount of Olives opposite the temple, he gave to four of them his prediction of the destruction of Jerusalem, the spread of the gospel, the suffering of his followers, and his own second advent (Matt. 24:4-36; Mark 13:5-37; Luke 21:8-36). This apocalyptic section, which appears to be a compilation of materials from various sources, concludes with a statement that the time of the end is unknown to all except God, and therefore in expectation of it one should always be watchful. The duty of watchfulness is then illustrated by the parables of the wise and foolish virgins and of the talents (Matt. 25:1-30). Finally, according to Matthew's account, Jesus drew a solemn picture of the last judgment, when the wicked shall be separated from the good (Matt. 25:31-46).

It is probable that during these days the plot was formed to destroy Jesus. Judas Iscariot, one of the Twelve, "went to the chief priests in order to betray him to them. And when they heard it, they were greatly pleased, and promised to give him money. So he began to look for an opportunity to betray him" (Mark 14:10-11). Why should one of Jesus' most intimate followers betray him? Judas was chosen originally, we may believe, because Jesus saw in him the potential qualities of a useful apostle. That he was a man of superior energy and administrative ability may be inferred from his having been made the treasurer of the apostolic group (John 12:6). Probably he had become a follower of Jesus in the hope of taking part in a political revolution and occupying a distinguished place in an earthly kingdom. But when Jesus refused to let himself be acclaimed as the worldly, national king of the Jews, and demanded instead commitment to purely spiritual values, Judas became more and more alienated from him and his teaching.

Though several motives may have been at work in Judas's diseased mind, the one that the Gospels single out as all-controlling was his love of money. Over the months he had gratified his avarice by petty pilferings from the common purse (John 12:6). He did not suddenly become the betrayer of his master for thirty pieces of silver. Greed was a cancer at the root of his character that gradually absorbed all that was excellent in him, and at the end became a tyrannical passion.

On Thursday of his last week, Jesus sent Peter and John into the city to prepare the Passover for him and the Twelve (Luke 22:8). Of all the Jewish holidays the celebration of the ancient Passover ritual, commemorating the deliverance of Israel from Egyptian bondage, was the most solemn. It involved a common meal at which the leader recalled to the participants the mighty acts of God in their earlier national history. It was in such a context that Jesus deliberately introduced a new element into the ancient liturgy, transforming it into the Christian Eucharist or Lord's Supper. After lifting the platter of unleavened bread and speaking the Aramaic formula prescribed in the ritual of the time ("This is the bread of affliction which our fathers ate in the land of Egypt. Let everyone who hungers come and eat; let everyone who is in need come and eat the Passover meal"), Jesus took up the Passover loaf, blessed it and broke it, and giving the pieces to his disciples, spoke words that went far beyond the prescribed ritual for the Passover; "Take, eat; . . . This is my body that is for you. Do this in remembrance of me" (Matt. 26:26 and 1 Cor. 11:24). At the close of the meal, after pouring the so-called "Cup of Blessing," Jesus again introduced some sentences into the ritual: "Drink from it, all of you; for this is my blood of the covenant, which is poured out for many for the forgiveness of sins. . . . Do this, as often as you drink it, in remembrance of me" (Matt. 26:27 and 1 Cor. 11:25). Then Jesus and his disciples sang antiphonally the concluding psalms prescribed for the Passover celebration (namely, Pss. 115–118).

Among serious-minded Jews, it was customary to remain together at table for several hours after the conclusion of the Passover meal and to talk about Passover miracles of the past and future. Jesus, too, no doubt remained for some time with his disciples, talking with them of things past and future, and explaining more in detail the significance of the new features that he had just introduced into the Passover ceremonial.

Then Jesus left the house and walked through the dark streets of the city and out into the Kidron Valley in order to reach the Mount of Olives. Here he sought a favorite spot of his for prayer and meditation, the garden of Gethsemane at the foot of the Mount of Olives (John 18:1). What Jesus endured there in spiritual agonizing we do not know, but the evangelists indicate that, being greatly distressed and sorrowful, he prayed that the cup of his sufferings might be removed from him (Matt. 26:36-44; Mark 14:32-39; Luke 22:40-44). According to an early Christian writer, Jesus' prayer was heard, not in the removal of the cup of suffering, but in his submitting to the divine will, which involved death and resurrection (Heb. 5:7-8). He attained a remarkable degree of tranquillity that accompanied him through his arrest and trial to his last moments on the cross.

5. THE ARREST, TRIAL, AND CRUCIFIXION OF JESUS CHRIST

Meanwhile, Judas brought a motley crowd of Jewish temple guards and servants of the high priest to search with lanterns and torches every hiding place. Such elaborate precautions, however, proved to be unneeded, for Jesus made no effort either to run away or to offer resistance to arrest. By a prearranged signal, Judas identified Jesus to the crowd by going up and greeting him with the usual salutation, "Rabbi," accompanied by a kiss on the head; this was the customary manner of greeting a respected teacher. Thus, the betrayal took the form of a kiss that was a sign of honor (Matt. 26:47-56; Mark 14:43-46; Luke 22:47-48).

The disciples had two swords among them (Luke 22:38), and Peter began to use one of them. But Jesus would not have this, declaring, "All who take the sword will perish by the sword" (Matt. 26:52). This was his forthright "no" to political and militant messianism.

Jesus was bound and the procession started. First the prisoner was taken to the palace of the high priest, and a preliminary examination was conducted while the Sanhedrin was being convened. The precise sequence of subsequent events is difficult to determine. It appears, however, that Jesus was taken before the Sanhedrin and accused of threatening to destroy the temple (Matt. 26:61; Mark 14:58). Earlier Jesus had foretold to one of his disciples that the temple would be destroyed (Mark 13:1-2), and this apparently had been circulating ever since in many forms and been giving rise to many interpretations. When, however, the witnesses against Jesus did not agree, another charge had to be found.

At last Caiaphas, the high priest, solemnly adjured him to say if he were the Messiah, the Son of the Blessed ("the Blessed" was a Jewish circumlocution for God). Thereupon Jesus replied, making the claim in the most explicit manner: "I am; and 'you will see the Son of Man seated at the right hand of the Power,' and 'coming with the clouds of heaven' " (Mark 14:62). To the high priest the answer was sheer blasphemy—a Galilean carpenter calling himself "Son of Man" in the exalted sense of Daniel 7:13 and saying that he would sit at the right hand of God and come "with the clouds of heaven"! The high priest tore his mantle—the custom of the judge who heard blasphemous words—and condemned him as worthy of death (compare Lev. 24:16). No further witnesses were needed, for the members of the Sanhedrin had heard with their own ears the defendant's sacrilegious claim. The unjust spirit of his judges appeared in the ribald mockery to which he was subjected (Matt. 26:67-68; Mark 14:65; Luke 22:63-65).

During the trial before Caiaphas, Peter had been in the courtyard of the high priest's palace, waiting and watching to see what would happen to his master. Though he had plucked up enough courage to follow at a distance, when he was challenged he thrice denied that he ever knew Jesus (Matt. 26:69-75; Mark 14:66-72; Luke 22:56-62; John 18:17, 25-27).

Shortly after dawn the official plenary session of the Sanhedrin took place. This formal meeting was required in order to confirm the results of the previous trial, for it was the law that decisions of the Sanhedrin must be made in the daytime.

But the Jewish Sanhedrin did not possess the power of life and death. Before Jesus could be executed, therefore, the findings of the Sanhedrin had to be ratified by Pilate, the Roman governor.

It appears that some revision of the charges needed to be made in order to convince Pilate that Jesus was worthy of death, for a Roman official could understand the significance of insurrection better than blasphemy. According to Luke 23:2, the Jewish leaders now accused Jesus of leading the nation astray (compare Deut. 13:1-5), of forbidding the payment of taxes to the emperor (compare Mark 12:13-17), and of calling himself an anointed king. All four evangelists record that Pilate found it difficult to believe that these charges were valid (Matt. 27:24; Mark 15:14; Luke 23:22; John 19:4); he forthwith declared that he found no fault in Jesus and would let him go. When the crowd fiercely demanded Jesus' crucifixion, he fell back on various weak expedients to shift the responsibility. Having learned that the prisoner was from Galilee, Pilate sent him to be examined by Herod Antipas, the tetrarch of Galilee (Luke 23:6-12), who happened to be in Jerusalem for the festival.

But this hearing also was without decisive result, for Herod refused to exercise jurisdiction.

Meanwhile the crowd had increased, and the governor appealed to them to say which prisoner he should release, as was his custom at the Passover. He may have hoped that the popularity of Jesus would rescue him from the chief priests. But the latter persuaded the rabble to ask for the release of a notorious criminal named Barabbas (Matt. 27:15-26; Mark 15:6-15).

At last Pilate yielded to the importunity of the Jewish leaders and the mad shouts of the crowds, who had turned against the one whom formerly they had honored, and he condemned Jesus to be crucified.[9]

Before the execution, as was customary, the prisoner was cruelly scourged and mocked by the Roman soldiers, who plaited a crown of thorns and hailed him as king of the Jews. Thereafter, the prisoner was compelled to bear the heavy wooden beam on which he was to die, but when his strength gave way, because of the scourging, a certain Simon of Cyrene was pressed into service (Matt. 27:32; Mark 15:21; Luke 23:26).

The place of crucifixion was a short distance outside the city at a spot called Golgotha, which means "the place of a skull" ("Calvary" is from the Latin translation). Here the Roman execution squad, in charge of a centurion, nailed Jesus to his cross, and then dropped the cross into a hole prepared for it. With him were crucified two criminals, one on either side of him.

The four evangelists include among their several accounts of the Crucifixion seven words (that is, sentences) that came from the lips of Jesus while on the cross.[10] In their traditional order they are as follows:

(1) "Father, forgive them; for they do not know what they are doing" (Luke 23:34)—a prayer of intercession in behalf of those who were responsible for his death.

---

9. Much has been debated concerning the fixing of responsibility for the crucifixion of Jesus. According to the New Testament, the guilt of bringing about his unjust death was shared by the Jewish Sanhedrin of the time, by the crowds in Jerusalem, and by the Roman governor, Pontius Pilate. To harbor feelings of dislike or enmity toward the descendants of those who put Jesus to death is to forget that while he was dying on the cross, he prayed, "Father, forgive them; for they do not know what they are doing" (Luke 23:34). Since to err is human, and not only Jewish or Roman, in a very profound sense all are implicated in the totality of evil that disclosed itself in the crucifixion of the Son of God.

10. Luke and John each record three sayings; Matthew and Mark each record one saying—the only one common to more than one Gospel.

(2) "Truly I tell you, today you will be with me in Paradise" (Luke 23:43)—a promise given to one of the two criminals, crucified with him, who had implored of Jesus, "Remember me when you come into your kingdom" (Luke 23:42).

(3) "Woman, here is your son. . . . Here is your mother" (John 19:26-27)—a word of loving concern, spoken to Jesus' mother and to the disciple whom Jesus loved (traditionally identified with John).

(4) "My God, my God, why have you forsaken me?" (Matt. 27:46; Mark 15:34)—an appalling and mysterious word of desolate loneliness (quoted from Ps. 22:1). This cry of dereliction came, according to the evangelists' accounts, at the close of a period of unnatural darkness that enveloped the whole land—a fitting accompaniment of the horror of him who, though the sinless Son of God, was now without the consciousness of the sustaining comfort of the Father's presence as he tasted death for everyone (Heb. 2:9).

(5) "I am thirsty" (John 19:28)—a pathetic cry of physical anguish and helplessness.

(6) "It is finished" (John 19:30)—a word of accomplishment and victory.

(7) "Father, into your hands I commend my spirit" (Luke 23:46)—a prayer of confidence and trust.

With these final words of prayer to the Father, Jesus breathed his last. The centurion in command of the execution was standing facing Jesus, and when he saw how he died, he was moved to exclaim, "Truly this man was God's Son!" (Mark 15:39).

According to the generally accepted chronology, Jesus died late Friday afternoon, April 7, A.D. 30. Arrangements for the burial of his body were made by a certain Joseph of Arimathea, who had been a secret disciple of Jesus. According to all four evangelists, this man, a respected member of the council, took courage and went to Pilate and asked for the body of Jesus (Matt. 27:57-61; Mark 15:43; Luke 23:50-56; John 19:38-42). After Pilate had satisfied himself that Jesus was already dead, he gave permission for burial. Then Joseph, joined by Nicodemus, took the body, wrapped it in a linen shroud, and laid it in his own rock-hewn tomb, over the mouth of which a great stone was rolled. According to Matthew, the Jewish leaders set a guard at the tomb for several days (Matt. 27:62-66).

6. THE RESURRECTION AND ASCENSION OF JESUS CHRIST

The evidence for the resurrection of Jesus Christ is overwhelming. Nothing in history is more certain than that the disciples believed that after being crucified, dead, and buried, Christ rose again from the tomb on the third day, and that at intervals thereafter he met and conversed with them. The most obvious proof that they believed this is the existence of the Christian church. It is simply inconceivable that the scattered and disheartened remnant could have found a rallying point and a gospel in the memory of him who had been put to death as a criminal, had they not been convinced that God owned him and accredited his mission by raising him from the dead.

It is a commonplace that every event in history must have an adequate cause. Never were hopes more desolate than when Jesus of Nazareth was taken down from the cross and laid in the tomb. Stricken with grief at the death of their Master, the disciples were dazed and bewildered. Their mood was one of dejection and defeat, reflected in the spiritless words of the Emmaus travelers, "We had hoped that he was the one to redeem Israel" (Luke 24:21). A short time later the same group of disciples was aglow with supreme confidence and fearless in the face of persecution. Their message was one of joy and triumph. What caused such a radical change in these men's lives? The explanation is that something unprecedented had occurred: Jesus Christ was raised from the dead! Fifty-some days after the Crucifixion the apostolic preaching of Christ's resurrection began in Jerusalem with such power and persuasion that the evidence convinced thousands.

Divergences in detail are certainly to be found in the accounts of the first Easter, but these are such as one would expect from independent and excited witnesses.[11] If the evangelists had fabricated the resurrection narratives, they would not have left obvious difficulties and discrepancies—such as those involving the number of

---

11. It is a notorious fact of ancient history that Polybius, the Greek historian, and Livy, the Roman historian, represent Hannibal in his invasion of Italy as crossing the Alps by completely different routes—routes that can by no stretch of the imagination be harmonized; yet no one doubts that Hannibal most certainly arrived in Italy. The discrepancy is there—but so is the quite undeniable fact. Discrepancies in the accounts of the resurrection of Jesus cannot be used as evidence to prove that the Resurrection did not take place.

angels at the tomb, the order of Jesus' appearances, and similar details. That the accounts have been left unreconciled, without any attempt to produce a single stereotyped narrative, inspires confidence in the fundamental honesty of those who transmitted the evidence.

The evangelists, moreover, give the impression of being unconcerned to provide all of the evidence on which the church rested its belief. That is, they offer only a part of the proof by which belief in the Resurrection was created and sustained. According to these fragmentary accounts, during the forty days following the Resurrection Jesus appeared to his followers at various times and places. Taken as a whole the narratives imply that Jesus' body had passed into a condition new to human experience. The reader gathers that the risen Lord was not living at any one place in Jerusalem or Galilee. Put in another way, he had no post-office address where he could always be found. Instead he had passed into a mode of being out of which he "appeared," superior to all obstacles, and into which he disappeared again. Since we have no category from personal experience of such a mode of being, theologians are accustomed to speak of the mystery of Christ's resurrection.

(i) Theories Concerning the Resurrection of Jesus

Over the centuries several theories have been put forward to explain the resurrection of Jesus. Perhaps the oldest is that the disciples stole the body of Jesus and then pretended that he had risen from the dead (Matt. 28:12-15). But it is acknowledged even by those who are not believers that so pure an ethical movement as Christianity cannot have originated in a deliberate fraud on the part of the disciples. Furthermore, if the Romans or the Jews had removed the body from the tomb, it would have been an easy matter for them to silence the Christians' claim by simply producing the body. We may be sure that they did not, because they could not.

Another theory is that the early followers of Jesus experienced hallucinations that led them to believe that Jesus was still alive. But against such a supposition there are two decisive objections. To begin with, it has no explanation for the empty tomb, witnessed by all four Gospels. In the second place, the psychological predisposition necessary for such hallucinations was not present. So far from being intensely preoccupied with expectations of Jesus' resurrection, the disciples are depicted as amazed and even skeptical when his resurrection is first announced to them (Matt. 28:17; Mark 16:11-14; Luke 24:11, 25, 37-38; John 20:25). Furthermore, the possibility of the occurrence of hallucinations is lessened in inverse proportion to the number of persons to whom Jesus is represented as having appeared. It is impossible to make such a theory account for the experiences of the various groups who witnessed his appearing, one of which numbered more than five hundred persons (1 Cor. 15:6).

Somewhat similar is the theory that God granted objective visions to the disciples, in order to assure them that the spirit of Jesus survived death. This view, though less offensive than the previous one, is also unsatisfactory. Not only is the empty tomb still unexplained, but the theory ignores the real character of the faith of the first disciples. Those who had seen the risen Christ did not believe merely that his spirit was still alive; they were convinced that he had risen from the grave. They regarded the Resurrection not as an illustration of spiritual survival, but as an event that resulted in an empty tomb.[12]

No theory will be found to satisfy the data in the records except the traditional explanation of a corporeal resurrection. The documentary evidence declares that the body of Jesus somehow disappeared from the rock-tomb. Unlike the myths of a dying and rising deity in the ancient mystery religions, typifying the recurrent vegetative cycle, the belief of the early Christians was that at the Resurrection the body of Jesus was changed from one of flesh and blood into one that was spiritual and incorruptible, in such a way that there was no trace left of the corruptible body that had been laid in the grave.

At the same time it should be observed that the disciples' certainty of the resurrection of Christ was based upon the appearances of their risen Lord, and not upon the empty tomb. The empty tomb is not appealed to in Acts or the Pauline Letters as a proof for the Resurrection. When, therefore, the Gospels mention the empty

---

12. The suggestion that on Easter morning the woman mistakenly went to the wrong tomb, which they found empty, is psychologically and historically improbable in view of their having observed three days earlier where Jesus' body had been laid (Matt. 27:61; Mark 15:47; Luke 23:55). Furthermore, such a mistake, even if made once, would be the kind that neither the friends nor the enemies of Jesus would have allowed to go uncorrected.

tomb, they do so not because it is an added legendary feature used to prove the Resurrection—for the sepulcher played no part in the early missionary preaching—but because it was actually empty and, therefore, served as the historical framework for understanding the Easter faith. But this faith was born with the self-manifestation of the risen Christ, and without this the empty grave remains mute.

Two different philosophical objections are sometimes raised against the bodily resurrection of Jesus Christ. On *a priori* grounds it is alleged that the resurrection of a material body is irrelevant to the reality of Christ's conquest of death, and its inclusion in the New Testament arises from ideas that must be discarded in the light of modern knowledge. But this contention ignores the difference between ideas of the immortality of the soul, which were well known in the contemporary world, and the quite distinct Christian doctrine of the resurrection of the dead, according to which not a disembodied spirit but the complete personality, consisting of body and soul, ultimately possesses eternal life. In short, a resurrection that is not a bodily resurrection is a contradiction of terms.

The other objection to the resurrection of Christ is less sophisticated. It amounts to saying that it is just unbelievable that a man should rise from the dead. The early Christians would certainly have agreed that there is a tremendous presumption against the resurrection of an ordinary man—for those who lived in the first century were quite as skeptical as those who live in the twenty-first that a dead person would rise. But in the case of Jesus Christ, so the early Christians held, the presumption was exactly reversed, for they had come to perceive that he was unlike any ordinary man in his moral purity and spiritual strength. During his public ministry he had made the most stupendous claims—claims that set him apart as a person who was entirely unique. Whereas, therefore, it is unlikely that any ordinary man would rise, it is unlikely that this man would not rise.

In conclusion, it is apparent that a methodological principle is involved. If the narrative of Jesus Christ's resurrection is separated from the account of his public ministry and teachings, one is left with something resembling a myth. But when one takes the evidence for the Resurrection along with the total picture of Jesus' life and the impression made by him during his ministry, a consistent account emerges of one who, as Peter declared seven weeks later at Pentecost, was raised from death "because it was impossible for him to be held in its power" (Acts 2:24).[13]

(ii) The Ascension of Jesus Christ

The forty days between the Resurrection and the Ascension formed a transition period, during which the disciples were being trained for their future ministry. The records contain numerous references to Jesus' giving instruction to them concerning the continuity of God's work in the past and in the present, and the fulfillment of Old Testament scripture by his death and resurrection (Luke 24:44-48; John 20:21-23; 21:15-22; Acts 1:3-8). Moreover, the experiences during those six weeks assisted the disciples to think of their Lord as absent and yet living; as invisible and yet near them; as risen to a new life and yet retaining the same nature that they had loved; as exalted but still the same (compare Heb. 13:8).

The ascension of Jesus Christ should not be regarded as an ascent by a celestial balloon from earth to God in heaven. Just as the Incarnation is not to be thought of as the passage from God's space into ours, so the statement that Christ "ascended up on high" does not mean that he was elevated so many feet above sea level in order to return to God. It means that he entered a higher sphere, a spiritual existence, what the Christian calls heaven, where God is and whence he had come to visit the earth in humility.

Doubtless one of the purposes of Jesus' ascension was to convince his followers that the transition period had now come to an end. Though Jesus did not *need* to ascend in order to return to the immediate presence of God, the book of Acts relates that he *did* ascend a certain distance into the sky, until a cloud received him out of sight (Acts 1:9). By such a dramatic rising from their midst, he taught his disciples that this was now the last time he would

---

13. Among noteworthy discussions of the resurrection of Jesus, see Pinchas Lapide, *The Resurrection of Jesus: A Jewish Perspective*, Wilhelm C. Linns, trans. (Minneapolis: Augsburg, 1983) (an Orthodox Jewish scholar defends the historical facticity of Jesus' resurrection); William Lane Craig, *Assessing the New Testament Evidence for the Historicity of the Resurrection of Jesus* (Lewiston, N.Y.: Edwin Mellon Press, 1989); and David Catchpole, *Resurrection People: Studies in the Resurrection Narratives of the Gospels* (London: Darton, Longman & Todd, 2000).

appear to them, and that henceforth they should not sit about waiting for another appearance, but should understand that the transitional period had come to an end. The didactic symbolism was both natural and appropriate. That the lesson was learned by the primitive church seems to be clear from the fact that the records of the early centuries indicate that his followers suddenly ceased to look for any manifestation of the risen Lord other than his second coming in glory. It appears that some event had taken place that assured them that the period of the resurrection appearances had now come to an end. Whatever else that event may have been, it is certain that Jesus Christ parted from the disciples in such a way that they thereby became more assured than ever of his royal power and divine rule.

Several early Christian theologians expressed the meaning of the Resurrection and Ascension in terms of the lordship of Christ. With joyful certainty they declared: He no longer lies mouldering in a tomb; he is seated at the right hand of God on high (Eph. 1:20; Heb. 1:3; 1 Pet. 3:22). What is God's right hand? This is symbolic language for divine omnipotence. Where is it? Everywhere. To sit, therefore, at the right hand of God does not mean that Christ is resting; it affirms that he is reigning as king, wielding the powers of divine omnipotence. It is altogether appropriate, therefore, that in the closing lines of the First Gospel the risen Christ says to his followers: "All authority in heaven and on earth has been given to me. Go therefore and make disciples of all nations" (Matt. 28:18-19).[14]

APPENDIX: MIRACLES IN THE GOSPELS

The Gospels report that Jesus wrought many wonderful cures on people's bodies and souls, and exercised on occasion an extraordinary control over what we call "inanimate nature." These deeds are not regarded as interferences with the so-called laws of nature, but as tokens of a new order of life inaugurated by the coming of Christ.

---

14. For further discussion concerning the significance of the Ascension, one may consult my article "The Meaning of Christ's Ascension" in the Festschrift *Search the Scriptures: New Testament Studies in Honor of Raymond T. Stamm*, edited by J. M. Myers, et al. (Leiden: E. J. Brill, 1969), pp. 118-28.

The words used most often to describe Jesus' miracles are "mighty works" and "signs." The former, which is used chiefly by the Synoptic Gospels, signifies acts of power. He who performs such acts is the possessor of a certain power, whether it be of divine or demonic origin (Matt. 12:27; Luke 11:19). The Gospel of John prefers to describe Jesus' miracles by the word "signs" (for example, John 2:11; 4:54; 20:30), a term that calls attention to the spiritual significance of the "mighty works." Thus, when Jesus multiplies the loaves to feed the five thousand (John 6:1-59) or restores sight to a man who was born blind (9:1-41), the fourth evangelist understands the individual work as also a symbol of Jesus' continuing ability and willingness to feed his followers with the bread of life and to open the eyes of the spiritually blind.

Accounts of thirty-seven miracles of Jesus are included in the four Gospels. Of this number, eighteen are narrated in one Gospel only, six in two Gospels, twelve in three Gospels, and one (the feeding of the five thousand) in all four Gospels. Contrary to what is sometimes supposed, the latest Gospel does not multiply the reports of Jesus' miracles; actually John describes only seven or eight miracles of Jesus. In Mark, the earliest Gospel, 209 verses out of a total of 661 (that is, more than 30 percent) deal directly or indirectly with miracles. Even Q, though primarily devoted to sayings of Jesus, not only includes the account of at least one miracle (see p. 83), but also reports Jesus' response to John the Baptist's question as to whether he was really the long-expected Messiah: "Go and tell John what you hear and see: the blind receive their sight, the lame walk, the lepers are cleansed, the deaf hear, the dead are raised, and the poor have good news brought to them. And blessed is anyone who takes no offense at me" (Matt. 11:4-6; Luke 7:22-23).

The implication of these words is that the miracles are not a mere addendum to the messianic work of Jesus, but are an integral part of it. They attest the beginning of the era of salvation in which, according to Old Testament prophecy (Isa. 35:3-6), illness and misery are to cease and liberation from sin is to become a reality.

Other passages in the Gospels also preserve Jesus' own testimony concerning his powers of healing and exorcism. For example, both Matthew and Luke record Jesus' reply to those who had charged that his ability to effect exorcisms was derived from Beelzebub (= Satan): "If Satan casts out Satan, he is divided against himself; how then will his kingdom stand? . . . But if it is by the Spirit of God that I cast out demons, then the kingdom of God has come to you" (Matt. 12:26, 28; compare Luke 11:18, 20). Again, there is a saying from the special Lukan material, "Go and tell that fox [that is, Herod] for me, 'Listen, I am casting out demons and performing cures today and tomorrow' " (Luke 13:32). Likewise, when Jesus sends out his disciples on a mission, be commands them to cure the sick and cast out demons (Mark 3:15; Luke 10:9)— clearly a further confirmation of his having performed such things himself.

It should not be thought, however, that the canonical Gospels exhibit an insatiable craving for the miraculous. Though Matthew and Luke occasionally heighten the Markan account of Jesus' power to effect cures (see pp. 98-99), they are not interested in the miraculous simply for the sake of the miraculous. Neither of them retained, for example, two striking miracle stories of Mark—the healing of the deaf stammerer (Mark 7:31-37) and the restoration of sight to a blind man (Mark 8:22-26).

If it were true, as some have suggested, that the evangelists invented the stories of Jesus' miracles, it is strange that they over-looked many an opportunity where pious imagination might well have embroidered the narrative. On the contrary, sometimes the evangelist's account is told in such a matter-of-fact style, stripped bare of all embellishments, that the reader cannot be certain whether a miracle is intended or not (as, for example, Jesus' escape from the angry mob, reported in Luke 4:30).

In short, the canonical Gospels, unlike the later apocryphal accounts, do not tell of a miracle worker who performs as many wonders as possible, but of one who refuses to perform mighty works merely for the sake of a spectacle (Matt. 12:38-39; Mark 8:11-12; Luke 11:29; 23:8-9). Indeed, according to the Synoptic Gospels, Jesus frequently charged those whom he had healed to say nothing about it (for example, Matt. 9:30; Mark 5:43; 7:36; Luke 5:14).

Practical principles for evaluating the stories of Jesus' miracles include the following:

(a) One should take into account the consistency between the meaning ascribed to Jesus' miracles and the rest of his ministry and message.[15]

(b) Even Jesus' enemies acknowledged that he possessed more than human power. Though they attributed it to his being in league with the devil (Matt. 12:24; Luke 11:18), or to his utilizing black magic (see the reference in the Talmud, p. 92), they did not deny the reality of the power.

(c) All the strata of the Gospels identified by literary criticism testify to Jesus' ability to work miracles. Even the narratives of Jesus' temptations (Matt. 4:1-11; Luke 4:2-17) presuppose that he had miraculous powers. We are not tempted to change stones into bread, because we cannot change stones into bread. Such a proposal can be a temptation only to one who has the possibility of complying. It is incredible that anyone should have told such a story about himself to persons who knew that he had never done a mighty work; it is equally incredible that anyone should invent such a story about a person who had never been known to do anything miraculous.

(d) Conversely, to acknowledge that Jesus possessed divine power does not relieve one of the necessity of examining the credentials of each narrative, canonical or apocryphal, that reports a miracle. Miracles are established, not by the number of witnesses, but by the character and qualifications of the witnesses. The apocryphal story about the boy Jesus who gave life to clay sparrows (see p. 121) is obviously quite different in character from Jesus' miracles reported in the New Testament.

(e) Just as some of Jesus' sayings were modified in the course of their transmission, so it is possible that an occasional nonmiraculous account has been transformed into a miracle story. For example, some scholars think that what was originally a parable lies behind what is now an account of the miraculous withering of the fig tree that Jesus had cursed (Matt. 21:18-22; Mark 11:12-14, 20-22).

---

15. Particularly thoughtful is A. E. Harvey's evaluation of "The Intelligibility of Miracle," in his volume *Jesus and the Constraints of History* (Philadelphia: Westminster Press, 1982), pp. 98-119, where he shows the consistency between the meaning ascribed to Jesus' miracles and the rest of his ministry and message. For other discussions of grounds for believing that miracles have occurred, see C. S. Lewis's *Miracles, a Preliminary Study* (New York: Macmillan, 1947) and Colin Brown's *Miracles and the Critical Mind* (Grand Rapids: Eermans, 1984). For an encyclopedic discussion of the history of interpretation, see H. van der Loos's *The Miracles of Jesus* (Leiden: E. J. Brill, 1968).

(f) There is also the possibility that occasionally early Christians transferred to Jesus whole stories of foreign origin. For example, the story of the demons going into a herd of pigs (Mark 5:1-17) is thought by some to be originally a non-Christian story that was appropriated by the early church and woven into an account of one of Jesus' exorcisms.

(g) It is obvious that doubt about any individual miracle story in the Gospels does not discredit all of them. Though there may be difficulties and uncertainties about the details of this or that miraculous account, it cannot be denied that as a whole they represent the *kind* of thing that Jesus used to do.

(h) It should be observed that to the Gospel writers the miracles have a close connection with Jesus' announcing the coming of God's kingdom. Jesus' works of healing were not merely acts of compassion, though he was certainly concerned about human suffering. The deepest meaning of the miracles lies in their testimony to the reality of God's love and power that Jesus brings into human life: "If it is by the finger of God that I cast out the demons, then the kingdom of God has come to you" (Luke 11:20; compare Matt. 12:28). Because his miracles were signs through which the kingdom was revealed, in its preaching the early church recounted the deeds as well as the words of Jesus in order to awaken saving faith in him as the true Messiah of God.

CHAPTER 6

ASPECTS OF THE TEACHING OF JESUS CHRIST

I. THE FORM OF JESUS' TEACHING

Before analyzing some of the leading ideas of Jesus' teaching, it is necessary to examine the literary form in which that teaching was communicated. In such an examination, the question to be asked is not what Jesus said, but how he said it. More than once it will be found that the meaning of his teaching is conditioned by the literary forms in which he expressed himself. In the following paragraphs attention will be given to such forms of Jesus' teaching as picturesque speech, puns, proverbs, poetry, and parables.

1. PICTURESQUE SPEECH

It is a truism that persons of different national temperaments express the same emotions in quite different ways. Thus, a person from southern Europe, looking at a masterpiece hanging in an art gallery, may say, "It is magnificent; it is truly grand, wonderful, utterly unsurpassed!" However, someone from northern Europe, wishing to express wholehearted appreciation of the same artistic masterpiece, may say simply, "Aye, it's not bad." And both persons will be expressing, in his or her own characteristic manner, a high approval of the work of art.

Jesus spoke differently from the way an Italian or a Scotsman would put things. The fact that he grew up in the Near East and spoke to Near Easterners affected both the matter and the manner of his speech. Along with his contemporaries, Jesus delighted in sharp contrasts and extreme statements—what the rhetorician calls hyperbole and exaggeration. His teaching is characterized not by grays and halftones, but by contrasting black and white. Using colorful speech he shows the ridiculous and ludicrous elements in everyday situations. For example, instead of saying in prosaic terms that some people are inconsistent when judging others and themselves, Jesus put it thus:

> Why do you see the speck in your neighbor's eye, but do not notice the log in your own eye? Or how can you say to your neighbor, "Let me take the speck out of your eye," while the log is in your own eye? You hypocrite, first take the log out of your own eye, and then you will see clearly to take the speck out of your neighbor's eye (Matt. 7:3-5).

By taking into account the presence of picturesque expression in Jesus' teaching, we can sometimes avoid misinterpreting his meaning. For example, the hard saying preserved in the Third Gospel, "Whoever comes to me and does not hate father and mother, wife and children, brothers and sisters, yes, and even life itself, cannot be my disciple" (Luke 14:26), must be understood in the light of what has just been said about overstatement as characteristic of the speech of Near Easterners. Obviously Jesus' statement does not mean what it says; he does not wish to increase the sum total of hatred in the world. Here Jesus states a principle in a startling, categorical manner, and leaves his hearers to find out whatever qualifications are necessary in the light of his other pronouncements. The saying means that if one is to follow Jesus, one must be prepared to choose between natural affection and loyalty to the Master. The same idea is expressed in Matthew's less rigorous version of Jesus' saying, "Whoever loves father or mother more than me is not worthy of me; and whoever loves son or daughter more than me is not worthy of me" (Matt. 10:37).

A warning is appropriate here against attempting to discover overstatement in Jesus' teaching when it is not present. One must beware of diluting his uncompromising statements simply because we find them unpalatable. For example, Jesus' command to the rich man who inquired as to what he should do to inherit eternal life, "Sell all that you own and distribute the money to the poor, and you will have treasure in heaven; then come, follow me" (Luke 18:22), must not be taken as hyperbole meaning, perhaps, "Sell part of what you have." The context makes it absolutely clear that the questioner as well as the disciples, all of whom were Near Easterners, understood Jesus' words in their literal sense.

2. PUNS

For centuries the Jews, like their surrounding Semitic neighbors, enjoyed making and hearing puns, or plays on words (for examples in the Old Testament, see the notes in the New Revised Standard Version at Jer. 1:11-12 and at Amos 8:1-2). The Greek Gospels contain more than one instance where the original Aramaic of Jesus' mother tongue is thought to have involved a wordplay. It is understandable that very few such puns in Aramaic could be reproduced in Greek. There is one, however, in the Gospel of John where it happens that the Greek word *pneuma*, just as the Aramaic *ruha'*, means both "wind" and "spirit." Jesus is quoted as saying to Nicodemus, "The *pneuma* blows where it chooses, and you hear the sound of it, but you do not know where it comes from or where it goes. So it is with everyone who is born of the *pneuma*" (John 3:8).

In other passages, the Greek text of the Gospels can reproduce only imperfectly, or not at all, the jingle that probably was present in Aramaic. In his condemnation of the inconsistency of scribes and Pharisees, Jesus charged them with "strain[ing] out a gnat but swallow[ing] a camel" (Matt. 23:24). Since in Aramaic the word for "gnat" or "louse" is *qalma'* and the word for "camel" is *gamla'*, the pun provides added piquancy to the picturesque speech of Jesus: he is describing a Pharisee who, in view of Leviticus 11:41-42, which forbids the eating of things that swarm or crawl on the earth, is careful to strain out a *qalma'* that may have fallen into his wine, but is quite unconcerned about gulping down a whole *gamla'*!

One of the most noteworthy of Jesus' sayings about the church involves a play on words. According to Matthew 16:13-18 at Caesarea Philippi, in response to Jesus' having asked his disciples who they thought he was, Simon Peter confessed, "You are the Messiah, the Son of the living God." After declaring that Peter spoke this by a divine revelation, Jesus retorts, "And I tell you, you are Peter [Greek *Petros*], and on this rock [Greek *petra*] I will build my church." The play on words in the Greek text between the proper name *Petros*, meaning "Rock," and the common noun *petra*, meaning "a rock, a stone," is even closer in Jesus' mother tongue. In Aramaic the word *kepha'* serves as a proper name (Cephas) and also means "a rock, a stone." Jesus' statement therefore would have been as follows: "And I tell you, you are *Kepha'*, and on this *kepha'* I will build my church."[1]

3. PROVERBS

Every language has pithy sayings or maxims that express a truth crisply and forcefully. Because proverbs frequently express only one side of a truth, it happens that mutually contradictory proverbs may circulate, each of which is true when applied to the intended circumstances. The saying "penny wise, pound foolish" correctly describes an individual in Great Britain who is scrupulous about small transactions, but extravagant in great ones. However, the proverb "Take care of the pennies, and the dollars will take care of themselves" is also true. More than once the Bible presents two proverbs, which, though contradictory, are both true when applied to appropriate circumstances. In Proverbs 26:4, the writer cautions his reader, "Do not answer fools according to their folly, or you will be a fool yourself"; in the very next verse, however, he advises, "Answer fools according to their folly, or they will be wise in their own eyes." It is left to the reader to discern when it is appropriate to heed one or the other of these two contradictory proverbs.

It is not surprising that Jesus frequently cast his teaching in the form of proverbs. Since these brief salty sayings stress one side of a truth, they should not be exalted as maxims of inflexible conduct. On the contrary, one categorical statement must be interpreted in the light of another, which may teach the opposite. For example, Jesus' command, "Do not judge, so that you may not be judged" (Matt. 7:1), must not be taken as a blanket prohibition against making judgments concerning right and wrong, good and evil. In the same context, Matthew includes another of Jesus' pithy sayings, one that presupposes the necessity of forming judgments: "Do not give what is holy to dogs; and do not throw your pearls before swine" (Matt. 7:6). To obey this command against desecrating what is holy, one must judge who is doggish and who is swinish. Spiritual prudence will know when it is appropriate to follow one precept and when it is appropriate to follow the other.

---

1. There remains a difference of gender; the common noun is feminine and the proper name, of course, masculine; compare French "pierre" (f.) and "Pierre" (m.).

Similarly, Jesus' proverb-like statement, "Do not resist an evil-doer" (Matt. 5:39), must not be taken to mean that his disciples are never to resist evil in any kind of way. In the light of Jesus' other teachings, as well as his use of force to drive out the money changers from the temple, it is clear that the principle he inculcates in this crisp maxim is nonretaliation for a malicious wrong inflicted on one by a personal enemy. In other words, Jesus' statement regarding nonresistance has to do with the motive and manner of the resistance. Truth will always resist falsehood, but it will resist by its own pure and truthful ways. It will resist by being itself.

4. POETRY

Hebrew poetry, illustrated, for example, in the book of Psalms in the Old Testament, is characterized by a parallelism of members. Rhythm is achieved, not by the succession of long and short syllables, with end rhyme, but by putting statements side by side that either echo one another or are antithetic. For example, what is called synonymous parallelism is found in the opening lines of Psalm 19:

> The heavens are telling the glory of God; and the firmament proclaims his handiwork.

An example of antithetic parallelism, where the idea is expressed by drawing a contrast, is found at the close of Psalm 1:

> For the LORD watches over the way of the righteous, but the way of the wicked will perish.

In view of Jesus' frequent quotations from and allusions to the Psalms, it is not surprising that he cast much of his teaching into the mold of Semitic poetry. Synonymous parallelism appears in his saying recorded in Luke 6:27-28:

> Love your enemies, do good to those who hate you, bless those who curse you, pray for those who abuse you.

Antithetic parallelism is illustrated by Mark 8:35:

> Those who want to save their life will lose it, and those who lose their life for my sake, and for the sake of the gospel, will save it.

Besides these basic varieties of parallelism, several other types have been identified. What is called step parallelism occurs when the second line takes up a thought contained in the first line, and, repeating it, makes it, as it were, a step upward for the development of a further thought, which is the climax of the whole. An example is found in Luke 9:48:

> Whoever welcomes this child in my name welcomes me, and whoever welcomes me welcomes the one who sent me.

Rhythmical structure is also observable in larger units of the teaching of Jesus. Sometimes elaborate aggregates of text fall into a kind of compound parallelism. The five verses of Luke 17:26-30 divide into two parallel stanzas:

> Just as it was in the days of Noah, so too it will be in the days of the Son of Man. They were eating and drinking, and marrying and being given in marriage, until the day Noah entered the ark, and the flood came and destroyed all of them. Likewise, just as it was in the days of Lot: they were eating and drinking, buying and selling, planting and building, but on the day that Lot left Sodom, it rained fire and sulfur from heaven and destroyed all of them—it will be like that on the day that the Son of Man is revealed.

(For other passages that exhibit an elaborate rhythmical pattern, see Matt. 6:19-21; 23:16-22; Mark 2:21-22; 9:43-48; Luke 11:31-32.)

5. PARABLES

In all the teaching of Jesus, there is no feature more striking than his parables. Whether we consider them in themselves or according to their influence in human life, they are incomparable. They have supplied inspiration to poets, artists, and moralists. Many an expression in common parlance has come directly from these matchless stories. Everyone knows what is meant by "hiding one's lamp under a bushel," or "he's a good Samaritan." No one had previously spoken of natural endowments as "talents" until Jesus told his parable of the talents; today this specialized sense of the word is better known than the original meaning of "talent," which referred to a certain weight of gold or silver.

Jesus was not unique in the use of parables. Several occur in the Old Testament (for example, 2 Sam. 12:1-14; Ezek. 17:1-10), and contemporary Jewish rabbis occasionally included parabolic stories in their teaching. But both in quantity and in excellence, Jesus' parables are acknowledged to be an outstanding feature of his teaching.[2] About sixty parables, out of what was probably a larger number, have been preserved in the Synoptic Gospels. The Fourth Gospel nowhere uses the word "parable," but it contains several parabolic sayings in the form of allegories.

The old definition of a parable as "an earthly story with a heavenly meaning" contains a certain amount of truth, but one must beware against seeking an elaborate allegorical meaning in every parable. The proper method of interpreting Jesus' parables is to make a thorough inquiry into the "life-setting" in his ministry when the parable was first uttered, and to seek out the chief point that it was intended to teach. Usually the details in a parable provide nothing more than the necessary background for the parable, and are not to be assigned special meanings in the fashion of an allegory.

An analysis of Jesus' parables reveals that most of them are intended either *(a)* to portray a type of human character or disposition for our warning or example, or *(b)* to reveal a principle of God's government of the world and humankind. In other words, Jesus' parables usually teach either a certain kind of conduct that his hearers are to emulate or to avoid, or they disclose something of the character of God and his dealings with individuals. The interpreter must be alert to discover in each case which is the primary intention of the parable.

By paying attention to the context in which the parable has been placed, as well as to internal hints, one can usually avoid interpreting a theological parable as though it were intended to teach ethics, and vice versa. For example, the parable of the Good Samaritan (Luke 10:29-37) has often been misinterpreted as though it were intended to teach the plan of salvation. According to Augustine and many after him, the opening statement, "A man was going down from Jerusalem to Jericho," refers to Adam, who

---

2. That it is not easy to draw up a significant parable, anyone can discover by trying to compose several!

fell from heavenly blessedness (the city of Jerusalem) into mortal sin (Jericho). The robbers, who stripped and beat him, are the devil and his angels. The priest and the Levite, who saw him and passed by, represent the Law and the prophets of the Old Testament, which are unable to save the sinner. The good Samaritan who rescues the traveler, taking him to an inn, is Christ himself, who takes him to the church. The two denarii that the Samaritan gives to the innkeeper (that is, to the apostle Paul) are either the two precepts of love, or the promise of this life and that which is to come. Finally, the promise of the Samaritan to return teaches the second coming of Christ.

Although this theological interpretation of the parable is rather ingenious, it is entirely arbitrary. The context makes it clear that Jesus intended the parable to teach, not the plan of salvation, but how his followers should live. Both the beginning and the ending of the parable ("Who is my neighbor?" . . . "Go and do likewise") indicate unmistakably that the parable has to do with our relationship toward others. Briefly, the parable depicts three basic philosophies of life. The philosophy of the robbers is, "What is yours is mine"; that of the priest and the Levite is, "What is mine is mine"; and that of the Samaritan, "What is mine is yours." The primary purpose of the parable is to stimulate the hearers to action—to avoid the immoral and the selfish attitudes exemplified by the brigands and the religious leaders, and to imitate the self-denying concern shown by the Samaritan.

Other parables of Jesus have as their chief purpose the teaching of theology—what God is like and how he deals with us. For example, the parable of the laborers in the vineyard (Matt. 20:1-16) begins by declaring, "For the kingdom of heaven is like a landowner who went out early in the morning to hire laborers for his vineyard." It goes on to tell of the unexpected generosity of the owner of the vineyard, who pays a full day's wage (a denarius) to all alike, whether they have worked twelve hours, nine hours, six, three, or even only one hour! The parable has nothing to do with ethics or economics (for example, that each worker should be paid a living wage); the point of the parable is clearly disclosed in the opening words, namely that God is like this landowner who does not bargain and haggle, trying to give as little as possible. God never gives less than he has promised, and frequently gives more. His extravagant benevolence is not limited; in his goodness he gives according to our needs and not according to what we deserve. God's free grace is liberal beyond our expectations.[3]

Taken all together, Jesus' parables were governed by a single purpose: to show, directly or indirectly, what God is and what we may become, and to show these things in such a way that they will reach our hearts if it is possible to reach them at all.

II. BRIEF SUMMARY OF THE TEACHING OF JESUS CHRIST

Even a casual acquaintance with the Gospels reveals that Jesus was more of what we would call a preacher than a teacher. Instead of giving a lecture in which he defined the terms, surveyed the data, and then drew generalizations, his method was to deal with specific situations. In this respect, Jesus stood characteristically in the tradition of the Old Testament prophets. Instead of being abstract and speculative, his teaching was concrete and in terms of personal involvement.

It must also be obvious that Jesus' teaching is not developed with systematic completeness. Whatever ideas Jesus shared with the majority of his audience he did not belabor. Where, for example, does he attack idolatry and what are his arguments for monotheism? The fact that he says nothing about these subjects certainly does not mean that he was a polytheist—it means that there was no need to convince his hearers on such matters as these. He assumes that God had already revealed himself in terms of ethical monotheism through the prophets and lawgivers of the Old Testament. An important corollary of this feature of Jesus' teaching is that the full sweep of his intention cannot be understood if we isolate his teachings from their context within contemporary Jewish thought derived from the Old Testament.

1. JESUS' TEACHING CONCERNING GOD

The Greek philosophers speculated about God as pure being, the cause of all becoming, the unmoved first mover. Such ideas of God

---

3. If it be asked whether any of Jesus' parables are intended to teach both ethics and theology, the answer is that perhaps a few do so. For example, the parable of the prodigal son

are limited to those who can think abstractly. Jesus' teaching about God, on the contrary, is in simple terms of proclamation—that in such a situation God acts thus. He said that God is interested even in the sparrow that falls (Matt. 10:29). He said that God has counted the hairs of a person's head; in other words, that he knows all about us (Matt. 10:30). God is extravagantly benevolent, like a landowner who hired laborers and paid them far beyond what they deserved (Matt. 20:1-15). Furthermore, God's benevolence is not limited to people of any one class, race, or religion. The prayer of the self-righteous Pharisee pleases God less than the cry for mercy from the lips of the crooked, but then repentant, tax collector (Luke 18:9-14).

An element of novelty in Jesus' teaching about God is to be found in his emphasis on the divine fatherhood. To be sure, the Old Testament occasionally speaks of God as Father. Usually the reference is to God as the Father of Israel as a nation (Deut. 14:1; 32:6; Isa. 63:16; Jer. 3:19; 31:9, 20), but in one or two passages God is referred to as the Father of individuals. Thus, the psalmist declares, "As a father has compassion for his children, so the LORD has compassion for those who fear him" (Ps. 103:13), and the prophet Malachi asks, "Have we not all one father?" (Mal. 2:10).[4] Likewise in the intertestamental literature and among contemporary rabbis in Jesus' day, God was sometimes referred to as Father. But Jesus' teaching concerning God as Father differs from these in two respects: the relative frequency with which he spoke of God as Father, and the degree of tenderness and warmth that be put into the word.

Every stratum of source material in the Gospels contains at least several instances of Jesus' referring to God as Father, and two of the four evangelists emphasize this aspect of Jesus' teaching (Matthew has 44 references and John has 120). Typical are such passages as: "Love your enemies, . . . so that you may be children of your Father in heaven" (Matt. 5:44-45); "Your Father knows what you need before you ask him" (Matt. 6:8); "So it is not the will of your Father in heaven that one of these little ones should be lost" (Matt. 18:14); "Abba, Father, for you all things are possible; remove this cup from

---

(Luke 15:11-32) holds up the character of the self-righteous elder brother as a rebuke to the Pharisees, and the father who welcomes and forgives the no-good but repentant son represents God, who is gracious and loving beyond our deserving.

4. It is possible, however, that the reference here may be to Abraham as the father of the nation.

me; yet, not what I want, but what you want" (Mark 14:36); "Do not be afraid, little flock, for it is your Father's good pleasure to give you the kingdom" (Luke 12:32); "Father, forgive them; for they do not know what they are doing" (Luke 23:34); and "The works that I do in my Father's name testify to me" (John 10:25).

From Mark 14:36 we may conclude that the word that Jesus used in his mother tongue for father was *abba*. This Aramaic word was the everyday word used by Palestinian children in speaking to their earthly father; it meant "daddy" as well as "father." When the rabbis on occasion referred to God as Father, they always used *abbi*, a modified form of the simple *abba*, meaning "my Father," for they felt that it was unfitting to speak of God or to God in the same familiar and intimate way in which one spoke of or to one's earthly father. Jesus, however, abolished this distinction; he used *abba* of God and taught his followers to do likewise.

One must beware, however, against reading into Jesus' teaching more than the records warrant. So far from teaching the multitudes that God is the Father of all, there is general agreement among all the sources that Jesus spoke of this subject only to his disciples. When Jesus addressed the general public, he seems almost never to have referred to God as Father. Of all the passages where Jesus mentions the fatherhood of God, in only one is he represented as speaking to the crowds as well as to his disciples: "You have one Father—the one in heaven" (Matt. 23:9, compare verse 1). From the mass of evidence, therefore, it appears that, instead of teaching the universal fatherhood of God, Jesus spoke of God as Father only (1) in terms of his own relation to God and (2) in terms of the relation of his disciples to God. Apparently, therefore, Jesus restricted the right to call God "Father" to those who had shown by their loyalty to himself to be entitled to regard themselves as children of God.

In this connection one must beware of the ever-present peril of modernizing Jesus. When Jesus spoke of God and used the everyday household word *abba*, meaning "father," he did not think of the "papahood" of God. Nothing in Jesus' teaching depicts God as a weak and indulgent "papa" who spoils his children by granting their every whim and never chastising them. On the contrary, as will be pointed out in a subsequent section on Jesus' teaching concerning our duties, he taught plainly that the Father in heaven is none other than the Lord God Almighty, who must be both loved and feared (that is, revered).

2. JESUS' TEACHING CONCERNING THE KINGDOM OF GOD

Odd though it may seem, the expression "the kingdom of God" occurs nowhere in the Old Testament or in the Apocrypha. But, though the term itself is absent, the idea is present throughout. Every part of the Old Testament contains such statements as the following: "The LORD will reign forever and ever" (Exod. 15:18); "You are God, you alone, of all the kingdoms of the earth" (2 Kings 19:15); "The LORD sits enthroned as king forever" (Ps. 29:10); "The LORD has established his throne in the heavens, and his kingdom rules over all" (Ps. 103:19); "I am the LORD, your Holy One, the Creator of Israel, your King" (Isa. 43:15).

The Old Testament concept of God's kingship, when we examine it more closely, always has a double aspect. *(a)* On the one hand, it is assumed that God is already king; he made the world and governs it in righteousness. God is reigning now, above all the world's tumult. In this knowledge his servants can trust him and wait patiently for him. *(b)* On the other hand, it is recognized that God's kingship lies in the future. He is the one true God whose will must prevail, but as yet he is known only to his people. They look for a coming day when he will overcome all usurping powers and assert himself as King of kings.

Both these aspects reappear in Jesus' teaching about the kingdom of God (or kingdom of heaven).[5] Some of his sayings refer to the kingdom as already present in his own person and deeds. He invites children to come to him, declaring that to such belongs the kingdom of God (Matt. 19:14; Mark 10:14; Luke 18:16). Its power appears palpably and visibly in his casting out of demons (Matt. 12:28; Luke 11:20). However, in many other sayings the kingdom is

---

5. No distinction of meaning should be sought between these two expressions in the Gospels (compare, for example, Matt. 5:3 and Luke 6:20). The Jews used the word "heaven" as a substitute for the word "God," which was considered too sacred a word to be uttered lightly. Matthew, who addresses himself primarily to Jewish and Jewish Christian readers, speaks for the most part of the kingdom of heaven, whereas Mark and Luke always speak of the kingdom of God, which was more intelligible to non-Jews. We may assume that Jesus made use of both expressions, depending in part upon the nature of his audience.

represented as still in the future (for example, Matt. 8:11; 20:21; Mark 9:1), and he bade his disciples pray to God, "Your kingdom come" (Matt. 6:10; Luke 11:2).

The implications of a present kingdom and a future kingdom seem to be contradictory, and therefore some have sought to eliminate one of them. It has been argued that Jesus always spoke of the kingdom as future, and the idea that he had also spoken of it as present was the product of early Christian theology introduced into the Gospels. On the other hand, sometimes it has been urged that he always spoke of it as present and spiritual, and the idea that he had also spoken of it as future and material was taken over from Jewish apocalypses. These attempts, however, have not been successful; the two representations are so thoroughly interwoven in the evangelists' reports that we must conclude that both are genuine elements in Jesus' teaching concerning the kingdom.

The seeming contradiction is resolved by a closer examination of the term "kingdom of God" and the verbs that are used with it in the Gospels. The word *kingdom,* when referring to God's kingdom, suggests the idea of "kingly rule" or "reign" and not at all the idea of "territory" or "domain." The kingdom of God in its essence is the reign of God, the personal relationship between the sovereign God and the individual. Thus there is no point in asking whether the kingdom is present or future, just as there is no point in asking whether the fatherhood of God is present or future. It is both. Therefore, it is natural that in his teaching Jesus urged his hearers to recognize God's sovereignty as a present reality, to be acknowledged by a personal response, and that he also led them to hope for a new age in which human hardness of heart would no longer prevent God's sovereignty from finding universal and complete response.

The verbal concepts that in the Gospels are associated with the kingdom are in accordance with this twofold aspect of the kingdom. One looks in vain for such ideas as "building" the kingdom, "advancing" the kingdom, or "promoting" the kingdom's interests. The kingdom is not referred to as merely a new social order, nor is it identified with the church. Instead, the Gospels refer to the kingdom as something near at hand, into which people can enter (Mark 1:15; Luke 19:52). It is given as a gift (Luke 12:32), and may be inherited (Matt. 25:34). At the same time it is not a national or racial privilege of the Jews, and it may be taken away from them (Matt. 8:12; 21:43). The necessary condition for entry into the kingdom is the doing of God's will (Matt. 7:21-23). The indispensable requirement is that one repent and be "converted," that is, be completely changed in one's disposition and point of view (Matt. 4:17; Mark 1:15), break resolutely (Luke 9:62) with earthbound interests (Matt. 22:1-4), and, as a child, receive the kingdom (Matt. 19:14; Mark 10:15; Luke 18: 16). The kingdom must be a person's first concern (Matt. 6:33; Luke 12:31), for the sake of which one must be prepared to give up everything (Matt. 13:44-48).

At the same time, there are mysteries concerning the kingdom (Matt. 13:11), and certain people are unable either to understand the kingdom (Mark 4:11-12) or even see it (John 3:3). In the future there will be a glorious manifestation of the power of the kingdom (Mark 9:1) when the Son of Man will come with his angels in the glory of his Father (Matt. 16:27). This kingdom, appointed by the Father to Jesus, is to be enjoyed by those whom Jesus appoints as worthy to share its joys (Luke 22:29-30). The duality of the kingdom (its present obscurity and its future glory) forms the subject matter of "the parables of the kingdom," particularly the parables of the sower and the seed, the mustard seed, and the leaven (Mark 4:1-32 and parallels).

Figure 6.1. A Palestinian Farmer Sowing Seed
(Courtesy of Bastiaan Van Elderen.)
In Palestine, sowing the seed preceded working the ground with a plow (see Joachim Jeremias, *The Parables of Jesus*. New York: Charles Scribner's Sons, 1962, 11)

In short, the kingdom of God as it is presented in the teaching and work of Jesus is essentially God's sovereign reign. It begins in the personal relation between God as king and individuals as subjects. Though in establishing this relationship God takes the initiative, human effort is not lacking: "Strive for his kingdom, . . . for it is your Father's good pleasure to give you the kingdom" (Luke 12:31-32); "Not everyone who says to me, 'Lord, Lord' will enter the kingdom of heaven, but only the one who does the will of my Father in heaven" (Matt. 7:21). In other words, to be in the kingdom presupposes a relationship of obedience to God.

3. JESUS' TEACHING CONCERNING HIMSELF

What significance did Jesus ascribe to himself? Did he regard himself as merely a teacher who, like other contemporary Jewish teachers, instructed his followers in matters of doctrine and ethics? Or did he think of himself as the Messiah, the anointed of God, to whom the hopes of his people pointed? How far did he adopt for himself previous categories, such as "Son of God," "Son of Man," "the Messiah," and how far did he give, by what he said and did, a distinctive interpretation of his person and work?

It should be recognized that the topic, what Jesus taught about himself, is different from the other topics that are considered in this chapter. In the case of Jesus' teaching about God, or the kingdom, or human beings, he dealt directly with the subject matter; in this case, however, we shall find that he taught nothing directly that might be called a "Christology." What we must look for are the presuppositions that underlie his comments concerning his person and work. These presuppositions of course were not proclaimed from the housetops; when we consider the matter it is obvious that we could not expect that Jesus would, for example, walk up to a person and say, "Look here, I want you to know that I am God's Son, the Messiah!" In the nature of the case, the only way in which he could convey such an idea convincingly was to give his disciples indirect hints concerning his mission and destiny, both through what he did as well as through what he said.

(i) The Messiah

The title "Messiah" is a Hebrew word meaning "anointed," which in Greek becomes *Christos* and in English *Christ*. The term was applicable to any person who had been anointed with the holy oil, as for example the high priest (Lev. 4:3, 5, 16) or the king (2 Sam. 1:14, 16). During the latter part of the Old Testament period the title "Messiah" acquired a special reference and denoted the ideal king, anointed by God (that is, empowered by God's spirit) to deliver his people and to establish his kingdom in righteousness (Dan. 9:26-27). In the period between the Old and New Testaments these ideas were considerably expanded and diversified by several Jewish sects and parties.

When we turn to the New Testament we find that the Greek word *Christos* occurs 55 times in the four Gospels and 474 times in the rest of the New Testament. The remarkable thing about these instances, which testify to the widespread use of the term in the early church when referring to Jesus, is the limited use of the term by Jesus himself. The word does not appear at all among the sayings of Jesus that belong to the source Q. Of its seven occurrences in Mark, only three appear in sayings attributed to Jesus (9:41; 12:35; 13:21), and in none of these does Jesus apply the name directly to himself. In Matthew, Luke, and John, the word is seldom found on the lips of Jesus, and almost never with reference to himself (only Matt. 23:10; two post-Resurrection sayings in Luke 24:26, 46; and John 17:3). We must conclude from these data that, though the members of the early church frequently spoke of Jesus as "the Christ" (the word appears in every book of the New Testament except 3 John), Jesus was reluctant to use the title of himself.

This reluctance does not mean that Jesus did not believe himself to be the Messiah, for when others directly confronted him with a statement or a question regarding his messiahship, he acknowledged it. Thus, at Caesarea Philippi he accepted Peter's declaration, "You are the Messiah" (Mark 8:29; compare Matt. 16:16), and at his trial he replied to Caiaphas's question, "Are you the Messiah, the Son of the Blessed One?" (Mark 14:61) with a clear affirmative, "I am." Similarly in John's Gospel, Jesus responds to the woman of Samaria's statement about the Messiah with the words, "I am he, the one who is speaking to you" (John 4:26).

Jesus' reluctance to adopt the title "Messiah" doubtless arose from the political and nationalistic expectations that had come to be associated with it in the minds of his contemporaries. More than once during his ministry he had cautioned others, both those who had been healed as well as his disciples, against public proclamation of his messiahship (Mark 1:25; 5:43; 7:36; 8:30; 9:9). Consistently repudiating the political overtones of might and grandeur, it is quite in harmony with his entire ministry that, when on the day of palms he accepted the plaudits of those who acclaimed him as the long-expected deliverer of Israel, he rode into Jerusalem not on a war horse, but on a lowly donkey, the beast of burden (Matt. 21:2-11). Later, though acknowledging to Pilate that he was a king, he declared that his kingship was not of this world (John 18:36-39).

(ii) The Son of Man

Instead of using the term *Messiah*, Jesus preferred to refer to himself as "the Son of Man." This expression occurs eighty-one times in the Gospels, and is present in all of the five traditions of Jesus as identified by scholarly investigation (one example from each will suffice): the Q source (Matt. 8:20 and Luke 9:58), Mark (2:10), the material found only in Matthew (25:31), the material found only in Luke (17:22), and the Johannine tradition (5:27). One of the striking features about all of the many occurrences of the expression in the Gospels is that, with one seeming exception, it always comes from the lips of Jesus himself, and is never used by his disciples, followers, petitioners, or enemies.[6] Furthermore, outside the Gospels it appears in the rest of the New Testament only four times (Acts 7:56; Heb. 2:6; Rev. 1:13; 14:14). Obviously, therefore, in this expression we have striking testimony to Jesus' own usage and preference, transmitted, as it appears, with great fidelity by the evangelists and other New Testament writers.

The previous Jewish usage of the expression "son of man" shows that it had a variety of meanings. It frequently means a human being being in general. In the book of Ezekiel, where "son of man" (rendered "mortal" in the NRSV) occurs more than ninety times, it describes the prophet as a frail human creature in the sight of God Almighty. A third usage of the phrase occurs in Daniel 7:13-14, where the prophet describes a vision that he had:

---

6. The one seeming exception is John 12:34, where, however, the people merely echo Jesus' earlier use of the expression.

I saw one like a human being [literally, "like a son of man"] coming with the clouds of heaven. And he came to the Ancient One [= Almighty God] and was presented before him. To him was given dominion and glory and kingship, that all peoples, nations, and languages should serve him. His dominion is an everlasting dominion that shall not pass away, and his kingship is one that shall never be destroyed.

Here the phrase stands for the personification of the saints of the Most High (7:18, 27). In later apocalyptic literature, such as the Similitudes of Enoch (Enoch, chaps. 37–61) and 2 Esdras 13, "the Son of Man" has become a superhuman being, the Elect One, destined to appear as the messianic ruler of the kingdom of God.

Which of these three Old Testament meanings of "Son of Man" influenced Jesus most in his own use of the expression? An examination of the passages in the Gospels where the expression occurs reveals that apparently Jesus identified himself with the heavenly Son of Man of Daniel's vision, but that at the same time he clothed the term with new and enriched meaning. Typical examples of the expression in the Gospels are the following, which fall into three groups:

(*a*) Some instances occur in contexts that relate to Jesus' activity during his public ministry. Thus, when he heals the paralytic (Mark 2:10), or justifies his disciples' activity on the sabbath (Mark 2:28), or replies to one who wished to follow him (Matt. 8:20 and parallel Luke 9:58), or contrasts himself with John the Baptist (Matt. 11:19; Luke 7:34-35), he refers to himself as the Son of Man.

(*b*) In other passages the expression refers to the future coming of the Son of Man on the clouds of heaven (Matt. 24:27; Mark 13:26-27; 14:62; Luke 17:24-30). The motif of exaltation is probably derived from the passage in Daniel 7:13-14.

(*c*) In a third group of sayings concerning the Son of Man, we find that Jesus deliberately modified and enlarged the meaning of the expression. In these sayings he refers to the necessity of his approaching sufferings, death, and resurrection (Matt. 20:18, 28; 26:45; Mark 8:31; 10:33; 14:21, 41; Luke 18:31; 19:10). Furthermore, he identifies himself with the suffering servant of the Lord depicted by Isaiah (Isa. 53:10-12), and declares that "the Son of Man came not to be served but to serve, and to give his life a ransom for many" (Mark 10:45).

The new thing, then, in Jesus' use of this phrase is his combining the motif of humiliation, suffering, and death with that of the future exaltation of the Son of Man. It is plain that he preferred to use an expression whose meaning was ambiguous, and which, therefore, he could define more precisely in order to express the mystery of his person and his ministry. As used by Jesus, the term "Son of Man" is intrinsically a paradox. It binds Jesus to humanity, yet it singles him out from other men. It predicates of him both supramundane glory and earthly humiliation. It includes the thought that the Man from heaven who will appear at the end of the world must first be hidden for a time. In short, his reference to himself as Son of Man carried with it the claim that he would some-day be acknowledged as Ruler, Messiah, and Redeemer.

(iii) The Son of God

In contrast with "Son of Man," which is used in the Gospels only by Jesus, and with "Messiah" (= "Christ"), which is used of him by others, "Son of God" or "the Son" is a title employed on both sides. In the Gospel of John, the evangelist frequently uses the more technical "the Son of God" (1:34, 49; 5:25; 9:35; 10:36; 11:4, 27; 19:7; 20:31), as well as the simple or absolute "the Son" (3:17, 35-36; 5:19-23, 26; 6:40; 8:36; 14:13; 17:1), and the form peculiar to John, "the only[7] Son" (3:16-17, compare 1 John 4:9-10). Throughout his Gospel the fourth evangelist is concerned to show that he who had been in the beginning with God, and who was indeed God, has now become incarnate in human flesh (John 1:1, 14). Identifying the Son of God as the King of Israel (1:49), the author repeatedly declares that Jesus claimed a unique relationship with God. More than once the Jews sought to kill Jesus for blasphemy, "because he was not only breaking the sabbath, but was also calling God his own Father, thereby making himself equal to God" (John 5:18, compare 10:30-33). By means of a series of unparalleled statements, such as "I am the bread of life" (John 6:35), "I am the light of the world" (8:12), and "I am the resurrection and the life" (11:25), Jesus is represented as utilizing the theophanic formula that in the Old

---

7. The characteristic adjective in John, which is traditionally translated "only begotten," means literally "unique in kind," and hence "only."

Testament is reserved for the most exalted descriptions of Jehovah (i.e., Yahweh; see Exod. 3:14 margin). It is not surprising that this Gospel concludes with an account in which the risen Jesus not only accepts the apostle Thomas's words of adoration, "My Lord and my God!" but also pronounces a blessing on all who make a similar confession (John 20:28-29).

Though the language used by the Synoptic Gospels concerning Jesus as the Son of God differs from that of the Fourth Gospel, the impression that they make on the reader is the same: Jesus both claims and receives the honor that is rendered only to the Deity. In addition to a dozen or so Synoptic passages where the title "the Son of God" is applied to him by others, with his express approval (such as Matt. 16:16; Mark 3:11; 5:7; 14:61; Luke 8:28), both Q and Mark represent Jesus as speaking of himself as "the Son" or calling God his Father in a new and unique way (see the discussion of *Abba*, pp. 171-72). Both directly (in his acknowledgment before Caiaphas, Mark 14:62) and indirectly (in the parable of the wicked tenants, Mark 12:1-9) Jesus makes claim to be not only God's son, but the one beloved Son of the Father, who will come with the clouds of heaven. In one of the most important christological passages in the New Testament, preserved in Q (Matt. 11:27; Luke 10:22), Jesus speaks of his "unshared sonship": "All things have been handed over to me by my Father; and no one knows the Son except the Father, and no one knows the Father except the Son and anyone to whom the Son chooses to reveal him." Here, in the oldest literary stratum of the Synoptics, and with language that is every bit as exalted as that used in the Fourth Gospel, Jesus claims not only that he alone stands in a special relation to God, but also that he is the only one through whom others can be brought into a similar relation.

In addition to such direct claims of Jesus as the foregoing to be the unique Son of God, the Gospels contain also many indirect testimonies that point in the same direction. More than once Jesus implies that in his person and work something new and joyous and wonderful has come into the world. When he is reproved because his disciples do not observe the traditional Jewish fasts, he replies that so long as he is with them, fasting is as inappropriate as it would be at a wedding (Matt. 9:14-15; Mark 2:18-19; Luke 5:33-35).

On another occasion when referring to King Solomon and his reputation for wisdom, Jesus declares that in himself and his kingdom "something greater than Solomon is here!" (Matt. 12:42; Luke 11:31).

Jesus takes for granted that he has the authority to forgive sins, a prerogative that his enemies correctly recognize belongs to God alone (Mark 2:5-7; Luke 5:21). He quietly assumes that all people will one day stand before him to be judged, not only as to their deeds, but also as to their motives, which only God can discern (Matt. 7:22-23; 25:31-46). He makes demands that individuals give themselves in utter self-committal to himself, as one who knows his cause to be the cause of God. For example, "Everyone therefore who acknowledges me before others, I also will acknowledge before my Father in heaven" (Matt. 10:32), and "Whoever loves father or mother more than me is not worthy of me; and whoever loves son or daughter more than me is not worthy of me; and whoever does not take up the cross and follow me is not worthy of me" (Matt. 10:37; compare Luke 14:26-27). In these and similar sayings, the whole worth of a person's life and destiny hinges upon that person's relation to Jesus.

The "I" sayings, often thought to be characteristic solely of Johannine theology (see p. 144), are present also in the Synoptic record. Jesus' Sermon on the Mount represents him as putting his own pronouncements on a par with those attributed by the Old Testament to God himself ("You have heard that it was said . . . but I say to you," Matt. 5:21-22, 27-28, 31-32, 38-39, 43-44). The same sovereign "I," suggestive of Jesus' self-consciousness, appears in many other sayings; for example, "I will give you rest" (Matt. 11:28); "I have come to call not the righteous but sinners" (Mark 2:17); and "I came to bring fire to the earth" (Luke 12:49). These are amazing statements whose wonder we often fail to appreciate because familiarity has dulled our perception.

Even Jesus' characteristic use of the word *amen,* usually translated into English as "verily" or "truly," implies a finality and an authority of his message quite unparalleled elsewhere. The entire range of Jewish literature knows of no example of a scribe or rabbinical teacher prefacing his remarks with the expression, "Verily *(amen),* I say to you. . . . " This solemn formula, however, appears thirty times in Matthew, thirteen times in Mark, six times in Luke, and twenty-five times in John (who usually doubles the word, "Verily, verily . . . "). The sayings that are thus prefixed are of varied individual content, but most of them have to do with Jesus' own person, either as Messiah or as demanding faith in his messiahship in spite of outward appearances and mistaken views. The point of the *amen* before such sayings is to show that their truth is guaranteed because Jesus himself, in his *amen*, acknowledges them to be his own sayings, thus making them valid. The whole implication is that through this characteristic mode of speech Jesus affirms his unique authority, presenting himself as one who speaks in the name and with the sanction of God himself. The reader is not surprised, therefore, to be told at the close of Jesus' Sermon on the Mount that "the crowds were astounded at his teaching, for he taught them as one having authority, and not as their scribes" (Matt. 7:28-29).

From what has been said it will be seen that an exalted view of Jesus' person is pervasive throughout all four Gospels. His words and attitudes reported in the earliest literary strata of the Synoptic Gospels are not different in kind (though many are different in language) from his testimony reported in the Fourth Gospel. After making the most rigorous examination of the sources, one must conclude that Jesus of Nazareth, in his bearing as well as in his words, made claim to be the unique Son of God.[8]

It was because of this lofty claim that Jesus was condemned to death by those who regarded him guilty of blasphemy (Mark 14:61-64). Of all of Jesus' teaching, therefore, none can be said to be more surely grounded in history, for without this element there is nothing in his life that can satisfactorily account for the inveterate acrimony and hostility that pursued him to the death. The attitude of orthodox Jewish piety is summed up in the taunt that was flung at him as he hung on the cross, "If you are the Son of God, come down from the cross" (Matt. 27:40; compare verses 41-44).

---

8. It has often been pointed out that Jesus' claim to be the only Son of God is either true or false. If it is true, (1) he is properly worshiped as God. If it is false, he either knew the claim was false or he did not know that it was false. In the former case, (2) he was a liar; in the latter case, (3) he was a lunatic. No other conclusion besides these three is possible.

4. JESUS' TEACHING CONCERNING ONE'S DUTIES AND RELATIONSHIPS

According to Jesus, one's duties are twofold—those that concern one's relation to God and those that concern other people. When he was asked which was the primary commandment, Jesus declared that the love of God and the love of one's neighbor sum up all of one's obligations.

> The first [commandment] is, "Hear, O Israel: the Lord our God, the Lord is one; and you shall love the Lord your God with all your heart, and with all your soul, and with all your mind, and with all your strength." The second is this, "You shall love your neighbor as yourself." There is no other commandment greater than these. (Mark 12:29-31, quoted from Deut. 6:4 and Lev. 19:18)

(i) One's Relationship to God

If the command to love God stands first in one's relationship to God, it does not stand alone. Not only must one love God; one must also, says Jesus, fear God. "I tell you, my friends, do not fear those who kill the body, and after that can do nothing more. But I will warn you whom to fear: fear him who, after he has killed, has authority to cast into hell. Yes, I tell you, fear him!" (Luke 12:4-5). Here the reference is not to the devil, who nowhere in Jesus' teaching is represented as having "authority to cast into hell," but to God, who alone has sovereign power to give life and to withhold life. The fact that God has had mercy on someone and has not cast him or her into hell does not alter the basic presupposition that in God's hands are one's eternal destinies, and therefore one's attitude toward God must be one of fear, that is, profound awe and reverence. To those who lack such awe and reverence the question is directed, more in warning than in threat, "How can you escape being sentenced to hell?" (Matt. 23:33).

Related to the attitude of awe that one must have toward God is Jesus' teaching that all persons are sinners. Jesus never speaks of sin in the abstract, but always of specific sins, which are called "debts" (Matt. 6:12) or "trespasses" (Matt. 6:14-15). He describes people of his generation as sinful and faithless (Mark 8:38; 9:19), and takes for granted that this is their natural condition (Matt. 7:11).

Jesus' conception of the essence of sin differs from that prevalent in Judaism. Instead of regarding sin as basically the violation of a law of God, he taught that its heinousness lies in one's refusal to live in accordance with the will of God. It is not enough, he taught, for one merely to refrain from those actions that violate the negative commandments of the Old Testament; one must also seek to fulfill positively the purpose that God had in mind when he expressed his will in negative commands. Thus, Jesus taught that the inward preliminary attitude of anger against another or of lustful thoughts is sinful, even though it may not eventuate in the overt act of murder or adultery (Matt. 5:21-22, 27-28). Merely to refrain from outward acts that violate negative commands does not make one righteous in God's sight; one must fulfill God's positive purpose in behalf of the other person's welfare when God forbade murder and adultery. It is in this sense that one must understand Jesus' declaration, "For I tell you, unless your righteousness exceeds that of the scribes and Pharisees, you will never enter the kingdom of heaven" (Matt. 5:20).

A significant part of Jesus' teaching about one's relationship to God concerns the development of the spiritual life. Always opposed to insincerity in the name of religion, he insisted that prayer and almsgiving should not be done for show (Matt. 6:1-8), nor should fasting be ostentatious (Matt. 6:16-18). In accordance with his disciples' request (Luke 11:1), Jesus composed and taught his followers a model prayer, commonly called the Lord's Prayer. They were to use this along with other prayers and benedictions current in contemporary Jewish piety and the synagogue service.

Two forms of the Lord's Prayer have been preserved, one in Matthew 6:9-13 and the other in Luke 11:2-4. The Matthean form is the longer of the two, and was taken over by the church universal.

According to the Matthean form, after the invocation the body of the prayer falls into two main parts, one containing three petitions concerned with God's glory, and the other containing petitions concerned with our personal needs. The concluding doxology, which is not present in the earliest manuscripts of the New Testament, was added by the ancient church for liturgical reasons; it is modeled after a prayer of David in the Old Testament (1 Chron. 29:11-13). A traditional wording of the Matthean form of the Lord's Prayer with the concluding doxology, is as follows:

(Invocation)	Our Father who art in heaven,
(First part)	hallowed be thy name.
	Thy kingdom come.
	thy will be done,
	on earth as it is in heaven.
(Second part)	Give us this day our daily bread.
	And forgive us our debts,
	as we forgive our debtors.
	And lead us not into temptation,
	but deliver us from evil.
(Doxology)	For thine is the kingdom, and the power,
	and the glory, for ever. Amen.

Several points in the prayer deserve special comment:

(*a*) It is to be observed that the prayer is cast in such a form as to imply that Jesus' disciples are not to pray for themselves without praying for others at the same time. Thus, in addition to addressing God as "our Father," petitions are made in terms of "our bread" and "our debts."

(*b*) The phrase, "on earth as it is in heaven," is probably to be taken with all three petitions of the first part, and not merely with the third petition. The sense, then, is: "Hallowed be thy name, on earth as it is in heaven. Thy kingdom come, on earth as it is in heaven. Thy will be done, on earth as it is in heaven."

(*c*) Two different forms of the fifth petition are in current use, going back to different English translations of the Bible. "Forgive us our trespasses, as we forgive them that trespass against us" is essentially William Tyndale's rendering of 1526, which, having been adopted by the Anglican *Book of Common Prayer,* gained wide currency. Most other English translations of the Bible, including the King James Version of 1611, read, "Forgive us our debts, as we forgive our debtors." *Debts* is the literal rendering of the Greek word used in the Matthean text of the Lord's Prayer; *trespasses* is an interpretative rendering of the same Greek word. The translation *debts* suggests that sins are acts by which a person robs God of God's rights and therefore incurs an obligation or debt for which one can only appeal to God's mercy. The translation *trespasses* emphasizes the idea that one's sins violate the divine commandments by going beyond what is prescribed.

This petition embodies Jesus' characteristic doctrine that divine forgiveness can come only to those who themselves show a forgiving spirit. By itself our refusal to forgive others prevents our obtaining forgiveness from God, but our forgiving others will not, by itself, secure forgiveness from God. God's grace is given, not earned.

(d) The words, "this day our daily bread," make it clear that Jesus intended that the prayer should be used every day. "Bread" signifies the necessities of life; nothing is said about luxuries.

(e) The word "but" in the last petition shows that it is in two parts. Temptation is always in the way: therefore we pray, not that it may not exist, but that it may not affect or overpower us.

(ii) One's Relationship with Others

The ethical demands of Jesus upon his followers are summed up in what has come to be called "the Golden Rule" ("golden" because it is considered to be excellent or supreme). The negative form of the Golden Rule was enunciated long before the Christian Era by Chinese, Hindu, and Greek philosophers. Nearer to Jesus' day it also appears in Jewish intertestamental literature. Tobit gives advice to his son in terms of refraining from evil: "What you hate, do not do to anyone" (Tobit 4:15). Jesus, however, phrases the rule positively: "In everything do to others as you would have them do to you; for this is the law and the prophets" (Matt. 7:12). The positive formulation in the mouth of Jesus surpasses the negative formulation of previous teachers just as far as "to help and to benefit" surpasses "not to injure."

An ethical ideal such as this cannot in the nature of things be reduced to precise rules of conduct; it is basically a matter of personal attitude. At the same time Jesus left no excuse for supposing that a vague feeling of benevolence is all that is required. Good intentions without action are not sufficient (Matt. 7:15-27). Jesus appealed to the imagination by concrete examples illustrating the kind of conduct to which a right attitude would lead. Thus, "if anyone strikes you on the right cheek, turn the other also"; "if anyone forces you to go one mile, go also the second mile"; "give to everyone who begs from you, and do not refuse anyone who wants to borrow from you" (Matt. 5:39, 41-42; Luke 6:29-30). These are not legal regulations. If they were, it would be relevant to point out that to turn the other cheek may in some circumstances be a most provocative act, that to help a robber or a murderer on their way is not philanthropic conduct, and that indiscriminate charity may have disastrous effects. They are proverb-like maxims (see pp. 164-65), which are intended to stimulate the imagination in making concrete the kind of action called for by the statement, "Be merciful, just as your Father is merciful" (Luke 6:36).

Such teaching offers the hearer not an ethic of precept but an ethic of principle. Instead of drawing up a code of detailed regulations, Jesus laid on his disciples the responsibility of making individual application of the underlying principle. Thus, when Jesus concluded his parable of the good Samaritan by saying, "Go and do likewise" (Luke 10:37), he did not mean, "Wait until a precisely identical situation turns up, and then obey my instructions"; he meant that everyone should live in such a spirit that he or she will respond almost instinctively to meet the varied needs of others.

That this was Jesus' intention is shown most clearly in the Beatitudes, which Matthew places at the beginning of the Sermon on the Mount. Each of these pithy sayings describes the character of the citizen of the kingdom of heaven. The emphasis is not so much on doing such and such things, but on being such and such persons: "Blessed are the poor in spirit, . . . the meek, . . . the merciful, . . . the pure in heart" (Matt. 5:3-9).

The chief danger in working out an ethic is that one may imagine that by keeping certain precepts one has earned God's graciousness. It was to counteract such an assumption that Jesus told his parable of the Pharisee and the tax collector (Luke 18:10-14). Here he contrasts the attitude of the self-righteous man who speaks boastfully of his own pious conduct, and the attitude of one who is conscious of his unworthiness in God's sight and who humbles himself before God. So far from being proud of their accomplishments, the disciples are admonished by Jesus, "When you have done all that you were ordered to do, say, 'We are worthless slaves, we have done only what we ought to have done!'" (Luke 17:10).

From what has been said thus far, it is clear what we can expect and what we cannot expect to find in the moral teaching of Jesus.

That he had no idea of initiating legislation, for his own time or the future, is evident from the character of his sayings; these could—most of them—never be embodied in laws. When his enemies tried to force from him some political pronouncement, he was content with the profound but enigmatical reply, "Give . . . to the emperor the things that are the emperor's, and to God the things that are God's" (Matt. 22:21; Mark 12:17; Luke 20:25). Here he seems to suggest that honor and taxes must be paid to lawfully constituted government (compare also Matt. 17:24-27).

When Jesus was asked for his opinion concerning the grounds on which divorce might be secured (Mark 10:2-12), he sided with neither of the two current views. The followers of Rabbi Shammai interpreted the Mosaic legislation strictly (Deut. 24:1) and permitted divorce only on the grounds of unchastity; the followers of Rabbi Hillel interpreted the same statute broadly and allowed a man to divorce his wife for the most trivial of reasons—including even that of putting too much seasoning in his food! Going behind the established framework of legal technicalities of divorce, Jesus offers a new and creative interpretation of God's institution of marriage. To his questioners he says, in effect: Your whole idea of marriage, with its possibility of remarriage after divorce, is wrong. From the beginning God's will has been that marriage shall be life-long. You forced Moses to make concessions to suit your hardness of heart. But to divorce and remarry during the lifetime of your partner is to commit adultery (Mark 10:6-12; Luke 16:18).[9] Here

---

9. Matthew differs from Mark and Luke in his report of Jesus' teaching about divorce, and inserts the words "except for unchastity" (Matt. 19:9; compare also 5:32), thus representing Jesus as siding with the view of Shammai. The addition of this excepting clause, as it is called, reflects an attempt in the early church to adjust the high ideal of Jesus' interpretation of the indissolubility of marriage to suit the exigencies of those whose hearts, like men's hearts in the days of Moses, were still hard! Such an adjustment of Jesus' teaching fell within the power to bind and loose given to the apostles—that is, power to adapt laws and make exceptions (Matt. 16:19 and 18:18; see p. 62).

Two reasons, among others, why the Matthean form of Jesus' saying on divorce must be regarded as a modification of his teaching are: (1) If it is original, then the report without the excepting clause in Mark and Luke represents an advance made by the early church upon the standards set by Jesus—and this is not likely to have happened; and (2) the excepting clause does not harmonize with the context in Matthew. (If Jesus sided with the Shammites, why should the disciples be amazed at the strictness of his teaching and exclaim, "If such is the case, . . . it is better not to marry" [Matt. 19:10]? And in the context of Matthew 5:32, Jesus is substituting the perfect standard of God for the standard recognized by the Jews of his day [Matt. 5:17-48]; but if the exceptive clause is retained, his teaching is no higher than Shammai's.)

Jesus is not thinking of marriage as a civil institution, universal in human society in some shape; but of marriage as it was intended to be in God's purpose, and in the hearts of those who enter into it with that purpose in mind. Those who are thus joined are no longer two but one, and so divorce is unthinkable.

On other questions of sexual morality Jesus teaches more by example than by explicit prescription. Naturally, he has nothing tosay on homosexuality (which was very rare among the Jews), or on birth control or premarital incontinence. But could anything go further than his identification of the licentious gaze with the licentious act? ("Everyone who looks at a woman with lust has already committed adultery with her in his heart," Matt. 5:28.) Likewise his courtesy to all the women with whom he came in contact—from his own mother to the much married Samaritan woman (John 4:18) and the woman of the streets (Luke 7:36-50)—involved, primarily, a condemnation of the contemporary disparagement of women, an attitude that even his own disciples appear to have shared (Matt. 19:13); and indirectly it raised all women to a level where it was impossible to regard them either as playthings or instruments to fulfill the desires of men. At the same time Jesus was no prude. Unchastity appeared to fill him with a sense of shame (John 8:6), yet he never inveighed against it as he inveighed against pharisaic hypocrisy. He gave his friendship to the unchaste, and by his friendship he redeemed them. In short, by his attitude toward women, as also toward Samaritans and other outcasts, he undermined the contemporary Jewish ethic that placed womankind and foreigners on a level inferior to that of the sons of Jacob.[10] For Jesus every individual was equally important in the sight of God.

---

10. The daily prayer of all male Jews during the early centuries of the Christian Era included the following:

"Blessed art thou, O Lord our God, King of the universe, who hast not made me a heathen.

"Blessed art thou, O Lord our God, King of the universe, who hast not made me a bondman.

"Blessed art thou, O Lord our God, King of the universe, who hast not made me a woman."

It may be added that these blessings remain part of the Orthodox Jewish liturgy today. In the widely used volume *Daily Prayer,* edited by Rabbi M. Stern (New York: Hebrew Publishing Co., 1928), the rubric after the last mentioned blessing directs women to say, "Blessed art thou, O Lord our God, King of the universe, who hast made me according to thy will."

(iii) Rewards for Doing God's Will

Finally, something should be said about Jesus' teaching concerning rewards for doing the will of God. More than once he spoke to his disciples about laying up for themselves treasures in heaven and about the rewards that those who follow his teaching may expect to receive here and hereafter (Matt. 5:12, 46; 6:20; Mark 9:41; 10:21; Luke 6:23, 35). It is sometimes objected that such a doctrine is merely a cloak for prudent self-betterment, and that one ought to believe in and practice virtue for virtue's sake and not for the sake of a reward.

A fuller examination of Jesus' ethical teaching, however, will reveal that he completely reoriented the idea of the nature of rewards as well as the question of their being inducements (or bribes) for living the good life. When Jesus advised his followers, "Store up for yourselves treasures in heaven" (Matt. 6:20; Luke 12:33), his meaning is not: Take steps to get in heaven the things people treasure on earth; but, learn to treasure, to love, and delight in the things of heaven. Those who hunger and thirst for righteousness will be rewarded by increasing in righteousness (Matt. 5:6), nor will one who really thirsts for righteousness expect something else as a reward. The rewards offered by Jesus to the righteous are not simply tacked on to the activity for which they are given, but are the activity itself in consummation.

Furthermore, Jesus' doctrine of reward is completely unmercenary. In the parables of the laborers in the vineyard (Matt. 20:1-15) and of the slave who has no claim to the thanks of his master (Luke 17:7-10), Jesus distinctly opposes all human calculation of rewards from God and denies that anyone can have any kind of claim before God. Precisely these parables, which speak of reward, make it especially clear that reward is, after all, a gift of God's grace. Moreover, in the parable of the last judgment (Matt. 25:31-46), those accounted worthy of eternal life are amazed to find it so, for they are completely unaware of having done anything to deserve it. The others, however, are rejected because, as indeed their excuses make plain, without the prospect of reward they could not be moved to do a deed of love for those in need. In short, Jesus promises reward to those who are obedient to God's will without thought of reward.

APPENDIX: THE ORIGINALITY OF
JESUS' ETHICAL TEACHING

Some have argued that the teaching of Jesus on moral questions lacks originality and merely repeats the Jewish ethic of his predecessors. Thus Rabbi Joseph Klausner, in his book *Jesus of Nazareth, His Life, Times and Teaching,* says emphatically, "Throughout the Gospels there is not one item of ethical teaching which cannot be paralleled either in the Old Testament, the Apocrypha, or in the Talmudic and Midrashic literature of the period near to the time of Jesus."[11]

It may readily be granted that Jesus owes much to the tradition of his people, but this is not the whole story. In taking over the traditional ethic, he transformed it into something new in at least the following respects:

(1) Jesus selected from the enormous accumulation of traditions of the elders those elements that he deemed vital. The Mosaic legislation as understood by the Pharisees was cleared of all irrelevant side issues and reduced to its controlling principles. Certainly genius is involved in making a wise selection!

(2) Though Jesus adopted certain current Jewish maxims, sometimes in identical words, he gave them a different emphasis. He threw the weight on inward motive rather than on outward prescription. Both he and contemporary scribes spoke of the law of God, but the latter commonly stressed the word *law* whereas he emphasized the word *God.*

(3) Not only did he single out the cardinal principles, but he grasped them in their ultimate bearings. He took up the old command to love one's neighbor—which meant love for one's fellow Israelite (Lev. 19:18)—and showed that it implied love and concern for *all* people, exercised without reserve.

(4) In the last analysis, what is important concerning the originality of Jesus' teaching is not the amount of new material, whether great or small, that he brought; it is the way in which he has linked this teaching with a new religious conception and a new religious experience. The end of all ethical teaching is not knowledge but action. Everyone recognizes that the chief problem is how to change

---

11. Rabbi Joseph Klausner, *Jesus of Nazareth, His Life, Times and Teaching* (New York: Macmillan, 1925), p. 384.

knowledge into performance. The important element in the ministry of Jesus is that he inspired others to follow his teaching.

How is one to explain the dynamic quality in his message? To this question no final answer is possible, but it is not difficult to perceive that the power of his teaching was partly due, at any rate, to his intense realization of the reality of what he taught. The truths might themselves be old, but no one before him had grasped them with such absolute conviction. Others had applied the name "Father" to God, but the point is that when Jesus called God "Father" he *knew* him as the Father. He was able to communicate to others his personal assurance of the truth of what he taught.

A second reason that accounts in great measure for Jesus' power as a teacher is that he so identified himself with his teaching that obedience to it became a matter of personal loyalty to him. There are few who can follow an abstract ideal; all are capable of devotion to a person. It was the supreme achievement of Jesus as a teacher that he exemplified in himself all that he taught. Thus he made it possible for his disciples to identify the moral law with a personal leader who evoked their love and confidence. The ultimate secret of Jesus' originality and power is intimately related to who he was and what he accomplished in behalf of his followers.

PART THREE

THE APOSTOLIC AGE

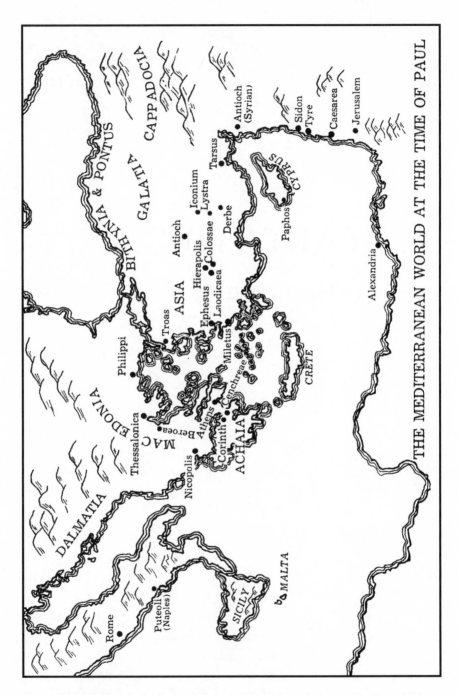

THE MEDITERRANEAN WORLD AT THE TIME OF PAUL

(from The New Testament: Its Background, Growth, and Content *by Bruce Metzger*
© 1965-1983 *by Abingdon Press. Used by permission.)*

CHAPTER 7

THE SOURCES AND THE CHRONOLOGY OF THE APOSTOLIC AGE

For our knowledge of Christianity in the apostolic age—a period that extended from about A.D. 30 to about A.D. 100—the historian is dependent practically upon the books that compose the New Testament. To be sure, there are several extracanonical sources, but these furnish little, if any, detailed information. The disputed passage concerning Jesus Christ in Josephus's *Antiquities* (see p. 90) concludes with the comment, "And even to this day [i.e., about A.D. 93] the tribe of Christians, who are named after him, has not died out." The Roman writers of the early Christian period who mention the new religion (see pp. 93-94) do so from an external point of view, and are valuable chiefly in corroborating what can be learned in far greater detail from documents written by early Christians.

Of noncanonical Christian writings produced during the second and succeeding centuries, those known as apocryphal acts of the apostle (such as the Acts of Paul, the Acts of Peter, the Acts of John, the Acts of Thomas, and the Acts of Andrew) refer to persons and events in the apostolic church. It will be obvious, however, to anyone who reads these apocryphal acts that they are merely romanticized and legendary accounts that tell us far more about the interests and mentality of their unknown authors of the second and succeeding centuries than they do about the first-century apostles whose deeds they purport to record.[1]

---

1. An English translation of most of the apocryphal acts is provided by M. R. James, *The Apocryphal New Testament,* and the other books mentioned in the note 15 on page 118. For a translation and discussion of the episode of Paul and the Baptized Lion, reference may be made to B. M. Metzger, *An Introduction to the Apocrypha* (New York: Oxford University Press, 1957), pp. 252-62. For a variety of recent studies, one may consult *The Apocryphal Acts of the Apostles: Harvard University Divinity School Studies,* ed. by François Bovon, et al. (Cambridge, Mass.: Harvard University Press, 1999).

The most important documents that provide information concerning the origin, expansion, and experiences of the early church are the Acts of the Apostles and the twenty-one letters that are included in the New Testament. The several authors of these letters record, each from his own point of view, aspects of the life and witness of Christianity in the eastern and north central areas of the Mediterranean world. Information about each of these letters will be given in chapters 10 and 11; it is enough to say here that, as a literary form, letters offer an opportunity for the author to combine in one document profound theological content with a direct personal approach to the reader. The historian today especially values ancient correspondence because it supplies information not only concerning the thinking of the writer, but also concerning the circumstances of the recipients.

I. THE ACTS OF THE APOSTLES

The chief source for our knowledge of the primitive church is the anonymous treatise known as the Acts of the Apostles, which now stands in the New Testament as an appropriate link between the preceding four Gospels and the following twenty-one letters. Because it is dedicated to Theophilus[2] the same person to whom the Gospel of Luke is addressed (Acts 1:1; Luke 1:1-4), and because the style and vocabulary of both books are strikingly similar, it is generally held that the two were written by the same author. According to early tradition this was Luke, a physician and companion of the apostle Paul (Col. 4:14; 2 Tim. 4:11; Philem. 24). From the way in which Paul mentions Luke, seeming to differentiate him from those who were of Jewish background (Col. 4:11 compared with verses 12-14), it appears that Luke was of Gentile birth. If so, he is the only known Gentile whose writings are included in the Bible. According to a tradition preserved in a second-century prologue to the Third Gospel, Luke was a Syrian of Antioch, who became a Christian convert in midlife after the church had been established at Antioch.

---

2. The name Theophilus means "dear to God," "friend of God." The title given to him, "most excellent" (Luke 1:3), marks Theophilus as a man of considerable social standing, perhaps the holder of a high political position (compare Acts 23:26; 24:3) or a member of the aristocracy.

1. LUKE AS A HISTORIAN

To write a historical work the author must obtain information. Whether he writes a good history depends upon two things: his raw materials, or sources, and his own powers of analysis and synthesis. How does Luke's reputation as a historian fare in these respects?

From the prologue to the Third Gospel (Luke 1:1-4) we learn that Luke made an effort to ascertain from eyewitnesses a reliable account of the life and ministry of Jesus Christ. By examining how he dealt with the Gospel of Mark we can see that he proceeded in a highly intelligent way to utilize for his own purposes a previously written source. In the opening sentence of his second volume, Luke indicates that he is writing a sequel to his first book, telling what happened to the Christian movement after Jesus' ascension (Acts 1:1-2).

It was no easy task to write the first history of the Christian church. The new religion had spread rapidly to many lands around the northeastern Mediterranean world. Within thirty or forty years after the death of Jesus, every major city of Asia Minor, Greece, and Italy had one or more Christian congregations. To learn who were the chief leaders in the missionary work and to sift the more significant events from those of merely local importance required not only the collecting of information, but also the arranging and evaluating of materials. Considering the difficulties that faced him, Luke prepared a remarkably well-ordered account. Instead of providing merely a chronicle of events and a list of the names of new converts, Luke simplified and arranged his materials as regards both geography and biography.

(a) The range of Luke's geographical interests is indicated by his mentioning in Acts no fewer than thirty-two countries, fifty-four cities, and nine of the Mediterranean islands. These are not introduced indiscriminately or haphazardly, but in an orderly way as he traces the story of the Christian movement from Jerusalem, the small and utterly provincial city of the Jews, to the arrival of the apostle Paul at Rome, the dazzling capital of the Roman Empire. Within these two termini, and spanning a period of about a third of a century, Luke arranges his material in what has been described as six "panels," each concluding with a summarizing comment that

197

looks back over the events just related and sums up the success attained. An analytical outline of his book is as follows (it must be remembered that all such outlines are of modern construction and may not always coincide with the original author's intentions):

First period (Acts 1:1–6:7). Early episodes in the Jerusalem church, including the coming of the Holy Spirit at the day of Pentecost and the subsequent preaching of Peter: summary, "The word of God continued to spread; the number of the disciples increased greatly in Jerusalem, and a great many of the priests became obedient to the faith" (6:7).

Second period (6:8–9:31). Extension of the church through Palestine; the preaching of Stephen, culminating in his martyrdom; troubles with the Jews: summary, "Meanwhile the church throughout Judea, Galilee, and Samaria had peace and was built up. Living in the fear of the Lord and in the comfort of the Holy Spirit, it increased in numbers" (9:31).

Third period (9:32–12:24). Extension of the church to Antioch; the preaching of Peter and the conversion of Cornelius; further troubles with the Jews and persecution by Herod Agrippa I: summary, "But the word of God continued to advance and gain adherents" (12:24).

Fourth period (12:25–16:5). Extension of the church to southern and central Asia Minor; Paul's first missionary journey to Cyprus and several cities of Asia Minor; controversies with Jewish Christians and the convening of the apostolic council at Jerusalem: summary, "So the churches were strengthened in the faith and increased in numbers daily" (16:5).

Fifth period (16:6–19:20). Extension of the church to Europe; Paul's second and third missionary journeys to such great centers as Philippi, Athens, Corinth, and Ephesus: summary, "So the word of the Lord grew mightily and prevailed" (19:20).

Sixth period (19:21–28:31). Extension of the church to Rome; Paul's arrest and subsequent hearings in Jerusalem and Caesarea; his voyage to Rome, where he was kept under house arrest, but was free to preach to any who came to him: concluding summary, "He lived there two whole years at his own expense and welcomed all who came to him, proclaiming the kingdom of God and teaching about the Lord Jesus Christ with all boldness and without hindrance" (28:30-31).

(b) Luke also simplifies his narrative as regards biography; though ninety-five different persons[3] are mentioned in the book of Acts, only a few are singled out for special attention. The first three sections of his book are dominated by Peter, and the last three sections by Paul. The only other persons in Acts who are at all individualized are Stephen and Philip in the first half of the book, and Barnabas and James the brother of Jesus[4] in the second half. It is remarkable that of these six leaders in the early church only one of them (Peter) had been a member of the original band of twelve apostles.

From what has been said thus far of Luke's work, it will be appreciated that he writes with skill and intelligence. Indeed, the import of the preface to his Gospel (Luke 1:1-4) shows that he was concerned to write a historical work that would command respect among cultured persons. But the successful writing of a historical document, as was mentioned earlier, requires not only literary competence on the part of the author; it is also necessary that the historian have access to reliable source material. What were the sources, both written and oral, available to Luke? The following have been suggested, with more or less probability, as sources lying behind the book of Acts.

(1) In three sections of Acts (16:10-17; 20:5–21:18; and 27:1–28:16) the author changes his style from the third person ("he," "him," "they," "them") to the first person plural ("we," "our," "us"). These "we" passages give the impression that the author was present and participated in the events that he describes. It may be that in these passages, which contain a wealth of details, Luke utilized notes that he had kept in diary form. If this is so, the "we" passages rest upon written sources drawn up by an eyewitness.

(2) At Antioch a copy of the decrees of the apostolic council (Acts 21:25) may have been available to Luke.

(3) It is not improbable that there were written archives in the possession of the church at Jerusalem that Luke would have been able to consult.

---

3. Of the ninety-five persons, sixty-two are not mentioned by any other New Testament writer and twenty-seven are nonbelievers (chiefly civil or military officials).

4. On the brothers of Jesus, see note 1 on page 288.

The "we" sections provide evidence of the author's presence in a variety of places and in company with various persons, from whom he could have secured additional information for his history of the church. Among the possible oral sources that have been suggested are the following:

(4) While living at Antioch Luke may have received information concerning the Herodian dynasty from Manaen (Acts 13:1), an Antiochian Christian who was a member of the court of Herod the tetrarch. In this way one could account for the fact that among the four Gospels the one by Luke contains the most detailed information about the Herodian family.

(5) Luke's intimate acquaintance with Paul would have enabled him to secure information concerning the earlier life and work of the apostle before they became companions.[5]

(6) At Caesarea Luke stayed in the home of Philip the evangelist (Acts 21:8), from whom he could have learned about events that led to the appointment of the Seven (Acts 6:1-6), as well as Philip's experience with the Ethiopian official (8:26-40).

(7) In Acts 21:16 reference is made to the author's lodging with a certain "Mnason of Cyprus, an early disciple." It is possible that Luke learned from him concerning affairs of the church in Cyprus, which, so far as we know, Luke himself had never visited.

(8) While in Jerusalem, Luke would have had opportunity to consult with James, from whom he may have learned about the apostolic council (Acts 15:1-29) and other events in Judea of importance concerning the growing church.

(9) Finally, from remarks made by Paul at the close of several of his letters (e.g., Colossians and Philemon), it appears that Silas and Timothy were with Paul when Luke was also present. From these and other leaders in the early church Luke would have had opportunity to glean further information.

2. LUKE'S PURPOSE AND SPECIAL INTERESTS

A careful examination of the two-volume work of Luke-Acts will disclose something of the author's purpose and special interests.

---

5. However it may be explained, Luke does not seem to have used any of Paul's Letters as source material.

(a) It is obvious that Luke wishes to prove that Christianity is not politically dangerous. He does this by citing favorable judgments of governors, magistrates, and other authorities in various parts of the empire. In his Gospel, Luke mentions that the governor Pontius Pilate had three times declared that Jesus was not guilty of sedition (Luke 23:4, 14, 22), and in the Acts he emphasizes that similar charges against Christians could not be sustained. For example, though Paul and Silas are imprisoned at Philippi for interfering with the rights of private ownership of a slave girl, the magistrates (praetors) finally release them and apologize for their illegal arrest (Acts 16:39). When Paul and his companions are accused of sedition before the city officials (politarchs) of Thessalonica, the latter require no more than the assurance of citizens of that place who will guarantee the missionaries' good behavior (17:6-9). Later when Jewish leaders of Corinth accuse Paul of propagating an illicit religion, the proconsul Gallio dismisses the case (18:12-17). The town clerk of Ephesus exonerates Paul from the charge of blaspheming the Ephesian goddess Artemis (19:37-41). In Judea, the tribune Claudius Lysias (23:29), the governor Festus (25:25), and King Herod Agrippa II (26:31-32) agree that Paul had done nothing to justify the indictment brought against him by his opponents, the Jewish leaders in Jerusalem. Thus Luke repeatedly emphasizes that Christianity is not politically dangerous; obviously his purpose is to win sympathy and remove any prejudice against the new religion.

(b) Another of Luke's interests in writing Acts is to show the activity of the Holy Spirit in the founding and growth of the church. The book might appropriately be entitled "The Acts of the Holy Spirit," for the dominating theme is the power of the Spirit manifested in the members of the early church. The outpouring of the Spirit at Pentecost (2:1-13) is described as a supernatural event that sent the apostles into the streets of Jerusalem and far beyond with a message of new power and conviction. Those who carry on Jesus' work of preaching and healing are described as being "full of the Spirit" (Acts 6:3, 5, 8; 7:55; 11:24). By the prompting of the Spirit new areas of evangelistic work are opened; thus, Philip (8:29, 39), Peter (10:19-20), Barnabas and Paul (13:2), and Paul and his companions (16:6-10) are guided by the Spirit to more extended service. Furthermore, besides the apostles and teachers in the early church there seems to have been also a special group known as prophets (Acts 13:1; compare 1 Cor. 12:28-29; Eph. 4:11). Like the prophets of ancient Israel, they exercised a double function of proclamation and prediction. By the Holy Spirit a prophet named Agabus foresaw an impending famine and issued spiritual guidance to the church (Acts 14:27-29). On another occasion the Holy Spirit prompted Agabus to predict the persecutions that lay in store for Paul (21:10-11).

It should not be imagined that Luke's emphasis on the activity of the Holy Spirit and his concern to show that Christianity was not a menace to Roman law and order have diminished the trustworthiness of his book as history. Though his special interests have controlled the selection and presentation of the facts, the detailed accuracy of his work has been confirmed more than once by archaeological discoveries. One of the most impressive examples of Luke's care for details is in the titles of Roman officials who are mentioned throughout his work. The variety of the forms of local and provincial government in the Roman Empire meant that various places were governed by such officials as asiarchs, politarchs, praetors, procurators, consuls, client kings, and so forth. Furthermore, when the status of a Roman province was changed, the titles of provincial governors also changed. It is a noteworthy fact that time after time such references in Acts prove to be just right for the place and time in question.[6] Furthermore, with a minimum of words Luke manages to convey the true local color of widely differing cities mentioned in his account. Even in the use of technical terms relating to ancient seamanship Luke exhibits a remarkable acquaintance with the special lingo of sailors and navigators. The sum total of these many instances of appropriate terminology is impressive testimony not only to Luke's wide knowledge but also to a native accuracy of mind.

3. SPEECHES AND SERMONS IN THE BOOK OF ACTS

About one fifth of the book of Acts is made up of the reports of speeches and sermons of early Christian leaders. With remarkable literary skill Luke conveys to the reader a variety of nuances that

---

6. For examples of Luke's use of seven of these titles, see section (a) on p. 201.

were appropriate to the several speakers and circumstances. Since Paul's sermon at Miletus (Acts 20:18-35) stands in a "we" section, it has been concluded that Luke himself heard the apostle's message; in any case, it is a fact that no part of Acts is closer to the Pauline Letters in wording and thought. Paul's celebrated Areopagus address (17:22-31) is a supreme example of a missionary discourse to cultured pagans; it begins by referring to inscriptions whose existence at Athens is attested by archaeology, and contains references to contemporary Stoic philosophy. Quite different in literary flavor are the sermons in the first half of Acts, where the discourses of Peter preserve Aramaic turns of expression and theological ideas appropriate to the early Palestinian stages of the development of Christian theology. Yet another point of view is conveyed in Stephen's speech (chap. 7), which reflects the militant stand of certain Jewish Christians who had made a decisive break with traditional Judaism.

In short, the speeches in Acts are literary masterpieces and deserve the most careful attention from the historian and the literary analyst. Those that occur in the "we" sections may embody notes made by Luke at the time; others are no doubt based on information derived from eyewitnesses whom Luke sought out as informants; still other speeches may well be Luke's own free composition, drawn up in accordance with what he judged to be appropriate for the occasion. In the last category must also be placed, as it seems, the contents of the letter written by Claudius Lysias to Felix (23:26).

By comparing the reports in the Acts of the Apostles of the sermons preached by Peter and Paul and other leaders of the early church, scholars have ascertained the common core present in all of them. The following points are emphasized:

(1) The promises of God made in Old Testament days have now been fulfilled, and the Messiah has come;

(2) He is Jesus of Nazareth, who

(*a*) Went about doing good and executing mighty works by the power of God;

(*b*) Was crucified according to the purpose of God;

(*c*) Was raised by God from the dead;

(*d*) Is exalted by God and given the name "Lord";

(e) Will come again for judgment and the restoration of all things.

(3) Therefore, all who hear the message should repent and be baptized.[7]

When one makes an evaluation of Luke as a historian, it must be admitted that the book of Acts has certain limitations. It is incomplete in the sense that it carries the reader up to Paul's two-year imprisonment at Rome, but says nothing of the outcome and the subsequent history of the church. Perhaps, as some scholars have suggested, Luke published his work just at this time (about A.D. 63), and therefore could not describe what had not yet happened. It is possible, however, that the book may have been published somewhat later in the first century, and if this is so, we must acknowledge that we do not know why Luke chose to bring it to such an unsatisfactory conclusion—unsatisfactory, that is, from the standpoint of those who are curious to know more.

Even for the period of time that Acts covers, the narrative has great gaps. We hear nothing about the church in Egypt or in Mesopotamia, nor are we told when or how the gospel first reached Rome (Christian believers greeted Paul when he arrived at Rome). Luke is interested chiefly in the expansion of the church and pays little attention to the inner life and development of local congregations.

Furthermore, in chronology Luke's work is deficient, particularly in the first half, which has only one precise date (11:26). A comparison of Acts with Paul's Letters discloses divergences of detail and orientation, some of which are extremely perplexing, such as the relationship of the events recorded in Acts 15 with those in Galatians 2.

Despite such admitted limitations, however, we must be grateful to Luke, who occupies a unique place in the New Testament. Though he had predecessors when he wrote a Gospel (Luke 1:1), as church historian Luke was a pioneer; it may be said that he is the father of church history. His skill as a historiographer, when his accomplishments are judged in the light of his sources, is of a high

---

7. The technical name given by modern scholars to this core of early Christian preaching is *kerygma*, a Greek word meaning "the proclamation." The basic publication was by C. H. Dodd, *The Apostolic Preaching and Its Development* (London: Hodder & Stoughton, 1936). This study was carried further by Eugene E. Lemcio, showing there is a central kerygmatic core that integrates the manifold plurality of the New Testament; see the appendix "The Unifying Kerygma of the New Testament" in Lemcio's monograph *The Past of Jesus in the Gospels* (Cambridge: University Press, 1991), pp. 115-31.

Figure 7.1. The Ruins of the Tribunal at Corinth
(Courtesy of John McRay.)
It was here at the *bema* (the public rostrum) that Paul was brought to trial
before Gallio, the Roman proconsul of Achaia (Acts 18:12-17). In the background
is the Acrocorinth, celebrated for its extensive view.

order. From every point of view the New Testament would be infinitely poorer without this first book of church history.

II. THE CHRONOLOGY OF THE APOSTOLIC AGE

In order to ascertain the chronology of the apostolic age, scholars
start with those events recorded in the book of Acts to which a
fixed date can be assigned from Roman or Jewish sources. Then,
reckoning backward and forward, the approximate dates of other
events relative to these fixed points can be determined.

Of the events described in Acts, only a few can be dated with
certainty.

(1) The most certain date is that of the death of Herod Agrippa I
(Acts 12:23). According to evidence from Josephus *(Antiquities,*
XIX.v.1 and viii.2), Agrippa was appointed king of all Palestine
soon after the accession of Claudius as emperor (in January, A.D.

41), and he reigned over this territory for three years. The date of his death, therefore, must be placed about A.D. 44.

(2) The date of the famine mentioned in Acts 11:28 depends on information supplied by several ancient authors (Josephus, Tacitus, and Suetonius) and by evidence preserved in Egyptian papyri concerning the high price of grain. When these various pieces of evidence are combined, it appears that a general famine occurred during the rule of Tiberius Alexander as procurator of Judea, that is, either A.D. 46 or 47.

(3) An edict of Claudius banishing the Jews from Rome is mentioned in Acts 18:2. According to Orosius, a fifth-century historian, this edict was issued in A.D. 49 or 50. It is, however, rather precarious to place much confidence in such a late historian as Orosius.

(4) According to Acts 18:12, Paul was brought to trial before Gallio, proconsul of Achaia. (See Fig. 7.1) Fortunately a Latin inscription found at Delphi enables us to date Gallio's proconsulship sometime between A.D. 51 and 53. Whether the episode that was brought to the attention of Gallio came at the beginning, middle, or end of his term of office, is not known.

The following table provides dates for some of the chief events of the apostolic age. It must be remembered that in many cases the dates are more or less approximate, and that frequently a plausible case can be made for another dating of the same event.

The outpouring of the Spirit on Pentecost fifty days after the resurrection of Jesus (Acts 2:1-4)	May 28, A.D. 30
The stoning of Stephen (Acts 7:54-60)	about A.D. 33–34
Paul's conversion to Christianity (Acts 9:1-19)	about A.D. 34–35
Paul's first missionary journey (Acts 13–14)	between A.D. 46 and 48

The apostolic council at Jerusalem (Acts 15:1-29)	A.D. 48 or 49
Paul's second missionary journey (Acts 15:36–18:23)	between A.D. 49 and 53
Paul's third missionary journey (Acts 18:23–21:17)	between A.D. 54 and 58
Paul's arrest in Jerusalem (Acts 21:27-33)	A.D. 58
Paul's imprisonment in Caesarea (Acts 24:27)	A.D. 58–60
Accession of Porcius Festus	about A.D. 59–60
Paul is taken to Rome for trial	autumn A.D. 60–spring 61
Paul remains for two years under house arrest (Acts 28:30)	A.D. 61–63

Here the book of Acts ends; the following events and dates are based on patristic traditions of the second and third centuries.

Paul's release from his first Roman imprisonment	A.D. 63
Paul's subsequent missionary journeys (including perhaps a visit to Spain; compare Rom. 15:24-28)	A.D. 64–67
Paul's second Roman imprisonment and subsequent death	A.D. 67–68
John's death at Ephesus	shortly after A.D. 98

CHAPTER 8

PRIMITIVE JEWISH CHRISTIANITY

I. PENTECOST AND THE EARLIEST EVANGELISM

The forty days between the resurrection and ascension of Jesus Christ formed a period of transition during which the apostles were being prepared for their subsequent work. According to the book of Acts, at his final meeting with his followers the risen Lord promised that they would receive power when the Holy Spirit had come upon them, and would become his "witnesses in Jerusalem, in all Judea and Samaria, and to the ends of the earth" (Acts 1:8). Devoting themselves to prayer, the little group of believers, numbering about one hundred and twenty (Acts 1:15), waited in eager expectancy.

After a lapse of ten days, the Spirit came with power upon the apostolic band. The occasion was the Jewish festival of Pentecost, which fell on the fiftieth day after Passover (hence the name "Pentecost," which means "fiftieth"). Originally the festival was held in celebration of the completion of the grain harvest, and in the Old Testament it is called the festival of harvest (Exod. 23:16) or of weeks (Exod. 34:22) and the day of the first fruits (Num. 28:26). Special offerings were made in the temple, and multitudes of Jews, not only from Palestine, but from abroad, attended the celebration. Among the later Jews the festival commemorated the giving of the Mosaic Law at Sinai. Both in its original meaning as well as in its later modification, gladness and gratitude were the keynotes of the festival.

1. THE DAY OF PENTECOST

According to Luke's account, the disciples, being assembled together, suddenly heard a sound "like the rush of a violent wind," which "filled the entire house where they were sitting," and something that had the appearance of a small tongue of fire rested on each of them. At the same time their minds were filled with joyous exultation and spiritual enlightenment, and they broke forth into ecstatic praise of God, speaking "in other languages, as the Spirit gave them ability" (Acts 2:2-4). It is obvious that the whole narrative is intended to describe the inauguration of the Christian church by the supernatural operation of the Spirit of God. By means of the symbols of wind and fire, both emblems of the effective power of the Spirit, Luke suggests that the energizing power of the Spirit imparted to the disciples a fluent enthusiasm that was contagious to all who heard their testimony.

The foreign-born Jews who, from motives of piety, had come to Jerusalem in order to celebrate the feast of weeks were amazed at the outburst of spiritual exuberance. Like the glossolalia that was manifested later in the primitive church at Caesarea (Acts 10:4), at Ephesus (Acts 19:6), and at Corinth (1 Cor. 12 and 14), the phenomenon of speaking in tongues at Pentecost involved a kind of spiritual intoxication (compare Acts 2:15) analogous to the rhapsodic "frenzy" described by certain poets. At the same time, those who heard Peter and the other disciples were able to catch phrases in their own native languages, which the same Spirit interpreted to their spiritual understanding.

The summary that Luke gives of Peter's sermon on the day of Pentecost (Acts 2:14-36) includes first an explanation of the unusual happening. It was, Peter declared, the fulfillment of the oracle given through the Old Testament prophet Joel concerning the outpouring of the Spirit upon Israel before the messianic judgment should take place (Joel 2:28-32). Then Peter proclaimed Jesus to be the Messiah whose death and resurrection were in accordance with "the definite plan and foreknowledge of God" (Acts 2:23). The conditions for receiving the promised gift of the Spirit, the apostle declared, were repentance for sin and baptism in the name of Jesus Christ.

As a result of Peter's sermon, faith was awakened in many who heard, and the close of the day of Pentecost saw the little band of one hundred twenty expanded into a company of about three thousand. These persons, we are informed, "devoted themselves to the apostles' teaching and fellowship, to the breaking of bread and the prayers" (Acts 2:42). Here the reference to "the apostles' teaching" alludes to the authoritative instruction concerning aspects of Jesus' life and teaching in the light of the Old Testament. The expression "the breaking of bread" refers to the common meals that believers shared in their homes (compare Acts 2:46), climaxed by the celebration of the Lord's Supper; such meals were called "love feasts" (Jude 12).

From what Luke tells us about the early church, it is clear that the members were a closely knit group within the Jewish community. The earliest Christians were all either born Jews or proselytes to Judaism (Acts 2:5-10). Though the church regarded itself as the true Israel of God (Gal. 6:16) and as the people of God's new covenant (2 Cor. 3:6), outwardly it differed little from the numerous separate synagogues that existed in Jerusalem. Like members of other synagogues, its members took part in the regular worship of the temple (Luke 24:53; Acts 2:46; 3:1), observed the Jewish festivals, and in general kept the Mosaic Law.

According to the early chapters of Acts, the Christian believers were favorably regarded by the populace of Jerusalem (Acts 2:47), and the converts they won included both priests and adherents of the sect of the Pharisees (Acts 4:4; 5:14; 6:7; 15:5). It is nowhere suggested that such priests ceased to be liable to the sacerdotal duties in the temple, or that Pharisaic converts ceased to observe their strict traditions. It was thus within the framework of Judaism that the members of the new group met daily for "the prayers" (Acts 2:42), which as Jews they had been accustomed to offer but which now obtained new import in the light of faith in Jesus as the divinely appointed Messiah.

The inward cohesion of the Christian community was expressed in what has been called "an experiment in communism." Communism in the strict sense it was not, for private control of property was not abrogated (Acts 5:4). But under the impulse of that love for one another that Jesus had inculcated, holders of real estate sold it and voluntarily handed over the proceeds to the apostles, who formed a common fund from which the poorer members of the community were assisted (Acts 2:45; 4:34-35). The practice was an impressive demonstration of Christian fellowship.[1] But it

---

1. How far the practice of "communism" in the early church was influenced by the pattern of communal life that the Essenes followed (see p. 52) is not clear. In any case, the most characteristic features of the Essene mode of life do not appear among the disciples of Jesus.

lent itself to abuse (Acts 5:15; 6:1), and the dissipation of capital left the church at Jerusalem without resources when hard times came. It is noteworthy that Paul, while accepting and emphasizing the principle of mutual economic responsibility among Christians (Rom. 12:13; 15:27; Gal. 6:2), enjoined that the common fund should be supplied out of earned income (Eph. 4:28; compare 2 Thess. 3:10).

The obligation to provide for the poor by the sharing of resources became a permanent principle in the church, but the earlier methods adopted at Jerusalem were modified through experience. During Paul's missionary activities among Gentile believers throughout the Greco-Roman world, the apostle stressed the need of liberality in contributing to the relief fund that he was collecting for the poor of the mother church at Jerusalem (Rom. 15:16, 25-27; 1 Cor. 16.1-4; 2 Cor. 8:1-15; 9:1-5; Phil. 4:18). Wherever the blame might lie for the impoverished condition of the Judean Christians—whether it was caused by famine, persecution, or the unwise experiment in communism—Paul saw in it a golden opportunity for impressing on his converts the practical implications of the maxim that "individually we are members one of another" (Rom. 12:5).

2. THE EARLIEST EVANGELISM

At the festival of Pentecost there were in Jerusalem Jews of many nations. The list of countries of their origin (Acts 2:9-11) corresponds almost exactly with what was considered by ancient geographers to be the sum total of all known nations. In his account of the phenomenon of speaking in tongues, Luke doubtless wished to emphasize the universality of the earliest evangelism. Rabbinical tradition held that the Mosaic Law had been proclaimed on Sinai in the seventy languages of humankind, though only Israel heard and obeyed. At Pentecost—so Luke seems to imply—the good news of the gospel was proclaimed in words that representatives of all nations could understand.

The rapid expansion of the church in many parts of the Roman Empire during the middle decades of the first century has often been a cause of amazement. Without detracting from the achievements of subsequent missionaries of the new faith, it should be pointed out how natural it was that newly made converts at

Pentecost should return to their own countries as evangelists of the gospel. Even though only some of them may have continued to be active in the propagation of their faith, within a relatively short time many Christian congregations would have been established far and wide.

Besides emphasizing the universality of the gospel message in the events that took place at Pentecost, Luke also symbolizes the suitability of the new faith for all races of people by including accounts of the conversion of three persons of different nationalities: an Ethiopian, a Jew from Tarsus, and a Gentile from Rome. In successive chapters he tells how the treasurer of the Ethiopian Candace, or queen, believed and was baptized by Philip (Acts 8:26-40); how Saul of Tarsus, intent upon the persecution of the early church, was converted and became Paul the apostle (Acts 9:1-19; compare 22:4-16; 26:9-18); and how Cornelius, a pious Roman centurion stationed at Caesarea, heard of Jesus Christ through the testimony of Peter, and received the gift of the Holy Spirit (Acts 10:1-48). In this way Luke calls attention to the diverse backgrounds (i.e., Africa, Asia, and Europe) of those who became members of the early Christian church.

II. THE CHURCH'S CONFLICT WITH JUDAISM AND THE MARTYRDOM OF STEPHEN

In the previous section it was pointed out that the first Christians were Jews, and that they did not cease to be Jews after their experience at Pentecost. On the contrary, their new enthusiasm led them to be regular in attendance at the temple, and their religious practices were sufficiently orthodox to allay any fears or suspicions that the Pharisees may have entertained about them. No breach of the Mosaic Law was involved if a group of Jews chose to consider a revered teacher as the Messiah.

The first opposition to Christians came from the Sadducees, the party to which most of the nobility belonged, and especially the branches of the high priestly family. The contagious enthusiasm of the new sect was obnoxious to them for several reasons, particularly because it threatened their own position of power. Since the chief priests had been active in securing the crucifixion of Jesus, they naturally were fearful that the disciples' proclamation of Jesus as the Messiah, accompanied by miracles[2] that they attributed to his power, could lead to undesirable excitement, in the course of which the populace might be moved to avenge the death of Jesus upon those responsible for it.

The occasion for official opposition was the healing of a man who was lame by the apostle Peter at the gate of the temple called the Beautiful Gate. A great concourse of people followed Peter to Solomon's Portico, on the east side of the temple area, where he preached to them (Acts 3:11-26). The temple guard, at the command of the Sadducees, arrested Peter, as well as John, who was with him, on the charge of fomenting tumult (4:1-3). The next day, when the Sanhedrin was convened in order to try the case, Peter made a brave address proclaiming Jesus as the Messiah through whom alone is salvation (4:8-12). The presence of the man who had been healed, the boldness of the apostles, and the obvious sympathy of the people, prevented the Sanhedrin from taking any further action than to command the apostles to discontinue their teaching (Acts 4:13-22). But so far from discontinuing, the disciples prayed for divine strength to enable them to speak with all boldness in the face of opposition (Acts 4:29-31).

Subsequently the Sadducees took more active measures in another attempt to put a stop to what they regarded as a politically dangerous movement. By their order, the apostles were imprisoned a second time (Acts 5:17-18). But in the night they were released, Luke says, by an angel of the Lord, and morning found them back in the temple proclaiming the faith. They were rearrested and brought before the Sanhedrin once again. In reply to the high

---

2. The evidence in Acts that in the early church miracles of healing were performed by apostles and others (such as Stephen and Philip) is supported by several references in the Pauline Letters. It is psychologically inconceivable that Paul would have appealed to the miracles wrought by the Spirit of God among the Galatians (Gal. 3:5), as a desperate argument to prevent his readers from going over to Judaism, if he knew that the answer would be that his readers had never heard of any such miracles. Similarly, he could hardly have written so confidently to the Romans of what Christ had done through him in performing signs and wonders if there had been none (Rom. 15:18-19). In the Corinthian correspondence, Paul alludes, almost incidentally, to his ability to perform "signs and wonders and mighty works" (2 Cor. 12:12; compare 1 Cor. 12:10).

How far the process of legendary accretion, inevitable in an age that expected miraculous cures and regarded them as a vindication of theological truth, may have been at work on the stories of Acts is variously estimated. Despite the possibility, however, of a certain amount of heightening of the miraculous, it is certain that, through the apostles, healings occurred that were attributed to the power of Jesus Christ.

priest's charge, which betrayed an uneasy conscience about the Crucifixion ("you are determined to bring this man's blood on us"), the apostles once more affirmed their allegiance to Christ, saying, "We must obey God rather than any human authority. The Jesus whom you killed has been raised up by God as Leader and Savior, and we are witnesses to these things, and so is the Holy Spirit" (Acts 5:29-32, in substance).

It was a bold answer, and the Sanhedrin, being enraged, wanted to kill the apostles. But Gamaliel, a leader of the Pharisaic party and a man of great reputation both for his learning and his wisdom, counseled moderation. If the new movement was of God, he said, there was no use in fighting against it; if it was from human origin, it would fail of itself, as other messianic movements had failed (Acts 5:33-39).

Gamaliel's policy of watchful waiting prevailed so far as any attempt at inflicting the death penalty was concerned. To placate the Sadducees the apostles were flogged as a precautionary measure and were ordered once more not to speak in the name of Jesus. The suffering and shame, however, did not daunt their spirits. Rejoicing that they were counted worthy to suffer dishonor for the name of their Master, the apostles continued their work in public and in homes, proclaiming Jesus as the Messiah (Acts 5:40-42).

The whole situation, however, was suddenly changed by an event that roused the anger of the Pharisees even more than of the Sadducees, and thus brought upon the disciples the hostility of the whole Sanhedrin. Among the Hellenists (that is, Greek-speaking Jews) who had been converted to the Christian faith was a man named Stephen. According to Luke's account, Stephen was a notable leader who stood out from the others in faith, spiritual power, and wisdom (Acts 6:5, 8, 10). Besides helping to superintend the distribution of the church's relief funds, Stephen was conspicuous in working miracles and preaching the gospel among the Hellenistic Jews in Jerusalem. His activity aroused opposition to the church among foreign Jews who, having returned to the holy city, were especially zealous for the honor of the Mosaic Law. Those most active against him were members of "the synagogue of the Freedmen (as it was called), Cyrenians, Alexandrians, and others of those from Cilicia and Asia" (Acts 6:8-9).

Stephen appears to be the first Christian to make a clear distinction between Judaism and Christianity, and to proclaim a Christianity that was emancipated from Jewish national limitations. Failing to refute Stephen's arguments, his opponents produced witnesses who accused him of blasphemy against Moses and God. This was a wholly new charge against a disciple, and it moved the Pharisees and affected the disposition of the people. Stephen was brought before the Sanhedrin, where a more specific indictment was lodged, charging him with teaching that Jesus of Nazareth would destroy the temple and overturn the Law of Moses (Acts 6:14).

Stephen's speech in his own defense appears on the surface to be an innocuous recital of Old Testament history from the call of Abraham to Solomon's dedication of the temple (Acts 7:1-53); its purpose, however, is clearly to undermine the accepted foundations of Jewish religion by claiming the church to be the true Israel and by disowning contemporary Judaism as apostate. Instead of appealing primarily to Old Testament prophecies, as Peter had done, Stephen emphasizes the providential acts of God throughout the centuries, and finds their culmination in Christianity as the intended goal of the whole history of the Hebrews. He makes a case, supported with quotations from the Old Testament itself, that in the past God had not restricted revelations of himself to persons in the holy land, but had made his presence known to his faithful servants in whatever part of the world they happened to be, whether Mesopotamia, Haran, Egypt, Midian, or Sinai. Then he points out that until the time of Solomon their fathers had not had the temple, but only the tent of witness made by Moses from a divine pattern, and that it was Solomon, not God, who wanted a temple (Acts 7:44-47). Even Isaiah condemned the temple as a denial of the true nature of God and spoke of the inwardness of true worship (Isa. 66:1-2; Acts 7:48-50).

Having carried his hearers along with him in his argument for the provisional and temporary character of a merely nationalistic interpretation of religion, Stephen launched into a denunciation of his judges, who having killed Jesus Christ, the Righteous One, proved themselves heirs of the murderers of the prophets and violators of the law of God (Acts 7:51-53).

The reaction of the Sanhedrin to this provocative speech was understandably one of unbridled fury, a fury that was intensified when Stephen broke into an ecstatic description of Jesus as "the Son of Man standing at the right hand of God," presumably as Stephen's advocate or witness in his defense (Acts 7:56). No formal sentence of death was pronounced against Stephen; instead, the trial turned into a riot during which he was dragged outside the city and stoned to death. The parallelism between Stephen's trial and subsequent death and that of Jesus is heightened by Stephen's prayer for his murderers ("Lord, do not hold this sin against them," 7:60, compare Luke 23:34). At this point Luke skillfully introduces as a witness of the lynching a young rabbi named Saul, who was later to become Paul the apostle (Acts 7:54–8:1).

To judge from the amount of space that Luke devotes to recounting Stephen's address (it is the longest of the speeches in Acts), he must have regarded it as especially significant and as marking the transition of Christianity from its earliest Jewish form to its extension among the Gentiles. The reader can detect in the speech overtones of a growing awareness that the new faith could not be limited by Judaism and that it was the true goal of Hebrew history. The seeds of theological revolution lie within Stephen's challenge against the alleged privileges of the Jews, and the logic implicit in his argument opened the way for a Christian mission to the Gentiles. In short, Stephen stands for a Christianity that was coming to realize its independence and self-sufficiency and was beginning to feel that it must either absorb Judaism or break with it.

The decidedly Semitic cast of Stephen's speech, so noticeable in the Greek text of Acts, suggests that Luke has managed to present a faithful echo of Stephen's argument. It would also seem that certain of the teachings of Jesus had made a deep impression on Stephen's mind. He describes Jesus by the term "Son of Man," which in the Gospels is Jesus' favorite description of himself. Hitherto, the Jerusalem Christians had emphasized those elements in the teaching of Jesus that united them with Judaism; now Stephen draws attention to those elements that had brought Jesus into controversy with the religious authorities. He saw that the characteristic features of Jesus' teaching must inevitably lead to a rupture with Judaism as well as to a spiritual interpretation of the Mosaic Law.

How far Stephen's theological insights were shared by others in the primitive church we cannot tell. Some years later, however, the author of the Letter to the Hebrews embodied in his treatise an elaboration of the principles inherent in Stephen's address. The theme of this letter, which contains the longest sustained argument of any book in the New Testament, is the superiority of Christianity over Judaism. It appears that certain Jewish Christians, confronted with religious persecution, were beginning to think that they had made a mistake when they left their ancestral religion. The letter was written in order to convince them that Christ is preeminent over the prophets of the Old Testament, over the angels, and over Moses himself (Heb. 1:1–4:13); that Christ's priesthood is superior to the Jewish priesthood in the succession from Aaron (Heb. 4:14–7:28); and that Christ's sacrifice of himself for sin inaugurated the new covenant, predicted by Jeremiah (Jer. 31:31-34), and provides the culmination toward which all of the Old Testament types were intended to point (Heb. 8:1–10:18). Important aspects of Stephen's theology were thus carried to their logical conclusion, and exercised a profound influence upon the growing Christian church.

The speech and subsequent death of Stephen had other important consequences, some of which were more immediately apparent than the underlying logic of his theology. As the first Christian martyr,[3] Stephen's death was a signal for the outbreak of a general persecution against the Christian community at Jerusalem, and "all except the apostles were scattered throughout the countryside of Judea and Samaria" (Acts 8:1). Contrary to the expectation of the Jewish persecutors, however, so far from suppressing the new religion, this scattering resulted only in the wider spread of the gospel. Everywhere they went the persecuted disciples proclaimed the faith for which they suffered.

Eventually some of the refugees traveled as far as Phoenicia and Cyprus and Antioch. Throughout their work of evangelism these nameless men and women appear to have made appeal primarily to Jews, or to Gentiles who had previously become Jewish proselytes. At Antioch, however, for the first time, as it appears, the gospel was preached to Gentiles ("Greeks") who had had no

---

3. The Greek word *martyr* means "witness." Others had witnessed to the person and death of Jesus Christ by their words; Stephen now witnessed also by his death.

previous contact with the synagogue (Acts 11:19-20). The establishment of the first mixed church at Antioch is a landmark in the history of early Christianity.

The city of Antioch, situated on the Orontes River, north of the Lebanon range, had been the capital of the Syrian kingdom, and was then the residence of the Roman governor of the province. Recent archaeological investigations have confirmed its cosmopolitan character, where persons of all races and creeds met and mingled. Lying just outside Palestine and at the entrance to Asia Minor, connected also by trade and politics with the whole empire, Antioch formed a natural base of operations from which the new faith, if it was to be separated from Judaism, could go forth to make converts in the Gentile world. It was here that the disciples were

Figure 8.1. Antioch on the Orontes River
(Courtesy of John McRay)

In apostolic days, Antioch of Syria was a great city of over 250,000 inhabitants. It was here that the disciples were first called "Christians" (Acts 11:19-26). The city also became the birthplace of foreign missions when the Church there sent out Barnabas and Saul on a missionary journey (13:12). Of all ancient cities, only Antioch could boast of street illumination at nighttime.

first given the name *Christians* (Acts 11:26). In the subsequent period of the expansion of the church, Antioch came to assume a more important role than even Jerusalem, and strongly supported Paul's anti-Judaizing policy. The development of Gentile Christianity, however, is another story, which must be told in the following chapter.

CHAPTER 9

THE EXPANSION OF CHRISTIANITY THROUGH THE WORK OF THE APOSTLE PAUL

I. PAUL'S EARLY TRAINING AND CONVERSION

One of the heroic figures in the life of the early church was the apostle Paul. Dramatically converted from being an archpersecutor of Christians into an indefatigable missionary of the gospel, the impact of his personality upon the church was both widespread and permanent. Besides founding new congregations of believers in Asia Minor, Macedonia, Greece, and other lands, this "apostle to the Gentiles" found time to write a sheaf of letters that now comprise about one-fourth of the bulk of the New Testament. Even if we conclude, as many scholars do, that Paul did not write the Pastoral Letters (1 and 2 Timothy and Titus), he remains second only to Luke in the amount of material contributed to the New Testament by one person.

Paul, whose Jewish name was Saul, was born near the beginning of the Christian Era at Tarsus, an important metropolitan center of Cilicia in southeastern Asia Minor. Under the Seleucids the city of Tarsus was fully hellenized and grew into a center of learning, surpassed only by Athens and Alexandria. One of Paul's contemporaries at Tarsus was the Stoic philosopher Nestor, who had been the tutor of Tiberius and whose school was widely influential. Though Paul was brought up in the strict observance of the Hebrew faith and traditions, his father having been a Pharisee (Acts 23:6), he was born a Roman citizen (Acts 22:28). We do not know by what means his father obtained citizenship; it may have been for service to the state or possibly by purchase. However acquired, Paul's Roman citizenship, a highly prized privilege possessed by only a few in the provinces of the empire, proved to be of great importance later in his Christian work and more than once saved his life.

Most of Paul's youth was spent not in Tarsus but in Jerusalem, where he received religious instruction from the famous Jewish teacher Gamaliel (Acts 22:3). At Gamaliel's feet, Paul became versed not only in the teachings of the Old Testament, but in the subtleties of rabbinical interpretation. Unlike the temperament of the peaceable Gamaliel whose counsel of moderation had prevented the Sanhedrin from attempting to kill the apostles (Acts 5:34-39), Paul's zeal for the traditions of his ancestors brought him eventually into bitter conflict with the followers of Jesus Christ. Whether Paul ever saw Jesus in person while both were at Jerusalem has been debated at length (2 Cor. 5:16 does not seem to imply such a meeting). It has also been debated whether Paul had ever been married. In view of the fact that very few Jews remained unmarried, it is highly probable that Paul had been married. Since, however, nothing is said in his letters about his wife, it is natural to conclude that she had died sometime before Paul undertook his extensive missionary journeys.

Paul first appears in Christian history in association with the persecutors of the Christian church (Acts 7:58). As a staunch and conscientious Pharisee he was filled with horror at the blasphemous sect that proclaimed a crucified malefactor as the promised Messiah of Israel. Soon after Stephen's martyrdom we find him taking a leading part in the fierce religious crusade against the Christians (Acts 8:3; 22:4; 26:10-11; 1 Cor. 15:9; Gal. 1:13; Phil. 3:6). Not content with waging the persecution in Jerusalem, he asked of the high priest letters to the synagogues of Damascus that he might bring from there any Christian Jews whom he could find (Acts 9:1-2). According to his own testimony as reported by Luke, Paul was a conscientious inquisitor, thinking that he was doing God service by his intense efforts to stamp out the new sect (Acts 22:3; 26:9).

Such was the person who became one of the most influential leaders of the early church. Possessing some acquaintance with Hellenic thought, Paul was chiefly characterized by an ardent devotion to the Pharisaic interpretation of the Hebrew Law. His mental aptitudes were varied and vigorous. Capable of discussing profound theological ideas, he was also a practical man of affairs, born to be a leader of others. Though at first a formidable foe, he became a correspondingly strong protagonist for the new faith.

Luke obviously regarded the conversion of Paul to be one of the most important events in the history of early Christianity, for he includes three separate accounts of it in the book of Acts; one is narrated by Luke (9:3-19) and two are put on the lips of Paul himself (22:6-16; 26:12-18). Each account is controlled by the immediate purpose of the narrator. Luke, with primarily a historical motive, briefly relates the event itself. Paul's first account, introduced in connection with his defense before the Jews, emphasizes the part that Ananias, described as "a devout man according to the law and well spoken of by all the Jews living there" (Acts 22:12), had in the transaction. When addressing Agrippa, however, Paul does not mention Ananias and condenses certain other details. Such variations are natural and even assure us of the veracity of the reports.

From these three accounts we learn that it was on the way to Damascus, in order to continue his inquisitorial work there, that Paul experienced an encounter with the risen Jesus. Paul and his companions, probably on horseback, had been following the usual road across the desert from Galilee to the ancient city of Damascus. Suddenly at midday a light from heaven, brighter than the sun, streamed round about them, and overwhelmed by its brilliance, Paul fell upon the ground. Out of the light he heard a voice saying to him in the Hebrew language, "Saul, Saul, why are you persecuting me? It hurts you to kick against the goads" (Acts 26:14). To Paul's question, "Who are you, Lord?" the reply was, "I am Jesus whom you are persecuting." Utterly overcome by this disclosure of the heavenly nature of the one he had despised, and temporarily blinded by the light, Paul was led by the hand into Damascus, where he lodged in the house of a certain Judas. There he continued three days in fasting and prayer, meditating on the revelation that had been made to him. On the third day a Jewish Christian named Ananias interpreted to him the significance of these events in relation to his future mission (9:10-19; 22:10-16). Thereupon he regained his sight and was baptized as a Christian.

The apostle's own references to his conversion, like the accounts of the external event reported in Acts, represent attempts to understand the significance of an experience that transcended ordinary categories of explanation. More than once in later years Paul described his conversion as a work solely of divine power and favor by which he was transformed into the opposite of what he had been before (1 Cor. 9:17; 15:10; Gal. 1:15; and so forth). He was convinced that he had seen the risen Jesus and had thus been qualified for apostleship (1 Cor. 9:1; 15:8; compare Acts 1:22).

According to Paul's own comments, as well as the accounts in Acts, his conversion experience had both an objective and a subjective side. The former, however, is represented as the basis of the latter; that is, a visible appearance of Jesus and a verbal declaration of his will form the basis for his own subjective enlightenment, so that he received the new truth and willingly devoted himself to it. The accounts do not describe the change, on its subjective side, as entirely instantaneous. It was not magical. Three days of prayer were required to complete his conversion. But the objective revelation is always represented by the apostle as unforeseen and peremptory, and he always ascribes the change wrought in him to the sovereign exercise of divine power.

How far was Paul's Christian theology determined by his conversion experience? Quite different answers have been given to this question, and the truth probably lies between them. Some have supposed that, except for an initial stimulus, Paul received little or no substantive truth, and only during later years worked out a more or less coherent system of thought. Others have maintained that at the moment of conversion Paul came into possession of all his major insights into Christian truth, which remained with him for the rest of his life.

In either case, it must not be forgotten that Paul, having a rich acquaintance with the Old Testament, already possessed certain basic religious concepts. These included not only monotheism, but belief in salvation as consisting in the possession of righteousness before God, as well as the doctrines of expiation of sin by sacrifice, of a future judgment, a resurrection of the body, and a messianic kingdom of glory. It is altogether natural that these ideas constituted the molds into which his new faith would run and to which it would adjust itself.

What, then, were the fundamental beliefs that now gripped the mind and soul of the converted persecutor?

First and foremost, Paul became certain that Jesus of Nazareth was alive. The crucified Messiah was no longer dead, but living and ruling as the heavenly Lord. This glorious certainty so overwhelmed Paul's consciousness that he never forgot it afterward; all of his letters witness again and again to his awareness of the real presence of the risen and reigning Christ.

Of equal importance for Paul's subsequent thinking was the fact that he had been called into his new life by the pure favor of God, shown to him while he was actively persecuting the followers of Jesus. So far from earning his standing before God by keeping the Mosaic Law, Paul discovered that his efforts to obey it had led him into the greatest sin. Instead of choosing God, Paul was chosen by God; instead of punishing him for his opposition to the work of Christ, God had mercifully pardoned him.

All of Paul's thinking thereafter revolved around these two foci: faith in Jesus as the living and exalted Messiah, and the recognition of God's favor and grace that had called and transformed a persecutor of the church into an apostle of Jesus Christ. Some very important consequences followed from Paul's reorientation. Now Paul came to realize that one's relation to God rested on God's overflowing goodness, not on one's success in conforming to the Old Testament Law. It followed that Gentiles, who did not observe the Jewish precepts regarding the sabbath, kosher foods, and a host of other legal minutiae, were not thereby excluded from God's favor. Thus, through Paul's own experience of divine grace in Christ, the man and the doctrine were prepared that were destined to help release the new faith from nationalistic Judaism and to interpret it to the Gentile world.

II. PAUL'S FIRST MISSIONARY JOURNEY

As soon as he was converted to Christianity, Paul began evangelistic work in the synagogues of Damascus. So successful was he in proclaiming the faith, which a short time before he had sought to stamp out, that opposition was raised against him from the Damascene Jews, who were aided by the governor of the city. Learning of a plot against his life, Paul escaped from the city at night, being let down by his disciples in a basket from a window in the city wall (Acts 9:23-25; 2 Cor. 11:32-33).

Figure 9.1. Wall of Damascus
(Courtesy of Studium Biblicum Franciscanum, Jerusalem)
An ancient wall of Damascus, thought to be the place where Paul escaped from the city (Acts 9:23-25).

Paul's movements during the next several years are not altogether clear. Apparently he went from Damascus into Arabia and later returned to Damascus (Gal. 1:17). We do not know where he went in Arabia, or how long he stayed, or what he did there. It is often thought that Paul spent the time chiefly in meditation upon the great change that had come over his life and the implications of his newly acquired faith. It was not until the third year after his conversion that Paul returned to Jerusalem, where as Peter's guest (Gal. 1:18) he undoubtedly received more of the tradition about Jesus' life and ministry, which he later handed on to his churches (1 Cor. 11:23; 15:3).

At first the members of the church at Jerusalem were afraid of Paul, remembering his reputation as a persecutor. The friendly intercession, however, of a Christian from Cyprus named Barnabas (Acts 9:27; compare 4:36-37) assured them that Paul's conversion was genuine and not a crafty trick to gain admission to their meetings. While in Jerusalem Paul also sought out his old friends, the

Greek-speaking Jews, and boldly proclaimed to them the gospel of faith in Jesus Christ. Enraged at what they doubtless regarded as a renegade to their cause, these Hellenists at once plotted against his life. The threatening danger was so great that his new Christian friends took Paul to Caesarea, on the seacoast, and sent him from there to Tarsus (Acts 9:29-30).

Of Paul's stay in Tarsus we know nothing. Presumably he spent these "silent years" engaged in missionary work, for we can scarcely imagine a man of Paul's zeal and sense of mission remaining inactive for any great length of time. Some scholars, who believe that Paul's Letter to the Galatians was written to churches in north-central Asia Minor, suppose that Paul established those churches during this period. Likewise, many of the hardships and persecutions that Paul describes in 2 Corinthians 11:23-27 are often placed during the same period.

Meanwhile, Barnabas had not forgotten Paul, and when the newly established church at Antioch in Syria needed help, he went to Tarsus and persuaded Paul to join him in the work at this important crossroads of the Near East (Acts 11:22-26).

As was mentioned at the close of the previous chapter, the Antiochene church was a mixed church, in which Gentile members soon came to outnumber Jewish members. That it continued, however, to maintain close ties with the mother church in Jerusalem is shown by the decision of the Antiochene disciples to send relief when, about A.D. 46, famine threatened the Christians of Judea (Acts 11:27-30). Those who were entrusted to take the gift were Barnabas and Paul.

Soon after Barnabas and Paul had returned to Antioch from their visit to Jerusalem, the seed of a daring new idea for the missionary enterprise took root in the minds of five of the prophets and teachers of the church there. Four of them—Barnabas; Symeon, who was called Niger (the epithet means "black" and may imply that he was of African origin); Lucius of Cyrene; and Paul—were Hellenistic Jews. The fifth, named Manaen, one of the few men of worldly rank in the primitive church, was a member of the court of Herod the tetrarch. The point to be noted is that they belonged to the circle that had already taken the deepest interest in the expansion of the faith. It was one of the decisive moments in the history of

Christianity when the church at Antioch, impelled by a profound sense of the guidance of the Holy Spirit, solemnly consecrated Barnabas and Paul for a program of invading the Greco-Roman world with the gospel (Acts 13:1-3).

Taking with them John Mark, the young cousin of Barnabas, they set out, probably in the spring of either A.D. 46 or 47, for a region familiar to Barnabas, namely the island of Cyprus, his birthplace (Acts 4:36). Landing at Salamis, they preached in the synagogues, and gradually traversed the whole length of the island.

Luke says nothing of the success of their mission until they reached Paphos, at the western extremity of Cyprus. There the Roman proconsul himself, named Sergius Paulus, embraced the faith (as it happens, this is the first convert of Paul who is mentioned by name). From now onward Luke, who previously had referred to the apostle by his Jewish name, Saul, consistently refers to him by his Roman name, Paul (Acts 13:9). Thus Luke, with delicate literary art, appropriately introduces the apostle's Gentile name when his missionary work began among the Gentiles, by whom he would of course be known as Paul. Of the two names, the apostle himself doubtless preferred to be called Paul, for he invariably uses this name in all his letters.

After leaving Cyprus for Asia Minor, Paul stepped into the place of leadership, and Mark, perhaps because of illness or resentment against Paul for overshadowing Barnabas, who was Mark's kinsman, left them and returned to his home at Jerusalem.

Landing at Perga in Pamphylia, the missionaries made their way some miles northward into the highlands of Phrygia. At Pisidian Antioch, in accordance with what was to be his strategy in most of the cities that he visited, Paul sought out the synagogue. Here, as a visiting teacher, he was given opportunity to speak. From Luke's summary of Paul's address, the first recorded specimen of the apostle's preaching (Acts 13:16-41), we can observe a general similarity with the main points made by other early Christian leaders, such as Peter, Stephen, and Philip. After reviewing God's providential guidance in Old Testament days, Paul related the testimony of John the Baptist regarding the Messiah, and the rejection of Jesus by the Jewish authorities, but declared that God had raised him from the dead, and that only through faith in him could one be freed from sin. The outcome of the preaching mission was the rejection of Paul by the leading Jews of the synagogue, who, Luke says, were jealous of the huge following that he had attracted, and the establishment of a congregation of Christian believers, made up chiefly of Gentiles (Acts 13:42-48).

Being driven out of Pisidian Antioch by a persecution instigated by the Jews, Paul and Barnabas went to Iconium, to Lystra, and to Derbe, all of which, with Pisidian Antioch, were in the southern part of the great Roman province of Galatia. More than once the missionaries encountered opposition, and at Lystra Paul was stoned and dragged out of the town and left for dead (Acts 14:19). But, regaining consciousness, he was able to get on his feet, and soon departed with Barnabas to Derbe, a town at the southeast limit of the province of Galatia. It would have been possible for the missionaries to cross the mountains into Cilicia and so go directly, by way of Tarsus, back to Syrian Antioch. But they resolved to return by the way they had come, in order to strengthen the converts and to appoint elders in the young churches they had founded (Acts 14:21-23). Having done this they returned to the church at Syrian Antioch, where they reported "all that God had done with them, and how he had opened a door of faith for the Gentiles" (Acts 14:27).

III. THE APOSTOLIC COUNCIL AT JERUSALEM

The more the church spread to the Gentile world, the looser became its ties with Judaism. Those members of the Palestinian church who lived in accordance with the customs of the Pharisees watched this development with profound regret and made a valiant attempt to keep the church from breaking with Judaism. The threatened split, they believed, could be prevented or mitigated only when all the churches and all their members agreed to observe the Mosaic Law.

Not long after the return of Paul and Barnabas from their missionary journey, emissaries from the church at Jerusalem arrived at Antioch and declared that unless the converted Gentiles submitted to the rite of circumcision according to the custom of Moses, they could not be saved. The issue was far from trifling, and Luke records that it aroused "no small dissension and debate" (Acts

15:2). Each side seemed to have good reasons for holding to its views. The Judaizers, who in effect demanded that Gentiles first become Jews before becoming Christians, could urge that the Old Testament was the revealed word of God and therefore its commands were obligatory upon all who sought to live in accordance with the divine will. However, Paul could argue that the observance of such external rites had proved unavailing in his own spiritual odyssey, and that even the Old Testament spoke of Abraham as justified by his faith long before the Mosaic Law had been promulgated.

So disturbing to the peace of the church was this dispute that Paul and Barnabas, with some of their Gentile converts, were appointed to go to Jerusalem in order to confer with the leaders of the mother church (Acts 15:1-29; Gal. 2:1-10). In the council that was convened, about A.D. 48 or 49, to consider the crisis, Peter took the side of the men from Antioch, reminding the others that when he had preached the gospel to Cornelius, the Roman centurion, the whole Gentile household received the gift of the Holy Spirit and was admitted into the church by baptism without undergoing the rite of circumcision (Acts 10:44-48). James, the brother of Jesus, also spoke in favor of the more liberal policy, pointing out that Old Testament prophets had foretold the calling of the Gentiles (Isa. 45:21; Jer. 12:15; Amos 9:11-12).

The result of the deliberations was the formulation of a letter in which the Jerusalem council recognized the Gentile converts as "brethren" and repudiated the position of the Judaizers. Instead of requiring that converts from paganism be circumcised and fulfill the other ceremonies of the Mosaic Law, the council declared that it was the mind of the Holy Spirit and of themselves to lay nothing further upon Gentile believers than certain minimum restrictions in the interest of harmony between the two wings of the church. Formulated by James, these restrictions touched upon certain practices in contemporary paganism that were particularly abhorrent to Jewish feeling. Specifically, converts from paganism were admonished to abstain from eating food that had been sacrificed to idols and then used for human consumption, from eating blood or meat that had been slaughtered without draining out the blood, and from sexual laxity (Acts 15:29).

Thus the decision of the council was essentially a prudent and tactful restraint laid upon Gentile Christians. It asked them to make certain justifiable concessions to Jewish sensibilities so that fellowship between the two groups could be maintained. Instead of formulating a system of doctrine bearing on the relation of law and grace, the decree of the council regulated only the behavior of pagan converts by showing them what the Christian ethic was. In granting freedom from the observance of the Mosaic Law as a requirement for salvation, the council saw that it was necessary that Gentile believers not use this freedom in such a way as to scandalize Jewish feeling by participating in offensive pagan customs.

The importance of this first church council is hard to overestimate. Had the Judaizers been successful in their insistence that Gentiles must become Jews before they could become Christians, the church would have remained an adjunct of the synagogue. By refusing to impose on Gentile converts the ritual act of circumcision and the observance of Mosaic ceremonial rules as a means of salvation, the council opened the way for the establishment of universal Christianity not tied to any national group.

IV. PAUL'S SECOND MISSIONARY JOURNEY

The apostolic council was a significant step in the progress of Christian liberty. It gave hearty commendation to the missionary policy of Paul and Barnabas, and acknowledged the freedom of Gentiles from the Mosaic Law. But many practical difficulties still remained to be solved.

One such difficulty appeared at Antioch soon after the meeting of the council (Gal. 2:11-21). The council had established the freedom of the Christians from the Mosaic Law, but it had not been determined that Jewish Christians should give up the Law. Furthermore, in order that the ceremonial requirements of the Law might be observed, the Jews had always been accustomed to avoid table companionship with Gentiles. What should be done, therefore, in churches that were composed of both Jewish Christians and Gentile Christians? How could Jewish Christians in such churches continue to observe the ceremonial law, and still hold table companionship with their Gentile brethren? The question was particularly important in view of the custom of celebrating the Lord's Supper in connection with a full meal, or love feast. The unity of the church, symbolized by partaking of one loaf and one cup, was threatened by pharisaically minded Jewish Christians who had conscientious scruples against eating with Gentile Christians.

It appears that the church at Antioch practiced "open communion," that is, that the Jewish dietary regulations had been dropped as an obstacle to Christian fellowship, and Jews and Greeks were allowed to sit at the same table and eat the same food. While visiting in Antioch, Peter, who had supported Paul and Barnabas at Jerusalem, conformed to local usage in eating at the same table with Gentile Christians. But when certain other visitors came to Antioch from Jerusalem, claiming the authority of James, Peter was afraid to be seen transgressing the Jewish ceremonial law, and he withdrew from having table companionship with Gentile Christians (Gal. 2:12). At length Barnabas and others joined him.

Paul sensed that a vital principle was at stake, and that Peter's course of action nullified the liberty that had been conceded by the Jerusalem council. For him there could be no compromise. Either Gentiles were to be admitted unconditionally to full Christian fellowship, or the church was essentially a Jewish institution, and this to him was to misunderstand the gospel. In his indignation he charged Peter and Barnabas with cowardice and hypocrisy (Gal. 2:11-14). His words of censure, deserved though they were, may well have left scars on his friendship with Barnabas and given Paul the uncomfortable feeling that his old comrade could not be trusted when the going became rough. After that, it would take only a slight matter to dissolve their association.

Such an occasion arose when Paul began to make preparations for another missionary journey. Barnabas wanted to take his cousin John Mark with them again. But Paul questioned the wisdom of taking one who had previously lost heart and returned home soon after the first journey had begun (Acts 13:13). Paul felt that they could not depend upon him—Barnabas was determined that he should be given a second chance (Acts 15:36-38). The upshot of the dispute was that the two apostles went their separate ways. Barnabas took Mark and sailed for Cyprus, while Paul set out, about A.D. 49, on a much wider mission with a new companion, Silas, otherwise known by his Roman name, Silvanus. The account of their journey in Acts 16 gives the impression that Paul now felt himself to be free as he had never been before, with all the world before him.

While revisiting towns of south Galatia in order to strengthen the churches that he had established on his first missionary journey, Paul found at Lystra the youthful Timothy, son of a Greek father and a Jewish-Christian mother, and persuaded him to come with them (Acts 16:1-3). Whether the three proceeded northward through the upper part of Galatia, establishing churches there, and then turned westward to Troas, or whether they went directly to Troas is difficult to determine from the brief account in the book of Acts. In any case, once at Troas, a seaport near the mouth of the Hellespont, the missionaries were led providentially, as they believed, to cross over into Europe. In response to a vision that Paul saw at night of a man of Macedonia beseeching him and saying, "Come over to Macedonia and help us," immediately the party took ship for Europe, and landing at Neapolis, went inland about ten miles to the city of Philippi (Acts 16:6-11).

Philippi was the leading city of the district of Macedonia. Luke describes it as a Roman colony (Acts 16:12), a status it acquired when Augustus Caesar sent to that city a group of Roman citizens, who, while retaining their Roman citizenship, formed the aristocracy of the place.

On the sabbath day, Paul preached to a group of earnest Jews and proselytes who had met for prayer at a spot alongside the Gangites River. The first convert was a prominent merchant woman from Thyatira named Lydia, apparently a Gentile proselyte, who with her household was baptized and later welcomed the missionaries into her home. The generosity of this presumably well-to-do woman set the pattern for the liberality of the Philippian church in later years (Phil. 4:14-20).

Paul's days in Philippi were cut short by an encounter with the city authorities. A slave girl possessed by a spirit of divination was being exploited by her owners to satisfy the superstitious desire of the pagan Philippians for soothsayers. Paul exorcized the spirit from the girl; whereupon, enraged by the financial loss, her owners had Paul and Silas arrested (Acts 16:16-24). Luke reports that even while in prison Paul and Silas bore such testimony to their Christian faith that the Philippian jailer was converted (Acts 16:25-34). The next day, invoking his rights of Roman citizenship, Paul, with Silas, was released, and accompanied by Timothy took to the highway again.

Thus began the first church established by Paul on European soil. It became Paul's favorite, the only one that he allowed to give him financial assistance (Phil. 4:15-16), and to which he later wrote what is perhaps his most affectionate letter.

Figure 9.2. Stone Crypt
(Courtesy of John McRay)
Stone crypt near the forum at Philippi in Macedonia, long identified as the place where Paul and Silas had been imprisoned (Acts 16:19-34).

Passing through towns that had no sizeable Jewish population, Paul and his companions traveled westward about one hundred miles to Thessalonica, where there was a synagogue. Strategically situated on the Thermaic Gulf, now called the Gulf of Salonika, the city of Thessalonica was one of the most important cities of Macedonia. Once again Paul's missionary work was successful; within a few weeks' time a church was established made up of some Jews, a great many of the devout Greeks, and "not a few of the leading women" (Acts 17:4). During Paul's residence in Thessalonica he found himself a job at his own trade of tentmaking in order to pay his way (1 Thess. 2:9). After a stay shorter than had been intended, persecution instigated by Jews drove the missionaries out of the city. The church, however, continued to thrive, and not long afterward Paul was able to say in a letter to the Thessalonians, "You became an example to all the believers in Macedonia and in Achaia" (1 Thess. 1:7).

Leaving Silas and Timothy in Macedonia to carry on the work at Beroea, Paul went on to Athens, the cultural center of the ancient Greco-Roman world. Here, in the historic cradle of philosophy, Paul preached not only in the synagogue but also directly to whoever happened to be in the marketplace. Several Epicurean and Stoic philosophers (see pp. 75-76) became superficially interested in the Christian teacher, though they regarded him more with amused contempt than with serious desire to learn what he had to say. He was, however, invited to expound his doctrines formally before the councilors of the Court of the Areopagus, which had among its police powers the duty of passing upon the competence of new religious lecturers. Paul's address before them as recorded in Acts is a classic of tact and courage. Taking as his starting point an inscription that he had chanced to see on an Athenian altar, "To an unknown god" (Acts 17:23), Paul stresses the work of God as creator and preserver of the world and of humankind. Whereas the apostle shows his appreciation of the truths that the gospel had in common with Stoicism and even includes quotations from two pagan writers (Acts 17:28), he finishes his address with the proclamation of the coming day of judgment of the world, when Jesus, whom God raised from the dead, is to be the universal judge. Paul's mention of the Resurrection divided his audience; some ridiculed the idea whereas others politely said that they would hear him at some other time.

Though Luke lists a few converts at Athens, there is no evidence that the apostle succeeded in establishing a church there, nor is the city mentioned in any of his correspondence. It appears that Paul left Athens disappointed at the meager results of his efforts to make Christianity appealing to philosophically minded sophisticates; at any rate he moved on to Corinth, resolved, as he later declared, to know nothing "except Jesus Christ, and him crucified" (1 Cor. 2:1-2).

Corinth, the capital of the Roman province of Achaia (Greece), was a great commercial metropolis, located on the seacoast about fifty miles west of Athens. This city, with a population of half a million persons, was notorious for its profligacy. The worship of fertility goddesses flourished in the most voluptuous and sensual forms, making Corinth a notorious center of immorality. Indeed, its reputation was so bad that the expression "to live like a Corinthian" meant to live an utterly dissolute life.

Paul's mission in Corinth, unlike that in Athens, was one of the most fruitful in the history of the early Christian church. During the course of his ministry there, congregations of believers were established not only in Corinth itself, but churches were formed also in adjacent towns (Rom. 16:1; 2 Cor. 1:1; 2 Thess. 1:4). As the Christian community grew, several distinguished persons became converts, including a certain Crispus, the ruler of the Jewish synagogue (Acts 18:8; 1 Cor. 1:14). On the whole, however, it appears that most of the church members had come from the lower strata of Corinthian society (1 Cor. 1:26; 6:9-11), and many were with difficulty separated from their pagan customs; some years later the apostle still addressed them as but "infants in Christ" (1 Cor. 3:1-2).

Paul's work in Corinth was also made notable for all time by the composition there of his earliest extant letters, the two written to the church at Thessalonica. In the opening salutations of the letters he names as his associates Silvanus and Timothy (1 Thess. 1:1; 2 Thess. 1:1), the latter of whom had recently come from Thessalonica with a report of the church there (1 Thess. 3:6). Since Paul had been obliged to leave Thessalonica before he had intended, he was anxiously wondering whether his work in that city had proved to be permanent. Overjoyed by the news of the progress of the church in Thessalonica, Paul wrote as a pastor to express his satisfaction and to answer some of the problems that concerned the young church there. (See the next chapter for a summary of the contents of the two letters.)

After eighteen months in Corinth, Paul once again turned eastward. Aquila and his wife Priscilla sailed with him as far as Ephesus (Acts 18:18-19), where he left them, promising to return after he had once again visited the church in Antioch, from where he had originally started (Acts 18:22). Thus was completed Paul's second missionary journey, extending from about A.D. 49 to about 53. During this period Christianity became established in Europe, and a long step forward had been taken in the evangelization of the Roman Empire.

V. PAUL'S THIRD MISSIONARY JOURNEY

Though Paul must have felt the need for a period of rest after the labor and anxiety of his second mission, such rest was not to be his. Still more insistent was what he interpreted to be a divine call to fulfill his ministry as an apostle to the nations. Feeling that he had been entrusted with a commission from God, he declared, "Woe to me if I do not proclaim the gospel!" (1 Cor. 9:16). Within several months after his return to Antioch, therefore, Paul began his third mission (probably A.D. 54). He first "went from place to place through the region of Galatia and Phyrgia, strengthening all the disciples" (Acts 18:23), and then settled in Ephesus.

Situated on the west coast of Asia Minor, Ephesus was the capital of the Roman province of Asia and one of the more influential cities on the main trade route from Rome to the East. Its magnificent open-air theater seated 24,500 spectators, and its great marble temple of the goddess Artemis (in Latin, Diana), with a floor area of more than 10,000 square feet, consisted of 100 columns of marble, each 55 feet in height, the 18 at each end sculptured. The cella, or inner sanctuary, which these columns surrounded, was 70 feet wide and 105 feet long. Its interior ornamentation was of surpassing splendor, adorned with the work of the greatest painters and sculptors of the Greek world. Generally regarded as one of the

Figure 9.3. The Theater at Ephesus
(Courtesy of Bastiaan Van Elderen.)
It was here that, according to Acts 19:34, for nearly two hours a tumultuous crowd kept shouting, "Great is Artemis of the Ephesians!" in order to protest the effects that Paul and his coworkers were having on the city, and especially on the economy connected with the temple of Artemis (called Diana in Latin).

seven wonders of the world, the temple drew many visitors from far and wide. In view of the strategic importance of Ephesus, it is understandable that the apostle for three years made it the center of his operations (Acts 20:31).

Paul's work in Ephesus followed a familiar pattern. After his initial preaching in the synagogue had aroused antagonism (Acts 19:8-9), he hired a lecture hall of a rhetorician named Tyrannus. Here he held forth daily, proclaiming the gospel to all and sundry between 11 A.M. and 4 P.M. These were the only possible hours, for the rhetorician would have lectured in the morning, and it was only when his class was over that the hall was available. Moreover, the apostle had to earn his daily bread, and since the working day began at sunrise and ended an hour before the sultry midday, it was only in the afternoon that he was free to preach and the populace to hear.

Such was the beginning of Paul's ministry at Ephesus—and a stirring and fruitful ministry it proved to be, penetrating the entire Roman province of Asia (Acts 19:1-20). Luke's brief account of the events of Paul's stay conveys vividly the superstitious regard of populace for black magic and astrology. One of the dramatic

Figure 9.4. Coin Issued by Hadrian Showing the Temple of Artemis
(Cambridge, Fitzwilliam Museum)
Coin of Ephesus (enlarged), issued under Hadrian (A.D. 117–138), depicting the famed temple of Artemis, the mother goddess of Ephesus (Acts 19:23-41). For many other examples of numismatic evidence, see Bluma L. Trell, *The Temple of Artemis at Ephesos* (New York: American Numismatic Society, 1945).

episodes of the apostle's ministry occurred when the practitioners of the black arts consigned their cabalistic books of charms and incantations to the flames "and burned them publicly" (Acts 19:19). That one person should have been able to do so much to combat ignorance and superstition is one of the marvels of the story of Christianity.

One of the results of Paul's preaching was the economic repercussion arising from the falling away of sales of silver shrines of Artemis. Demetrius, a silversmith, addressed a group of similar artisans, concluding, "There is danger not only that this trade of ours may come into disrepute but also that the temple of the great goddess Artemis will be scorned, and she will be deprived of her majesty that brought all Asia and the world to worship her" (Acts 19:27). When they heard this, they were enraged and began to shout, "Great is Artemis of the Ephesians!" As a result, the city was filled with confusion, and people rushed together to the theater dragging with them Gaius and Aristarchus, Macedonians who were Paul's traveling companions. For two hours the crowds kept

Figure 9.5. A Statue of the Ephesian Artemis (Courtesy of Bastiaan Van Elderen)

Several statues of Artemis (Diana) have been found at Ephesus, one of them twice life-size. All the statues depict multiple breasts (or eggs), emphasizing the goddess's fertility.

shouting in unison, "Great is Artemis of the Ephesians!" It was only with difficulty that the town clerk managed to quiet the crowd, and Paul and his companions were released (Acts 19:34-41).

It was while Paul was busy in Ephesus that bad news reached him from Galatia. Jewish Christian agitators had come among the churches of Galatia and taught Paul's converts that it was necessary for them to keep the Mosaic Law, as well as have faith in Christ, in order to be assured of God's favor. Perceiving that this was a recrudescence of the Judaizing heresy, Paul wrote an impassioned letter in which he set forth the first formal statement and discussion of the doctrines of grace and of justification by faith. (For a summary of the Letter to the Galatians, see the next chapter.)

While Paul was in Ephesus, news of the condition of the Corinthian church also occasioned him much anxiety. In reply to inquiries from Corinth he wrote a letter, now lost,[1] concerning relations of believers to the pagan society about them (1 Cor. 5:9). But later reports showed that more serious troubles had arisen. When we recall Corinth's reputation as the cesspool of Greece, and the circumstance that many of the earliest Christian converts at Corinth had come from the lower strata of society, it is not surprising that after Paul's departure, irregularities, both ethical and liturgical, had arisen. In order to set these straight, Paul wrote the letter that we know today as 1 Corinthians. To read this letter at this point (or the summary of the letter given in the following chapter) is to realize how vast were the odds against which Paul was fighting, how intensely practical was his approach to the Christian life, and how certain he was that God's providential care and love would ultimately prevail, despite the setbacks.

The dispatch of this letter did not end the apostle's anxiety about the Corinthian church. It would seem that the letter was too kindly—at all events it did not have the desired effect. Many think that Paul, after writing 1 Corinthians, himself made a flying visit to Corinth for disciplinary purposes (compare 2 Cor. 12:14; 13:1). The visit was so distressing that he returned to Ephesus much troubled. Conscious of his failure to heal the crisis, Paul seems to have sent a sharp letter by Titus, warning the Corinthians that he meant to

---

1. Unless, as some scholars hold, a fragment of it is preserved in 2 Corinthians 6:14–7:1, a section that interrupts the thought of the passage in which it now stands.

come again. (What is now 2 Cor. 10:1 through 13:10 may be a part of this severe letter, which is referred to in 2 Cor. 2:3-4; 7:8).

Paul left Ephesus full of anxiety about the effects of his severe letter. Hurrying on to Troas and thence to Macedonia, he there met Titus, who reported that the Corinthians had repudiated and punished the recalcitrant members and that the crisis was over (2 Cor. 2:12-13; 7:5-16). The apostle was overjoyed and wrote yet another letter, sending it by Titus to Corinth. (This fourth letter appears to be preserved today as 2 Cor. 1:1 through 9:15 and 13:11-14; for a summary see the next chapter).

From Macedonia Paul himself went on to Corinth where he resided for some three months (Acts 20:2-3). Luke records no incidents of this stay in Corinth (probably during the winter of A.D. 57–58). It is altogether likely, however, that during this visit the apostle completed the discipline and organization of the Corinthian church. The visit, moreover, is memorable because it was then that Paul wrote the Letter to the Romans. In it the apostle sets forth completely the conception of Christianity as the way of salvation. From its pages we also discover that the gospel was being preached vigorously in the world's capital, and that the Roman Christians possessed the gifts of the Spirit and some amount of organization (Rom. 12:6-8). Yet the letter is not addressed to "the church at Rome," but "to all God's beloved in Rome," a phraseology that suggests that their organization was not compact or unified.

The beginnings of Christianity at Rome are shrouded in obscurity. It is possible that some of the "visitors from Rome" (Acts 2:10) carried it back after Pentecost. It is possible that some of the disciples who fled from Jerusalem after the death of Stephen traveled as far as Italy (Acts 8:4). Though Paul had never visited Rome, as "a minister of Christ Jesus to the Gentiles" he evidently considered the church there to be under his care (Rom. 15:15-16). He had long wished to preach in Rome (Acts 19:21; 2 Cor. 11:16), and to go on from there to Spain (Rom. 15:28), but thus far had been prevented (Rom. 1:13). Now when he was about to return to Jerusalem with a liberal offering from Gentile churches for the relief of the poor Christians of Judea, Paul wrote a letter to pave the way for a visit to Rome, which he hoped to make in the near future.

Since the Christians of Rome had never seen his face and knew him only by reputation, Paul no doubt felt that he must give them a more or less formal account of his teaching—something much more complete than he would need to give a congregation that he had established himself. Thus it comes about that the Letter to the Romans is a didactic treatise presenting the fullest account of Paul's theology that we have. (For a summary of the Letter to the Romans, see the next chapter.)

Accompanied by friends from several Gentile churches, Paul now set out on his last journey to Jerusalem (Acts 20:4). At Philippi Luke joined the group (Acts 20:6), and he describes the subsequent journey in considerable detail (Acts 20:7 to 21:6).

At Tyre and again at Caesarea, where he stopped off to visit with groups of Christian believers (Acts 21:4, 12), Paul was warned of the dangers arising from antagonistic Jews and Jewish Christians that would confront him in Jerusalem. But he resisted all efforts to dissuade him from going, and at length came to Jerusalem, thus completing what is known as his third missionary journey, extending from about A.D. 54 to 58.

VI. PAUL'S ARREST AND IMPRISONMENT

The forebodings of Paul's friends for his safety in Jerusalem proved to be well founded. Though James and the elders of the Jerusalem church received Paul cordially enough, they were anxious about his reception by others in view of persistent reports that in his mission work he had taught Jews to forsake Moses (Acts 21:17-21). It was proposed, therefore, that he should show publicly his respect for Jewish customs by joining in the temple rites of a Nazirite purification about to be performed by four believers, and by paying their expenses. To this he consented, for while Paul insisted that no Gentile should observe the cultic Law of Moses, and while be maintained that no Christian Jew was bound to observe it, he found no fault with Jews who chose to observe it (Acts 21:22-26).

The act of conciliation, however, resulted in the very trouble it was intended to prevent. Fanatical Jews from the Roman province of Asia, seeing Paul in the temple, raised a hue and cry. They falsely charged him with having brought Gentiles into the temple, thereby defiling the sacred precincts. At once a fierce riot broke out, and Paul would probably have lost his life had not the commander of the Roman garrison in the adjacent castle of Antonia, which served as a barracks, run up to quell the howling mob. The tribune, Claudius Lysias, arrested Paul as the manifest cause of the disturbance, had him chained to a couple of soldiers, one on each side, and then asked the bystanders what he had been doing. Some shouted one thing and some another, and as he could make nothing of their statements, he ordered Paul taken away into the barracks. The mob, disappointed in its effort to make an end of him, followed shouting, "Away with him!" (Acts 21:27-36).

As Paul was about to be brought into the barracks, he requested permission of the tribune to address the crowd from the castle steps. The crowd listened to his defense until he uttered the word "Gentiles"—then tumult broke out afresh (Acts 22:21-22). The tribune thereupon hurried Paul into safety inside the barracks and gave orders to have him examined under the lash, to get the truth out of him as to what all the outcry was about. By appealing, however, to his Roman citizenship, Paul was saved from the flogging (Acts 22:24-29).

On the following day, Paul was brought to trial before the Jewish Sanhedrin, but that body came to no conclusive adjudication of the case, thanks to a stratagem on Paul's part to divide his enemies (Acts 23:6-10). Then some forty men, obviously Sicarii or Assassins (see p. 55), conspired to lie in ambush for Paul, having bound themselves with an oath not to eat or drink until they had killed him. But Paul's nephew heard of the plot and managed to warn his uncle and the Roman tribune (Acts 23:12-22). This lurid story did not appear to the tribune in the least improbable, and he gave orders that Paul should be taken to Caesarea that very night under a strong guard of nearly five hundred of the military. The fact that Paul was a Roman citizen made Lysias anxious to transfer him to the custody of Felix, the Roman procurator, at a safe distance from the local insurrectionists (Acts 23:23-35). The sixty-mile trip being made, two hearings before Felix still brought no decisive result. Owing to Felix's procrastination in disposing of the case, Paul was left in prison at Caesarea for two years, until Porcius Festus arrived in A.D. 59 or 60 as successor to Felix (Acts 24:1-27).

Thus, as the result of a minor collision with the Jewish revolutionaries at Jerusalem, Paul's liberty came to an end, and with it all the great plans of wider missionary work that he had in view. It would be interesting to know how the apostle was occupied during his Caesarean imprisonment.[2] Probably he was able in a certain measure to continue to direct the affairs of churches, for Luke says that his friends were allowed to visit him (Acts 24:23). Furthermore, Felix and his wife Drusilla, who was a Jew, would on occasion send for Paul and listen to his teaching about faith in Christ, and about uprightness, self-control, and coming judgment. When the preaching became too personal and alarming, Felix would dismiss the apostle only to recall him another day (Acts 24:24-26).

As soon as Felix was replaced by Porcius Festus, the Jews besought the new procurator to have Paul returned to Jerusalem for trial. Festus, however, bade them send their representatives to Caesarea, and when they came, they were unable to substantiate their charges (Acts 25:1-8). Nevertheless Festus, wishing to conciliate the Jews, asked Paul if he was willing to go to Jerusalem to be tried. Thereupon the apostle, realizing the hopelessness of securing justice in Palestine, made a dramatic appeal as a Roman citizen to the emperor's court in Rome (Acts 25:9-12). That would at least put him beyond the reach of the Jewish Sicarii who were so relentlessly on his trail in Palestine. Furthermore, to argue his defense in person in Caesar's court would provide this intrepid missionary with an opportunity of proclaiming the gospel before the most exalted audience in the world.

Before arrangements could be made to send him to Rome, however, Festus was paid a state visit by King Herod Agrippa II and his sister Bernice, who came over from Chalcis, northeast of Galilee, to welcome him to his new post. Partly as a compliment to Agrippa, who was the titular king of the Jews, and partly to learn what account of Paul he ought forward to Rome, Festus proposed that together they should hear the prisoner's defense (Acts 25:14-22). Accordingly, Paul was given the opportunity of delivering to a

---

2. Though some scholars have suggested that several of Paul's extant letters were written while he was in prison at Caesarea, internal evidence points rather to their composition during the apostle's subsequent Roman imprisonment.

distinguished audience his most famous apologia (Acts 25:23–26:23). Festus's verdict was that Paul was insane, and Agrippa's reaction was to ask superciliously whether Paul was trying to convert him. Both agreed privately that there was no substance in the Jewish charges against the prisoner, and no reason he should remain in custody. But Paul had appealed to the emperor, and to the emperor he had to go (Acts 26:24-32).

Luke's description of the voyage to Rome is narrated with a degree of picturesque detail that suggests that it had come from an eyewitness. Since the account is told in terms of "we" and "us," it appears that Luke himself embarked on the ship that was carrying Paul and certain other prisoners to Italy (Acts 27:1). Setting out from Caesarea in the early autumn of A.D. 60, the vessel encountered a fierce storm that resulted in its being shipwrecked on the island of Malta (Acts 27:9). Setting out again the next spring in another ship, Paul and his captors finally landed at Puteoli in the bay of Naples (Acts 28:11-13). News of his coming had preceded him, and delegations from the Roman Christians met him as he approached the city along the Appian Way (Acts 28:14-15).

Paul had achieved one of his great ambitions, to visit the capital of the empire. It was not, however, as a traveling evangelist, but as the emperor's prisoner awaiting trial. Guarded by a soldier, to whom he was manacled by a chain, Paul was kept in custody under house arrest. He was free to receive visitors, although he could not move about freely himself (Acts 28:17-31).

Appeals to the emperor were slow processes, and for two years the case continued on the list of trials still pending. At this point Luke's narrative ends with surprising abruptness. But more light is thrown on this period of Paul's life by the correspondence that he carried on during the months of enforced idleness. In spite of his imprisonment, he continued to instruct, admonish, and encourage congregations and individuals in Macedonia and Asia Minor. As "an ambassador in chains" (Eph. 6:20) he dispatched letters to the churches at Ephesus and Colossae through Tychicus, who was accompanied by Onesimus, by whose hand Paul also sent a letter to Philemon. Later, toward the close of the two-year period, Paul wrote a letter to his beloved church at Philippi. Looking back upon his months of confinement he declares to the Philippians, "I want you to know, beloved, that what has happened to me has actually helped to spread the gospel, so that it has become known throughout the whole imperial guard and to everyone else that my imprisonment is for Christ; and most of the brothers and sisters, having been made confident in the Lord by my imprisonment, dare to speak the word with greater boldness and without fear" (Phil. 1:12-14). (For summaries of these four letters written during his Roman imprisonment, see the next chapter.)

What happened to Paul at the end of the two-year imprisonment, we do not know. A tradition preserved in a letter of Clement of Rome, written about A.D. 95–96, implies that the apostle was released and went to Spain. Two of the three Pastoral Letters (1 Timothy and Titus) allude to certain of Paul's activities in the East that cannot be fitted into the narrative of Acts. It has often been supposed, therefore, that Paul was acquitted, or at any rate released from imprisonment, that he fulfilled his long cherished wish to visit Spain, and that subsequently he continued his evangelistic work in the eastern Mediterranean world. Since 2 Timothy contains references to Paul's being in prison, it is assumed that he was rearrested about A.D. 67, and sent to Rome, where according to tradition he was beheaded by order of the emperor Nero.

Because the three Pastoral Letters differ somewhat from the generally acknowledged Pauline Letters in literary style and vocabulary, as well as in doctrinal emphases, some scholars believe that they either were written by an amanuensis[3] to whom the apostle gave considerable freedom in their composition, or that they were drawn up toward the end of the first century by a devoted follower of Paul, who may have incorporated some fragmentary letters of the apostle that otherwise would have been lost. No matter who was responsible for the composition of the Pastoral Letters, they attest the apostle's release from his (first) Roman imprisonment and his subsequent missionary activity followed by imprisonment once again. (For a summary of the Pastoral Letters, see the close of the next chapter.)

---

3. The presence of certain similarities as regards significant words, phrases, and ideas between the three Pastoral Letters and the Third Gospel and Acts has led some scholars to suggest that it was Luke who served as Paul's amanuensis; see S. G. Wilson, *Luke and the Pastoral Epistles* (London: SPCK, 1979).

The use of computers recently to make comprehensive and accurate counts of stylometric features (like proportions of sentence lengths, variations of sentence lengths, and position of key words) has led to new interest in the question of the authorship of the Pauline Letters. On the basis of some ninety different stylistic indicators, Sir Anthony Kenny has summed up the matter as follows:

> What is to be said of the authorship of the Epistles is in the end a matter for the Scripture scholar, not the stylometrist. But on the basis of the evidence in this chapter [on the Pauline corpus] for my part I see no reason to reject the hypothesis that twelve of the Pauline Epistles are the work of a single, unusually versatile author.[4]

---

4. Sir Anthony Kenny, *A Stylometric Study of the New Testament* (Oxford: Clarendon Press, 1986), p. 100. In referring to twelve rather than thirteen epistles of Paul, Kenny acknowledges that "the most serious limitation of the statistical study of literary texts concerns the difficulty of applying stylometric methods to short passages. This affects the confidence both about short works (such as the Epistle to Titus) or about short passages alleged to be interpolated (such as the final chapter of Romans)" (p. 188).

CHAPTER 10

PAUL'S LETTERS TO CHURCHES AND INDIVIDUALS

I. PAUL'S LETTERS IN GENERAL

After the apostle Paul had established churches during his missionary journeys, it was his custom to oversee the spiritual growth of the new congregations either by revisiting them or by writing letters to them, or both. The form of his letters was the same as that of secular letters of the period. These normally contain an introductory paragraph giving the name of the writer, the name of the recipient(s), and a greeting ("health"); the middle portion of the letter contains the main message; a concluding paragraph bids farewell and often gives messages from friends. Though Paul followed the conventional letter pattern, he made certain changes that stamp his correspondence as characteristically Christian. Thus, instead of using the nonreligious greeting "health," he opens his letters with the salutation "grace and peace" [from God and Christ be with the recipients], and in the conclusion he modifies the secular "farewell" into some form of benediction, such as "the grace of our Lord Jesus Christ be with you." In the majority of his letters the main part is divided into two sections, the former dealing with points of doctrine and the latter dealing with practical problems confronting the recipients of the letter.

Paul usually followed the custom of dictating his letters to an amanuensis or secretary. In Romans 16:22, the amanuensis adds a greeting of his own and discloses his name as Tertius. We may picture Tertius, or some other amanuensis on another occasion, sitting and writing as Paul paces the floor. Doubtless the apostle gesticulates with his hands, speaking now rapidly and now slowly as he strives for the clearest expression of his thought. It is interesting to conjecture where interruptions may have come, and where dictation was resumed again, perhaps on another day. The sharp break in the progress of thought in the midst of Philippians 3:1 may be accounted for in this way.

In antiquity trained amanuenses made use of a system of Greek shorthand; a letter taken down in this form would, of course, need to be transcribed later in ordinary Greek script. One wonders how thoroughly Paul edited the completed work of the amanuensis. At least it was his custom to close every dictated letter with a sentence or two in his own handwriting, both as a token of special affection and as a sign of genuineness (1 Cor. 16:21; Col. 4:18; 2 Thess. 3:17).

It is possible that Paul followed the contemporary practice of keeping a copy of each letter in a special letter book and that he referred to it from time to time when composing subsequent letters. This would help account for certain similarities of ideas and phraseology in, for example, his letters to the Ephesians and the Colossians. When Paul quoted passages from the Old Testament, how far did he consult a copy of the text and how far did he rely upon his memory? From the freedom with which he quotes, adapts, and combines texts it appears that he usually did so from memory. Quotations from the Hebrew text are very rare; for the most part Paul followed the Greek translation of the Old Testament known as the Septuagint.

In antiquity there was no organized system for the carrying and delivery of private letters. Early in the Roman Empire Augustus instituted a postal service *(cursus publicus)*, but this was reserved for official dispatches, and only rarely were nonofficials allowed to make use of it. Private letter writers, therefore, had to rely on special messengers or friendly travelers. When such a person arrived bearing a letter from Paul to a church that the apostle had founded some years previously, what a variety of emotions must have stirred in the hearts of his friends! One thinks what it must have meant to hear the leader read to the congregation, for the first time, such sentences as, "If I speak in the tongues of mortals and of angels, but do not have love, I am a noisy gong or a clanging cymbal" (1 Cor. 13:1), or, "Work out your own salvation with fear and trembling; for it is God who is at work in you, enabling you both to will and to work for his good pleasure" (Phil. 2:12-13). We may be sure that such a letter was put away in the archives of the little community, and that it was read and reread to the congregation. It appears, too, that Paul intended copies of his letters to be circulated among churches other than the one originally addressed. Thus, at the conclusion of his letter to the church at Colossae, he directs: "When this letter has been read among you, have it read also in the church of the Laodiceans; and see that you read also the letter from Laodicea" (Col. 4:16).

A significant characteristic of Paul's correspondence is that he writes as an authority whom the recipients are bound to obey (1 Thess. 4:2; 2 Thess. 2:15; 3:6-14). He assumes that the same authority will be attached to his words as to a revelation of the Spirit (1 Cor. 2:13), or to a command of the Lord (1 Cor. 14:37). Paul bases the authoritative character of his words not on his own inherent superiority—for he calls himself the least of the apostles (1 Cor. 15:9)—but on the divine commission that he had received from Jesus Christ himself (Gal. 1:12).

The letters traditionally ascribed to Paul may be arranged in accordance with various orders and classifications. The sequence in which they stand in the New Testament has very little practical utility; they are arranged roughly according to their length, the longest (Romans) standing first and the shortest (Philemon) last. As it happens, in this order the nine letters to seven churches (Romans, Corinthians, Galatians, Ephesians, Philippians, Colossians, Thessalonians) fall into one group, and the four letters to three individuals (Timothy, Titus, Philemon) fall into another group.

Another way of classifying the Pauline Letters is to arrange them in chronological order. In such a sequence they reveal something of the historical development of Paul's thinking and preoccupation during that part of his career—lasting about a dozen or fifteen years—when he wrote the letters that are preserved today. It is obvious that the apostle touches upon a wide variety of topics in his correspondence, topics that fall into theological, ethical, administrative, and devotional categories. These elements are combined with great freedom, and no strict line can be drawn between them. At the same time, the proportion in which they are blended, and the preponderance of one kind of concern or another, give to each letter its special complexion.

When the traditional Pauline Letters are examined in their chrono-logical sequence, so far as this can be ascertained, they fall into four groups, each of which has a special theological emphasis or concern. The first letters that he wrote (the two to the church at Thessalonica)[1] deal primarily with problems bearing on eschatology—the second coming of Christ and the end of the age. A few years later, during his third missionary journey, Paul sent four of his most weighty letters to the churches in Galatia, Corinth, and Rome. Amid the variety of theological topics considered in these four, the apostle's preoccupa-tion is with soteriology--the doctrine of the way of salvation. Several years later, while Paul is in prison at Rome, his letters to Christians at Ephesus, Colossae, and Philippi deal primarily with Christology—the doctrine of the person and work of Christ. In this period also falls the very brief personal note to Philemon. Finally, whoever may have been responsible for the present form of the three Pastoral Letters, which are traditionally associated with Paul's second Roman imprisonment (1 Timothy, Titus, 2 Timothy), it is obvious that their chief concern is with ecclesiology—the duties of a pastor in providing instruction and leadership for the local church.

II. SUMMARIES OF PAUL'S LETTERS

In the following pages, the gist of each of Paul's Letters is set forth within the historical context of the local church to which it was sent. Since the recipients of the letters were already Christian believers, the apostle needed only to recall the preaching they had received (1 Cor. 15:1), and he devotes most of his letters to teaching the application of the gospel to the diverse conditions of everyday life. In writing, Paul naturally takes for granted much of the back-ground and local situation, which would be well known to the recipients; for us today, however, it is sometimes difficult to recon-struct the details of the motives, circumstances, and problems that called forth his correspondence.

1. PAUL'S FIRST LETTER TO THE THESSALONIANS
Founded during Paul's second missionary journey, the church at Thessalonica in Macedonia consisted of a few Jewish converts and

---

1. Some scholars have thought that Paul's Letter to the Galatians was his first extant letter, but this view is not widely held today.

a large number of converted pagans (Acts 17:4; 1 Thess. 1:9). Paul had been obliged by bitter persecution to leave Thessalonica before he had assured himself that the young church there was mature enough to be left without apostolic guidance. Moving on to Greece, Paul was filled with anxiety lest his work in Thessalonica would not be permanent. Every human probability was against the maintenance of Christian testimony in the face of Jewish opposition and pagan corruption. While in Corinth Paul received his first news from Thessalonica, and the news was good news. Timothy brought him a report of the satisfactory spiritual health of the young Thessalonian church despite persecution arising from the leaders of the synagogue who were attempting to discredit the authority of the Christian missionaries. He also brought two questions, possibly in writing, that were agitating the minds of some in the Thessalonian church and needed an immediate answer. One concerned the date of the parousia, or second coming of Christ, and the other concerned the fate of other believers who, by their premature death, could not possibly be witnesses of the parousia.

In the course of answering these questions, Paul also took occasion to urge his converts to live a diligent and orderly life. The letter is remarkable for the glimpse it gives us of the personality of Paul and of his genuine concern for the welfare of his converts.

Summary of 1 Thessalonians

After the opening salutation Paul expresses his gratitude to God for the steadfastness of the Thessalonian Christians, for their endurance despite much affliction, and for the influence they had already exerted as "an example to all the believers in Macedonia and in Achaia" (1:7). The apostle next surveys the relations between himself and the congregation (2:1–3:13). He reminds them of his unself-ish and devoted work in their midst ("You remember our labor and toil, brothers and sisters; we worked night and day, so that we might not burden any of you while we proclaimed to you the gospel of God," 2:9), and of the enthusiasm with which they had received his preaching and steadfastly endured persecutions (2:13-16).

After having left Thessalonica Paul had longed to return for another mission (2:17–3:5), and now he rejoices at the good news that Timothy brought back (3:6-10). The apostle concludes the first part of his letter with a prayer that he may be permitted to return to them and that God may make them "increase and abound in love to one another and for all" (3:11-13).

Turning to the questions that were troubling the Thessalonians, Paul first exhorts them to lead lives of purity in the relation of the sexes (4:3-6), and to work quietly, minding their own affairs, so that they "may behave properly toward outsiders and be dependent on no one" (4:9-12). Concerning believers who have already died, the apostle assures his readers, on the authority of a special revelation that he had received (4:15), that at the parousia they will rise first and be caught up with the living to be united with the Lord. Those who have died in Christ thus will not fail to enjoy the glories of the kingdom (4:13-18).

In the final section, Paul reiterates his previous teaching among them that no one knows the date of Christ's second coming; Christians should, therefore, lead lives of constant watchfulness and sobriety (5:1-11). He concludes with a variety of exhortations, including respect for officers of the church, consideration for those in need, cultivation of spiritual gifts, and other duties of the Christian life (5:12-28).

2. PAUL'S SECOND LETTER TO THE THESSALONIANS

The obsession of some of the members of the church at Thessalonica concerning the end of the world, so far from subsiding after receiving Paul's first letter, had become more serious. The hysteria over the imminence of Christ's coming had reached such a pitch that some had given up earning their livelihood and were living off the generosity of more sober-minded believers. The agitation was apparently increased by alleged revelations of an ecstatic individual and also by a letter purporting to be from Paul containing such teaching (2:2). Confronted by an acute situation, the apostle hastened to correct misunderstandings by writing a second letter in which he describes certain signs that must first be seen before the end of the world comes. If Paul had been challenged that this contradicts his statement in 1 Thessalonians that the time of the parousia is uncertain, he doubtless would have explained that the "signs" form one unit with the parousia, and the whole is to come unexpectedly.

Summary of 2 Thessalonians

After the opening salutation, Paul expresses his thanksgiving to God for the fidelity of the Thessalonian Christians amid persecution; he assures them that at the second coming of Christ divine judgment will come upon those who now afflict them (1:1-12).

Turning to what is obviously the main reason for his letter, Paul begs his readers not to be disturbed by the idea that the second advent of Christ is all but upon them. He reminds them that before that day comes there will be an apostasy, culminating in the appearance of "the man of lawlessness," who will impiously claim the homage due to God alone (2:1-4). For the present, the development of this apostasy is being restrained from achieving its full effect. At the end of time, however, "the lawless one" (Antichrist) will be manifested in satanic power and with "signs" and "lying wonders" will lead astray "those who are perishing"; but he will be destroyed by Christ at his second coming (2:5-12).

In the second part of his letter, Paul expresses thanksgiving for his readers' election to salvation, and prays that they may stand firm in their Christian profession (2:13-17). He appeals for their prayers on his behalf (3:1-3), and, assuring them of his confidence in their obedience (3:4-5), repeats his injunction that they imitate him in leading a sober and industrious life (3:6-9). He denounces shirkers who sponge off their neighbors' generosity. Give them nothing, he says bluntly (in crisp paraphrase, "No loaf to the loafer!"), and hunger will bring them to their senses (3:10-13). Severe measures are to be taken against those who are recalcitrant, yet it should always be remembered that even the black sheep in the congregation are still members of the family (3:14-15).

In view of the circulation of a letter purporting to be from him (2:2), Paul calls attention to his signature, which was added by his own hand as a token of genuineness to every letter of his (3:17).

3. PAUL'S LETTER TO THE GALATIANS

The region of Galatia, which is in the interior of Asia Minor, was settled by migrating Gauls in the third century B.C. Amyntas, the last king of Galatia, died in 25 B.C. and bequeathed his kingdom to the Roman Empire. The Romans made it a province, adding a number of other districts on the south, including Pisidia, Isauria, Phrygia, and parts of Lycaonia.

In view of the ambiguity of the term *Galatia*, which may be used ethnically or politically, the question arises whether Paul's letter was addressed to the descendants of the Gauls in the northern part of the province (North Galatian theory) or to the people in the southern part of the province (South Galatian theory). If the second theory is correct, we know that Paul evangelized the area on his first missionary journey with Barnabas (Acts 13 and 14). If the first theory is correct, it is not certain when Paul evangelized the area; perhaps he did so on his second journey (compare Acts 16:6). Each of the two theories has been vigorously defended; the absence of proof, however, that the people who belonged to the parts of the province outside the region of Galatia proper were ever described or addressed as Galatians makes the South Galatian theory the less probable.

The occasion for Paul's writing this impassioned letter was the disquieting news that the Galatians had begun to fall away from the true gospel of the sufficiency of faith in Jesus Christ, and were following the opinions of certain Judaistic agitators. These teachers held that to please God it was necessary to keep the Law of Moses in addition to believing in Jesus Christ. Before a man could become a Christian, they maintained, he had to undergo the rite of circumcision, keep the sabbath and other Jewish days, eat only kosher food, and observe the other ceremonial laws of the Old Testament. In short, the Judaizers declared that a person is saved by faith and works, whereas Paul held that one is saved through faith alone.

Paul saw that the controversy was not a minor one; great issues were at stake. He knew from his own bitter experience that salvation is God's free gift to those who have faith in Christ, not something to be earned by keeping certain rules.

So serious was the crisis that Paul dispenses with the customary expression of thanksgiving and commendation, with which he opens all his other letters, and plunges directly into a vigorous defense of his apostolic authority and the validity of his teaching (1:1–2:21). The central part of the letter is an exposition of the doctrine of justification by faith alone (3:1–4:31). Lest any should imagine that this doctrine leads to a life of indifference to the moral code, Paul concludes with certain practical applications of his teaching (5:1–6:18).

The importance of this letter, sometimes called the Magna Carta of Christian liberty, is hard to overestimate. In it Paul sets forth, with impassioned eloquence, the true function of the Mosaic Law and its relation to God's will revealed in Jesus Christ. The great point is that the Christian life is founded on God's grace (compare "gratis" = "given free"), not on any good actions (works) that one does. The declaration of the principles reiterated in these six brief chapters made Christianity a world religion instead of remaining a sect within Judaism.

Summary of Galatians

Opening abruptly and without his usual cordiality, Paul's salutation emphasizes his divinely given authority as an apostle and the atoning death of Jesus Christ, "who gave himself for our sins . . . according to the will of our God and Father" (1:1-5). He expresses his astonishment that the Galatians have so quickly fallen away from the true gospel, and he anathematizes the Judaizing teachers who have misled them (1:6-9).

In the historical part of the letter (chapters 1 and 2), Paul tells the story of his conversion and commission as an apostle. Both the gospel message and his apostolate come not from humans but from God—facts that the Jerusalem church and the original apostles recognized (1:10-24). Furthermore, the leaders of the mother church at Jerusalem expressed formally their approval of his evangelistic work among the Gentiles (2:1-10). To illustrate that his authority as an apostle was unchallenged, even by one of the older apostles, he adds an account of his rebuking Peter at Antioch (2:11-21; see p. 232).

In the doctrinal part of the letter (chapters 3 and 4) the apostle argues that it is faith, and not the Mosaic Law, that brings a person into right relation with God. He discusses the difference between the faith principle and the works principle, showing that both cannot be essential conditions of salvation, which the experience of the Galatians themselves proves, for they had received the gift of the Spirit through faith and not because they observed the Mosaic Law (3:1-5). Even the Old Testament itself, to which the Judaizers so confidently appealed, teaches that Abraham was justified through faith, not by works (3:6-14). The Mosaic Law, which came much later than Abraham, cannot annul the faith principle that underlay God's dealings with Abraham (3:15-18).

What, then, is the purpose of the Old Testament Law? Paul answers that one of its purposes is to make people realize that sin is a transgression of God's commandments (3:19-20). In this function the Law does not contradict God's promises; on the contrary, the Law serves as a kind of tutor to bring people to Christ, that they may be justified through faith; and now that faith has come, the tutor's function has ceased (3:21-25). So Christ has freed individuals from the Law and made them children of God and heirs (3:26–4:7). As an interlude in his theological argument, the apostle makes a warm personal appeal to the Galatians, reminding them of their earlier enthusiastic affection for him (4:8-20).

Besides referring to the history of Abraham himself, Paul adduces another illustration from the Old Testament to show the primacy of faith over works. He reminds his readers that Abraham had two wives—one a slave (Hagar), and one a free woman (Sarah). By means of an allegory, a form of argument that would carry conviction with the Judaizers, he declares that the children of the slave woman correspond to the children of the present Jerusalem, whereas the children of Sarah resemble Isaac, a son granted her by the gracious promise of God (4:21-31).

In the third part of the letter (chapters 5 and 6), Paul warns against the misapplication of his teaching. Christian freedom is not a license to indulge the desires of the flesh; it involves moral obligations that are fulfilled through love for the other believers (5:1-15). God has given Christians the Holy Spirit, and the Spirit should control their lives, producing "the fruit of the Spirit" (5:22-23).

Paul concludes his letter with practical counsel concerning the obligation of Christians to help one another (6:1-5), to support their teachers, and to "work for the good of all, and especially for those of the family of faith" (6:7-10). A postscript is added, in the apostle's own handwriting, in which he sums up the main points of the letter (6:11-18).

4. PAUL'S LETTERS TO THE CORINTHIANS

During Paul's third missionary journey, disquieting news came to him concerning the state of the church at Corinth, and he wrote a letter warning the Corinthians against associating with immoral persons (1 Cor. 5:9). This (first) letter to Corinth is now lost, unless, as some scholars hold, a portion of it has been preserved as 2 Corinthians 6:14–7:1, a section that interrupts the thought of the passage in which it now stands.

Instead of subsiding, the irregularities in the Corinthian congregation multiplied. Information concerning the condition of the church was reported to Paul by members of the household of a certain Chloe (1 Cor. 1:11), by a deputation of three leaders from the church there (1 Cor. 16:17), and in a letter from the church asking Paul's judgment on various questions (1 Cor. 7:1). As a result, Paul wrote one of the most intensely practical of all his letters. In chapters 1 through 6 of what is called 1 Corinthians, he deals with disruptive factions in the church, a case of gross immorality, and the lawsuits that some members had instituted against others (these were the things of which he had heard by word of mouth). In chapters 7 through 16 he answers the questions that the Corinthians had put to him in their letter. He refers to each point in turn with the same formula:

"Now concerning the matters about which you wrote" (7:1-24).

"Now concerning the virgins" (7:25-40).

"Now concerning food sacrificed to idols" (8:1–11:1).

"Now concerning spiritual gifts" (12:1–14:40).

"Now concerning the collection for the saints" (16:1-12, combined with some personal matters).

Apparently 1 Corinthians was ineffective in correcting the irregularities in the Corinthian church; at any rate, Paul subsequently wrote a third letter, exceedingly severe in its rebuke of the wrongdoers (2 Cor. 2:3-4; compare 7:8). Not long after, having heard that there had been a change for the better, in a cheerful spirit the apostle sent the church a fourth letter, in which we can detect his satisfaction that disciplinary action had been taken. In view of the marked change of outlook between the first nine chapters of

2 Corinthians from the rest of the letter, which is much more sharp in tone, many scholars believe that 2 Corinthians 10:1–13:10 preserves a portion of the third or "severe" letter. It would have been easy for the two letters, both sent to Corinth about the same time, to become joined together as one when Paul's correspondence was copied out after his death, before our New Testament was put together.

In any case, what is called 2 Corinthians is not an easy letter to understand, because it is nearly all a reply to things that other people said or felt, most of which are not explicitly detailed. But 2 Corinthians is particularly valuable for the insights it gives us into the mind and heart of the apostle Paul.

Summary of 1 Corinthians

After the introductory greeting and an expression of Paul's thanksgiving for their spiritual riches (1:1-9), the apostle proceeds to reprove the strife and party spirit that had split the church into cliques. He declares that the division of the community into four rival groups—a Paul party, an Apollos party, a Cephas party, and a Christ party—is absurd, for Christ is not divided (1:10-17). He contrasts his own simple preaching of the cross of Christ with the pretentious philosophizing that the immature Corinthians delight to hear (1:18–2:16). Actually all Christian evangelists have the same task, namely to build on Jesus Christ, the foundation that Paul has laid (3:1-23). Christian teachers therefore are not important in themselves, but are only the instruments of God, and responsible to Christ (4:1-21).

Turning to the moral abuses in Corinth, Paul deals with a case of incest where a man married his stepmother. The apostle censures his readers for allowing such a person to retain membership in the church, and instructs them to excommunicate the offender (5:1-13). Next the apostle reproves the Corinthians for carrying their disputes about ordinary affairs before pagan courts; such a course is entirely unworthy of Christians (6:1-11). Paul concludes this section of his letter by a general reminder that Christian freedom does not allow unchastity: "Do you not know that your body is a temple of the Holy Spirit within you, which you have from God, and that you are not your own? For you were bought with a price; therefore glorify God in your body" (6:12-20).

In reply to the problems raised in the letter from the Corinthian church, Paul discusses aspects of sex, marriage, and celibacy. In accordance with Christ's command (Mark 10:11-12), divorce is not permitted for Christians. Even where one partner is a Christian and the other remains a pagan, Paul's advice is against dissolving the marriage. But if the non-Christian partner breaks the marriage bond by desertion, the believer is released from the bond (7:1-16). Though Paul frankly discloses his own preference for the unmarried state "in view of the impending crisis" (7:26), he upholds the sanctity of marriage and its place in the Christian life (7:25-40).

Some of the Corinthians were troubled by another problem, namely the propriety of eating food that had previously been offered in pagan sacrifice (8:1). Here Paul's directions are bold and tactful. He lays down the principle that since the idol is nothing, such food is as good as any, and might be eaten freely. At the same time, for the sake of the conscience of "weak" Christians, who had scruples against eating such food, Paul declares that he will forgo his freedom, "so that I may not cause one of them to fall" (8:13). Indeed, Paul declares that in his whole apostolic ministry he has been careful to subordinate his own rights and has made himself the servant of all (9:1-27).

Paul next seeks to correct certain abuses that existed in public worship, particularly at the celebration of the Lord's Supper (11:2-34). In a lengthy section about various spiritual gifts (12:1–14:40), the apostle points out that none would be of value without the others, so that there is no reason for pride in a particular gift. The best gift of all is Christian love, which is described in lyrical terms in the famous chapter 13. The least edifying of the spiritual gifts was that of "speaking in tongues" (glossolalia). During a service of worship, first one and then another would fall into a trance and pour out, sometimes simultaneously, a flood of excited but unintelligible speech. When the ecstasy was past, someone with a kindred gift of interpretation would explain the message, if that was possible. In order to prevent outsiders from concluding that the Corinthian Christians are out of their minds (14:23), Paul orders that in each service not more than two or three should speak in a tongue, and each in turn. If, however, no one is present to interpret "let them be silent in church and speak to themselves and to God" (14:28).

Finally, Paul takes up the one doctrinal subject about which some at Corinth were disturbed—the resurrection of the dead. After reviewing the apostolic testimony concerning the reality of Christ's resurrection (15:1-11), the apostle declares that the future resurrection of believers will take place at the second coming of Christ, and will be part of the Son of God's completed victory over death (15:12-28). Answering questions concerning the "how" and the "what" of the resurrection body, Paul teaches that believers will share in Christ's resurrection, not in their present natural bodies, but in new and glorious bodies given by God.

The letter closes with directions about the weekly collection of gifts for the relief of the poor Christians at Jerusalem.

Summary of 2 Corinthians

What is called 2 Corinthians falls into three main divisions. After the introductory greeting and thanksgiving to God for comfort in troubles (1:1-11), Paul explains his actions and gives the Corinthians news of his activities. The omission of the visit to Corinth that he had threatened to make and the sending of the previous letter (the "severe" letter) were due, he explains, to his loving consideration for the Corinthian church (1:12–2:4). Paul is pleased to learn of the disciplinary action taken against the guilty one, and advises that the penitent be shown forgiveness and love (2:5-11). He then describes the greatness of the apostolic office, which involves the ministry of reconciliation (5:18-21). This work, despite all its hardships (4:7-18; 6:3-10), is the only thing he lives for, and to his joy in it is now added the happiness over the restoration of good relations between himself and the Corinthians, his children in Christ (7:2-16).

In the second main division (chapters 8 and 9), the apostle asks his readers to contribute generously to the relief fund for the church at Jerusalem. He appeals to the Corinthians not to let themselves be outstripped in their giving by the generosity of the churches in Macedonia (i.e., Philippi, Thessalonica, and others). "The point is this: the one who sows sparingly will also reap sparingly, and the one who sows bountifully will also reap bountifully. Each one of you must give as you have made up your mind, not reluctantly or under compulsion, for God loves a cheerful giver" (9:6-7).

In the third main section (10:1–13:10), which differs so markedly in tone from the previous chapters, and which (as was explained on p. 260) is thought by some to preserve Paul's earlier "severe" letter, the apostle confronts his adversaries and the community that tolerates them. He rejects the charges brought by his opponents (10:1-18), and, in a magnificent outburst of indignation, enumerates his apostolic qualifications in comparison with those of his rivals (11:1–12:13). The lengthy list of the persecutions, hardships, and sufferings that he underwent for the sake of the gospel (11:23-27) not only makes us realize how relatively little Luke was able to include in his summary of Paul's life in the book of Acts, but also provides some measure of the apostle's indomitable courage and endurance.

Paul closes with an announcement of his forthcoming visit to Corinth, warning them, that if need be he will exercise his authority, but pleading rather for their repentance and submission (12:11–13:10). The final blessing, which is one of the fullest of Paul's benedictions at the end of his letters, is in trinitarian form: "The grace of the Lord Jesus Christ, the love of God, and the communion of the Holy Spirit be with all of you" (13:14).

5. PAUL'S LETTER TO THE ROMANS

If Paul's letter to the Galatians can he called the Magna Carta of universal Christianity, his letter to the Romans is its constitution. Unlike most of his other letters, this one was not written to meet a particular emergency, but is rather a calm exposition—as nearly systematic as anything written by Paul could be—of the essentials of the gospel that he preached. The great theme developed in this treatise is that righteousness is the free gift of God, and faith in Jesus Christ is the only way of salvation for Jew as well as Gentile. At the same time, because the Roman Christians were already converted, the apostle does not have to give them the whole Christian message; he concentrates on things he particularly wants to say by way of introducing himself and his message to a church he had not founded, or even visited.

The content of his letter to the Romans was not the flash of the moment of writing, but had been maturing in Paul's thinking and teaching over many years. Therefore what he sets forth in one part of the letter cannot be isolated from what he has said, or is going to say, in another part. Sometimes he will begin to answer an objection only to break off and leave it for fuller treatment later (for example, 3:1-4 is continued in chapters 9–11, and 3:5-8 is developed in chapters 6 and 8 and in 12:1–15:13).

Summary of Romans

The letter falls into two main divisions, doctrinal (1–11) and practical (12–16). After the introduction (1:1-7) and the apostle's thanksgiving to God for the faith of the Roman Christians (1:8-15), Paul epitomizes the message of the gospel: "It is the power of God for salvation to everyone who has faith. . . . For in it the righteousness of God is revealed through faith for faith" (1:16-17).

The first point that Paul makes is the universal need of righteousness (1:18–3:20). All the world is astray from God and under his condemnation. The Gentiles are guilty of idolatry and many other sins (1:18-32); the Jews are really no better, for they have come short of the standard set them in the Mosaic Law (2:1–3:20). The Law only increases the consciousness of sin (3:20).

The good news of the gospel is that God in his grace has acquitted the guilty through the redemptive and sacrificial work of Christ, "whom God put forward as a sacrifice of atonement by his blood, effective through faith" (3:25). There is thus a twofold manifestation of God's righteousness, both in condemning sin and in conveying pardon to all who by faith appropriate the benefits of Christ's atoning work.

Turning to the Old Testament, Paul adduces scriptural proof (Gen. 15:6) to show that Abraham was justified by faith, not by works; he likewise declares that all who share the faith of Abraham belong to the people of God (4:1-25). The consequences of justification through faith in Christ are peace and joy and the certitude of redemption, guaranteed by the Holy Spirit that has been given to believers (5:1-11). Taking Adam as the representative of mankind without the gospel, Paul draws a contrast: "Just as by the one man's [Adam's] disobedience the many were made sinners, so by the one man's [Christ's] obedience the many will be made righteous" (5:19).

The apostle next discusses, and refutes, three objections that could be brought against the doctrine that one's salvation rests upon the work of Christ and is received through faith alone. To those with evil impulses such a gospel may seem to be an invitation to sin as much as possible, so that God may get more credit for saving them. Such an argument, Paul replies, is unthinkable, because faith in Christ involves vital union with him and sharing in his righteous life (6:1-14). The second objection is that Paul's doctrine of freedom from the Old Testament Law releases one from moral obligation, to which he replies no, because the believer accepts a new and higher obligation of loyalty to Christ and therefore will be devoted to doing the will of God (6:15–7:6). The third objection is that Paul's teaching makes the law of God an evil thing, because the Law not only makes us conscious of sin (compare Gal. 3:19), but also subtly incites us to sin (by suggesting what we must not do). To this Paul replies that the reason the Law cannot save is not that the Law is evil, but that we are sinful and cannot keep it (7:7-25).

Turning again to the positive exposition of the gospel, Paul describes the confidence and inner tranquillity of "those who are in Christ Jesus." By union with Christ, believers have been made children of God and are guided by the Holy Spirit. There is therefore to them "no condemnation," and nothing in this world or the next shall separate them from the love of Christ (8:1-39).

Paul then discusses the problem of how it is that the Jews deny and reject what he declares to be the teaching of their own scriptures. Three complementary answers are given: (a) God is absolute sovereign of all people, and he can choose or reject in accordance with his good pleasure (9:6-29). (b) God's rejection of Israel is because of Israel's own deliberate faithlessness (9:30–10:21). (c) There is a faithful remnant (the small body of Christian Jews), and the whole nation will, at the coming of Christ, receive the fulfillment of all the Old Testament promises (11:1-36).

The practical portion of the letter now commences, and in it Paul exhorts his readers to cultivate the several Christian graces (chap. 12), to be obedient to duly constituted civil authority (chap. 13), and to show mutual charity and forbearance, especially as regards the question of nonkosher foods (14:1–15:13). He closes with a long list of greetings and personal messages (15:14–16:23), and a final doxology.[2]

Figure 10.1. Erastus, the City Treasurer
(Courtesy of John McRay)

Among those who joined Paul in sending greetings to believers in Rome was "Erastus, the city treasurer" (Rom. 16:23). Since Paul was writing from Corinth, Erastus was a Christian in high official position in that city. Perhaps he is the person referred to in a broken Latin inscription found at Corinth last century (the largest of the three parts is shown in the figure; several letters still contain their original lead inlay): "Erastus laid this pavement at his own expense, in appreciation of his election as Aedile."

Aediles were primarily financial and business managers in a Roman colony, responsible for the upkeep and welfare of the city's public buildings and works.

6. PAUL'S LETTER TO THE COLOSSIANS

Colossae was a rather insignificant town of Phrygia in Asia Minor, about one hundred miles east of Ephesus. The church at Colossae had been founded not by Paul, who had never visited the place (2:1), but by one of his helpers, a Colossian named Epaphras who had probably been converted during Paul's ministry at Ephesus. Now in prison (4:10), Paul writes a letter to the Colossian Christians, chiefly to correct some serious errors that had obtained a foothold in the community, and to instruct them in the Christian life.

---

2. One of the puzzling features in the transmission of Paul's Letter to the Romans is the variation in the manuscripts concerning the position of the doxology. The oldest known copy of Paul's Letters (the Chester Beatty papyrus II, which was written about A.D. 200), places it after 15:33. In other ancient manuscripts it occurs after 14:23 or after 16:23, and in some it appears in both places. In a few witnesses it is lacking altogether.

The Colossian heresy—so far as its nature can be inferred from Paul's criticism of it in the letter—was a syncretistic movement, combining Jewish ritualistic observances (2:16) with features drawn from pagan mythology and philosophy (2:8, 18). The Christian religion was in danger of being transformed into a theosophical or Gnostic speculation concerning "the elemental spirits of the universe" (2:8, 20).[3] These were apparently conceived of as angelic beings that exercise power over those who are subject to them by reason of birth and fate. The false teachers were urging that, in addition to honoring Jesus Christ, Christians should also worship these angelic creatures (2:18).

The seriousness of the Colossian heresy lay in its compromising the absolute preeminence of Christ as the only Mediator and Redeemer. Hence in his letter, Paul stresses the uniqueness of Christ, describing him as the majestic head of both the cosmos and the church (1:15-20), in whom all the fullness of God was pleased to dwell, and by whose death and resurrection a decisive and final victory was gained over all opposing forces (2:9-15).

Summary of Colossians

The letter falls into two main parts, the doctrinal section (1:1:34) and the practical exhortations (3:5–4:18). After the opening salutation, Paul expresses his thanks to God for the Colossians' faith and love, and prays for their further progress in their life in Christ (1:1-14). At this point the apostle's references to prayer and thanksgiving merge into an exalted description of the person of Christ, which, in its turn, leads back again to a contemplation of his reconciling work and of its results among the Christians who are addressed (1:15-23).[4] In this passage we find Paul's fullest statement concerning Christ's person before the Incarnation (compare also 1 Cor. 8:6). The Son is the image of the invisible God, and everything created, whether earthly or heavenly, is founded in him, for he is the agent, sustainer, and goal of all (1:15-17). Through the work of such a Christ, Paul declares, we are freed from the fear

---

3. For other forms of Gnosticism see page 78 and pages 296-97.

4. It may be, as some have suggested, that in 1:15-20 Paul has adopted and adapted an early Christian hymn in honor of Christ. In any case, even in English translation the reader can sense the rhythmic nature of the language and the parallelism between verses 15-16 and verses 18-19.

of all those hostile forces that have dominated our existence, and from the burden of our guilt (1:20-22).

As the apostle to the Gentiles Paul realizes that he has an obligation even to the Phrygian communities, whom he does not know (1:23–2:7). He therefore undertakes to warn the Colossians of the false teaching among them: "See to it that no one takes you captive through philosophy and empty deceit, according to human tradition, according to the elemental spirits of the universe, and not according to Christ" (2:8). The person who is incorporated in Christ needs nothing more, and must neither adopt ascetical practices nor practice ritual observances (2:10-23).

In the second part of the letter, the apostle urges that the everyday conduct of the Colossians ought to reflect their exalted position in Christ (3:1–4:6). He exhorts them to put to death what is earthly in them—the old nature with its practices—and to put on the new nature with all of the Christian graces (3:1-17). Special instructions are directed to wives and husbands, to children and parents, and to slaves and masters (3:18–4:1). The concluding words include admonitions to "continue steadfastly in prayer" and to show Christian tactfulness in witnessing before non-Christians (4:2-6). After sending greetings from himself and from his helpers, Paul takes the pen from his amanuensis and adds his signature and final message: "I, Paul, write this greeting with my own hand. Remember my chains. Grace be with you" (4:18).

7. PAUL'S LETTER TO PHILEMON

This brief letter, a private note concerning an incident of domestic life, gives us a glimpse of what must have been a steady stream of such correspondence from the apostle to his wide circle of associates and acquaintances. Philemon was a well-to-do Christian of Colossae, whose house was large enough to serve as a meeting place of the members of the church in that place.[5] A slave named Onesimus had run away from Philemon and had somehow been

---

5. There is no evidence that separate "church" buildings existed prior to the second century. Before that time Christians met together in "house-churches," of which there might be several in a community. This partly explains the great attention that Paul pays in his letters to matters of family life (for example, Col. 3:18–4:1). It also helps account for the existence of party strife in the apostolic age, growing out of personal or domestic rivalries (see, for example, 1 Cor. 1:11-12).

brought in touch with Paul at Rome. The details of the story are not known, but apparently Onesimus had either damaged some of Philemon's property or had stolen some of his valuables (see verses 11 and 18). At any rate, as the result of his being with the apostle, Onesimus was converted and wished to make restitution for the wrong he had done to his master, Philemon. As a runaway slave Onesimus could be punished very severely, and therefore he besought Paul to write a conciliatory letter to Philemon in his behalf. Paul accedes to his request, and appeals to Philemon, for the sake of his friendship with Paul, to receive Onesimus kindly, not as a slave but as a Christian brother.

All in all, this letter is a model of the art of letter writing, revealing, as it does, simple dignity, refined courtesy, and warm sympathy. It also illustrates the way in which ordinary human relationships may be made the means of expressing Christian love. Though it was to be many generations before the institution of slavery would be abolished in the Roman Empire, when Paul in this letter put the relationship of master and slave on the new plane of Christian brotherhood (v. 16), he enunciated a principle that in the long run was destined to reorganize ancient society.

Summary of Philemon

After the salutation (vv. 1-3), Paul expresses thanksgiving for what he had heard of Philemon's faith in Christ and charitable deeds to other believers (vv. 4-7). He delicately intercedes for Onesimus, who now is true to his name (which means "helpful"); though as an apostle, Paul has the right to command, he prefers to leave the matter to Philemon's free choice (vv. 8-14). As for anything that Onesimus may have damaged or stolen, Paul says magnanimously, "Charge that to my account" (v. 18).

Paul closes the letter with a gentle hint that Philemon should release Onesimus from servitude: "Confident of your obedience, I am writing to you, knowing that you will do even more than I say" (v. 21). In the next sentence the apostle adds a personal request. "One thing more—prepare a guest room for me, for I am hoping through your prayers to be restored to you" (v. 22). In other words, after his release from prison he can visit Philemon's home where he will see for himself how far his petitions in behalf of Onesimus have been granted!

Paul's final words include greetings from several friends and the concluding benediction, "The grace of the Lord Jesus Christ be with your spirit" (v. 25).

8. THE LETTER TO THE EPHESIANS

The Letter to the Ephesians presents a variety of problems concerning its authenticity and destination. Though the apostle Paul had spent three years preaching in Ephesus, and though he had a warm affection for the church there (compare Acts 20:17-38), the letter that purports to be his to these same Ephesians is strangely impersonal and lacking in any local color. The writer sends no greetings to individuals and makes the curious statement that the recipients have presumably heard of his ministry (3:2). To account for these features, as well as the fact that the letter contains a number of words and phrases not present in the letters that are unquestionably Paul's, scholars have suggested that it was written by a later admirer of the apostle, perhaps as a "covering" letter for the first collection of the apostle's correspondence. Though this is not impossible, it is certainly improbable that two persons in the early church were so similar in both native genius and exalted spiritual insight as Paul and his otherwise unknown counterpart. Even stranger is the total absence of any independent historical evidence for the existence of such an "alter ego" of the apostle Paul.

The many similarities between the letters to the Colossians and the Ephesians, despite the presence of certain differences, make it likely that the two letters were written by the same person at about the same time, though perhaps through different amanuenses. Instead of being intended only for Ephesus, what we call "to the Ephesians" may have been a circular letter or encyclical sent to a group of churches, of which Ephesus was one. This would explain why it is more like a sermonic meditation than the other Pauline Letters, and why it does not deal with the mistakes or needs or personalities of one particular congregation. Such a theory also accounts for the fact that in the earliest and best manuscripts the words "in Ephesus" are absent from the salutation (1:1).

In any case, whoever wrote the letter and wherever it was addressed, Ephesians is one of the most exalted of the writings in the New Testament. Its theme is God's eternal purpose in establishing and completing the universal church of Jesus Christ. Though drawn from various backgrounds and nationalities, the members of the church have been brought together into a unity that is described as the building or temple of God (2:20-22), the Body of Christ (1:22-23), and the bride of Christ (5:23-32).

Summary of Ephesians

The letter falls into two parts, one doctrinal in content (1:1–3:21) and the other hortatory (4:1–6:24). After an unusually brief salutation (1:1-2), the writer expresses his thanksgiving for all that he has heard of the faith and good works of his readers (1:3-14). This is followed by a prayer that they may come to an even deeper appreciation of the spiritual gifts imparted to believers through God's work in Jesus Christ (1:15-23). The readers are reminded that, as Gentiles, they have been raised by grace from a state of spiritual death to a state of spiritual life in the risen Christ (2:1-10); though formerly they had been "strangers to the covenants of promise, . . . and without God in the world," now they are united with believing Jews in the one structure of the church, whose cornerstone is Jesus Christ (2:11-22). It was God's good pleasure to entrust the writer with the stewardship of proclaiming what had formerly been hidden in the counsels of God, namely that the Gentiles are fellow heirs of the promises made long before through the prophets to the chosen people (3:1-13). He prays for the continued indwelling of Christ in their hearts through faith (3:14-19), and ascribes praise to God, to whom "be glory in the church and in Christ Jesus to all generations, forever and ever" (3:20-21).

In the second part of the letter, the writer develops the implications of God's plan to unite all people and all things under Christ's lordship. He urges them to use their diverse spiritual gifts for the building up of the one body whose head is Christ (4:1-16). In their personal conduct they must make a clean break with their former pagan customs, ignorance, and sensuality. The Christian life means living in conformity with the mind of God and walking in the steps of Christ (4:17–5:20). In their relations with one another, a proper subordination must be recognized, on the pattern of the subordination of the church to Christ. This principle holds in the relation of wife and husband, children and parents, slaves and masters (5:21–6:9).

A final exhortation urges the readers to put on God's armor (compare Isa. 11:5; 59:17) and to wage an unrelenting battle against the spiritual forces of evil in the universe (6:10-18). With an appeal for prayers in his behalf and a commendation of Tychicus, the bearer of the letter, the apostle closes with a blessing upon "all who have an undying love for our Lord Jesus Christ" (6:19-24).

9. PAUL'S LETTER TO THE PHILIPPIANS

This letter, one of the most cordial and affectionate we have from Paul's hand, was addressed to the Christians at Philippi in Macedonia. According to the book of Acts they were the first congregation to be established through the apostle's preaching on European soil (Acts 16:11-15). Paul's relations with the Philippians in all the years afterward seem to have been extraordinarily close and happy. More than once they had sent him money or supplies when he was at Thessalonica (see 4:16), and now that he was in prison at Rome, as soon as they could they appointed a messenger, Epaphroditus, to take him several things he needed (4:18). After some time Epaphroditus wanted to return to Philippi (2:25-29), and Paul took the opportunity of sending with him this letter to express his warm affection for his friends at Philippi, to thank them for their gifts, and to give them news and encouragement.

The entire letter breathes Paul's radiant joy and serene happiness in Christ, even while in prison and awaiting trial (2:2; 3:8-14; 4:11-13). The letter also contains an important statement about Christ, who was "in the form of God" and enjoyed "equality with God" before he came to earth as a man, and who is now exalted as Lord of all (2:5-11).

Summary of Philippians

After the opening salutation, in which Timothy joins him (1:1-2), Paul expresses his heartfelt gratitude for the Philippians' constancy in the Christian faith, and prays for their continued growth in grace (1:3-11).

The apostle reassures his readers that his imprisonment has not hindered the preaching of the gospel in Rome. On the contrary, the local missionaries have become much more bold to witness on behalf of Christ from his example of evangelizing even among the whole imperial guard (1:12-18). He declares that whether his trial results in life or death, it will be a blessing for him (1:19-22); he desires to "depart and be with Christ," yet for the sake of the Philippians he wishes and hopes to remain alive (1:23-26).

In the exhortations that follow, we hear echoes of Paul's customary homilies delivered during services of worship in his churches (1:27–2:18). He urges his readers to maintain spiritual unity, through self-forgetfulness and love, according to the example of Jesus Christ. To illustrate his point the apostle introduces what may have been part of a hymn concerning the incarnation of Christ (2:5-11). He also exhorts them to work out their salvation with fear and trembling, and thus to prove that it is God who is at work in them (2:12-13).

Turning next to personal messages, Paul indicates that as soon as he is sure about the outcome of his trial he will send them Timothy, his loyal fellow worker (2:19-24). Meanwhile he is sending back Epaphroditus, who had been very ill but has recovered his health (2:25-30).

Paul then digresses to warn them against Judaistic agitators, who preach a religion of meritorious works. Whereas the Judaizers would say, "If you do not live rightly, you will not be saved," Paul taught, "If you do not live rightly, you have not been saved" (compare 3:1–4:1).

Next the apostle refers to a personal quarrel between two prominent women in the Philippian church (4:2-3); he characteristically makes it the occasion of a final appeal to be tolerant, to be diligent in prayer, and to concentrate on the big things that really matter (4:4-9). Finally Paul thanks the church for the gift they had sent him; at the same time he lets them know that he has learned to rely on spiritual resources, declaring, "I can do all things through him who strengthens me" (4:10-20).

Among those who join Paul in sending greetings are "those of the emperor's household"—an illuminating comment on Paul's successful preaching of the gospel to those in the service of Nero himself (4:21-23).

10. THE PASTORAL LETTERS: 1 AND 2 TIMOTHY, AND TITUS

The main purpose of the Pastoral Letters is to warn against unorthodox teachings and to provide guidance for the administration of local churches. Timothy had been closely associated with the apostle from the time that Paul recruited him for missionary service at Lystra, to take the place of John Mark on the second of his campaigns (Acts 16:1-3). From internal evidence in the letters it appears that Paul had left Timothy in charge of the church at Ephesus (1 Tim. 1:3), a post of responsibility and difficulty, especially for one who was still a relatively young man (1 Tim. 4:12). Titus, who, though not mentioned in the book of Acts, is frequently referred to in Paul's correspondence as one of his trusted helpers, had been left in Crete to superintend the organization of the churches in that island (Titus 1:5). Later, according to 2 Timothy 4:10, Titus went, perhaps on a mission, to Dalmatia (modern Croatia).

From internal indications 2 Timothy appears to be the latest of the three Pastoral Letters; it was written at Rome (1:17), where Paul, in chains like a criminal, was in prison for a second time (1:8; 2:9). Expecting to be executed soon (4:6) and with no friend to stand by him, the apostle longed for the companionship of Timothy. He therefore resolved to write him for the last time, bidding him come to him with all speed before the winter storms would close the Mediterranean (4:21). Whatever theory is adopted concerning the composition of the Pastoral Letters, it can scarcely be doubted that in such personal details as these we hear the apostle's own voice, lonely yet undaunted.

As was mentioned at the close of the previous chapter, many scholars doubt the authenticity of the Pastoral Letters; others also have similar doubts concerning 2 Thessalonians, Colossians, and Ephesians, designating them as "deutro-Pauline." It is significant, however, that recent stylometric study of the New Testament (see p. 248) as well as a growing number of present-day New Testament scholars, representing differing theological backgrounds, disagree and have set forth reasons for believing that Paul was responsible for the whole corpus of thirteen letters.[6]

---

6. For example, Donald Guthrie, *New Testament Introduction*, 4th ed. (Downers Grove, Ill.: InterVarsity Press, 1990); Luke Timothy Johnson, *The Writings of the New Testament: An Interpretation*, rev. ed. (Minneapolis: Fortress Press, 1999), especially pp. 267-73; and Bo Reicke, *Re-Examining Paul's Letters: The History of the Pauline Correspondence*, ed. by David P. Moessner and Ingalisa Reicke (Harrisburg: Trinity Press International, 2002).

Summary of 1 Timothy

Although Paul hopes to see Timothy soon at Ephesus, he writes him this letter because of the possibility that his journey there may be delayed (1 Tim. 3:14; 4:13). The letter, which is rather loosely constructed, begins by recalling the charge committed to Timothy and urges him to defend the truth against heretics (1:1-20). The apostle then lays down certain rules for Timothy's guidance concerning the offering of prayer for all persons, especially those in authority (2:1-7); the conducting of public worship (2:8-15); and the qualifications required of bishops (3:1-7) and of deacons (3:8-13). He then gives more detailed instructions concerning false teachers who will infiltrate the church (4:1-5); concerning Timothy's conduct in the discharge of his duties (4:6-16); and concerning widows (5:3-16), elders (5:17-25), and slaves (6:1-2).

In the concluding section, the author denounces again the heretical teachers, whose chief concern is to make money (6:3-10), and adjures Timothy to "fight the good fight of the faith" (6:11-16). The rich are urged to make good use of their wealth (6:17-19), and Timothy is once again warned to beware of the false doctrines of Gnostic teachers (6:20-21).

Summary of Titus

After an earnest apostolic salutation (1:1-4), the writer advises Titus concerning the kind of persons qualified to be elders (who are also called bishops) in the church (1:5-9). One of their main functions is to check the spread of false teaching, arising particularly from Judaizers (1:10-16). He next lays down certain Christian precepts for various groups in the church (older men, 2:1-2; older women, 2:3-5; younger men, 2:6-8; and slaves, 2:9-10), all to the effect that Christians, in view of Christ's work of redemption on their behalf, should be zealous for good deeds (2:11-15).

The concluding section deals with the duty of Christians to society; they are bidden to respect authority and to be good citizens because of God's grace shown to them (3:1-7). Once again the apostle stresses the importance of right beliefs as an incentive to good deeds, and warns against becoming entangled in theoretical arguments that distract the attention and divert energy from the Christian cause (3:8-15).

Summary of 2 Timothy

After the salutation (1:1-2), the apostle expresses thanksgiving for Timothy's loyalty to the faith, which is like that of Timothy's mother Eunice and grandmother Lois (1:3-7). The writer then exhorts Timothy to be bold in his evangelistic efforts and to bear suffering cheerfully (1:8-14). Referring to examples of desertion and of loyalty on the part of other Christian leaders (1:15-18), he charges Timothy to be strong, to choose his assistants carefully, to disseminate the traditional teaching of the apostles, and to take heed to his own spiritual life, avoiding any kind of behavior that would impair his testimony as the Lord's servant (2:1-26). To press home his points, the apostle quotes some lines from what appears to be a fragment of a very early Christian hymn:

> If we have died with him, we will also live with him;
> if we endure, we will also reign with him;
> if we deny him, he will also deny us;
> if we are faithless, he remains faithful—
> for he cannot deny himself. (2:11-13)

The writer continues with a warning that in the last days every kind of evil will be rampant and false teachers will seek to corrupt the truth of the gospel (3:1-9). Timothy should remember the example of steadfast endurance that Paul himself had shown him and the teaching of the inspired scriptures of the Old Testament, in which he had been trained (3:10-17).

As his farewell message Paul exhorts Timothy with all possible solemnity to be faithful to the duties of his office (4:1-5). Referring to his own expectation of martyrdom and joy in it (4:6-8), he expresses a desire to see Timothy again (4:9), and closes with sundry details of news and greeting (4:10-22).

APPENDIX: LEADING IDEAS IN PAUL'S THEOLOGY

Amid the variety of subjects that the apostle Paul deals with in his correspondence with churches and with individuals, several large and luminous ideas recur again and again. Some of these ideas are identical with those that appear in the teaching of Jesus; others are doctrines that developed in the early church or that were special contributions from Paul's own deep spiritual insight.

God as Father. Paul, like Jesus, taught that God *is* the Father, and people *become* his children–for the father-child relationship is neither necessary nor physical as though based on the creator-creature status; it is ethical and spiritual, based on God's gracious choice and one's response in faith (Rom. 8:14-17). According to Paul, God is first of all Father of the Lord Jesus Christ (Rom. 15:6; 1 Cor. 1:9; 2 Cor. 13), and through Christ, God is the Father of all believers (1 Cor. 8:6; 2 Cor. 1:3; 6:18). Only these believers can know God with such intimate and trustful confidence as to address him, "Abba! Father!" (Rom. 8:15; Gal. 4:6; for the Aramaic term, characteristic of Jesus' usage, see p. 171).

Humankind as sinners. According to Paul, all people, Jews and Gentiles alike (Rom. 3:9), have disobeyed God and stand guilty before him (Rom. 3:22-23). In bondage to sin, they are powerless to save themselves (Rom. 6:17, 20; 7:14). The whole person is subject to sin, which manifests itself not only in the grosser sins "of the flesh" (Gal. 5:19-20), but has defiled also the spirit (2 Cor. 7:1).

God's grace. Paul never tires of emphasizing that one does not earn a standing in God's sight by performing meritorious good works, but that, on the contrary, only through God's love and grace is the sinner forgiven and accepted into the household of faith (Rom. 3:24; 6:14; 1 Cor. 15:10; Gal. 1:15). In this respect also the apostle agrees with one of the fundamental doctrines that runs through the teaching of Jesus (compare Jesus' parables of the laborers in the vineyard, Matt. 20:1-17, and the Pharisee and the tax collector, Luke 18:9-14) and which was the root of Jesus' opposition to the scribes and Pharisees. It is because of God's love and grace that Paul can make the confident assertion, "We know that all things work together for good for those who love God, who are called according to his purpose" (Rom. 8:28).

Redemption. For Paul, Jesus is far more than a great teacher; he is the divine redeemer of individuals from sin and death. Since Jesus himself had spoken of giving his life "a ransom for many" (Mark 10:45), Paul was merely expanding the same idea of emancipating a slave from bondage when he declared that through the death and resurrection of Christ believers have been redeemed from enslavement to sin and now stand in "the glorious liberty of the children of God" (Rom. 8:21; Gal. 3:13; Col. 1:14).

Justification through faith. Prior to his becoming a Christian, Paul had been unable by the punctilious keeping of the Mosaic Law to attain righteousness, that is, a right relationship with God (Rom. 3:19; Gal. 3:10). But when he accepted the crucified Jesus as his Lord, all his burden of guilt and frustration was lifted; Paul felt himself a new person, at peace with God and with himself, and overflowing with joy and a sense of unlimited power (Rom. 7:25; 8:1). Thereafter the apostle opposed a religion of works—a religion that can open an account with God and seek to obtain salvation by merit. Adopting legal terminology Paul taught that every person, standing like a prisoner at the bar, is guilty. God, the judge, of his free grace acquits and "justifies the ungodly" (Rom. 4:5). Faith is the response of those who put their confidence and hope in what God has done for them in and through Jesus Christ (Rom. 4:6-8; Gal. 2:16-21).

Sanctification and the new life in Christ. If Paul knew that one is saved by faith alone, he knew also that the faith that saves does not remain alone—it is followed by good works that testify to its vitality. Lest justification be merely a legal fiction, it must lead to what Paul calls sanctification by union with the living Christ (Rom. 6:1-19; 1 Cor. 1:2, 30; 6:11). Christians can overcome sin because they are in Christ and Christ is in them (Gal. 2:19-20; Col. 1:27). This idea appears again and again in all of Paul's Letters, where he uses the expression "in Christ" (or "in Christ Jesus" or "in the Lord") more than one hundred times. All human relations and earthly events are transformed for the person who is "in Christ Jesus" (2 Cor. 5:15-17). Impurity is shunned as a defilement of "the temple of God" and an outrage upon the Holy Spirit (1 Cor. 6:19; 1 Thess. 4:8). The obligations of the family and the state are not destroyed for the Christian but assume a deeper meaning and a new sanctity (Rom. 12:1–13:10).

In working out the ethical implications of the gospel, Paul's teaching is strikingly similar to that of Jesus. Both, for example, regarded love as the fulfilling of the Law, and instead of imposing external rules bearing on minutiae of behavior, both stressed the great principles of justice and mercy. Instead of perpetuating triviality and the formalism that characterized much of contemporary Pharisaism (see pp. 50-51) Paul echoes Jesus' teaching and example when he writes of "love, joy, peace, patience, kindness, generosity, faithfulness, gentleness, self-control" (Gal. 5:22-23), or when he counsels his readers, "Bless those who persecute you; bless and do not curse them" (Rom. 12:14).

The Church. In addition to emphasizing the individual aspect of the new life in Christ, Paul took into full account its corporate aspect. The church is the community of believers who constitute one body in Christ (Rom. 12:5). All members of the body—eyes, ears, hands, feet—need one another, and together they constitute the Body of Christ, whose gifts and life-giving presence are supplied to individual members of the church (1 Cor. 12:12-31). Paul also refers to the church under the image of a building that serves as a temple of God (Eph. 2:21); individual believers are the building blocks, each in their own place, contributing to the growth and completeness of the whole (1 Cor. 3:10-17).

The kingdom of God, now and hereafter. The expression "kingdom of God" is not very frequent in the Pauline Letters, where much is said about the church; but it is used as though familiar to the readers, and when it does appear, it has the same meaning as in the teaching of Jesus. For Paul, as for Jesus, the kingdom is divorced from all political and materialistic associations. Though this may seem today to be something that should be taken for granted, it must not be forgotten that in Judaism of the first century such a view was revolutionary. Paul teaches that the implications of entrance into the kingdom are ethical: "Do you not know," he writes, "that wrongdoers will not inherit the kingdom of God?" (1 Cor. 6:9). Then Paul enumerates, as he does also in Galatians 5:19-21, a long list of sins that exclude a person from participation in the kingdom. Here again Paul is continuing faithfully the teaching of Jesus, who demanded repentance for admission into the kingdom (Matt. 4:17).

Moreover, for Paul, just as for Jesus (see pp. 172-73), the kingdom is regarded partly as present and partly as future. In the two passages just referred to, as well as in 1 Corinthians 15:50, it is future; whereas the present aspect is in view in such passages as Romans 14:17, "For the kingdom of God is not food and drink but righteousness and peace and joy in the Holy Spirit."

Eventually the kingdom will come in its fullness and power. Then the demonic powers and all enemies of God and of Christ will be vanquished (Eph. 6:10-13; 1 Cor. 15:24-27, 54-57). At the resurrection all will appear before the judgment seat of Christ (2 Cor. 5:10); those who have been of hard and impenitent heart will experience the wrath of God's righteous judgment (Rom. 2:5), and those who belong to Christ will be conformed to "bear the image of the man of heaven" (1 Cor. 15:49).

This brief summary of some of the leading ideas in Paul's teaching may be concluded with a comment on two questions that have engaged the attention of scholars. *(a)* How far do Paul's Letters indicate that over the years he changed his basic theological views? *(b)* How much influence from the mystery religions (see pp. 78-86) can be detected in his writings?

(a) Paul's literary activity covered a period of a dozen years (or about fifteen, if the Pastoral Letters are his). During this period the main doctrines that he taught, with one possible exception, show no evidence of modification or fundamental reorientation. There are, of course, differences of emphasis and concern (for some of these see pp. 254); but his teaching about God, Christ, humankind, grace, redemption, justification, sanctification, and much more remained constant. It is not surprising that this is so, for prior to the period represented by his extant letters, Paul had ample opportunity to think through these matters. Almost twenty years passed between Paul's conversion and his second missionary journey, during which he began to write the letters that are preserved today. On basic issues, therefore, the apostle had long since formulated, consciously or unconsciously, his distinctive views and terminology. The only area in which one finds traces of modification in his thinking over the years concerns the imminence of the second coming of Christ and the details of the resurrection and future judgment. Beginning with his Letter to the Philippians (1:20-23), Paul commences to reckon with the possibility that he may die before Christ comes (compare also 1 Thess. 4:13-18; 2 Thess. 2:1-12; 1 Cor. 15:35-57; and 2 Cor. 5:1-5).

(b) During the previous century it was fashionable in some circles to argue that Paul's theology shows evidence of having been influenced by the mystery religions. Particularly it was contended

that the sacrament of the Lord's Supper and the whole concept of a dying and rising god were obvious borrowings from contemporary pagan cults.

Today it is generally agreed that Paul's heritage, so far from being basically Hellenistic, was essentially rabbinical, and that his Christian orientation was broadly shared by his predecessors within the primitive Palestinian church. Furthermore, an analysis of Paul's vocabulary shows that of the score or more common words relating to the cultus and beliefs of the mysteries—words that one would expect to find in Paul if he had really developed a syncretistic amalgam—only the word *mystery* itself is used with any frequency, and even this word bears a different sense from that current in the mysteries. It thus appears that, so far from borrowing, Paul made a deliberate effort to avoid using expressions that had associations with paganism.

It is also generally agreed today that the celebration of the Lord's Supper in the Pauline churches had its antecedents in the last meal that Jesus had with his followers in Jerusalem at the Passover season (see pp. 144-45).

Unlike the savior-gods of the mysteries, who were mythological figures of dim antiquity, the divine Being whom the Christians worshiped as Lord was known as a historical person who had lived on earth only a few years before the earliest documents of the New Testament were written. In all the mysteries that tell of a dying deity, the god dies by compulsion and not by choice, sometimes in bitterness and despair, never in love. But according to Paul, God's redeeming love was the free divine motive for the death of Jesus Christ, who accepted with equal freedom that motive as his own.

For the pagan cults the world process is infinitely repeatable, being a circular movement leading nowhere. The rites of the mysteries that commenorate a dying and rising deity reflect the recurring seasons and the vegetative cycle. For Paul, on the contrary, the time process is a series of unique events, involving as the most important event the once-for-all character of the death and resurrection of Jesus Christ, who is to climax the world process at his return in glory. For a bibliography on the subject of the mystery religions, see note 1 on p. 78.

CHAPTER 11

THE GENERAL LETTERS AND THE BOOK OF REVELATION

Besides the letters traditionally ascribed to the apostle Paul, the New Testament contains eight letters written by five or six other leaders in the early Christian church. Most of them are addressed, not to a single Christian community, but generally to all. They are less like personal letters than most of Paul's, and more like official letters or sermons from a bishop or elder to a group of churches.

Without depreciating the very great role that the apostle Paul played as a leader and theologian, it must be said that the eight general letters supply evidence for the existence of a rich and broad leadership within the early Christian communities. Though Paul cannot be regarded as having a narrow or one-track mind, our New Testament would be infinitely poorer without the variety of emphases supplied by the general letters. Even the casual reader can see that the theology of the author of the Letter to the Hebrews is as different in its characteristic features from that of Paul's as both are different from the orientation of the three Letters of John or the Letter of James. As sunlight is composed of a variety of colors, so the spectrum of early Christian theology represented in the New Testament letters is remarkable for its diversity of emphases as well as for its unity in fundamentals.

I. THE GENERAL LETTERS

1. THE LETTER TO THE HEBREWS

In the King James Version of the Bible, the Letter to the Hebrews is headed "The Epistle of Paul the Apostle." Contrary to Paul's custom, however (see 2 Thess. 3:17), it has no salutation or conclusion giving his name, and there is nothing in the text of the letter to connect it with him, except that Timothy is mentioned (Heb. 13:23)—

but many other people in the church must have known Timothy. In short, the letter is anonymous, and in the earliest manuscripts the title is simply "To the Hebrews." At a later date the words "Epistle of Paul the Apostle" were added to the title when the letter was copied out by someone who guessed that it was written by Paul.

That guess, however, was wrong, as is plain when one compares the contents of the letter with those of unquestioned Pauline authorship. This author writes his sentences carefully and deliberately according to an elaborate outline; Paul tends to jump from one subject to another as a new idea strikes him. This author's theological emphasis is different from Paul's. *(a)* Paul uses the expression "Christ Jesus" about ninety times, including twenty-six instances in the Pastoral Letters; here it does not occur once. *(b)* Paul mentions the resurrection of Christ many times in his letters; here it is referred to only once, and then in a subordinate clause (13:20). *(c)* Paul's frequent reference to the believer's being "in Christ" is replaced here (2:11; 10:10, 29) by the believer's being "sanctified" through the work of one's priestly representative. Even when the two authors use the same words they argue differently. *(a)* Both speak of the Old Testament Law, but for Paul the Law is almost always the moral law; here the Law is chiefly ritual and sacrificial law. *(b)* Both regard the Law as weak, but Paul says it is weak through the flesh (that is, because of factors outside the Law; Rom. 8:3), while here it is said to be weak because it is a mere copy and shadow (10:1). *(c)* Even the word *faith* is used differently—for Paul it is personal commitment to Christ, who makes the believer one with him; here it is confident assurance of God's providential care, which undergirds the Christian's certainty of spiritual realities (11:1).

In addition to Paul many other guesses have been made about the author of the letter, including Barnabas (suggested by Tertullian, a church father who lived about A.D. 200), Apollos (so Luther), Luke (so Calvin), Aquila (so Henry Alford), and Priscilla (so Harnack). There is no compelling proof for any of these, and the only sure conclusion about the authorship of the letter is that it was not written by Paul.

We are not much better off concerning the identity of the original recipients of the letter. Apparently they were Jewish Christians, but whether they lived in Palestine or in Rome (as might seem to be implied from the greetings sent by "those from Italy," 13:24) or in some other locality is not clear. The time of writing is also disputed, though a strong argument can be made for a date prior to the destruction of the temple in A.D. 70. Since the author's chief purpose is to show that the Jewish modes of worship are obsolete and ineffective, it would have been a clinching argument if he had been able to point to the temple in ruins as an indication that God had no further use for it; that he does not make use of this argument is a strong presumption that he was writing while the temple was still standing.

The occasion for the writing of the letter is clear enough. The recipients had grown lax in their faith and remiss in attendance at divine service (10:23-25). Many of them felt themselves drawn to the Jewish liturgy, and were on the point of renouncing Christianity and returning to their ancestral Jewish faith.

Writing in the spirit and perhaps under the inspiration of the work of Stephen the protomartyr (see p. 218), the unknown author appeals to the intellect as well as the emotions of his readers, urging that Christ and his work are superior to anything that Judaism can offer. He develops a carefully constructed discussion in several stages, which are interspersed with exhortations and warnings.

Summary of Hebrews

In developing the theme of the superiority of Christianity over Judaism, the author makes three main points involving the preeminence of Christ, the preeminence of Christ's priesthood, and the preeminence of Christ's sacrifice (1:1–10:18).

The first point is developed in three ascending stages. After declaring that Christ as the Son of God is preeminent over the Jewish prophets (1:1-3), the author assembles a string of quotations from the Old Testament to show the preeminence of Christ over angels (1:4–2:18), who were regarded by contemporary Jews as the mediators of God's Law to Moses on Sinai (Acts 7:53; Gal. 3:19). As a climax he argues that Jesus Christ is superior even to Moses (3:1–4:13), seeing that he "was faithful over God's house as a son," whereas Moses was but a servant within it (3:1-6). This section concludes with a warning against losing the promised rest of God through apostasy, as Israel did under Moses (3:7–4:13).

In the second main argument, the author discusses the value of Christ's high-priestly office (4:14–7:28). Jesus Christ possesses the requirements for serving as high priest: compassionate sympathy for the ignorant and wayward, and a divine call appointing him as priest (4:14–5:10). Once again the readers are rebuked for their shortcomings and warned against falling away (5:11–6:20).

At this point the author launches into what may seem to modern readers to be a farfetched argument based on a comparison between the priesthood of Christ and that of Melchizedek, a mysterious figure mentioned twice in the Old Testament (Gen. 14:18-20; Ps. 110:4). We should not forget, however, that this kind of argument by analogy was not only normal in those days, but was probably the best suited to convince the original recipients of the letter. The gist of the discussion is that the characteristics of Jesus Christ as absolute high priest were prefigured in Melchizedek, an ancient priest-king of Salem. First the author draws a contrast between the Melchizedekian priesthood and the Levitical priesthood. The fact that Melchizedek received tithes from Abraham and also gave Abraham his priestly blessing (7:4-7) shows that he was superior to Abraham, and if superior to Abraham the patriarch, how much more to his descendants, Aaron and the priestly Levites (7:4-10). Christ's priesthood, however, is not according to the order of Aaron, but according to the order of Melchizedek, for like Melchizedek, Christ as priest has no successor (7:11-25), and unlike Aaron, the sinless Christ has no need to offer sacrifice for himself (7:26-28).

In the third main argument the author proves the superiority of Christ's sacrifice over the Levitical sacrifices offered in accordance with the Mosaic Law (8:1–10:18). Briefly, Christ is the priestly ministrant in the new tabernacle in heaven (8:1-6) whose mediatorial work is based on the conditions of a new covenant that supplants the old covenant (8:7-13). After describing the Mosaic sanctuary with its repeated sacrifices (9:1-10), the author sets forth the abiding efficacy of Christ's one sacrifice in cleansing the conscience and bringing the sinner to God (9:11–10:18). Among his points the author declares that Jesus' sacrifice was not offered in an earthly tabernacle (as are the Levitical sacrifices), but in heaven itself (9:5-24), nor does it need to be repeated (9:27-28), as do the Levitical sacrifices, which are not really effective (10:1-4). The crowning superiority of Christ's single sacrifice over the multiple sacrifices of dumb beasts lies precisely in his being a free moral agent who willingly offered himself as a single sacrifice for sins (10:9-10).

In the final section of the letter the readers are exhorted to avail themselves of the privileges and benefits of Christ's high-priestly work (10:19–12:29). The author urges them to be loyal to the Christian faith, declaring that those who deliberately renounce their faith in Christ have a fearful prospect of divine judgment (10:26-31). To encourage them to hold to that faith the author describes it as trusting in God, come what may, and illustrates it by tracing in the Old Testament notable examples of the triumph of faith over great obstacles (Heb. 11:1-40). After enumerating a stirring roll call of heroes of faith, the writer urges:

> Let us also lay aside every weight, and the sin that clings so closely, and let us run with perseverance the race that is set before us, looking to Jesus the pioneer and perfecter of our faith, who for the sake of the joy that was set before him endured the cross, disregarding its shame, and has taken his seat at the right hand of the throne of God. (12:1-2)

In a last magnificent exhortation, the author contrasts the gloom and terror of life under the Mosaic Law with the exhilaration of being caught up in the great company of saints of old and new Israel whose names are enrolled in heaven (12:12-29). By way of relating faith to daily life, the writer concludes with injunctions concerning the practice of mutual love, purity of life, freedom from greed, respect for good leaders, and above all loyalty to Jesus Christ (13:1-19). He closes his letter with personal greetings and a prayer that reflect his confidence that his readers will heed what he has written (13:20-25).

2. THE LETTER OF JAMES

The Letter of James is more like a sermon than a letter. Except for the opening greeting "to the twelve tribes in the Dispersion" (which probably means Jewish Christians wherever they may be), it has none of the other formal parts that were usual in ancient letters. The treatise is epigrammatic in style, hortatory in content; there are about 60 imperative verbs in a total of 108 verses. The author was a practical man, and his tract is about Christian conduct, with little or no doctrinal teaching. His short paragraphs of exhortation are linked, not by a logical development of argument, but by catchwords, a common Jewish mnemonic device for the preservation of material in oral tradition.

The book is saturated with Old Testament language and allusions (see the cross-references in any good reference Bible). It also discloses the author's familiarity with the Wisdom Literature of the intertestamental period. Thus James's advice, "Let everyone be quick to listen, slow to speak" (1:19), imitates Sirach's pithy proverb, "Be quick to hear, but deliberate in answering" (Sir. 5:11); and his question and answer, "What is your life? For you are a mist that appears for a little while and then vanishes" (4:14), reminds one of the statement in the apocryphal book the Wisdom of Solomon, "Our life will pass away like the traces of a cloud, and be scattered like mist" (Wis. 2:4).

Of all of the books in the New Testament other than the four Gospels, this one has the greatest number of parallels to the words of Jesus, particularly to his teaching in the Sermon on the Mount (Matt. 5–7). Among the chief parallels are the condemnation of these who are hearers only (1:22, 25 and Matt. 7:26); of censorious judgment of others (4:11 and Matt. 7:1-5); of the swearing of oaths (5:12 and Matt. 5:34-37); and of worldliness (1:10; 2:5-6 and Matt. 6:19, 24); the teaching about prayer (1:5 and Matt. 7:7) and about anxious concern for the future (4:13 and Matt. 6:34); and the references to moth and rust (5:2-3 and Matt. 6:19) and to the tree and its fruit (3:12 and Matt. 7:16).

Of the authorship and date of this treatise not much is known. The writer describes himself as "James, a servant of God and of the Lord Jesus Christ" (1:1). The name James (Greek *Iakobos*) is a form of the Hebrew name Jacob. Two of the apostles of Jesus had this common Jewish name (see Mark 3:17-18), as had also one of Jesus' brothers (Mark 6:3).[1] James the brother of Jesus became the leader

---

1. The names of Jesus' brothers are given as James, Joseph (or Joses), Simon, and Judas (Matt. 13:55; Mark 6:3). In what sense they were his "brethren" has been much disputed. Some have regarded them as children of Joseph by a former marriage. Others, wishing to maintain the perpetual virginity of Joseph as well as of Mary, have argued that they were Jesus' cousins on his mother's side (or on Joseph's side). In the light, however, of Luke 2:7, where Jesus is called Mary's "firstborn son," the most probable view is that they were the children of Joseph and Mary, born after Jesus. The brothers of Jesus were not disciples at first, for they naturally could not believe that God's Messiah had been a member of their family circle (Mark 3:20-33), but afterward they came into the church (Acts 1:14).

of the church at Jerusalem and presided over the apostolic council (Acts 15:13). According to patristic tradition it was this James who wrote the Letter of James sometime prior to his martyrdom about A.D. 62.

However, there are features that make it difficult to accept the traditional view, and many scholars think that the letter was written by an unknown Hellenistic Christian toward the close of the first century A.D. It is pointed out that the rhetorical style of the letter presupposes a good Greek culture, which is improbable for one born and bred at Nazareth. For several generations the ancient church showed no sign of acquaintance with this letter—a circumstance that is difficult to reconcile with its early composition by a well-known leader of the church. Likewise, the letter contains no hint of the Judaizing controversy that raged at the middle of the first century and in which James had been a central figure.

None of these objections, however, is quite conclusive. The atmosphere of the letter is clearly Jewish Christian, and the setting must be Palestine (for only there in ancient times did farmers employ hired labor rather than slaves; compare 5:4). There is no allusion to the Jewish war of A.D. 66–70 and its aftermath, and the uncertainties of life to which the author refers are those of peaceful times. The allusion to participation in worship in Jewish synagogues ("assembly" in 2:2 is literally "synagogue") suits the first generation of the church rather than a later date. In the light of such considerations as these, we may conclude that the letter contains a compilation of Jewish Christian teachings, part of which may go back to the preaching of James, the Lord's brother. In any case, the author had been deeply influenced by the moral teaching of Jesus and was impelled by a prophetlike compulsion to instruct and exhort his readers.

It is sometimes asserted that James is in conflict with Paul on the question of the relation of faith and works. James declares that "faith by itself, if it has no works, is dead" (2:17) and "a person is justified by works and not by faith alone" (2:24). Conversely, Paul is emphatic that "a person is justified not by the works of the law but through faith in Jesus Christ" (Gal. 2:16; compare Rom. 3:28).

The difference between the two, however, is largely one of emphasis and definition. For James "faith" means primarily an intellectual acceptance of a proposition about God, such as "God is one"—a belief that even demons possess without undergoing any moral change (2:19). Paul would have agreed with James that this kind of faith is insufficient to save a person. Faith, according to Paul, is far more than a mere intellectual assent to a doctrine, however orthodox that doctrine may be. For him faith is at once belief, trust, and loyalty, the means whereby the believer comes into mystical union with Christ and receives the gift of the Spirit. According to Paul, one is saved by faith alone, but the faith that saves is not alone—it is followed by good works that prove the vitality of that faith. In brief, Paul declares that the only thing that avails in bringing one into a right relationship with God is "faith working through love" (Gal. 5:6)—and in this he is merely rephrasing a saying of Jesus, "Not everyone who says to me, 'Lord, Lord,' will enter the kingdom of heaven, but only the one who does the will of my Father in heaven" (Matt. 7:21).

Summary of James

For the most part the letter consists of a series of little groups of maxims, warnings, and instructions that are rather loosely strung together without any apparent plan. The main themes, most of which recur several times throughout the letter, are the following:

Trials and temptation. After the opening address (1:1) James consoles his readers in their trials and exhorts them to be steadfast, relying on divine wisdom (1:2-8). In a bold paradox he insists on the joy that temptation brings, since by enduring it with fortitude a person "will receive the crown of life" (1:12-18).

The rich and the poor. Position and wealth are uncertain (1:9-11), and subservience to the rich and despising the poor are fundamentally opposed to the Christian ethic (2:1-4). The royal law is, "You shall love your neighbor as yourself" (2:8, compare Lev. 19:18), and to transgress that command in any respect is to transgress the whole law (2:5-13). The merchant in pursuit of wealth presumes on his own powers and forgets God. Life is transient, and the plans of mortals are futile until they submit to the will of God (4:13-16). Divine retribution will punish the godless rich employer who exploits his workers (5:1-6).

Faith and works. One must not only hear God's word but also obey it. The true service of God is care for widows and orphans and

moral self-control (1:22-27). Faith without works of practical charity is dead, as is proved by the examples of Abraham and of Rahab
(2:14-26). Anyone who knows what is right and fails to do it com-
mits a sin (4:17).

The tongue. The Christian must be "quick to listen, slow to speak,
slow to anger" (1:19-21). If any think they are religious but do not
curb their tongue, their religion is worthless (1:26-27). All living
creatures can be tamed, but no one can tame the tongue. "From the
same mouth come blessing and cursing. My brothers and sisters,
this ought not to be so" (3:1-12). Christians must not speak evil of
one another (4:11-12). Christians should renounce all oaths; they
should be so truthful and straightforward that their bare word will
suffice (5:12).

Patience and prayer. The readers are urged to persevere patiently
("for the coming of the Lord is near"—5:8), following the example
of Old Testament prophets and of Job (5:10-11). Prayer is the sufficient resource of the Christian in every need, for "the prayer of the
righteous is powerful and effective" (5:13-18).

The true wisdom of life. True wisdom comes from God, and manifests itself in peaceableness (3:13-18). Conflicts and feuds among
the readers arise from their love of the world—but friendship with
the world means enmity toward God. Penitence and humility pre-
cede exaltation (4:1-10). The surest way of saving our own souls is
to be concerned about the souls of others (5:19-20).

3. THE FIRST LETTER OF PETER

The first Letter of Peter was written to Christians living in districts of the northern and western part of Asia Minor (1:1). The
writer implies that he himself had not evangelized his readers
(1:12), who appear for the most part to be of Gentile origin (1:14, 18;
2:10; 4:3). He addresses them as "the exiles of the Dispersion in
Pontus, Galatia, Cappadocia, Asia, and Bithynia" (1:1), implying
thereby that they are the true people of God who, like ancient
Israel, live scattered among pagan communities but whose real
home is in heaven (compare Phil. 3:20; Heb. 13:14).

The purpose of the letter is to encourage the recipients to stand
fast in their Christian profession (5:12) despite trials and persecutions. The references to persecution (1:6; 3:14; 4:14; 4:19) do not

seem to imply a systematic, official attempt to suppress the church, but suggest rather the presence of widespread suspicion and hostility of the pagans against Christian believers, many of whom had withdrawn from social and religious gatherings that involved the countenancing of pagan worship and immorality.

The letter was written from "Babylon" (5:13), a term that appears to be (as also in the book of Revelation, 14:8; 18:2, 10, 21) a cryptic reference to Rome, the great capital of the pagan world.

In the introductory greeting, the author identifies himself as "Peter, an apostle of Jesus Christ" (1:1), and in 5:1 he claims to have been a "witness of the sufferings of Christ." The Petrine authorship, however, has been questioned on three grounds: (a) the Greek literary style of the letter is too refined to be the work of a Galilean fisherman whose native language was Aramaic; (b) certain passages reflect Pauline teaching (compare 2:6, 8 with Romans 9:32-33, and 3:1-7 with Ephesians 5:22-28); and (c) official persecution of the church in Asia Minor at so early a date is otherwise unattested.

The last objection, however, is not valid, for as was mentioned earlier, the persecutions seem to be privately instigated "pogroms" such as are reflected elsewhere in the New Testament (Mark 13:9). The other two objections are inconclusive, for (a) the writer explicitly states that he has made use of a Greek amanuensis named Silvanus (5:12), and (b) the so-called "Paulinism" may be either the primitive Christianity on which Paul depended as well as others, or it may be genuine echoes of Paul's teaching introduced by Silvanus who had been Paul's companion for several years. The author's description of Silvanus as "a faithful brother" (5:12) has been taken to suggest that Peter gave him an outline of the content of the letter and left him free to compose the wording; then, when the work was finished, Peter added a conclusion in his own hand (5:12-14).

The date of the letter has been disputed. According to church tradition, Peter perished in the Neronian persecution; if, therefore, it was written prior to his death, a date early in the 60s is most probable. However, those who think that the persecutions referred to were officially organized later against the church date the letter near the close of the first century.

Summary of 1 Peter

After the introductory greeting (1:1-2), the author praises God for the blessings of salvation (1:3-12). The body of the letter consists of three sections containing a variety of exhortations that are interspersed with doctrinal passages. It has been suggested that some of this material had originally been delivered as a sermon to candidates for baptism, urging them to stand firm in their new faith.

The first part (1:13–2:10) consists of exhortations of a general nature, in which the author calls upon his readers to lead a blameless life, following the example of Christ, by whose death they were ransomed from the futile ways inherited from their ancestors (1:13-21). Because they have been born anew by the living and abiding word of God, they are to put away "all malice, and all guile, insincerity, envy, and all slander," for now they are "a royal priesthood, a holy nation, God's own people" (2:1, 9).

The second part (2:11–4:6) consists of special injunctions for particular states of life. As pilgrims passing through this world, all Christians are to behave in such a way that the world may recognize that this is so (2:11-17). Slaves are to obey their masters—even unjust masters—enduring humiliation in the spirit of Christ (2:18-25). A Christian wife should seek to convert her pagan husband by the silent example of her attitude to life and by the standards she adopts for herself (3:1-6). Likewise the Christian husband must treat his wife with consideration and honor, since both he and she "are heirs of the gracious gift of life" (3:7). In short, whoever or wherever the Christian may be, the Lord's words and the Lord's ways must always be one's guide (3:8-22).

The third part consists of exhortations relating to the time of suffering that had befallen them and to the coming judgment (4:1–5:11). The proximity of the end of the age calls for an ordered and sober life; for mutual love, hospitality, and a right use of the gifts of grace for the glory of God (4:7-11). Christians are to show patience in adversity, for they who share in Christ's sufferings will be triumphant when his glory is revealed on the last day (4:12-19).

The elders of the church must discharge their duties faithfully, as shepherds with wisdom; the younger men must be subject to the elders; and all members of the community should be humble, sober, alert, and steadfast in the face of persecution, knowing that the same trials and suffering beset their brothers and sisters everywhere (5:1-11).

After a brief reference to Silvanus and a final exhortation to stand fast in the faith, the letter closes with greetings from the church in Babylon and from Mark, and with a benediction (5:12-14).

4. THE SECOND LETTER OF PETER

Although the author of this letter calls himself "Simeon Peter, a servant and apostle of Jesus Christ" (1:1), and makes reference to his being present at the transfiguration of Jesus Christ (1:18), several features of its style and contents have led nearly all modern scholars to regard it as the work of an unknown author in the early part of the second century who wrote in Peter's name.

Unlike the style of 1 Peter, which is written in fluent koine Greek, the style of 2 Peter is almost pseudoliterary. The wording is unusual, artificial, and often obscure; it is the one book in the New Testa-ment that gains by translation. Though some have suggested that the marked difference in style between the two letters might be accounted for by supposing them to be the work of different amanuenses, several passages of 2 Peter point to a date long after Peter's lifetime. Thus, the section dealing with the delay of the second coming of Christ (3:3-4) presupposes that the first generation of Christians—to which Peter belonged—had passed away. Furthermore, the letters of Paul, it appears, have not only been collected, but are referred to as "scripture" (3:16), a term that was not applied to them until some considerable time after the apostle's death. The second chapter of 2 Peter embodies most of the little Letter of Jude, which probably dates from the latter part of the first century. Moreover, 2 Peter is not definitely referred to by early church writers until the third century when Origen speaks of its disputed authenticity. In the light of such internal and external evidence one must conclude that 2 Peter was drawn up sometime after A.D. 100 by an admirer of Peter who wrote under the name of the great apostle in order to give his letter greater authority.

The letter is a general one addressed to all Christians in all places (1:1). An analysis of the contents shows that the author had two main purposes in writing: (*a*) to counteract the teaching of false prophets and heretics, and (*b*) to strengthen the faith of Christians in the second coming of Christ and make them live accordingly.

SUMMARY OF 2 PETER

After the introductory greeting (1:1-2), the writer refers to the reliability of God's promises, and exhorts his readers to exhibit a noble character, cultivating self-control, endurance, godliness, and love, thereby confirming their call and election (1:3-11). Speaking in the person of the apostle, he declares that his end is near, and appeals to the transfiguration of Christ in support of what he has taught about the second coming of Christ (1:12-21).

Adopting material from the Letter of Jude, the writer next warns his readers that false and licentious teachers will appear who will deny the Lord and cause many to apostatize (2:1-3). Their punishment, however, is certain, as can be deduced from three examples of punishment in olden times involving the fall of angels, the deluge, and the wicked cities of Sodom and Gomorrah (2:4-9). Audacious and self-willed, utterly debauched in sensual pleasures, the heretical teachers promise freedom, "but they themselves are slaves of corruption" (2:10-22).

Last, the writer dwells in solemn tones on the certainty of the future judgment at the second coming of Christ (3:1-7). Though punishment may be deferred, this delay is only a sign of the forbearance of the Lord, who does not want "any to perish, but all to come to repentance" (3:8-9). The day of the Lord will come suddenly and unexpectedly, like a thief, and will bring universal conflagration to be followed by renewal of the heavens and the earth (3:10-13). In view of the approaching end, therefore, it behooves Christians to live righteously and peacefully, as Paul also has written in all his letters (3:14-17). The writer ends, as he had begun, by calling on his readers to grow in grace and knowledge (3:18).

5. THE THREE LETTERS OF JOHN

The writer of these letters does not refer to himself by name, as did Peter, Paul, and James in their letters, but in the second and third letters he merely calls himself "the elder." Presumably he was a person sufficiently well known to do this. The term *elder* is used in New Testament letters interchangeably with the term *bishop* (see Titus 1:5-7), and refers to one who has (or shares) the spiritual oversight of a congregation. Since apostles might also be called "elders" (as 1 Pet. 5:1 shows), early tradition identified the author with John the apostle (the son of Zebedee), who after the fall of Jerusalem settled in Ephesus and became the acknowledged leader of the churches there. Many modern scholars, however, believe that the Fourth Gospel and the three Johannine Letters were composed by a disciple of the apostle John, who wrote as a pastor and friend of the churches in Asia Minor and who had come under John's care and instruction (see p. 115). Whoever the author was, he obviously held a position of authority in the church and writes as one who had known Jesus by actual bodily experience (1 John 1:1-3).

What is called the First Letter of John has none of the usual features of a letter. Not only does it lack (as was mentioned above) the writer's name, but nothing is said to identify its destination. There are no greetings at the end, nor does it contain any contemporary personal, historical, or geographical allusions. It is more like a sermon than anything else, in which the writer provides a practical application of the doctrines set forth in the Fourth Gospel. The style is simple, but occasionally baffling in its simplicity. Though the sentences are easy for a child to read, their meaning can sometimes be difficult for an adult fully to analyze. With spiraling sequence of thought, the author states and restates certain great Christian truths concerning the person and work of Christ, the love of God, eternal life, and love for one another, weaving them together like the leading refrains of a great musical composition.

The purpose of the letter is twofold: to deepen the spiritual life of its readers and to warn them against heretical teachings. Apparently some who boasted of special insight had separated themselves from their fellow Christians and formed their own sect (1 John 2:19), advocating a theosophical amalgam of Gnostic philosophy and Christianity. They declared that Christ had no physical human body but was a phantomlike appearance of God on earth (1 John 2:22; 4:2-3, 15). Since he only seemed to have a mortal body, he suffered no pain on the cross; he was not actually there at all, but only seemed to be crucified.[2]

---

2. For other forms of Gnosticism, see pp. 78 and 267.

The Second Letter of John is addressed to "the elect lady and her children" (v. 1). This does not refer to a Christian woman who provided lodging for wandering missionaries (compare v. 10), but is a picturesque way of speaking of some local church, probably in Asia Minor. The writer repeats in briefer form the main teachings of 1 John, and adds a warning against showing hospitality to false teachers, lest by so doing one further the growth of error (vv. 7-11). The letter closes with greetings from "the children of your elect sister" (v. 13). This is not a greeting sent by the nephews and nieces of the elect lady to their aunt, but from members of a sister church.

The Third Letter of John is a short personal letter to "the beloved Gaius" (v. 1), presumably a distinguished and perhaps well-to-do Christian who had been converted by the writer (v. 4). The letter reflects a period in the church's life when organization was loose and local congregations were bound together by letters from those in authority and by personal visits of their representatives and itinerant evangelists. The writer acknowledges the cordial hospitality that Gaius had shown to such missionaries, and encourages him to continue this practice.

The date of the composition of the three letters of John is thought to be near the end of the first Christian century.

Summary of 1 John

In a lengthy introductory sentence, the writer, having himself been an eyewitness, tells his readers of the divine life that was manifested on earth so that they also may have a share in his fellowship with the Father and the Son (1:1-4).

God is light; fellowship with God must, therefore, show itself in moral goodness. Only those who, having confessed their sins, are forgiven and cleansed through the atoning death of Jesus Christ have fellowship with God and with one another (1:5; 2:2). There can be knowledge of God and fellowship with him only by keeping his commandments. Union with God involves conformity to his character as revealed in Christ (2:3-6).

Those who profess to be in the light and yet disobey the old-new commandment of mutual love are still in darkness. True Christians must not love the world or the things in the world, which is doomed to destruction (2:7-17).

The appearance of many antichrists in the person of false teachers, who deny that Jesus is the Christ, is a sign of the approaching end of the age. True believers, however, will abide secure in Christ, for they have an anointing of the Holy Spirit (2:18-27).

God is righteous; hence fellowship with him involves doing righteousness, and this is an evidence of divine sonship. At the coming of the Lord the children of God will be made like him (2:28; 3:3). There is a marked contrast between righteousness and sin, between the children of God and the children of the devil. No one born of God sins habitually and constantly, for the divine nature abides in a child of God (3:4-10). Those who are of God do not merely talk about mutual love—they actively practice it (3:11-18). If the Christian's conscience is clear in this matter, God may be addressed in confidence, and the believer's prayers will be answered (3:19-24).

Not all spiritual activity is the work of God's Spirit; only those who confess that Jesus Christ has come in the flesh are of God. False prophets who deny this are of antichrist and must be repudiated (4:1-6).

Genuine love is of divine origin, and those who exhibit this love are children of God. God is love, and has proved this love for us by sending his Son to be the expiation for our sins; this obliges us to love one another (4:7-12). Such mutual love and confession that Jesus is the Son of God are the foundation and proof of our union with God (4:13-16). Perfect love drives out fear of judgment (4:17-19). Love for God and love for one's brothers and sisters are inseparable (4:20-21).

Faith in Jesus as the Christ and as the Son of God is the mark of everyone who is born of God; such a person will observe God's commandments and overcome the world (5:1-5). The threefold witness of Jesus' baptism, his death, and the Spirit authenticates Jesus as the giver of eternal life (5:6-12).

Christians can be confident that God will hear their requests, as well as their intercession on behalf of a believer who has sinned, unless it be a mortal sin (5:13-17). Christians can be certain (*a*) that the children of God are kept from sin, (*b*) that they are of God and the world is in the power of the devil, and (*c*) that the incarnate Son of God has brought true knowledge of God. Everything that takes the place of God in one's affections must be rejected (5:18-21).

Summary of 2 John

After the introductory salutation (vv. 1-3), the elder tells a local church how happy he is that some of her members are living good Christian lives (v. 4). He reminds his readers of the commandment from the Father—"that we love one another"—and begs them to obey it (vv. 5-6).

The elder warns them against false teachers, who do "not confess that Jesus Christ has come in the flesh," and exhorts them to remain true to the orthodox doctrine of Christ (vv. 7-9). Heretics should not be received into one's house, or even given any greeting, lest this be interpreted as a sign of approval (vv. 10-11).

After mentioning his hope of paying them a visit, the elder closes with greetings from members of the church where he is staying (vv. 12-13).

Summary of 3 John

After a brief salutation (v. 1), the elder expresses great satisfaction at the reports he has heard concerning the character and activity of Gaius (vv. 2-4). Gaius has given proof of his loyalty by offering hospitality to itinerant missionaries, who have refused to accept help from nonbelievers. The elder intimates that by fitting them out for the continuation of their journey, Gaius himself would be spreading the truth of the gospel (vv. 5-8).

The elder censures Diotrephes, an ambitious leader who excommunicated those who showed hospitality to the friends (vv. 9-10). Highly commendable, however, has been the conduct of Demetrius, as everyone testifies, and as his truly Christian behavior indicates (vv. 11-12).

A fuller explanation is not necessary because the elder hopes to see Gaius in the near future, when they can talk face-to-face. He closes with greetings from those who are with him, and wishes to be remembered individually to all his friends (v. 15).

6. THE LETTER OF JUDE

This brief writing, which in some ways is more like a tract or pamphlet than a letter, was sent to no particular church or locality, but is addressed quite generally to the whole body of Christian people

("To those who are called, who are beloved in God the Father and kept safe for Jesus Christ," verse 1). It is an energetic and indignant warning against a combination of sexual depravity and fantastic theology that threatened to undermine church doctrine and discipline.

The writer begins with the tantalizing statement that he was about to write concerning "our common salvation" (an expression that suggests that he was a Jewish Christian writing to Gentiles), but thought it necessary instead to send an appeal for his readers "to contend for the faith that was once for all entrusted to the saints" (v. 3; one wonders what the unwritten document would have contained). Jude does not mince words: with scathing denunciations he declares that the false teachers are immoral (vv. 4, 7, 16) and covetous (vv. 11, 16), and reject authority (vv. 8, 11). Grumblers, malcontents, loud-mouthed boasters (v. 16), they are crisply characterized as "worldly people, devoid of the Spirit" (v. 19). Their doom is sure; like their spiritual prototypes in the Old Testament— the disobedient Israelites, the fallen angels, and the wicked cities of Sodom and Gomorrah—they will certainly stand condemned at the judgment seat of God.

The writer of this impassioned tractate calls himself simply "Jude, a servant of Jesus Christ and brother of James" (v. 1). Of the half dozen persons in the New Testament who are named Jude (or Judas), probably the only one who could have identified himself by referring to his brother merely as James, without further specification, was the Lord's brother mentioned in Matthew 13:55 and Mark 6:3 (on the "brethren" of the Lord, see the footnote on p. 288). Scholars have debated whether this is a true identification on the part of the author, or whether some unknown Christian decided to compose a letter under the name of Jesus' brother. In favor of the authenticity of the letter is the unlikelihood that a later pseudepigrapher would have chosen to write under the name of so undistinguished and almost unknown brother of the Lord. Likewise in favor of the genuineness of the letter is the modest way in which the author speaks of himself with a complete lack of undue emphasis.

Apparently Jude wrote sometime during the closing decades of the first century, for he alludes to the words of the apostles as though they lived in a previous generation (vv. 17-18).

The historical value of the little Letter of Jude is out of proportion to its length. It is important for the light it sheds on the state of Christianity toward the close of the New Testament period, revealing that at that time libertine heresies were becoming a menace and a challenge to the church.

Furthermore, the author's use of such uncanonical Jewish works as the Assumption of Moses and the book of Enoch (vv. 6, 9, 14, 15) shows that Jewish apocalyptic literature (see p. 47) was popular in some parts of the church toward the close of the first century. If for no other reason, however, the preservation of Jude's letter in the New Testament is worthwhile because it contains what is perhaps the most exalted doxology in early Christian literature: "Now to him who is able to keep you from falling, and to make you stand without blemish in the presence of his glory with rejoicing, to the only God our Savior, through Jesus Christ our Lord, be glory, majesty, power, and authority, before all time and now and forever. Amen" (vv. 24-25).

Summary of Jude

The author greets his readers, praying that mercy, peace, and love may be theirs in fullest measure (vv. 1-2). The intrusion of false teachers who have wormed their way into the church makes it urgently necessary for Jude to write at once and appeal to his readers to join in the defense of the faith (vv. 3-4). Despite the warnings in sacred history of judgments that fell upon evildoers, these enemies of true religion continue in their wickedness. Their conduct is quite different from that of the archangel Michael (v. 9), who, though provoked to anger by the devil (who had charged that Moses, being a murderer, was not worthy of burial), did not presume to condemn him in insulting words. The heretics, however, are very free with intemperate language; they pour abuse upon things they do not understand, are blemishes on the Christian love feasts, where they eat and drink without reverence, and care for none but themselves (vv. 10-13).

Enoch prophesied of the punishment that awaits the ungodly, and the apostles foretold that such persons would arise in the last time (vv. 14-19). The author exhorts his readers to remain loyal to the faith, and instructs them how to work for the salvation of those enmeshed in error (vv. 20-23). He concludes with an ascription of praise to God, who alone can keep them from falling (vv. 24-25).

II. THE BOOK OF REVELATION

The last book in the New Testament is for many readers the most difficult, and has occasioned more misunderstanding and fantastic speculation than any other part of the Bible. Certainly the book is an unusual one; its language is sometimes cryptic, and its symbolism is often bizarre and even grotesque. It refers to altars that speak, an angel whose legs are pillars of fire, single stars that fall on all rivers and infect them with poison, locusts like horses arrayed for battle, a lamb with seven horns and seven eyes that takes a scroll and opens its seals, a monster from the sea with ten horns and seven heads, and other extraordinary creatures.

A clue to the proper interpretation of the book as a whole can be gained from a consideration of the literary genre to which it belongs. The book of Revelation, as its title in Greek states, is an apocalypse. Apocalyptic literature among the Jews contained weird symbols of mythological beasts representing nations and individuals. The meaning of such imagery must have been as clear to the original reading public of apocalypses as the significance is today of newspaper cartoons that depict the British lion, the Russian bear, the Republican elephant, or the Democratic donkey.

Jewish and Christian apocalypses have often been called, quite appropriately, tracts for bad times. They were intended to strengthen their readers to meet some crisis, some grim ordeal, or some impending calamity. To struggling and suffering people the message of apocalyptic writers was one of hope and encouragement. These writers affirmed in no uncertain terms that God Almighty rules and overrules in the affairs of humankind, and that despite the apparent success of earthly tyrants his righteous purpose will ultimately prevail.

Although today we do not understand in every detail what the author of the book of Revelation intended to convey through his symbolism, even a casual reader can appreciate something of the poetic power and beauty of its magnificent word-pictures of the cosmic struggle between Christians and their persecutors, between Christ and antichrist, between God and the devil. The Apocalypse offers its deepest truths to those who keep in mind the following considerations: (*a*) The book contains the substance of real visions that repeat with kaleidoscopic variety certain great principles of

God's just and merciful government of all creation. *(b)* Though the key for the understanding of some of the symbols has been lost, a comparison with the prophetic symbolism in the Old Testament, especially in the books of Daniel and Ezekiel, will often shed light upon the author's meaning. (In this connection use should be made of the cross-references provided in the margins of many Bibles.) *(c)* Instead of seeking to find a specific meaning in each detail of what is sometimes elaborate and dazzling symbolism, the reader should allow the total scene to make its impact upon his or her imagination.

It will be found that throughout the book the author employs a wide variety of images, some of which seem to be mutually exclusive, in order to express the richness of his theological ideas. In the first chapter, for example, the exalted Christ appears as an impressive human figure in a long robe, described in terms that suggest his royalty, eternity, wisdom, and immutability, and the penetrating power of his words (1:13-16). Later he is referred to as a lion, a root, and a lamb (5:5-6). He also rides forth from heaven as a warrior on a white horse (19:11). The lion symbolizes his kingly power; the root suggests his Davidic ancestry; the lamb recalls especially his sacrificial death for our salvation; and the warrior figure points forward to his final and complete triumph over all evil powers. In these metaphors the book of Revelation does not offer new doctrines about Jesus Christ that are not taught elsewhere in the New Testament; on the contrary, it presents the common faith of the early church, yet not in bald prose, but in striking images that are symbolized ideas.[3]

The author of the Apocalypse calls himself John (1:4; 22:8), with no title beyond brother (1:9) and prophet (22:9). Though traditionally identified with the apostle John (son of Zebedee), this is not stated in the New Testament itself. The author received his visions while exiled on the Mediterranean island of Patmos, but his familiarity with the life of churches in Asia Minor (chaps. 2–3) suggests that he was normally a resident there.

From various internal features it appears that the book was written at the close of the reign of the emperor Domitian (A.D. 81–96).

---

3. In this connection reference may be made to the present writer's book *Breaking the Code: Understanding the Book of Revelation* (Nashville: Abingdon Press, 1994).

It was then that Domitian began to demand that his subjects address him as "Lord and God" and to worship his image. For refusing to commit this act of idolatry, many Christians were put to death (Rev. 6:9; 13:15), others were exiled, and all were threatened. One reason for the author's couching his teaching in mysterious figures and extraordinary metaphors was to prevent non-Christians from understanding that his book is a trumpet call to the persecuted, assuring them that, despite the worst that the powers of evil can do, God reigns supreme in heaven, and Christ, the Lamb of God, who died and is alive forevermore (1:18; 5:6), has the power to overcome all evil, and his kingdom will triumph.

Certain aspects of the literary style and content of the book of Revelation are noteworthy. The original Greek text is unique in the number of instances where the author has disregarded the accepted usage of "good" grammar and committed atrocious violations of the rules of Greek syntax. These have usually been explained by supposing that the author was better acquainted with a Semitic language (Hebrew or Aramaic) than Greek, and would, therefore, lapse into non-Greek expressions.

In spite of such instances of disregard for the idiomatic usage of Greek, the book of Revelation is not lacking in literary power. It contains solemn and sonorous passages that are almost poetically rhythmical and have something of the Miltonic "organ-voice" about them, discernible even in English translation. Many of these sections contain hymnlike materials, sung by celestial choirs (for example, 4:11; 5:9-10; 7:15-17; 11:17-18; 15:3-4; 16:5-6). Presumably these sections are based on hymns actually used in Christian services of worship at the close of the first century.[4]

The power of this ancient apocalypse to inspire down through the ages some of the most sublime creations of the human spirit has been remarkable. Many of the hymnlike materials have been set to exalted music by such musicians as Handel and Brahms (for example, the "Hallelujah Chorus" in Handel's oratorio *Messiah*). Other parts of the book have inspired devotional writers such as Bernard of Cluny ("Jerusalem the Golden"), artists such as Michelangelo (*The Last Judgment* in the Sistine Chapel at Rome) and Holman Hunt

---

4. Compare what Pliny the Younger says of Christians in Bithynia who sang hymns to Christ as to a god (p. 93).

(The Light of the World), poets such as Dante and Milton, and unnamed medieval sculptors whose artistic works in stone and glass decorate the cathedrals of Europe.

Summary of the Book of Revelation

The book begins with John's commission from Christ to put in writing his visions of "what is and what is to take place after this" (1:19), and to send the account to seven churches in the Roman province of Asia, in western Asia Minor (1:1-20). The next two chapters (2:1–3:22) contain letters dictated by Christ to John for the seven churches, beginning with Ephesus and proceeding north through Smyrna to Pergamum, thence southeast to Thyatira, Sardis, Philadelphia, and Laodicea. All the letters follow a general pattern:

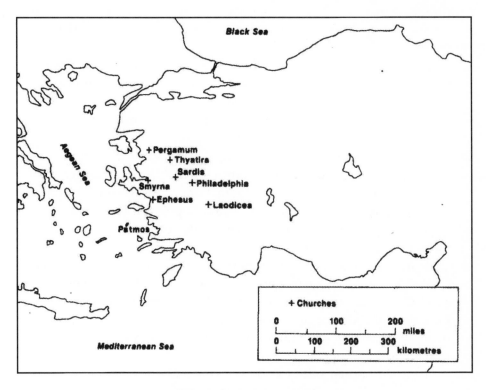

The Seven Churches of Asia
(Reprinted with the permission of Cambridge University Press)
Map showing the route of a letter carrier going from Ephesus to Laodicea with messages to each of the seven churches. See Colin J. Hemer, *The Letters to the Seven Churches of Asia in Their Local Setting* (Grand Rapids: Eerdmans, 2001).

The words of him who . . .
I know your works . . .
But I have this against you . . .
Repent . . .
Let anyone who has an ear, listen to what the Spirit says to the churches . . .
To the one who conquers I will give. . . .

Yet each letter is different from the others, and individually suited, as it seems, to the needs of the particular local church to which it is addressed. The gist of each of the brief letters is as follows:

(1) As invisibly present among his people, Christ rebukes the church in Ephesus, the most important city in Asia Minor, for the cooling of her first love. To those who overcome the special temptations to which they are exposed, he promises to give food from the tree of life (2:1-7).

(2) As conqueror of death, Christ exhorts the church in Smyrna, which had a large Jewish settlement, to steadfastness during an approaching persecution instigated by the "synagogue of Satan," and promises whoever conquers deliverance from the second death (2:8-11).

(3) As the wielder of the sword, Christ warns the church in Pergamum, a noted center of idolatrous worship, of the presence of the heretical Nicolaitans among them, but promises to give some of the hidden manna to support them and to give a mysterious white stone, perhaps as a kind of pass that would secure admission to the messianic feast (2:12-17).

(4) As God's Son, Christ pronounces divine judgment on "that woman Jezebel, who calls herself a prophet" but who had encouraged Christians to participate in idolatrous feasts sponsored by local trade guilds. He promises to the faithful in Thyatira a share in his own dominion over the Gentile nations, and the morning star to whoever conquers (2:18-29).

(5) As the source and guardian of spiritual life, Christ warns the church in Sardis, a city noted for its luxury and licentiousness, of the approach of spiritual death, but promises that those who keep themselves pure from moral pollution will not be expunged from the book of life (3:1-6).

(6) As the true steward over the household of God, Christ declares the right of Christians in Philadelphia, a small town in Lydia, to membership in God's family despite Jewish opposition. He promises them protection through the coming persecution and a permanent place ("a pillar") in the temple of God that is shortly to be revealed (3:7-13).

(7) Christ rebukes the church in Laodicea, a proud and wealthy city near Colossae, for her indifference and her self-satisfaction. He warns her to expect chastisement, but also invites her to repent, and thus be enabled to participate in the joys of the messianic banquet in the coming age and to share his own regal authority (3:14-22).

The preliminary or admonitory part of the revelation of Jesus Christ is now complete: he is seen to be the present and living judge and protector of all Christian communities. The principal or prophetic part of the book next sets forth the drama of the end of the present epoch and the coming of the future world era (4:1–22:5). John is granted a vision *(a)* of God on his throne in heaven, presiding over the destinies of the universe and accepting the acts of homage that representatives of all creation offer to him (4:1-11), and *(b)* of Jesus Christ who, as the Lamb of God, opens the sealed scroll of the divine decrees concerning the destinies of all (5:1-14).

Four of the seven seals of the scroll are opened, letting loose the "Four Horsemen of the Apocalypse" who bring disasters upon the world (6:1-8). The opening of the fifth seal discloses the souls of slain Christians asking how long judgment of the wicked is to be delayed (6:9-11). Further disasters follow upon the opening of the sixth seal (6:12-17). Between the opening of the sixth and seventh seals an episode is introduced that shows the security of the people of God amid the judgments that befall the world (7:1-17).

The opening of the seventh seal leads, after a dramatic half-hour's silence in heaven, to a vision of the seven angels with trumpets (8:2–11:19). The sounding of each trumpet is followed by a vision of destruction upon a sinful world, ending with the last judgment and the proclamation that "the kingdom of the world has become the kingdom of our Lord and of his Messiah, and he will reign forever and ever" (11:15).

In one sense the book is complete at this point. It is possible, however, to look at the same spiritual truths from a fresh point of view. Using, then, a variety of other symbols, the author describes a vision of the church, under the figure of a woman, bringing forth a male child, against whom the dragon, or Satan, wages war (12:1-17). This is followed by a series of visions of the monsters[5] that Satan will use as his agents (13:1-18), of the militant church (14:1-5), and of the angels with the seven bowls of the last plagues of God's judgment upon powers hostile to him (14:6–16:21). The destruction of Babylon, described as "the great whore" arrayed in purple and scarlet, is vividly portrayed (17:1–18:24). There follows the marriage supper of the Lamb, which is the occasion for rejoicing in heaven. Christ is represented as a warrior riding forth in triumph, and the beast and the false prophet are destroyed in one final battle (16:16; 19:1-21). Satan is bound for a thousand years (20:1-3), and finally thrown into the lake of fire and sulfur where he will be tormented day and night, forever and ever (20:10).

The book continues with a vision of the general resurrection and the last judgment (20:11-15), and the coming of the eternal kingdom of God, with the heavenly Jerusalem as its center, upon a new earth (21:1-2). The new creation is described as the abode of the presence of God, assuring perfect happiness and eternal life (21:3-8).

An account follows of the new Jerusalem in its grandeur and magnificence, touching upon its form, size, precious things, river of the water of life, and the tree of life (21:9–22:5).

The Apocalypse concludes with an epilogue, consisting of warnings and exhortations (22:6-17), and appends severe penalties for anyone who tampers with the contents of the book (22:18-19). The final sentence, "The grace of the Lord Jesus be with all the saints" (22:21), is a fitting conclusion to the book and to the Bible.

---

5. In 13:18, the name of one of these monsters is identified as being the equivalent of the number 666. The letters of the Hebrew and Greek alphabets are also used as numerals; the number of a name, therefore, is the sum of its individual letters. Of many solutions that have been proposed for 666, the most notable is *Neron Caesar* (in Hebrew letters), which, when spelled without the final "n," also accounts for the variant reading, 616, in some ancient manuscripts of Revelation.

CHAPTER 12

THE FORMATION OF THE CANON OF THE NEW TESTAMENT

Etymologically, the word *canon* comes from an ancient Semitic root meaning a reed or a stalk. The word came to be used to designate something that could measure lengths and make a straight line, and if it had dots along the edge it could measure different lengths. When applied to a group of several literary pieces, a canon of literature was the established critical standard of that material. The canon may be simply drawn up as a list of the titles of several different documents, or the word may refer to the assembled documents themselves. Thus the term *canon* has both these connotations: it is a list as well as the contents of what is comprised in that list.

Used with reference to the Bible, the term *canon* means the collection of books that are received as divinely inspired and therefore authoritative for faith and life. The recognition of the canon of the New Testament is one of the most important developments in the thought and practice of the early church; yet history is silent as to how, when, and by whom it was brought about. It is possible, however, to reconstruct some of the influences that must have contributed to the emergence of the New Testament canon.

The Bible of the earliest Christians was the Old Testament, and, with one possible exception, all the references in the New Testament writings to "the scriptures" refer to the Jewish Scriptures (the possible exception is the mention in 2 Peter 3:16 of "the other scriptures"). Like every pious Jew, Jesus accepted the Old Testament as the word of God and appealed to it. Thus, he proves the indissolubility of marriage from Genesis 1:27; 2:24 (Mark 10:6-12), states that the Holy Spirit had inspired David (Mark 12:36), and more than once bases arguments on the presupposition that scripture cannot be broken (Matt. 26:54; Luke 22:37;

John 10:35). Most significantly, in the several parts of the Old Testament he finds his coming, his work, and his death foretold (Luke 4:16-21; 24:24-27, 44-46; John 5:39).

In a similar vein, Peter (in Acts 1:16), James (James 4:5), Stephen (in Acts 7:38), and Paul (Rom. 3:2) refer explicitly or implicitly to the Old Testament as oracles of God that cannot be set aside. For the early church as a whole, as for Jesus, the Old Testament pointed forward to the coming of the Messiah, and its prophecies obtained their fulfillment in Jesus of Nazareth (John 5:39; Acts 17:2-3; 2 Tim. 3:15; Heb. 10:1). It follows that it can be rightly understood only with reference to this fulfillment.

For the early Christians the supreme authority was not the Old Testament but Jesus Christ, their true Master and risen Lord. The apostles and their helpers did not preach the Old Testament; they bore witness to Jesus Christ who had come to fulfill the law and the prophets (that is, to bring them to completion, Matt. 5:17) and who, in doing this, had given authoritative pronouncements concerning what is the true and most profound meaning of the Old Testament (Matt. 5:21-28; Mark 10:2).

We are not surprised, therefore, that in the early church the words of Jesus were treasured and quoted, taking their place beside the Old Testament and being held as of equal or superior authority to it (Acts 20:35; 1 Cor. 7:10, 12; 9:14; 1 Tim. 5:18). Parallel with the oral circulation of Jesus' teaching were apostolic interpretations of the significance of his person and work for the life of the church. It is natural that when these two kinds of authoritative materials (the remembered words of Jesus and the apostolic explanations of his person and work) were drawn up in written form, the documents would be circulated and read in services of worship (Col. 4:16; 1 Thess. 5:27; Rev. 1:3).

Just when it was that certain Christian writings began to be generally accepted as of equal authority with the Old Testament is not known. Presumably, as each Gospel was completed, it was approved (cf. John 21:24, "We know that his testimony is true") and used for public reading, first in the place of its composition, then copied and circulated to other churches. The collecting of Paul's Letters must have begun early, even in the apostle's own lifetime. He himself prescribed (Col. 4:16) that two churches interchange two of his letters (no doubt by making copies). From that point it was a natural step to collecting copies of his other letters as well.[1] The book of Acts doubtless shared the circulation and acceptance of Luke's earlier volume, the Third Gospel.

At first a local church would have only a few apostolic letters and perhaps one or two Gospels. During the course of the second century most churches came to possess and acknowledge a canon that included the present four Gospels, the Acts, thirteen letters of Paul, 1 Peter, and 1 John. Seven books still lacked general recognition: Hebrews, James, 2 Peter, 2 and 3 John, Jude, and Revelation. It is hard to say whether this was the cause or the effect of the divergent opinions concerning their canonicity. Certain other Christian writings, such as the first letter of Clement, the Letter of Barnabas, the Shepherd of Hermas, and the Didache, otherwise known as the Teaching of the Twelve Apostles, were accepted as scriptural by several ecclesiastical writers, though rejected by the majority.

We learn about the history of the recognition of the canon by examining what various writers in the early church have to say about these books and their collection. Already in the New Testament in 2 Peter (3:15-16), we find that the author refers to "our beloved brother Paul [who] wrote to you according to the wisdom given him . . . as he does in all his letters." We do not know how many are covered by "all," but it is several.

An important book for this kind of study is *The New Testament in the Apostolic Fathers,* prepared by a committee of the Oxford Society of Historical Theology.[2] This volume lists the quotations and echoes of the New Testament in the several documents known as the Apostolic Fathers.[3] The earliest of the Apostolic Fathers is a letter written about A.D. 96 by a Christian leader at Rome named Clement and sent from the church at Rome to the church at Corinth. In it he quotes from the Old Testament and also makes some remarks about Paul's (first) letter to the Corinthians, quoting some sentences from it. He also alludes to one or two other letters

---

1. See David Trobisch, *Paul's Letter Collection: Tracing the Origins* (Minneapolis: Fortress Press, 1994).

2. Oxford Society of Historical Theology, *The New Testament in the Apostolic Fathers* (Oxford: Clarendon Press, 1905).

3. Several English translations of the Apostolic Fathers are available; the most recently published is *The Apostolic Fathers: Greek Texts and English Translations*, rev. and ed. by Michael W. Holmes (Grand Rapids: Baker, 1999).

that Paul wrote. The quotations show that a copy of a letter that Paul had written in the late 50s to Corinth in Greece was also available in Rome in the year 96.

Among the dozen or so writings included in the corpus of the Apostolic Fathers is a letter attributed to Barnabas. This was not the Barnabas who was a companion of Paul, but another who wrote about A.D. 125 from the city of Alexandria concerning the way Christians should interpret the Old Testament. In this letter, Barnabas makes use of various parts of the New Testament, though he does not refer by name to any particular book of the New Testament.

Another of the Apostolic Fathers is Hermas, whose book *The Shepherd* was widely disseminated and appreciated by early Christian believers of the second and third centuries. This is a long and rambling narrative of parables and visions, which, once again, is found to contain allusions to several New Testament books, along with references to the Old Testament. Both the Letter of Barnabas and *The Shepherd* of Hermas were so highly regarded that the famous Codex Sinaiticus, a fourth-century copy of the Greek Bible and the earliest complete uncial manuscript of the New Testament, contains both of these writings following the ending of the New Testament.

From the middle of the second Christian century come the writings of an important Christian teacher known as Justin Martyr (ca. 100–ca. 165). He was born of pagan parents at Flavia Neapolis in Samaria, and was converted from pagan philosophy to Christianity about 130. He continued as a philosopher, but was now teaching Christianity, first at Ephesus, where he engaged in a disputation with a Jew named Trypho (ca. 135), and later at Rome, where he opened a Christian school. Here he wrote his "First Apology" (ca. 155), addressed to the emperor, Antoninus Pius, and soon afterward issued his "Dialogue with Trypho." His "Second Apology," addressed to the Roman Senate, was apparently written shortly after the accession of Marcus Aurelius (161). Justin and some of his disciples were denounced as Christians about 165, and on refusing to sacrifice were flogged and beheaded.

In Justin's writings he quotes freely from the three Synoptic Gospels, referring to them as the memoirs of the apostles. Whether he knew the Gospel of John is not evident from his writings, but he refers by name to the Revelation of John written on the island of Patmos. This is the first time that a church father refers by name to a document that is in our New Testament.

Toward the end of the second century, perhaps about 170, a Syrian Christian decided to weave together all four Gospels—Matthew, Mark, Luke, and John—into one narrative. This person was Tatian, a former student of Justin Martyr at Rome. Whether his work, called the *Diatessaron* ("Through the Four"), was published first in Greek at Rome or in the East in Syriac, we do not know. It was, however, widely disseminated among Eastern churches.

These are the beginnings of the slow, steady spread and recognition of books of the New Testament by various Christian writers, starting in the late–first century.

The first major period in the development of the New Testament canon is from about the year 180 to 200. The most prolific writer was Saint Irenaeus (ca. 130–ca. 200), Bishop of Lyons. Relatively little is known of his life. As a boy he had, as he delighted to point out, listened to the sermons of the great bishop and martyr Polycarp of Smyrna, who was regarded as a disciple of the apostles themselves. Here Irenaeus came to know, he says, "the genuine unadulterated gospel," to which he remained faithful throughout his life. Perhaps he also accompanied Polycarp on his journey to Rome in connection with the controversy over the date of celebrating Easter (A.D. 154). Later he went as a missionary to southern Gaul (France), where he became a presbyter at Lyons.

Actually, we know Irenaeus almost solely from his writings, and these have not been transmitted to us in their entirety. His chief work, *The Refutation and Overthrow of Knowledge Falsely So Called* (or, more briefly, *Against Heresies*), has been preserved in the Greek original in fragments and only in a literal Latin translation in its entirety. Another writing, *The Demonstration of the Apostolic Teaching*, has been made available to us only since the beginning of the twentieth century when an Armenian translation was discovered. From these two sources we can appreciate the importance of Irenaeus as the first great Catholic theologian, a champion of orthodoxy against Gnostic heresy, and a mediating link between Eastern and Western churches.

Irenaeus is the first among patristic writers who makes full use of the New Testament. The Apostolic Fathers largely reecho the oral tradition; the Apologists (such as Justin and Athenagoras) are content with quoting the Old Testament prophets and the Lord's own words in the Gospels as proof of divine revelation, but Irenaeus shows the unity of the Old and the New Testaments in opposition to Gnostic separation of the two. Unlike his predecessors, his citations from the New Testament are more numerous than those from the Old Testament. In his treatise *Against Heresies* he quotes 1,075 passages from almost all of the books of the New Testament: 626 from the Gospels, 54 from Acts, 280 from the Pauline Epistles (but not from Philemon), 15 from the General Epistles (but not from 2 Peter, 3 John, or Jude), and 29 from the book of Revelation. As against the multiplicity of new gospels produced by the Gnostics, the great church by the time of Irenaeus had ceased to recognize any but the four Gospels, or rather, as he puts it, one single gospel in four forms.

Toward the close of the second century, an African lawyer of Carthage named Tertullian (ca. 160–ca. 225) was converted to Christianity in midlife. He became the author of a long list of apologetic, theological, controversial, and ascetic works in Latin, as well as of a few writings in Greek. One of the heretics that he went after tooth and nail was Marcion, who lived in the mid–second century. According to the lengthy treatise that Tertullian wrote against him, Marcion had joined an abbreviated Gospel of Luke with several Pauline Letters as a kind of modified Christian canon. Tertullian attacks Marcion vehemently for having cut out the majority of the books from the New Testament.

Another prominent Christian writer of this period was Titus Flavius Clement (ca. 150–ca. 215). An Athenian by birth and of pagan parentage, in his adult years Clement embraced the Christian religion. After extensive travels in pursuit of learning he came to Alexandria about A.D. 180. Here he worked for the conversion of pagans and the education of Christians. As head of the catechetical school in Alexandria, Clement devoted himself to lecturing to his pupils and to writing many books, the majority of which have disappeared. Three of his major works have survived: the *Protrepticus,* or "Exhortation to the Greeks," was addressed to pagan readers; the *Paedagogos*, on Christian life and morality; and the *Stromata*, or Miscellanies. Throughout his writings Clement makes copious citations of both classical and biblical literature: the total number of citations is about eight thousand, more than a third of which come from non-Christian authors. Of this number about 1,575 quotations are from the four Gospels and about 1,375 from the Pauline Epistles. In the course of several treatises, Clement cites all of the books of the New Testament except Philemon, James, 2 Peter, and 2 and 3 John.

Thus from the works of Irenaeus, Tertullian, and Clement during the latter part of the second century, we have evidence for the wide-spread recognition of twenty of the twenty-seven books of the New Testament. Seven books are still lacking general recognition, namely, Hebrews, James, 2 Peter, 2 and 3 John, Jude, and Revelation.

Among ante-Nicene writers of the Eastern church, the greatest by far was Origen (ca. 185–ca. 254), both as a theologian and as a prolific biblical scholar. Born of Christian parents in Egypt, probably at Alexandria, he received a thoroughly Christian education in the house of his parents. He spent most of his life in Alexandria as head of the Catachetical School as successor to Clement, who had fled Alexandria during the persecution in 292. (During this period Origen's father, Leonidas, was killed, and Origen was prevented from seeking martyrdom only by a ruse of his mother, who hid his clothes.) At various times during his life Origen visited Antioch, Athens, Arabia, Ephesus, and Rome, and lived for a rather long period at Caesarea in Palestine, where he established a school that soon became famous, and where he continued his literary work and devoted himself to preaching. In 250, in the persecution of Decius, he was imprisoned and subjected to prolonged torture, which he survived only a few years.

Having traveled widely, Origen had the opportunity of observing the usage of churches and individual Christians as to the acceptance of books of the New Testament. Origen's witness is clear and forthright, declaring that one must distinguish between the acknowledged books, which all Christians accepted as scripture, and the disputed books, which some did not accept. As acknowledged books Origen lists the four Gospels, fourteen letters of Paul (including Hebrews and the letters to Timothy and Titus), the Acts of the Apostles, 1 Peter, 1 John, and the Revelation of John—twenty-two in all. Among the disputed books, which he himself accepted as belonging to the New Testament, were James, 2 and 3 John, Jude, and 2 Peter.

During the third century and part of the fourth century there continued to be a sifting of the disputed books; certain of them came to be acknowledged as canonical and others as apocryphal. Among the church fathers who made a careful study of the usage throughout the church was Eusebius of Caesarea, who quotes in his *Ecclesiastical History* the pronouncements of earlier writers concerning the limits of the canon. In summarizing the results of his investigations (book III, chap. 25), he divides the books into three classes: *(a)* twenty-two are generally acknowledged to be canonical, namely the four Gospels, Acts, the letters of Paul (including Hebrews), 1 John, 1 Peter, and Revelation (though see Eusebius's comment cited in *[c]* below); *(b)* five are widely accepted, though disputed by some (apparently all were accepted by Eusebius himself), namely James, Jude, 2 Peter (earlier regarded by Eusebius as spurious), 2 and 3 John; and *(c)* five are spurious, namely the Acts of Paul, Hermas, Apocalypse of Peter, Barnabas, and the Didache; Eusebius continues, "To these perhaps the Revelation of John should be added, for some reject it while others count it among the accepted books." It will be observed that this is virtually the canon as we know it today. After Eusebius's time (about A.D. 325) fluctuations in the canon are limited and only occasional.

In the East, Athanasius was the first to name (in his Festal Letter for A.D. 367) exactly the twenty-seven books of the New Testament as exclusively canonical.[4] In the West, at the African synods of Hippo Regius (A.D. 393) and Carthage (A.D. 397 and 419) the twenty-seven books of the New Testament were accepted. Augustine supported this canon, which through the Latin Vulgate translation of Jerome soon came into general acceptance throughout the Western church. Though in the East some continued to have doubts about the canonicity of the book of Revelation, eventually the canon of most of the Eastern churches came to be identical with

---

4. In Athanasius's list the book of Acts is followed immediately by the General Letters. This is their position also in the great majority of Greek manuscripts.

that of the Western church. The Syrian church, however, accepted only twenty-two books; 2 Peter, 2 and 3 John, Jude, and Revelation are lacking in the standard version of the Syriac Bible, called the Peshitta, dating from the early part of the fifth century. Among Western Syrians acceptance of these books was slow; they were finally included in Bibles of the sixth and seventh centuries (the Philoxenian version). The Eastern Syrian church, having lost contact with the rest of Christendom, continued much longer to hold to the shorter canon.

Various external circumstances assisted in the process of canonization of the New Testament books. The emergence of heretical sects having their own sacred books made it imperative for the church to determine the limits of the canon. Gnosticism posed a real danger to the fledgling church because it threatened to turn Jesus into a myth with its insistence that, as the true spiritual God, he could not have been truly human. He may have appeared to be human, but his body, they maintained, was not a real human body.

The full extent of this Gnostic threat to the church was not fully grasped until recently because our only documentary evidence came from refutations by orthodox authors, who destroyed all the Gnostic writings they could get their hands on after Christianity came to dominate the empire in the fourth century. In the mid–twentieth century, however, a considerable number of Gnostic writings turned up at Nag Hammadi in Egypt (see pp. 118-20), and our knowledge of various Gnostic teachings has grown rapidly since then.

Another external pressure that forced Christians to be certain which books were Scripture and which were not occurred during periods of persecution. In 303, when Christians were persecuted under Diocletian for their faith, it became a matter of utmost importance to know which books could and which could not be handed over to the imperial police for destruction without incurring the guilt of sacrilege.

As far as can be determined, the chief criterion for acceptance of particular writings as sacred, authoritative, and worthy of being read in services of worship was conformity to what was called the "rule of faith" (*regula fidei*), that is, the congruity of a given writing with the basic Christian tradition recognized as normative for the

church. Another criterion was apostolic authorship. This requirement, however, was not applied in a narrow sense, for in the case
of two of the Gospels, the tradition of apostolic atmosphere and
association (Mark with Peter and Luke with Paul) vouched for
their authority. Other tests of canonicity included the question of a
book's continuous acceptance and usage in the churches as a sign
of its value.

These three criteria (orthodoxy, apostolicity, and consensus
among the churches) came to be generally adopted during the
course of the second century, and were never modified thereafter.
At the same time, however, there would be some variation in the
manner in which the criteria might be applied. There were, no
doubt, different opinions as to which criterion should be allowed
chief weight. Sometimes the overriding consideration was the
opinion of a much-respected bishop, or the tradition of a leading
church of the area.

It is, therefore, not surprising that for several generations the
precise status of a few books remained doubtful. What is really
remarkable is that, though the fringes of the New Testament canon
remained unsettled, a high degree of unanimity concerning the
greater part of the New Testament canon was attained within the
first two centuries among the very diverse and scattered congregations not only in the Mediterranean world, but also over an area
extending from Britain to Mesopotamia.

When, toward the close of the fourth century, church synods and
councils began to issue pronouncements concerning the New
Testament canon, they were merely ratifying the judgment of individual Christians throughout the church who had come to perceive
by intuitive insight the inherent worth of the several books. In the
most basic sense neither individuals nor councils created the
canon; instead they came to recognize and acknowledge the self-
authenticating quality of these writings, which imposed themselves as canonical upon the church.

Put another way, instead of suggesting that certain books were
arbitrarily or accidentally excluded from the New Testament
(whether the exclusion was the activity of individuals, or synods,
or councils), it is more accurate to say that certain books excluded
themselves from the canon. Among the dozen or more gospels that

circulated in the early church (see pp. 118-22), the question how, when, and why our four Gospels came to be selected for their supreme position may seem to be a mystery—but it is a clear case of the survival of the fittest. In the words of a well-known Scottish author, "It is the simple truth to say that the New Testament books became canonical because no one could stop them doing so."[5]

---

5. William Barclay, *The Making of the Bible* (Nashville: Abingdon Press, 1961), p. 78. For further discussion of the subject, reference may be made to the present writer's book, *The Canon of the New Testament: Its Origin, Development, and Significance* (Oxford: Clarendon Press, 1978), and to David Trobisch, *The First Edition of the New Testament* (New York: Oxford University Press, 2000).

APPENDIX

THE TRANSMISSION AND TRANSLATION OF THE BIBLE

I. THE TRANSMISSION OF THE BIBLE

Until 1456, when Johannes Gutenberg first printed the Bible by means of moveable type, every copy of the Scriptures was produced by hand—a long and painstaking task. Books of all kinds were quite expensive, for it would take weeks or even months to finish a handwritten copy of a lengthy document. (The process gave us the word *manuscript*, derived from the Latin *manu* and *scriptum*, meaning "written by hand.")

Something of the drudgery of copying can be appreciated from the colophons, or notes, that scribes sometimes appended at the close of a manuscript. A typical example, found in many nonbiblical works, expresses relief: "As travelers rejoice to see their home country, so also is the end of a book to those who toil in writing." Another, appearing in more than one ancient classic, complains: "Writing bows one's back, thrusts the ribs into one's stomach, and fosters a general debility of the body." A colophon in an Armenian copy of the Gospels records that a heavy snowstorm was raging outside the monastery, that the scribe's ink froze, his hand became numb, and the pen fell from his fingers!

1. THE MATERIALS OF ANCIENT BOOKS

The two materials most widely used for making manuscripts in antiquity were papyrus and parchment. Papyrus is an aquatic plant of the sedge family that grew abundantly in the marshy lands of the Egyptian delta. Its stem, which resembles a stalk of corn (maize), was cut into sections about a foot in length, split open, and the core of pith removed. After the pith had been sliced into thin strips, these tapelike pieces were placed side by side on a flat surface, and another layer was laid crosswise on top. Then the two

Figure 13.1. Replica of One of Gutenberg's Printing Presses
(Courtesy of Institut für neutestamentliche Textforschung, Münster.)

The invention of printing with moveable type was the most important development in the transmission of literary works. All printing had previously been done with solid blocks of wood with the words engraved on them. But Gutenberg in the 1450s began to use a separate moveable metal type for each letter. The types he prepared comprised not only the 24 capital and 24 lower-case letters of the Latin alphabet, but 290 different characters (47 capitals and 243 lower-case letters). Gutenberg cast such a great number of types because he wanted to reproduce as accurately as possible the details of letters and combinations of letters used in sumptuous medieval Latin manuscripts—and, if he could, to surpass their beauty through his new art. According to most critics, Gutenberg's 42-line Bible is better proportioned and harmonized than any of the manuscripts, including those transcribed with the greatest care. Because he printed with a brilliant deep black ink, his Bibles retain their fresh luster to this day.

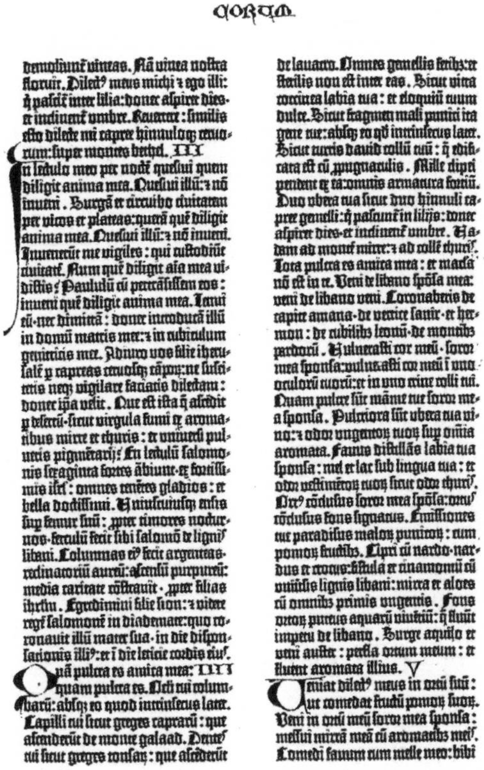

Figure 13.2. A Page from the Gutenberg Bible
(Courtesy of the Princeton Theological Seminary.)

Generally bound in two massive folio volumes, the Gutenberg Bible has no title page or colophon. It comprises 1,282 double-column pages, which are without numbers, each page measuring 15 1/2 by 11 1/8 inches. The headlines, the two-line first letter of every chapter, and the vertical accent added to the first letter of each sentence were in every case supplied by hand, and in varying degrees of beauty and excellence.

The figure shows a page containing the Latin text of the Song of Songs, from *demoliunt(ur)* of 2:15 to *bibi* of 5:1. Decorations are in red and occasionally blue. In the Roman numerals III and IIII the successive vertical units alternate red-blue-red; the numeral V is red, the initial letter at the beginning of chapter III is much enlarged, running on in the margin for eleven lines. This letter and the letter that begins chapter V are red; the other large initial letter is blue. On this page, each of the thirty-nine enlarged initial letters that begin new sentences has a vertical stroke of red. We do not know how many artists were employed to add, page by page, all these decorative features.

It is believed that approximately 150 copies were printed on paper and about 35 on parchment (vellum), for which about 6,000 calves were needed to supply enough vellum for the 35 copies. According to Don Cleveland Norman, *The 500th Anniversary Pictorial Census of the Gutenberg Bible* (Chicago: Coverdale Press, 1961), 154-55, 253-58, only 12 parchment and 36 paper copies are known to exist worldwide; four of the parchment copies are complete, as are 17 of the paper copies.

layers were pressed and pounded together with a shell or a flat stone, producing a sheet of "paper" that was remarkably durable. Even more durable as writing material was parchment. This was made from the skin of sheep, calves, goats, antelopes, and other animals. The younger the animal, the finer the quality of the skin. Vellum was the finest quality of extra-thin parchment, sometimes obtained from animals not yet born. After the hair had been removed and the surface dressed, such a sheet was lined by scoring the surface with a blunt-pointed instrument drawn along a ruler. It was sufficient to draw the lines on one side of the sheet (usually the flesh-side), since they were visible also on the other side. In many manuscripts these guide lines can still be noticed, as also the pinpricks that the scribe made first in order to guide him in ruling the parchment.

The most common ink used for papyrus was a carbon-based mixture made from soot, gum, and water. Since it does not stick well to parchment, another kind of ink was developed, using oak galls (gallnuts) and sulphate of iron. Other chemicals were added to produce a wide variety of colors. Titles were often written with vermilion ink, and today we still speak of the "rubrics" of a literary work (from the Latin word *ruber*, meaning "red") and of "red-letter" days (which were marked on the calendar in vermilion).

Vellum intended for deluxe volumes, such as presentation copies for royalty, would be dyed a deep purple and written with gold and/or silver ink. Some literary works were illustrated with exquisite miniatures, painted in the margins or on separate folios with lovely colors that even after centuries still dazzle the eye. These frequently depict scenes of the Bible, recording both the interest of the passage and the piety of the artist.

2. THE FORMAT OF ANCIENT BOOKS

There were two main forms of books in antiquity. The older form was the roll, made by fastening together sheets of papyrus or parchment side by side, and then winding the long strip around a roller of wood, bone, or metal. The maximum length of such a roll was about thirty-five feet; anything longer became excessively unwieldy to unroll while winding the strip around a second roller. The writing was placed in narrow columns, each about two and a half to three and a half inches wide, running parallel to the rollers. Usually only one side of the writing surface was utilized.

The other common form of books was the codex, or "leaf book." It was made of sheets of parchment or papyrus stacked upon one another and folded down the middle. Depending upon the size of book desired, one or more such quires, as they were called, would be fastened together at the back. Since the hair-side of parchment is darker in color than the flesh-side, the esthetically minded scribe was careful to place the sheets in such a way that wherever the codex was opened the flesh-side of one page would face the flesh-side of another page, and the hair-side face a hair-side. Similarly, in making a papyrus codex careful scribes would assemble sheets of papyrus in such a sequence that the direction of the fibers of any two facing pages would run either horizontally or vertically. Unlike the scroll, the codex could conveniently receive writing on both sides of a sheet.

It is obvious that the advantages of the codex form of a book greatly outweigh those of the scroll, which required the use of both hands while reading. Also the economy of production that resulted from using both sides of the sheet and the convenience of not having to unroll long portions to find a desired passage soon led the church to adopt the codex rather than the scroll for its sacred books. Another contributing factor may have been the desire to differentiate the external form of the Christian Bible from the Jewish scrolls used in the synagogue.

Sometimes, particularly during periods of economic recession when the cost of writing materials increased, the parchment of a worn-out codex would be used a second time. After the original text had been scraped or washed off and the surface resmoothed, a new text was written on the salvaged pages. Such a manuscript is called a palimpsest (which means "rescraped"). With modern chemical reagents and ultraviolet ray lamps, it is often possible to decipher the almost totally obliterated underwriting. An important palimpsest of the Scriptures is the fifth-century copy of the Greek Bible known as the Codex Ephraemi, which was erased in the twelfth century to receive the homilies of Saint Ephraem, a Syrian church father of the fourth century.

3. THE TRANSCRIBING OF MANUSCRIPTS

Two modes of producing manuscripts were in common use in antiquity. According to one procedure, an individual would procure writing material and make a new copy, word by word, letter by letter, from an exemplar of the literary work desired. It was inevitable (as anyone can see who tries to copy by hand an extensive document) that accidental changes would be introduced into a text as it was transmitted by successive generations of copyists. The accuracy of each new copy would depend, of course, upon the degree of the scribe's familiarity with the language and content of the manuscript that was being transcribed, as well as upon the care exercised by the scribe. But even for the best-trained and most conscientious copyist, the likelihood of error was compounded by certain features of ancient writing. For one thing, several letters in both the Hebrew and the Greek alphabets were similar and could be confused. Furthermore, the fact that ordinarily no space was left between words and between sentences would lead to several types of mistakes. One should remember also that eyeglasses were not invented until about 1374 (in Venice), but prior to that date copyists might be afflicted with various opthalmic disorders that impaired their vision.

The other mode of producing manuscripts was that followed at a scriptorium, where a lector would read aloud, slowly and distinctly, from an exemplar while several scribes seated about him would simultaneously write as many new copies as there were transcribers at work. Although it increased productivity, the dictation method also multiplied the kinds of errors that could creep into the text. A particular source of trouble arose from the circumstance that certain letters and words in Greek came to be pronounced alike (as in English, the words "grate" and "great," or "their" and "there"). For example, in later Greek the words for "we" and "you" and the words for "us" and "you" were indistinguishable to the ear. Consequently, in the Epistles of the New Testament it is sometimes difficult or impossible to decide on the basis of divergent evidence in the manuscripts which word was used originally by the author.

It should be noted, however, that among the Jews great care was taken to copy the Hebrew Scriptures with exactness, and the dictation method was seldom employed. Given the rapid expansion of the Christian church and the consequent demand for many copies of the Scriptures, the speedy multiplication of copies sometimes seemed more important than strict accuracy of detail.

In addition to inadvertent alterations, occasionally deliberate changes were introduced into the text. Thus, as the liturgy of the church and the ascetical practices of monastic communities became more highly developed, scribes would sometimes introduce changes into the text they were copying. In the earliest manuscripts of the Gospel According to Matthew, for example, the Lord's Prayer closes with the words, "And lead us not into temptation, but deliver us from evil" (6:13). It is only in later manuscripts that we find a liturgically appropriate doxology added at the end ("For thine is the kingdom and the power and the glory, for ever, amen").

Among ascetically prompted modifications that have crept into the text during the course of its transmission is the addition in later manuscripts of a reference to fasting in such passages as Mark 9:29, Acts 10:30, and 1 Corinthians 7:5. In these passages the King James Version translates the later, corrupted form of the Greek text.

Again, sometimes the copyist succumbed to the natural desire to fill out the account in one biblical book with a phrase from a similar passage in another biblical book. Thus, in Colossians 1:14 the later and less accurate manuscripts have the words "through his blood," which some well-meaning scribes introduced into this verse from having recollected the words in the parallel passage in Ephesians 1:7.

It should be mentioned that, though there are thousands of divergencies of wording among the manuscripts of the Bible (more in the New Testament than in the Old), the overwhelming majority of such variant readings involve inconsequential details, such as alternative spellings, order of words, and interchange of synonyms. In these cases, as well as in the relatively few instances involving the substance of the record, scholars apply the techniques of textual criticism in order to determine with more or less probability what the original wording was. In any event, no doctrine of the Christian faith depends solely upon a passage that is textually uncertain.[1]

---

1. Those interested in pursuing further the history and practice of textual criticism as applied to the New Testament may consult the present writer's book, *The Text of the New Testament: Its Transmission, Corruption, and Restoration*, 3rd ed. (New York: Oxford University Press, 1992).

4. IMPORTANT EARLY MANUSCRIPTS
OF THE NEW TESTAMENT

As regards the New Testament text, many important early manuscripts have come to light during the nineteenth and twentieth centuries. In 1859, the German scholar Constantine von Tischendorf discovered in a monastery on Mount Sinai the famous Codex Sinaiticus, a magnificent parchment copy of the Bible in Greek, dating from the middle of the fourth century A.D. It is now in London on display at the British Library. Another important manuscript, dating from the late fourth or early fifth century, is a parchment codex of the four Gospels in Greek, purchased in 1906 by Charles L. Freer of Detroit from a dealer in antiquities in Cairo. Today this manuscript is in the Freer Art Museum at the Smithsonian Institution of Washington, D.C. About 1930, a British collector of antiquities, A. Chester Beatty, acquired more than a dozen papyrus codices of Greek texts, including three that contain portions of most of the books of the New Testament. What makes these biblical manuscripts important is that they date from about the third century. They are now in the Beatty Museum at Dublin.

In 1935, a British paleographer, C. H. Roberts, edited a tiny fragment of the Gospel According to John, measuring only two and one-half by three and one-half inches, which belongs to a collection of papyri owned by the University of Manchester. On the basis of the style of handwriting, the fragment is dated to the first half of the second century, and is the oldest extant portion of the Greek New Testament. It contains about thirty words from the eighteenth chapter of the Gospel According to John.

Still more recently, the Swiss bibliophile, Martin Bodmer, acquired several papyrus codices of Greek authors, including several books of the New Testament. One of these codices, dating from about A.D. 200, contains most of the text of the Gospel According to John; another, dating from the third century, contains large portions of the text of both Luke and John. These examples of early and important Greek manuscripts of the New Testament are only a few of many others that might be mentioned. Some idea of the numbers of extant Greek manuscripts of part or all of the New Testament may be gained from the following statistics (as of 30 March 2001) supplied by the Institute for Textual Research at Münster, Germany.

Number of New Testament papyri 96
Number of parchment manuscripts:
    Uncial script (capital letters) 310
    Minuscule script (after ca. A.D. 750) 2,863
    Lectionaries (Church reading books) 2,414
Total number 5,519

About sixty Greek minuscule manuscripts contain all twenty-seven books of the New Testament. Among unical manuscripts, only Codex Sinaiticus has the complete New Testament.

In evaluating the significance of this rich store of manuscripts,[2] it should be recalled that the writings of many ancient classical authors

Figure 13.3. An Early Greek Manuscript of Revelation (Courtesy of the Princeton Theological Seminary)

This is a parchment leaf from a fourth-century pocket-sized codex of the book of Revelation, measuring 3 ¾ inches by 2 ⅞ inches and containing Rev. 3:19–4:2. Among the 301 Greek manuscript witnesses to Revelation currently known, eleven are uncials, of which only three are complete and three others (including this one) consist of a single leaf each.

---

2. For further information, including about forty life-size facsimiles of pages from New Testament Greek manuscripts, see the author's book *Manuscripts of the Greek Bible: An Introduction to Greek Palaeography* (New York: Oxford University Press, 1981). For new and complete transcriptions with photographs of pages from sixty-nine of the earliest New Testament Greek manuscripts prior to the beginning of the fourth century, see Philip W. Comfort and David P. Barrett, *The Text of the Earliest New Testament Greek Manuscripts* (Wheaton, Ill.: Tyndale, 2001).

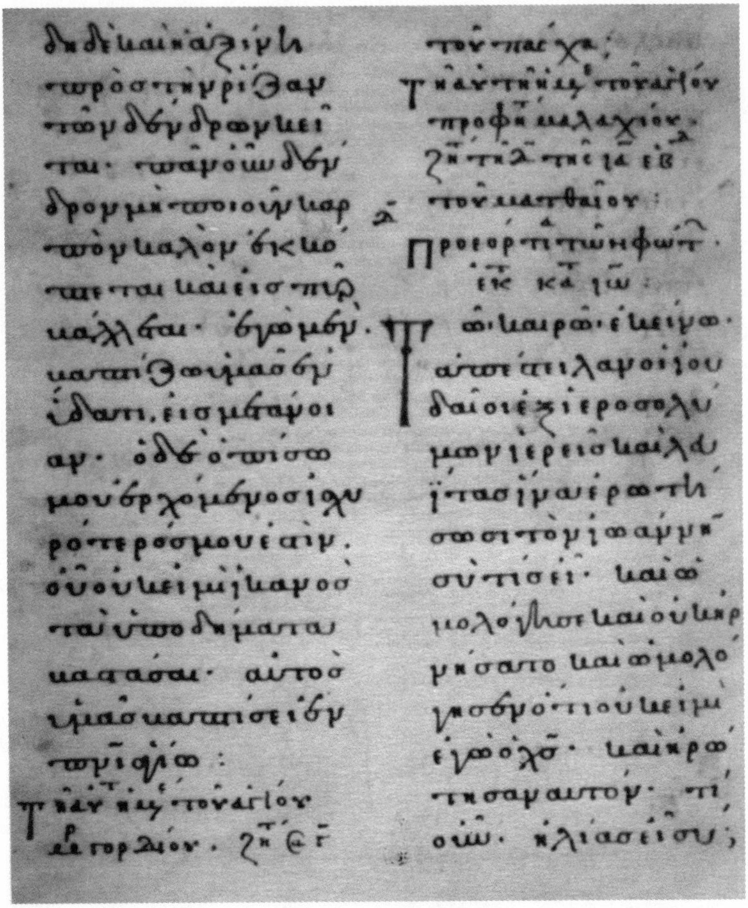

Figure 13.4. A Greek Gospel Lectionary
(Courtesy of the Princeton Theological Seminary.)

Greek Gospel lectionaries are in two sections, the synaxarion and the menologion. The former provides lections from all four Gospels, starting at Easter with John 1:1-17. The latter, which follows the civil calendar beginning with September 1st, is organized in celebration of festivals and saints' days.

The parchment page shown here, measuring 12 3/8 by 10 5/8 inches and written in minuscule script of about the twelfth century, presents Matthew 13:10-11 and John 1:19-21; the previous and the following pages contain additional material of the two lections.

The margin of the first folio contains in Greek and in Arabic: "No one has authority from God to take this [book] away under any condition, and whoever transgresses this will be under the wrath of the eternal Word of God, whose power is great. Gregory, Patriarch by the grace of God, wrote this."

A full account of the manuscript is given in the present writer's unpublished Ph.D. dissertation, "Studies in a Greek Gospel Lectionary (Greg. 303)" (Princeton University, 1942); for a shorter account, see "A Treasure in the Seminary Library," *Princeton Seminary Bulletin*, xxxvi, no. 4 (March 1943), pp. 14-19.

have survived in only a few copies, or even in only one. Furthermore, in many cases the earliest of these nonbiblical manuscripts date from the later Middle Ages and thus are separated from the time of the composition of the original work by more than a thousand years.

II. THE TRANSLATION OF THE BIBLE

During the early centuries of the Christian Era, as the church spread far beyond Palestine among peoples who could read neither the Hebrew of the Old Testament nor the Greek of the New Testament, the role of scribes in transmitting the Bible was supplemented by that of translators. By A.D. 600, the Gospels, as well as several other books of the Bible, had been rendered into Latin, Syriac, Coptic (several dialects), Gothic, Armenian, Georgian, Ethiopic, Nubian, and Sogdian. In all these languages, except Latin and Sogdian, the translation was the first written literature.[3] During the next eight centuries relatively few translations of the Bible were made. By the time that printing with moveable type was invented (1456), a mere 33 languages had any part of the Scriptures, and when the Bible Society movement began, about 175 years ago, the Bible existed in only 67 languages—a rather insignificant number when one considers that there are about 6,800 living languages and dialects throughout the world.

With the rise of the modern missionary movement in the nineteenth and twentieth centuries, the task of preparing new translations of the Scriptures—as well as revising earlier ones—got going in earnest. By the beginning of the year 2000, the entire Bible was available in 371 languages, the New Testament in 960 other languages, and at least one book of the Bible in 902 other languages, with about 600 translation projects, including revisions, currently under way throughout the world.

In the English-speaking world, new translations of the Bible, including revisions of earlier renderings, have burgeoned during the past century. There are three main reasons new English versions

---

3. For a detailed discussion of all versions of the New Testament made before A.D. 1000, reference may be made to the author's volume *The Early Versions of the New Testament: Their Origin, Transmission, and Limitations* (New York: Oxford University Press, 1977). A similar but briefer account by the same author is *The Bible in Translation: Ancient and English Versions* (Peabody, Mass.: Hendrickson Publishers, 2001).

are needed. Two of the reasons are related to the original texts, and one to the English language itself:

(1) New versions in English, including revisions of earlier English renderings, are needed because the English language is changing (only dead languages remain unchanged, and translations into living languages become dated as time moves on). In 1960, Ronald Bridges and Luther A. Weigle published *The Bible Word Book,* which lists and discusses nearly a thousand examples of words and phrases in the King James Version of the Bible (1611) that had become obsolete or archaic by the twentieth century.

In some cases, modern English usage is not only different from that of the seventeenth century, but it may actually convey the opposite meaning. For example, the word *suffer* is used by the King James Version in two quite different senses. It is used, of course, to translate the Hebrew and Greek verbs that mean "to endure hardship, pain, insult," and the like. But it is also used to translate Hebrew and Greek verbs that mean "to let, allow, or permit." Today some people misunderstand the King James rendering of Matthew 19:14, where Jesus says, "Suffer little children, and forbid them not, to come unto me." Modern English renderings quite properly eliminate the use of the word *suffer* in the sense of "let" or "permit," thus removing an ambiguity for which there is no warrant in the original language.

Another example involves two English verbs, both of which are spelled and pronounced exactly alike, but which come from two distinct Anglo-Saxon roots. The one verb *let* means "to hinder, impede, or prevent"; the other verb *let* means just the opposite, "to permit or allow." Both were current in 1611, but only the second remains part of ordinary English today; the first is now archaic except in the legal phrase "without let or hindrance" and in the game of tennis—where a "let" ball is one that has been hindered from going cleanly over the net. To persons who do not know the earlier usage, several passages in the King James Version now seem to be nonsense (Isa. 43:13; Rom. 1:13; and 2 Thess. 2:6-7).

(2) A second reason new English translations of the Bible are needed is related to the increase of knowledge of Hebrew and Greek lexicography. Most of the fifty or so translators of the King James Version were excellent scholars; some of them had begun the

study of Greek and Hebrew as schoolboys when they were six or seven years old. It is no denigration of their scholarship, however, to recognize that discoveries during the intervening centuries have increased our understanding of the meaning and usage of many words and phrases in these languages.

For example, the King James translators were at a loss when confronted with the Hebrew word *pim*, which, up to their time, was not known to occur anywhere except in 1 Samuel 13:21. They guessed from the context (which speaks of Israelite farmers taking their agricultural tools to Philistine blacksmiths to be sharpened) that the word meant "a file." This guess, however, turned out to be altogether wrong. During the twentieth century, archaeologists found at various places in Palestine sets of weights bearing inscriptions of Hebrew words, one of which is *pim*. Now the translation of the passage in most modern English versions correctly states that the Philistines charged a pim to sharpen a plowshare or a mattock.

Similarly, the past one hundred years have shed considerable light on our knowledge of the kind of Greek used by the New Testament writers—namely the koine Greek, which sometimes differs from that used by the earlier classical Greek authors. Beginning at the end of the nineteenth century, great quantities of Greek papyri were discovered in the dry sands of Egypt, involving all kinds of documents written during the first Christian centuries. They reveal that the language of New Testament authors, besides reflecting the special nuances of meaning derived from their study of the Old Testament, often reflects as well the colloquial usage of contemporary Greek.

(3) The most important reason for revising older translations of the Bible arises from the discovery of copies of Hebrew and Greek manuscripts of the Scriptures that are much older—and hence more accurate—than those previously available to translators. The King James scholars in 1611 had to use printed editions of the Greek New Testament that rested upon late Greek manuscripts, none of which was older than the tenth or eleventh century. Translators today use editions of the Greek New Testament that rest upon manuscript evidence from the third and fourth centuries. As concerns the Old Testament, until recently the earliest copy of any considerable portion of the Hebrew Bible was the Cairo man-

uscript of the Prophets written A.D. 895. But discoveries made during the mid–twentieth century, mainly in caves at Qumran near the Dead Sea, have brought to light much older manuscripts (most of them fragmentary) of every book of the Hebrew Bible, except Esther, written in the first century B.C. and the first century A.D.

III. ENGLISH TRANSLATIONS OF THE BIBLE

The multiplication of English-language translations presents to the modern reader a wide choice of styles of rendering and levels of English usage. During the first eighty years of the twentieth century more than seventy different English translations and revisions of the Bible or New Testament were published. Before one can consider the question of which is the best version, one must take into account its intended reading public and the use to which it will be put. The cadences of Shakespearian English in the King James Version probably remain unsurpassed for use in a traditional liturgy, in oratorios, and similar settings. However, a modern-speech version is preferable in contexts that call for a more colloquial—or at least a more simplified—literary style. In other cases the choice may depend upon a consideration of the religious sponsorship of the several versions, whether they were made by Protestant or Roman Catholic or Jewish teams of translators. The following descriptive comments are intended to help differentiate among several widely used English translations of the Bible currently available. They are listed in more or less chronological order of the date of publication.

King James Version. The most widely used English Bible up to the present time has been the King James Version of 1611. Although often called in Great Britain the Authorized Version, it was never formally authorized by any competent body of either church or state. In America, the 1611 version is more commonly referred to as the King James Version, a designation that is historically justified by the active part taken by King James I in arranging for the appointment of about fifty scholarly translators to do the work and in giving the finished product his approval—though some people who speak of the King James Version may imagine that he was the translator, if not indeed the original author!

The 1611 version was a revision of the Bishops' Bible of 1568, with adjustments in renderings adopted from the half dozen other English Bibles made earlier in the previous century. Like its predecessors, the new version included a translation of the books of the Apocrypha. Four years after its publication Archbishop Abbot of Canterbury forbade anyone to issue the King James Bible without the Apocrypha, on pain of a fine and one year's imprisonment.

The King James Bible was admirably suited for public reading. Produced by translators who had an instinctive feeling for good style, the version is characterized by felicitous rhythm and splendid cadences.

Curiously enough, at first the King James Version had to overcome opposition in certain quarters. The learned Dr. Hugh Broughton, a Hebrew scholar in the Church of England, excoriated the new version, saying, "I had rather be rent in pieces with wild horses, than any such translation, by my consent, should be urged upon poor churches." When the Pilgrims came to the shores of New England in 1620, they brought with them copies of their beloved Geneva Bible of 1560, for they mistrusted the 1611 version as being too modern. Eventually, however, the intrinsic worth of the King James Bible came to be widely acknowledged, and many people came to accept it as "the Word of God" in a sense in which no other version would be so accepted.

During the eighteenth and nineteenth centuries proposals were occasionally voiced as to the desirability of making corrections and other modifications in phraseology here and there in the King James Version. In 1758, John Wesley produced a revised version of the New Testament, with some twelve thousand alterations—but none of them, Wesley assured the reader, for altering's sake. In America, Noah Webster, the lexicographer, produced an amended edition of the Bible (1833). His purpose was, as he says, to correct mistranslations and grammatical infelicities, and to remove obsolete words and phrases, as well as those expressions that were, he felt, "offensive to delicacy, and even to decency."

Revised Version (1881–84). For the reasons mentioned earlier, the need for a thorough revision of the English Bible began to be more and more apparent. In 1870, both Houses of Convocation of the

Anglican Church in Great Britain adopted a recommendation that led to the preparation of a full-scale revision.

Soon after the work of revision had begun, an invitation was extended to American scholars to cooperate with the British committee in this work of common interest. Renderings that the American committee preferred but that the British committee rejected were printed in an appendix (for example, the Americans preferred "Jehovah" to represent the Hebrew tetragrammaton instead of the traditional rendering "LORD," printed with a capital and small capitals). The agreement was that after a certain number of years the Americans would be allowed to publish an edition of the Revised Version that incorporated into the text itself the several preferences previously listed in the appendix.

The fate of the Revised Version was disappointing. Complaints about its English style began to be made as soon as it appeared. Charles Haddon Spurgeon, the great English preacher at the close of the nineteenth century, put it tersely when he characterized the rendering of the New Testamemt as "strong in Greek, weak in English." The revisers were often woodenly literalistic, inverting the natural order of words in English to represent the Greek word order (for example, Luke 9:17 reads, "And they did eat, and were all filled; and there was taken up that which remained over to them of broken pieces, twelve baskets").

American Standard Version (1901). In accordance with the agreement made with the British translators, in 1901 the American committee issued the Standard American edition of the Revised Version. In order to protect the integrity of the rendering, which came to be called the American Standard Version (ASV), its text was copyrighted.

The *New American Standard Version* (1971), prepared by a group of anonymous scholars sponsored by the Lockman Foundation of California, is ostensibly the American Standard Version of 1901 purged of some of the archaisms taken over from the Revised Version of 1881–84. On the whole, however, it remains a severely literalistic rendering. In 1995 an Updated Edition of the New American Standard Bible was issued. This edition embodies about eighty-five changes that introduce gender inclusive language.

Jewish Versions. In 1917, the Jewish Publication Society of America published *The Holy Scriptures According to the Masoretic Text*, a rendering of the Hebrew text that frequently echoes the idiom of the King James Bible. A much more contemporary style of English characterizes the latest Jewish version, entitled *A New Translation of the Holy Scriptures according to the Masoretic Text*, the work of two committees of American Jewish scholars. In 1963, *The Torah: The Five Books of Moses* was issued, and in the following years translations of Isaiah, of Jeremiah, and of other prophetical books were made available. The project was completed in 1982 with the publication of the final section of the Hebrew Scriptures, entitled *The Writings: Kethubim*. In 1985, the several sections were issued in one volume under the title *Tanakh: The Translation of the Holy Scriptures According to the Traditional Hebrew Text*.

Revised Standard Version. In view of the woodenly literal rendering characteristic of the American Standard Version (1901), in the early 1930s it was decided to undertake a revision under the leadership of Luther A. Weigle of Yale Divinity School that would reintroduce some of the rhythm and cadences of the Tyndale-King James tradition while taking advantage of advances made in lexicography and textual studies. This revision of the Standard Version resulted in the Revised Standard Version (New Testament, 1946; Old Testament, 1952; the Apocrypha, 1957). Just as Martin Luther sought through continual revision to improve the accuracy and idiomatic quality of his German translation of the Bible, so the Standard Bible Committee continued its work, taking into account the progress made in lexical and grammatical studies, as well as the latest manuscript discoveries.

Contributing their work without financial remuneration, the members of the Standard Bible Committee, though predominately Protestant, included several Roman Catholic scholars, a Greek Orthodox member, and a Jewish scholar (who served on the Old Testament section). A second edition of the New Testament, embodying several larger and smaller improvements, was published in 1971 (see also pages 344-45).

The *Jerusalem Bible* (1960) is an English translation made by British Roman Catholic scholars. Based on the French *La Sainte Bible de Jérusalem* (1956), the work of Dominican scholars at École

Biblique in Jerusalem, it presents a vivid and lively rendering into English, particularly in its narrative passages. In the Old Testament it was decided to render the personal name of the God of Israel as Yahweh, even though (as the preface acknowledges) in the Psalms especially this form may be unacceptable. Occasionally the translators rearranged the sequence of verses so as to give what they regarded as a more meaningful order. The idiom is modern, and "thee," "thou," and "thine" are replaced by "you" and "your." The volume is furnished with introductions to the several books and with annotations on the text, and at the close there is an index of scriptural themes, useful to those undertaking a thematic study of the Bible. In 1973, a revision of the *Bible de Jérusalem* was issued by the Dominican scholars, and this became the basis of another English rendering, *The New Jerusalem Bible* (1985).

The New American Bible (1970) is the first English translation of the Bible to be made by Roman Catholic scholars from the original languages, earlier ones having been made from Saint Jerome's Latin Vulgate text. The version is the outcome of twenty-five years of work by almost fifty scholars, most of them members of the Catholic Biblical Association of America. It is more faithful to the original texts than the 1960 *Jerusalem Bible,* and the idiom reflects twentieth-century American speech. The annotations, like the brief introductions to each of the biblical books, reflect contemporary higher critical opinions regarding date, authorship, and composition of the Scriptures. New features of typography are introduced, such as printing the First Epistle of John in strophic format similar to free verse.

New English Bible (1970). In 1946 plans were formulated in Great Britain for producing a totally new English rendering of the original biblical texts without comparison with earlier translations. Completed in 1970 by a distinguished panel of Protestant scholars, the New English Bible with the Apocrypha was issued by the Oxford and Cambridge university presses. The rendering is free and vigorous, tending at places to be periphrastic with interpretative additions. Here and there the translators have rearranged the sequence of verses and sections of the text. As has been true with many another version, the New English Bible was greeted with mixed reactions. Although T. S. Eliot declared that it did not sound like the Bible to him and that he would not believe a person who used it to take an oath (!), many other readers have found it fresh and meaningful, pegged at about the level of the cultured diction used by university-trained British readers. In 1989, a revision appeared under the title *The Revised English Bible with the Apocrypha*. The panel of revisers avoided complex or technical terms wherever possible, and produced a rendering that is more suitable for liturgical use.

The Living Bible, Paraphrased (1971), prepared over the years from 1951 onward by Kenneth N. Taylor, differs from standard English versions in being throughout a mixture of translation and commentary. As compared with a literal rendering, a paraphrase tells the reader what the passage means, whereas a literal translation tells what the passage says. Of course, a paraphrase, like a commentary, has a legitimate place in the Bible student's library. The major problem connected with the use of such a volume, however, lies in the failure of many readers to realize its purpose, and hence to assume that it is a translation pure and simple. To avoid being misled, those who cannot consult the original languages of the Bible should always check a paraphrase against a literal translation.

As an example of the expanded detail that the Living Bible inserts into the text, one may compare the opening words of the book of Amos in the literal rendering of the King James Version with the expanded paraphrase in the Living Bible: "The words of Amos, who was among the herdmen of Tekoa, which he saw concerning Israel" (16 words), and "Amos was a herdsman living in the village of Tekoa. All day long he sat on the hillsides watching the sheep, keeping them from straying. One day, in a vision, God told him some of the things that were going to happen to his nation, Israel" (46 words).

The opposite of an expanded paraphrase was issued by the Reader's Digest Association in 1982, entitled *The Reader's Digest Bible*. As general editor, the present writer had been asked to suggest block cuts and the elimination of passages that are repeated elsewhere (for example, Psalm 14 and Psalm 53 are virtually identical wording). Unlike other "shorter Bibles," this edition does not omit any of the sixty-six books. The team of editors at the head-quarters in Pleasantville, New York, condensed the text by elimi-nating a few words here and there. For example, "he answered and said" can be reduced by 50 percent to "he answered." The resulting *Reader's Digest Bible* is about 60 percent of the complete Bible. It is not, of course, intended to take the place of the complete Bible, but to provide a simplified edition for beginners who may feel daunted by the size of the entire Bible.

The *Good News Bible* (1976). Persons who have only a limited facility in English—such as immigrants, or children, or those with little education—find the traditional language of the 1611 King James Bible forbidding, if not sometimes incomprehensible. It was for such readers that in 1966 the American Bible Society issued *Good News for Modern Man*, otherwise known as *Today's English Version of the New Testament*. Prepared by Dr. Robert G. Bratcher, the idiom is contemporary, and aims at "dynamic equivalence," that is, producing the same effect for the reader today that the Greek text produced for those who first read it. In order to accomplish this, the translator introduced qualifying words here and there, as well as occasional phrases that have the function of a commentary. The immediate popularity of the rendering led to the formation of a committee composed of seven translators who prepared a similar rendering of the Old Testament. The completed Bible, embodying here and there modifications of the New Testament, was issued in 1976 under the title *Good News Bible*. In 2001, the title was changed to *Good News Translation*.

The *New International Version* (1978) was prepared by more than one hundred scholars, working in groups on various sections of the Scriptures, in the United States, Canada, Great Britain, Ireland, Australia, and New Zealand. Its beginnings date from 1956 when the Christian Reformed Church appointed a committee of fifteen scholars to study the feasibility of producing a new translation. After work on that translation had begun, in 1968 the New York Bible Society assumed responsibility for the project, paying an hourly stipend to the translators. The number of translators was greatly increased, so as to represent eventually thirty-four different religious groups. Divided into twenty teams, each produced trial translations of their respective biblical books. These translations were screened and edited by two editorial committees, and then were finally examined and approved by a committee of fourteen scholars. The New Testament was published in 1973 and the Old Testament in 1978. The New International Version is more colloquial than the Revised Stardard Version, less free than the *New English Bible*, and more literary than the *Good News Bible*.

The *New King James Bible* (1982) is a revised edition that retains much of the phraseology characteristic of the 1611 rendering, minus many of its archaic and obsolete expressions. Several new features have been introduced, such as the use of quotation marks and the printing of the words of Jesus in red, neither of which typographical feature was used in 1611. Furthermore, it was decided to capitalize the initial letter of all pronouns that refer to God, Jesus, and the Holy Spirit—even though the Hebrew and the Greek texts do not indicate reverence in this way. Because a great number of revisers had a part in producing various sections of the version, attentive readers will discover occasional inconsistencies in the introduction of contemporary English expressions.

A *Common Bible*. As is generally known, the Old Testament as used by the Roman Catholic Church contains several books and parts of books, called Deuterocanonical writings, that are regarded by Protestant churches as Apocrypha.[4] A special edition of the Revised Standard Version of the Bible with the Apocrypha/ Deuterocanonical books was issued in 1973 by the Collins Bible publishers of Great Britain as a "Common Bible," endorsed by both Roman Catholics and Protestants.

Worthy as such a "Common Bible" may be, it failed to live up to its name, for it lacked the full canon of writings that are recognized as authoritative by Eastern Orthodox churches. The Greek, Russian, Ukrainian, Bulgarian, Rumanian, Serbian, and other Eastern

---

4. For a summary of each of these books as well as an account of their influence on poets, artists, and novelists over the centuries, reference may be made to the present writer's *An Introduction to the Apocrypha* (New York: Oxford University Press, 1957).

churches receive not only the traditional Deuterocanonical books, but also the Third Book of the Maccabees. Furthermore, the Greek Church accepts also the Fourth Book of the Maccabees and Psalm 151. In 1972 a subcommittee of the Revised Standard Version Bible Committee was commissioned to prepare a translation of 3 and 4 Maccabees and Psalm 151. Upon completion of the translation in 1976, the Oxford University Press in New York took steps immediately to incorporate these three texts in an Expanded Edition of *The New Oxford Annotated Bible with the Apocrypha* (1977). This expanded edition is the first printing of the Bible in English that contains all the books regarded as authoritative by all the major branches of the Christian church.

New Revised Standard Version (1990). In order to take into account information made available by the discovery of still more ancient Hebrew and Greek manuscripts of the Bible, as well as further investigation of linguistic features of the text, in 1973 the Standard Bible Committee was authorized to undertake a revision of the Revised Standard Version that would make necessary changes in accordance with the maxim "as literal as possible, as free as necessary." Finally, after seventeen years of work, the New Revised Standard Version was issued in 1990 by seven publishers in the United States and Great Britain under the title *The Holy Bible, Containing the Old and New Testaments with the Apocryphal/ Deuterocanonical Books.*[5] In 1996 this version was also issued by Thomas Nelson Publishers as a Common Bible.

In 1995 the Oxford University Press in England, which had already issued the New Revised Standard Version, issued the version also in an Anglicized Edition, for example, with British spelling, British punctuation (single, instead of double, quotation marks), and British grammar (e.g., "have got" for "have gotten"). In 2000, the Anglicized New Revised Standard Version was issued in a Catholic Students' Edition by the St. Paul's publishers, Manila, Philippines.

Thus, the story of the making of the New Revised Standard Version of the Bible is an account of the slow but steady triumph of

---

5. Copyright for the NRSV was obtained in 1989 so that several denominations planning to issue new hymn books in 1990 could include responsive readings from the new version.

ecumenical concern over more limited sectarian interests.[6] Now, for the first time since the Reformation, one edition of the Bible has received the approval of leaders of Protestant, Roman Catholic, and Eastern Orthodox churches alike.

6. For an account of the making of the New Revised Standard Version, with a picture of members of the translation committee, see chapter 8 in my autobiography, *Reminiscences of an Octogenarian* (Peabody, Mass.: Hendrickson, 1997), pp. 89-102..

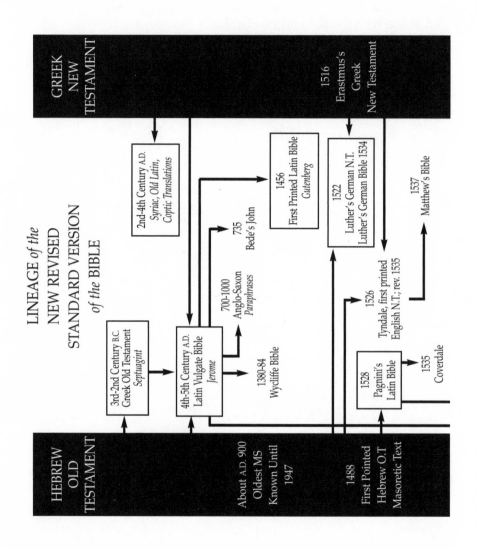

LINEAGE *of the*
NEW REVISED
STANDARD VERSION
of the BIBLE

GREEK NEW TESTAMENT

1516
Erastmus's
Greek
New Testament

2nd-4th Century A.D.
*Syriac, Old Latin,
Coptic Translations*

1456
First Printed Latin Bible
Gutenberg

1522
Luther's German N.T.
Luther's German Bible 1534

735
Bede's John

1537
Matthew's Bible

700-1000
Anglo-Saxon
Paraphrases

1526
Tyndale, first printed
English N.T; rev. 1535

3rd-2nd Century B.C.
Greek Old Testament
Septuagint

4th-5th Century A.D.
Latin Vulgate Bible
Jerome

1380-84
Wycliffe Bible

1528
Pagnini's
Latin Bible

1535
Coverdale

HEBREW OLD TESTAMENT

About A.D. 900
Oldest MS
Known Until
1947

1488
First Pointed
Hebrew O.T
Masoretic Text

Figure 13.5. Notable Versions of the Bible Through the Ages
This chart was originally drawn up by the present writer for use in enlarged
format on the wall of the Bible Room of the Interchurch Center, New York City
(used by permission).

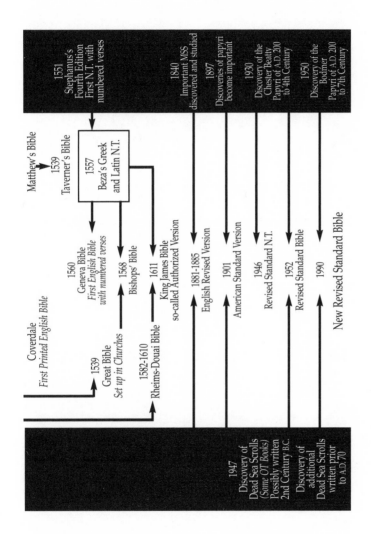

Matthew's Bible

1539
Taverner's Bible

1551
Stephanus's
Fourth Edition
First N.T. with
numbered verses

1557
Beza's Greek
and Latin N.T.

1840
Important MSS
discovered and studied

1897
Discoveries of papyri
become important

1930
Discovery of the
Chester Beatty
Papyri of A.D. 200
to 4th Century

1950
Discovery of the
Bodmer
Papyri of A.D. 200
to 7th Century

Coverdale
First Printed English Bible

1539
Great Bible
Set up in Churches

1560
Geneva Bible
First English Bible
with numbered verses

1568
Bishops' Bible

1611
King James Bible
so-called Authorized Version

1582-1610
Rheims-Douai Bible

1881-1885
English Revised Version

1901
American Standard Version

1946
Revised Standard N.T.

1952
Revised Standard Bible

1990
New Revised Standard Bible

1947
Discovery of
Dead Sea Scrolls
(Some OT Books)
Possibly written
2nd Century B.C.

Discovery of
additional
Dead Sea Scrolls
written prior
to A.D. 70

GLOSSARY

'Am ha-arets. A Hebrew expression meaning "people of the land," often used by elite Pharisees in referring disdainfully concerning common people who failed to observe the Mosaic Law. (See pp. 55-56).

Abba. The Aramaic word for "father," which occurs three times in the New Testament and always in address to God (Mark 14:36; Rom. 8:15; Gal. 4:6).

Amanuensis. A Latin word referring to one employed to take dictation or to copy a manuscript.

Apocalypse (Apocalyptic). A Greek term meaning literally "the revealing of what is hidden," especially applied to a form of literature that flourished among the Jews during the last two centuries B.C., and the first century A.D.

Apocrypha. A Greek term meaning "hidden." For reasons that are not altogether clear, the term came to be applied to books that are found in the Greek Old Testament but are not part of the Hebrew canon. (See pp. 44-47).

Apostle. The word "apostle" comes from the Greek and means "one who has been sent." Of the many disciples (literally "learners") who followed Jesus, "he appointed twelve, whom he also named apostles" (Mark 3:14).

Aramaic. A Semitic language closely akin to Hebrew. At least two dialectical forms of Aramaic were current in Palestine; Galilean Aramaic was recognizably different in pronunciation from the southern dialect spoken in and around Jerusalem (See pp. 39-40).

Ascension. The term used to describe the departure of Jesus from the earth as related in Acts 1:9-11. The word is not frequent in the New Testament (see John 20:17; Eph. 4:8-10). Other words are more common, for example, "was taken up" (Mark 16:19; Acts 1:2, 11, 22; 1 Tim. 3:16), "was lifted up" (Acts 1:9), "was carried up" (Luke 24:51). All these suggest that the power at work was God's. The space metaphors are used pictorially to convey the thought that Christ's resurrection body returned to the immediate presence of God, and so to the place of power and authority.

Asia. Nowhere in the New Testament does the word "Asia" refer to the great land mass commonly known by this name today. It refers always and only to one rather small part of what is now called Asia Minor. This was the Roman province of Asia, bounded on the north by Bithynia, on the east by Galatia, on the south by Pamphylia and Lycia, and on the west by the Aegean Sea.

Beelzebul or *Baal-zebub* (2 Kings 1:2). The title of a pagan deity, to whom the Jews ascribed the sovereignty of the evil spirits (Matt. 12:24; Mark 3:22); that is, Satan (Luke 11:18).

Caesar. The family name of Gaius Julius Caesar. In the New Testament, the title "Caesar" refers to the Roman emperor. Four holders of this office are mentioned: (1) Augustus (Luke 2:1); (2) Tiberius (Luke 3:1); (3) Claudius (Acts 17:7; 18:2); and (4) Nero (not mentioned by name, but referred to in Acts 25:11).

Calvary. This word, so well known as the name of the place close to Jerusalem, but outside the city walls, where Jesus was crucified, is actually found only once in the King James version (Luke 23:33). The Greek reads *kranion,* skull, where the other evangelists give the Aramaic word of the same meaning *Golgotha.* Calvary (from the Latin word for skull, *calvaria*) had become so familiar through the Latin Scriptures that the English translators kept the word in 1611.

(NT) Canon. This may be generally described as the collection of books that form the original and written rule of the faith and practice of the Christian Church. These books were not *made* canonical by the act of any council, but a council gave its sanction to the results of long and careful investigations as to what books were really of divine authority and thus expressed the universally accepted decisions of the church.

Christ from Greek *christos.* Literally the "Anointed One," corresponding to Hebrew "Messiah," which denoted the anointed king of Israel. Originally a title, it very soon came to be used by the followers of the risen Jesus as part of the personal name of their Lord, so much that they themselves came to be known as "Christians."

Codex. A quire of manuscript pages held together by stitching on the back to make the earliest form of a book, replacing the scroll and wax tablets of earlier times.

Colophon. An inscription at the end of the manuscript, often giving the name of the scribe.

Crucifixion. The act of fastening a victim to a cross for the purpose of inflicting capital punishment. Because Jesus was executed in this way, the cross (which previously had no religious significance) was spoken of by Paul as the means of salvation and has become the symbol of the Christian faith.

Cybele. In classical mythology, an earth-goddess of Phrygian and Cretan origin, identified by the Greeks with Rhea, wife of Cronus and mother of Zeus or Jupiter—hence called the Mother of the gods, or the Great Mother.

Cynic(s). Belonging to a sect of Greek philosophers founded by Antisthenes of Athens (born about 444 B.C.), who sought to develop the ethical teaching of Socrates, whose pupil he was. They advocated the doctrine that virtue is the only good, that the essence of virtue is self-control, and that pleasure is an evil if sought for its own sake.

Dead Sea Scrolls. The term denotes leather scrolls and fragments discovered for the most part between 1947 and 1960 in caves on the northwest and west shores of the Dead Sea near Qumran. Now comprising more than eight hundred biblical and nonbiblical texts, mostly fragmentary, in Hebrew, Aramaic, and Greek, they throw light on the state of the Hebrew text of the Old Testament at a time for which there had been no previous evidence (except the Nash papyrus) and assist our understanding of the history of the Hebrew language.

Decapolis. A district, east of the Jordan in north Palestine, dominated by ten allied Greek cities. The Greek population had come in the wake of Alexander's conquest. The ten cities originally included in the association were Scythopolis (Beth-shean), Hippos, Damascus, Gadara, Raphana, Kanatha, Pella, Dion, Gerasa, and Philadelphia. Other towns were afterward added.

Demon Possession. Apparent possession by spirits is a worldwide phenomenon. The New Testament records many cases of possession. The Gospel accounts show that Jesus distinguished between ordinary illnesses and those that accompanied demon possession. The former were healed by laying on of hands or anointing, the latter by commanding the demon to depart.

Denarius. A Roman silver coin used in Palestine during the New Testament period. It was the ordinary pay of an agricultural worker for a day (Matt. 20:2, 9-10, 13). This was the coin brought to Jesus by the Pharisees in connection with their question about the payment of taxes to the emperor (Mark 12:13-17).

Devil. The Bible speaks in terms of one central power of evil, a ruler of that world of darkness that is ruthlessly hostile to God and to his people. The Bible nowhere explains the origin of this evil power, or gives the reason for which God allows it to exist. But his time and power are limited. His end is to be totally destroyed (Rev. 20:10).

Dionysus. In Greek religion, the god of fertility and wine; also called Bacchus. Legends concerning him are profuse and contradictory. Votaries, through music, dancing, drinking, and through eating raw flesh and blood of sacrificial animals, attempted to merge their identities with that of the god.

Disciple (literally "learner"). A pupil (Matt. 10:24), especially the followers of a public teacher. Jesus in the Gospels is nearly always seen surrounded by groups of disciples. These were of two classes. The first class consisted of those who heard his word with pleasure and desired to obey it. These were many (Mark 2:15). The second class were the Twelve whom Jesus drew into closer intimacy with him, whom he commissioned to share his ministry (Matt. 10:1-4), and to whose training as apostles he devoted more and more time as his ministry drew to a close.

Doxology. An ascription of praise (Greek *doxa,* "glory, honor") to God. In the Psalms the word *hallelujah* is a Hebrew doxology translated as "Praise the Lord!" The best-known doxology of the Christian church is the angelic ascription of praise at the birth of Jesus (Luke 2:14).

Eleusinian. Relating to Eleusis in Attica, Greece: as in the Eleusinian mysteries and festival, held in honor of Demeter (Ceres), and celebrated at Eleusis.

Epicurean(ism). A follower of Epicurus (341–270 B.C.), who founded a school at Athens about 307 B.C. His philosophical system held that the external world is a series of fortuitous combinations of atoms and that the highest good is pleasure, interpreted as freedom from disturbance or pain.

Essene. A member of one of the three major Jewish sects in New Testament times, characterized by asceticism, celibacy (although some married), and joint holding of property. The claim sometimes advanced that Jesus and/or John the Baptist came from this sect has never been substantiated.

Glossary

Ethnarch. A title used in Greek antiquity with various meanings, but in general a person appointed to rule over a particular area or constituency on behalf of a king (2 Cor. 11:32 margin). See also "Tetrarch."

Eucharist (Greek, rendering of thanks, thanksgiving). The Lord's Supper, Holy Communion (with reference to the giving of thanks before partaking of the sacrament).

Form Criticism. A method of biblical criticism that concentrates on the pre-history of written documents or sources, classifying them according to their literary form or genre (e.g., stories, sayings, legends, pronouncements, and so forth).

Gemarah. A body of rabbinical comments and opinions on the Mishnah, and with it forming the Talmud. The Gemarah exists in two forms or recensions, receiving their name from the regions in which they were compiled, viz., the Jerusalem or Palestinian and the Babylonian, the former (in west Aramaic) having been completed in about the middle of the fourth century and the latter (in east Aramaic, closely akin to Syriac) about the end of the sixth century.

Glossolalia. Speaking in tongues, a form of ecstatic speech.

Gnostic(-ism). A member of any of certain sects among early Christians who claimed to have superior knowledge *(gnosis)* of spiritual things, and explained the world as created by powers or agencies arising as emanations from the Godhead.

Golgotha. Derived from the Aramaic word for a skull *(gulgulta),* the place where Jesus was crucified (Matt. 27:33; Mark 15:22; John 19:17, 18). Suggestions for the name "the skull" have been various—that it refers to the shape of the hill, that skulls were found there, that it was a place of execution, and that (according to an ancient tradition) the skull of Adam was found there.

Hasidean(s) (Hebrew = the pious). Ancient Jewish religious sect; the most rigid of adherents of Judaism in contradistinction to those Jews whom Hellenistic influences were beginning to affect. They developed between about 300 B.C. and 175 B.C. They were persecuted during the hellenizing campaign of Antiochus IV (175–163 B.C.), who required that they eat the flesh of swine and to offer sacrifice to Greek gods.

Hazzan. A permanent official subordinate to the ruler of a synagogue, whose duties, besides those of a sexton in charge of heating and lighting the building, included the assigning of seats, giving the signal for responses, replacing the sacred scrolls after the sabbath readings, and blowing the trumpet three times on Friday at sunset to announce the arrival of the sabbath.

Hellenism (-ic, -istic). The culture, ideals, and pattern of life of ancient Greece in classical times. Frequently it is contrasted with Hebraism—Hellenism then meaning pagan joy, freedom, and love of life contrasted with the austere morality and monotheism of the Old Testament. The Hellenic period came to an end with the death of Alexander the Great in 323 B.C., whose conquests had spread Hellenistic civilization over the Near East and far into Asia.

Hermeneutics (from the Greek *hermeneuo* "to interpret"). The science of the methods of exegesis, especially of the Scriptures. Whereas exegesis is usually the act of explaining a text according to formally prescribed rules, hermeneutics is the science (or art) by which exegetical procedures are devised.

Herodian(s). The Herodians were influential Jews (though not a religious sect like the Sadducees), who supported the dynasty of Herod, and particularly favored Herod Antipas. In the New Testament they are shown joining the Pharisees in an attempt to ensnare Jesus with their questions (Matt. 22:16; Mark 12:13).

Isis. A Nature goddess whose worship, originating in ancient Egypt, gradually extended throughout the lands of the Mediterranean world and became one of the chief religions of the Roman Empire. The worship of Isis, combined with that of her brother and husband Osiris and their son Horus, was enormously resistant to the influence of early Christian teachings, and her mysteries were performed as late as the sixth century.

Justification, justify. The Greek verb *dikaioo,* in legal language, means "acquit," "treat or account as righteous," and the noun *dikaiosis* signifies "justification" or "acquittal." These words in the New Testament refer to God's gracious act (Rom. 8:33), grounded in the death and resurrection of Christ (Rom. 4:25), by which sinners are accepted when they put their faith and trust in Christ (Rom. 3:21-26, 28; Gal. 2:16-21; 3:24).

Kerygma (Greek "a public declaration" as by a herald). The element of proclamation in the apostolic Christian message, as contrasted with "didache" or its instructional aspects.

L (Lukan Source). The abbreviation L is often used in New Testament source criticism for the solely Lukan material found in the Synoptic Gospels. How far any of this material can be traced back to written sources remains unclear.

Levite(s). Among the ancient Hebrews, a religious caste, descended from Levi, the third son of Jacob and Leah. This body was composed of all males of the tribe of Levi between thirty (or twenty-five) and fifty years of age, exclusive of the family of Aaron, which constituted the priesthood. In David's reign the Levites were divided into four classes: (1) Assistants to the priest in the work of the sanctuary; (2) Judges and scribes; (3) Gatekeepers; (4) Musicians.

Literary Criticism. In the broadest sense, literary criticism is the analysis of the meaning of a written text by means of the study of its style, and how that meaning is communicated by the author to the reader. It includes the analysis of how form is related to meaning and the aesthetic effects of language.

M (Matthean Source). The abbreviation M is often used in New Testament source criticism for the solely Matthean material found in the Synoptic Gospels. How far any of this material can be traced back to written sources remains unclear.

Maccabean(s). The members of the Hasmonean family of Jewish leaders that ruled Judea from 166 B.C. to 37 B.C. The epithet Maccabeus (meaning "the hammerer") was first given to Judas, third son of Mattathias (1 Macc. 2:4) but at an early date it was transferred to the entire family and to others who had a part in the defeat of the Syrians and the rededication of the temple in 164 B.C. (1 Macc. 4:52).

Martyr (Greek "a witness"). The term was originally used of the apostles as witnesses of Christ's life and resurrection (e.g., Acts 1:8, 22), but with the spread of persecution it was reserved to those who had undergone hardships for the faith, and finally it was restricted to those who had suffered death rather than renounce their religion.

Melchizedek. According to Genesis 14:18, Melchizedek was the "king of Salem" and "priest of God Most High," who offered Abraham bread and wine as he was returning from his defeat of the four kings. The only other mention of him in the Old Testament occurs in Psalm 110:4, where the king is described as "a priest forever according to the order of Melchizedek." Both passages are used by the author of the Letter to the Hebrews (6:20; 7:1) to prove the superiority of the priesthood of Christ, prefigured by Melchizedek, over that of Aaron and the Levites.

Messiah. The Hebrew term *mashiah* ("anointed one") was applicable to any person anointed with the holy oil, as the high priest (Lev. 4:3, 5, 16) or the king (2 Sam. 1:14, 16). In the time of Jesus many were hoping for a Messiah who would "restore the kingdom to Israel" (Acts 1:6). Some believed that he would be a spiritual leader (Luke 2:25-32). At the central point of Mark's narrative (8:29), Peter confesses Jesus as the Messiah. (The corresponding word in Greek is "Christ.")

Mishnah. The first of the two components of the Talmud, containing the oral law or body of ancient Jewish traditional teachings. Next to the Hebrew Scriptures it is the basic textbook for Jewish life and thought. It was reduced to writing about A.D. 200 by Rabbi Judah ha-Nasi. This material, expressed in postbiblical Hebrew, is arranged in sixty-three tractates divided into six orders. See also Gemarah.

Mithraism. The worship of Mithra, an ancient Indo-Iranian god adopted into the Roman Empire as the principal deity of a mystery religion that flourished in the second and third centuries. The cult is known primarily from its archaeological remains, many of them in excavated meeting places, and about one thousand dedicatory Latin inscriptions.

Mystery Religion(s). The variety of reports concerning ancient mystery cults makes it difficult to summarize them both briefly and accurately. Although the mystic rituals were kept secret, it was known that they required elaborate initiations, including purification rites, beholding sacred objects, accepting occult knowledge, and the acting out of a sacred drama.

Palestine. Historic region on the eastern shore of the Mediterranean between Syria and Egypt. In the Bible, Palestine is called Canaan before the invasion by Joshua; the usual Hebrew name is Erets Israel [land of Israel]. Its boundaries, never long constant, usually included at least some of the land between the Mediterranean and the Jordan River. So taken, the region is about 150 miles long and from about 30 to about 75 miles wide.

Palimpsest. When parchment writing material was expensive, writers sometimes took a piece that had been used, rubbed or scraped off the writing as much as possible, and then reused it by writing on it again. The result is a palimpsest. In some cases ultraviolet ray photography has made it possible to rediscover the original writing.

Papyrus. Writing material, made from strips of pith cut from the stem of the papyrus plant (or sedge) that grew abundantly in the Nile Delta. Buried in dry sand, papyrus manuscripts could remain intact for hundreds of years.

Parable. A simple story illustrating a moral or religious lesson.

Parchment. The skin of sheep or goats prepared for use as writing material and for other purposes. Vellum is a fine parchment made from the skins of calves, kids, and stillborn lambs.

Passion of Christ. The sufferings of Jesus both spiritually and physically in the period following the Last Supper and including the Crucifixion (2 Cor. 1:5; 1 Pet. 2:21; 3:18; 4:1; 5:1).

Passover. The Jewish festival celebrated every spring in remembrance of the Exodus from Egypt. According to the account of its institution in Exodus 12, a lamb was to be slain in each household and its blood sprinkled on the lintel and door posts of the house in memory of the fact that when the first-born in Egypt were slain, the Lord "passed over" the houses of Israelities that were so marked.

Pastoral Epistles. A common designation for the two Letters to Timothy and the Letter to Titus. The chief subject matter of these letters is the organization of a Christian ministry able to care for congregations and to combat false doctrine.

Pauline (Epistles/Letters). Of the twenty-one Epistles/Letters included in the New Testament, thirteen are attributed to the apostle Paul. Nine of these are directed to congregations (Romans through 2 Thessalonians), and four to individuals.

Pentecost (Greek = fiftieth). The Jewish Festival of Weeks (Exod. 23:14-17) that began on the fiftieth day (seven weeks) after the second day of Passover; celebrating the close of the grain harvest. On this day, fifty days after the resurrection of Christ, the Holy Spirit came upon the disciples at Jerusalem (Acts 2).

Pharisee(s). A member of a school or party among ancient Jews, noted for strict and formal observance of rites and ceremonies of the written Law and for insistence on the validity of the traditions of the elders.

Platonism. The philosophy of Plato (427–347 B.C.), pupil of Socrates and teacher of Aristotle, took many forms and influenced Christian theologians. Plato stressed the ideal over empirical reality and encouraged the use of the mind. (1) Atheism, (2) the view that the gods are indifferent to human conduct, and (3) the notion that the gods can be deterred from the execution of justice by human offerings, are all rejected as morally pernicious.

Praetorium (from the Latin word *praetor,* one of the chief civil magistrates in a Roman colony). The headquarters of the Roman military governor, wherever he happened to be.

Proconsul. An official who acted as governor of a Roman province that was administered by the Roman senate. Appointed for one year, he exercised most of the powers of a consul. He was attended by quaestors, who collected the revenues and paid them into the treasury managed by the senate.

Procurator (Latin, "administrator"). The agent of the Roman emperor; he resided in an imperial (as distinct from a senatorial) province, received the revenues, and paid them into the emperor's private exchequer.

Prodigal. A person who spends money extravagantly or without necessity; one who is profuse or lavish; a waster; a spendthrift. With the definite article *(the prodigal),* the term, taken from the ordinary chapter heading, is used to designate the younger son in Jesus' parable (Luke 15:11-32).

Glossary

Pseudepigrapha. Writings ascribed to someone other than the real author, generally with a view to giving them enhanced authority. Used of certain Jewish writings not included in the Septuagint version of the Old Testament.

Q. The initial letter of the German word *Quelle* (meaning "source") is commonly used to designate the presumed written or oral source for portions of the Gospels of Matthew and Luke that are similar to each other, but unlike anything in Mark.

Quadrans. The smallest Roman coin, one sixty-fourth of a denarius, worth about a penny.

Qumran. A site in Palestine, ten miles south of Jericho, on the shores of the Dead Sea, where the first Dead Sea Scrolls were found in a cave in 1947. Occupied from the eighth century B.C. to A.D. 135, but principally from 150 B.C. to A.D. 68.

Rabbi (Hebrew = "my master, my teacher"). A title of respect used by Jews in referring to their spiritual instructors. Another form of the title was Rabboni (John 20:16).

Redaction Criticism. A method of biblical research that focuses on identifying the work of compilers and/or editors of biblical books with a view to understanding their own particular beliefs or interests, the background against which they worked, the culture to which they belonged, and anything else that might have led them to make changes or adjustments in the text so as to arrange it in a particular way.

Resurrection (Latin *resurrectio,* "rising again [from the dead]," a translation of Greek *anastasis,* "rising [from the dead]." Unlike Greek thought, which believed in the natural immortality of the soul, the New Testament proclaims the resurrection of the body through the power of God. The usual emphasis is on the resurrection of the believer, but there is a reference in John 5:29 to the rising of "those who have done evil, to the resurrection of condemnation."

Sabbath (Hebrew *shabbat,* "rest"). The seventh day of the week, set apart for worship and rest (Exod. 20:8; Deut. 5:14). God, having completed the work of creation in six days, ceased from creative work on the seventh day (Gen. 2:1-3). During the exile and afterward the Jews saw sabbath observance as an important mark distinguishing them from their pagan neighbors (Neh. 10:31; Ezek. 20:12). From this time they began to study in detail how the sabbath was to be lawfully observed. Though the earliest Christians largely continued to keep the seventh day as a day of rest and prayer, the fact that the resurrection of Christ and the coming of the Holy Spirit had taken place on the first day of the week soon led to the observance of that day (i.e., Sunday), to the exclusion of the Jewish sabbath on Saturday.

Sadducees. A Jewish politico-religious party, opposed to the Pharisees. In the New Testament they appear to have taken a leading part against Jesus, whose teachings they opposed (Matt. 22:23-33). They also repeatedly attacked the apostles for teaching the resurrection of Christ (Acts 4:1-3; 5:17; compare 23:6-10). After the fall of Jerusalem they disappear from history.

Samaritans. Inhabitants of a district in ancient Palestine, between Galilee on the north and Judea on the south. Of mixed ancestry, the Samaritans accepted no more of the Old Testament than the Pentateuch, which further contributed to friction between them and the Jews. They claimed that God had chosen Mount Gerizim, and not Jerusalem, for the temple (John 4:20). Some of their descendants still live at Nablus (ancient Shechem) and continue to practice their religion.

Sanctification. The process of God's continuing work in Christian believers through the power of the Holy Spirit. They are thus purified from the guilt and power of sin and established in those dispositions and actions that conform to the will of God (Rom. 6:17; 1 Thess. 4:3; 2 Thess. 2:13; 1 Pet. 1:2). It may also refer to the state of consecration and moral wholeness that is the result of that process (Rom. 6:22).

Satan. In the Judeo-Christian tradition, the supreme embodiment of evil. The word in Hebrew means "adversary," and this original sense is still found in Jesus' application of the name to Peter in Matthew 16:23. An assembly of those who have grievously erred from the faith is the synagogue of Satan (Rev. 2:9; 3:9). There are depths in Satan that inexperienced Christians fail to fathom (Rev. 2:24). He is, moreover, so plausible that he seems to be an angel of light (2 Cor. 11:14). Jesus saw the overthrow of Satan's power (Luke 10:18).

Scribe. One of the group of Palestinian scholars and teachers of Jewish Law and tradition, who transcribed, edited, and interpreted the Hebrew Scriptures. Most of the scribes belonged to the party of the Pharisees, and the juxtaposition of scribes and Pharisees suggests that they were the scholarly representatives of that sect.

Scripture. Originally the Latin word *scriptura* meant simply anything written. In the Christian tradition, the Old and New Testament are considered Holy Scripture in that they are, or convey, the self-revelation of God. The term may refer to a single verse or the whole Bible.

Scroll. Documents in Old Testament and New Testament times were of papyrus or leather (including specially prepared skin called parchment), and were kept rolled up when not in use. The writing was done on the front or inside, and continued on the back if necessary (Ezek. 2:10).

Seleucid(s). Rulers of an empire founded by Seleucus I Nicator (ca. 358–281 B.C.), who had been a general in Alexander the Great's campaigns. The Greek dynasty of Seleucids (312–64 B.C.) governed a vast realm stretching from Asia Minor, via Syria and Babylonia, to Iran and thence to central Asia.

Septuagint (in abbreviation, LXX). The collection of Jewish writings that became the Old Testament of Greek-speaking Christians. They are mainly translated from the Hebrew (or Aramaic) Scriptures but include also some other pieces composed by Jews in the Hellenistic period, some in Greek and others translated from lost Semitic originals.

Shema' (Hebrew "hear"). The first word in Deuteronomy 6:4, which became the affirmation of the monotheism of the Old Testament. The Shema', however, was extended to include more than this verse and came to consist of Deuteroonomy 6:4-9; 11:13-21; and Numbers 15:37-41.

Shemoneh Esreh (Hebrew, "eighteen"). The collection of nineteen (originally eighteen) benedictions, from which are taken those recited with the Shema' at the daily services and at the additional services on Sabbaths and holy days. Their contents date in part from pre-Christian times; but apparently they were for long not written down and varied in number and wording, especially those in the middle section.

Stoicism. A Greco-Roman school of philosophy, founded at Athens by Zeno of Citium (335–263 B.C.). The system may be described as a form of materialistic pantheism or monism in contrast to Platonic idealism on the one hand and Epicurean hedonism on the other. Stoicism emphasized ethics, harmony with nature, the suppression of emotions, and divine law.

Synagogue. The Greek word meant simply "gathering together," but before the time of the New Testament it had come to mean (1) a gathering of people for religious worship, (2) the building in which this worship took place. The building served also for a local law court and school.

Synoptic(s), Synoptic Gospels (Greek *synoptikos,* "a seeing together"). The name given to Matthew, Mark, and Luke because they provide an overall conspectus or general survey, are similar in style and content, and can readily be compared with one another.

Talmud. The body of Jewish civil and canonical Law, consisting of the Mishnah, or text (in Hebrew), and the Gemarah, which is an Aramaic commentary on it. The Palestinian Talmud was completed in about the fourth century A.D. and a much longer and more highly regarded Babylonian Talmud in the fifth or sixth century A.D. The latter is normative for Judaism.

Tetrarch. A title meaning originally "ruler of a fourth" part of a kingdom or province.

Theosophical. Pertaining to a body of doctrine relating to deity, cosmos, and self, and held to rest on direct intuition by which initiates could master nature and guide their destiny.

Zealot(s). A Jewish political group in the first century A.D. According to Josephus the Zealots were one of the three factions who controlled Jerusalem in the last years of the Jewish revolt against Rome (A.D. 66–70).

BIBLIOGRAPHY
AIDS FOR THE STUDY OF THE NEW TESTAMENT

BASIC REFERENCE WORKS

Day, Colin A., ed. *Roget's Thesaurus of the Bible*. San Francisco: Harper & Row, 1998, 944 pages.
 A thesaurus that links together biblical passages with similar content in accordance with P. M. Roget's development of 990 general headings, with an index of passages and a subject index.

Finegan, Jack. *Handbook of Biblical Chronology: Principles of Time Reckoning in the Ancient World and Problems of Chronology in the Bible*, rev. ed. Peabody, Mass.: Hendrickson Publishers, 1998, 426 pages.

Pritchard, James B., ed. *The Harper Collins Concise Atlas of the Bible*. San Francisco: HarperCollins, 1997, 151 pages.
 With a historical commentary and index to the maps.

Whitaker, Richard E. and John R. Kohlenberger, III. *The Analytical Concordance to the New Revised Standard Version of the New Testament*. Grand Rapids Mich.: Eerdmans Pub. Co., 2000, 789 pages.
 An index to every occurrence of every significant word in the NRSV New Testament, with an analysis of which Greek word is being translated in each context.

BIBLE DICTIONARIES

Freedman, David Noel, ed. *The Anchor Bible Dictionary*. 6 vols. New York: Doubleday, 1992, 7,035 pages.
 Extensive scope of articles, including entries on individual Nag Hammadi tractates and specific Dead Sea Scrolls.

Freedman, David Noel, ed. *Eerdmans Dictionary of the Bible*. Grand Rapids, Mich.: Eerdmans Pub. Co., 2000, 1,474 pages.
 An excellent one-volume Bible dictionary with 5,000 entries, 134 illustrations, and 16 maps.

Metzger, Bruce M. and Michael D. Coogan, eds. *The Oxford Companion to the Bible*. New York: Oxford University Press, 1993, 874 pages.

Ranging beyond the scope of the traditional Bible dictionary, the *Companion* features, in addition, twenty interpretative essays on secular influence of the Bible on the ideas of Freud, Jung, Marx, as well as on the complex interplay between the Bible and such areas as art, dance, ecology, feminism, fortune-telling *(Sortes biblicae)*, law, literature, medicine, music, and American popular culture.

NEW TESTAMENT INTRODUCTION

Brown, Raymond E., S.S. *An Introduction to the New Testament.* New York: Doubleday, 1997, 878 pages.
A monumental piece of scholarship that speaks to experts and novices alike, making the New Testament intelligible and enjoyable.

Guthrie, Donald. *New Testament Introduction*, 4th ed. Downers Grove, Ill.: InterVarsity Press, 1990, 1,161 pages.
A detailed discussion with wide-bibliographical references.

Johnson, Luke Timothy. *The Writings of the New Testament: An Interpretation,* rev. ed. Minneapolis: Fortress Press, 1999, 694 pages.
A blend of thorough scholarship and a lively interest in religious experience.

Moule, C. F. D. *The Birth of the New Testament*, 3rd edition. San Francisco: Harper & Row, 1982, 382 pages.
A fresh and independent treatment.

Schnelle, Udo. *The History and Theology of the New Testament Writings.* Translated by M. Eugene Boring. Minneapolis: Fortress Press, 1998, 573 pages.
An advanced and technical discussion.

NEW TESTAMENT THEOLOGY

Caird, G. B. *New Testament Theology.* Completed and Edited by L. D. Hurst. Oxford: Clarendon Press, 1994, 340 pages.
Penetrating and insightful treatment.

Goppelt, Leonhard. *Theology of the New Testament.* Edited by Jürgen Roloff, Translated by John E. Alsup, 2 vols. Grand Rapids, Mich.: Wm. B. Eerdmans Pub. Co., 1982, 348 pages.
The variety and the unity of the apostolic witness to Christ.

Hengel, Martin. *The Four Gospels and the One Gospel of Jesus.* London: SCM Press, 2000, 354 pages.
A learned discussion of problems posed by the existence of several written Gospels together with Paul's preaching of the gospel.

Schlatter, Adolf. *The Theology of the Apostles: The Development of New Testament Theology.* Translated by Andreas J. Köstenberger. Grand Rapids, Mich.: Baker Books, 1998, 452 pages.
A perceptive discussion of the convictions upheld by Jesus' followers.

HISTORY OF THE CRITICAL STUDY OF THE NEW TESTAMENT

Hayes, John, ed. *Dictionary of Biblical Interpretation*, 2 vols. Nashville, Tenn.: Abingdon Press, 1999, 675 pages.
Schools of interpretation and individual biblical scholars throughout the centuries.

Kümmel, Werner Georg. *The New Testament: The History of the Investigation of its Problems*. Translated by S. McLean Gilmour and Howard C. Kee. Nashville, Tenn.: Abingdon Press, 1972, 510 pages.
Comprehensive and incisive.

Neill, Stephen and Tom Wright. *The Interpretation of the New Testament, 1861–1986*. New York: Oxford University Press, 1988, 464 pages.
Historical survey of New Testament criticism, somewhat uneven in its coverage.

NEW TESTAMENT BACKGROUND

Barrett, C. K. *The New Testament Background: Selected Documents*, 2nd ed. New York: Harper & Row, 1961, 361 pages.
English translations of Greek, Latin, Hebrew, Aramaic, and Slavonic documents, illuminating the background of the New Testament.

Bell, Albert A., Jr. *Exploring the New Testament World: An Illustrated Guide to the World of Jesus and the First Christians*. Nashville, Tenn.: Thomas Nelson Pub. Co., 1998, 322 pages.
A gold mine of information covering historical, political, philosophical, and religious matters.

Evans, Craig A. and Stanley E. Porter, eds. *Dictionary of New Testament Background*. Downers Grove, Ill.: InterVarsity Press, 2000, 1,328 pages.
Exact and detailed factual information, set out clearly.

ENGLISH TRANSLATIONS OF THE BIBLE

Gutjahr, Paul C. *An American Bible: A History of the Good Book in the United States, 1777–1880*. Stanford, Calif.: Stanford University Press, 1999, 256 pages.
Production and marketing of the Bible during the first century following American independence, with illustrations.

McGrath, Alister E. *In the Beginning; The Story of the King James Bible and How It Changed a Nation, a Language, and a Culture*. New York: Doubleday, 2001, 340 pages.
A comprehensive account that holds the interest of the reader.

Metzger, Bruce M. *The Bible in Translation: Ancient and English Versions*. Grand Rapids, Mich.: Baker Book House, 2001, 200 pages.
Discusses and evaluates briefly nearly sixty versions.

Bibliography

Opfell, Olga S. *The King James Bible Translators.* Jefferson, N.C.: McFarland & Co., 1982, 173 pages.
Information about individual translators.

Pope, Hugh. *English Versions of the Bible,* Revised and Amplified by Sebastian Bullough. St. Louis, Mo.: B. Herder Book Co., 1952, 787 pages.
A comprehensive account by a Roman Catholic scholar.

Rhodes, Erroll F. and Liana Lupas, eds. *The Translators to the Reader; The Original Preface to the King James Version of the 1611 Revisited.* New York: American Bible Society, 1997, 75 pages.
A presentation of the original preface in three forms: facsimile reproducing the 21 original printed pages; a transcription in modern typeface with modern spelling and punctuation; a translation in Modern English with Greek and Latin quotations given only in English, and obsolete words and archaic idioms replaced by equivalent modern expressions.

Sims, P. Marion. *The Bible in America: Versions That Have Played Their Part in the Making of the Republic.* New York: Wilson-Erickson, 1936, 394 pages.
Little-known facts about Bibles brought to America by the first colonists, as well as notable translations made subsequently.

Thuesen, Paul J. *In Discordance with the Scriptures: American Protestant Battles over Translating the Bible.* New York: Oxford University Press, 1999, 238 pages.
Discussion of modern Bible translation controversies.

Wegner, Paul D. *The Journey from Texts to Translations: The Origin and Development of the Bible.* Grand Rapids, Mich.: Baker Book House, 1999, 462 pages.
Includes photographs of many translators, 118 figures, 104 tables, and 6 maps.

Index of Principal New Testament References

GENERAL INDEX